P9-BYR-763

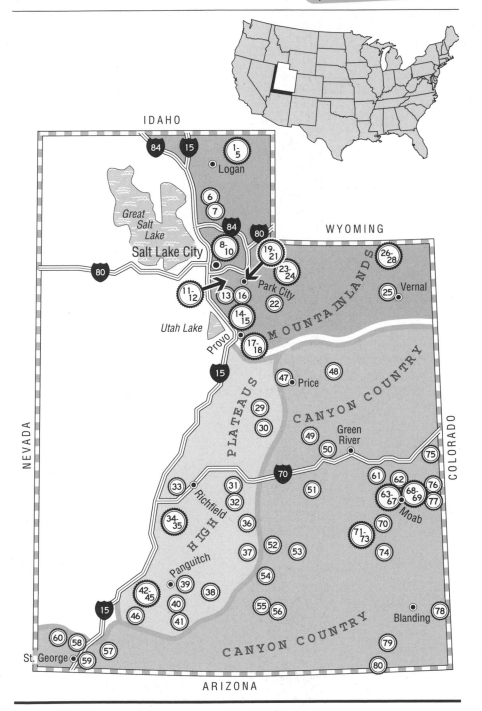

IDAHO

84 15

1-5
Logan

Great Salt Lake

6

7

84 80

WYOMING

8-10
Salt Lake City

80

19-21

26-28

23-24

25 Vernal

MOUNTAIN LANDS

11-12

13 16
Park City

22

14-15

Utah Lake

Provo

17-18

15

47 Price

48

PLATEAUS

CANYON COUNTRY

29

30

49 Green River

50

75

70

61

62

76

33 Richfield

31

51

63-67

68-69

77

32

Moab

34-35

36

70

NEVADA

COLORADO

71-73

74

37 52 53

HIGH

54

Panguitch

42-45 39 38

55 56

40

Blanding

78

46 41

79

60 58

57

80

St. George 59

CANYON COUNTRY

ARIZONA

iii

Table of Contents

THE MOUNTAIN BIKER'S GUIDE TO
UTAH

*Dennis Coello's America by
Mountain Bike Series*

Gregg Bromka

Foreword and Introduction
by Dennis Coello, Series Editor

MENASHA
RIDGE
PRESS

FALCON™

Library of Congress Cataloging-in-Publication Data
Bromka, Gregg.
    The mountain biker's guide to Utah / Gregg Bromka ; foreword and
introduction by Dennis Coello.—1st ed.
    p.   cm.
—(Dennis Coello's America by mountain bike series)
    "A Falcon guide"—CIP galley.
    ISBN 1-56044-287-5
    1. All terrain cycling—Utah—Guidebooks.   2. Utah—Guidebooks.
I. Title.   II. Series: America by mountain bike series.
GV1045.6.U8876   1994
796.6´4´09792—dc20   94-26656
                                            CIP

Photos by author unless otherwise credited
Maps by Tim Krasnansky
Cover photo by Gregg Bromka, Poison Spider Mesa

Menasha Ridge Press
3169 Cahaba Heights Road
Birmingham, Alabama 35243

Falcon Press
P.O. Box 1718
Helena, Montana 59624

WARNING:
    Outdoor recreation activities are by their very nature potentially hazardous. All partic-
ipants in such activities must assume the responsibility for their own actions and safety.
The information contained in this guidebook cannot replace sound judgment and good
decision-making skills, which help reduce risk exposure, nor does the scope of this book
allow for disclosure of all the potential hazards and risks involved in such activities.
    Learn as much as possible about the outdoor recreation activities you participate in,
prepare for the unexpected, and be safe and cautious. The reward will be a safer and
more enjoyable experience.

 Text pages printed on recycled paper

CENTRAL UTAH'S HIGH PLATEAUS   126

Captain Clarence E. Dutton   127

SOUTHERN UTAH'S CANYON COUNTRY   203

Slickrock   205

List of Maps

AMERICA BY MOUNTAIN BIKE   *MAP LEGEND*

Ride trailhead

Primary bike trail

Direction of travel

Optional bike trail and trailhead

Other trail

Hiking Only trail

Interstate highways (with exit no.)

U.S. routes

State routes

Hole in the Rock Rd.
Other paved roads

Unpaved, gravel or dirt roads (may be 4WD only)

U.S. Forest Service roads

Salt Lake City
Cities

Moab
Hite
Towns or settlements

Dam
Lake

Intermittent stream

Perennial stream

0   1/2   1
MILES
Approximate scale in miles

N
True North

DEAD HORSE POINT STATE PARK
Parklands

State Border

✈ Airport

♥ Archeological or historical site

Boat ramp

▲ Campground (CG)

≡ Cattle guard

Cemetery or gravesite

✝ Church

Cliff, escarpment or outcropping

Drinking water

Fire tower or lookout

Food

Gate

House or cabin

Lodging

Mountain or butte

Mountain pass

△ Mountain summit
3312 (elevation in feet)

✕ Mine or quarry

Mining tunnel

Observatory

Park office or ranger station

Picnic area

Power line or pipeline

Restrooms

Spring

Stable or horse farm

Swimming Area

Transmission towers

Tunnel or bridge

Dedicated to all those who . . .
"Eat, Sleep, Mountain Bike!"

Acknowledgments

This multi-year project would have not seen the light of day had it not been for the enthusiastic assistance of others. Due to the project's immensity, it was necessary to seek the advice and contributions of those who might be considered trail experts in a given locale. As you page through the following chapters, you will be introduced to these people by way of a short "biographic sketch." My sincere gratitude goes to Jeff Keller and the staff of Sunrise Cyclery, Logan; Ron Lindley, the mountain bike guru of Diamond Fork, Provo; Jan Wilking of Bicycle Utah, Park City; Charlie and Kathy Sturgis of White Pine Touring, Park City; Kevin Christopherson and the Wild Bunch Bike Club, Price; Steve Howe, Salt Lake City; Kevin and Jill James, Salt Lake City; Bill Murphy of Brian Head Cross Country Ski and Bike Shop, Brian Head; Dean Reader, Director of the Utah Travel Council, Salt Lake City; Mark McLaughlin of Bicycles Unlimited, St. George; Kent McDonald, St. George; Todd Campbell, Moab; and John Groo, Moab.

Considerable guidance was received from the various National Forest and Bureau of Land Management agencies including the Wasatch-Cache, Uinta, Ashley, Fish Lake, Manti–La Sal, and Dixie National Forests; and Moab, Cedar City, and Richfield District Offices of the Bureau of Land Management.

I would like to thank Bob Moyer for his companionship on numerous trips (both planned and blind reconnaissance varieties) and for patiently stopping for "just one more shot"; a tip of the helmet goes to fellow biker buddies and their companions for the same.

Of course I am thankful to Dennis Coello first for offering me "the challenge of a lifetime," and second for providing undying encouragement when the project was overshadowed by doubt.

To my mother, Irene, and family, I thank you all for encouraging me to follow my bliss.

And lest I forget, thank you, Tricia, for immeasurable patience and continued understanding of my two-wheeled obsession and the ceaseless hours this project required.

Gregg Bromka

Foreword

Welcome to America by Mountain Bike, a 20-book series designed to provide all-terrain bikers with the information they need to find and ride the very best trails everywhere in the mainland United States. Whether you're new to the sport and don't know where to pedal, or an experienced mountain biker who wants to learn the classic trails in another region, this series is for you. Drop a few bucks for the book, spend an hour with the detailed maps and route descriptions, and you're prepared for the finest in off-road cycling.

My role as editor of this series was simple: First, find a mountain biker who knows the area and loves to ride. Second, ask that person to spend a year researching the most popular and very best rides around. And third, have that rider describe each trail in terms of difficulty, scenery, condition, elevation change, and all other categories of information that are important to trail riders. "Pretend you've just completed a ride and met up with fellow mountain bikers at the trailhead," I told each author. "Imagine their questions, be clear in your answers."

As I said, the *editorial* process—that of sending out riders and reading the submitted chapters—is a snap. But the work involved in finding, riding, and writing about each trail is enormous. In some instances our authors' tasks are made easier by the information contributed by local bike shops or cycling clubs, or even by the writers of local "where-to" guides. Credit for these contributions is provided, when appropriate, in each chapter, and our sincere thanks goes to all who have helped.

But the overwhelming majority of trails are discovered and pedaled by our authors themselves, then compared with dozens of other routes to determine if they qualify as "classic"—that area's best in scenery and cycling fun. If you've ever had the experience of pioneering a route from outdated topographic maps, or entering a bike shop to request information from local riders who would much prefer to keep their favorite trails secret, or know how it is to double- and triple-check data to be positive your trail info is correct, then you have an idea of how each of our authors has labored to bring about these books. You and I, and all the mountain bikers of America, are the richer for their efforts.

You'll get more out of this book if you take a moment to read the Introduction explaining how to read the trail listings. The "Topographic Maps" section will help you understand how useful topos will be on a ride, and will also tell you where to get them. And though this is a "where-to," not a "how-to" guide, those of you who have not traveled the backcountry might find "Hitting the Trail" of particular value.

In addition to the material above, newcomers to mountain biking might want to spend a minute with the Glossary, page 356, so that terms like *hardpack,* *single-track,* and *water bars* won't throw you when you come across them in the text.

All the best.

Dennis Coello
St. Louis

Preface

For years now Utah has boasted having the "Greatest Snow on Earth," a motto displayed on its license plates, no less. Perhaps the time is appropriate to interject into this catch phrase, ". . . and Mountain Biking . . . ," for Utah has become the self-proclaimed mountain bike capitol of the world. Granted much of this honor has been generated by one particular town and its most unusual cycling experience, Moab and the Slickrock Bike Trail. Even if Utah did not have Slickrock or the canyon country that surrounds it, this state would still be an outstanding mountain bike destination, for its alpine regions, which are extolled as world-class winter playgrounds, define the term "mountain biking." But since good fortune *has* blessed Utah with the striking diversity of rugged mountains and spacious plateaus contrasted with the surrealistic glow of canyon country, the total package, which is decidedly Utah, separates this great state from other fat-tire locales. With the help of this guidebook both locals and visitors from distant abodes may discover, or rediscover, the pleasures of mountain biking in Utah.

It is likely that a guidebook of this nature will increase usage in certain areas and on specific routes; after all this is a "where-to" book. Consequently, there is a risk of visitors effectively loving a place to death. But visitation to a specific area is normally sparked by curiosity, which in turn fosters awareness and understanding of critical issues that pertain to the area. Conversely, withholding accurate and complete information may foster ignorance or disregard for these same issues.

The routes included in this guidebook were chosen carefully and all are deemed appropriate for mountain bike travel by the land management agencies and entities that oversee them. This guide revisits celebrated destinations while simultaneously directing the mountain biker to emerging venues and previously unknown locations. Most of all, this work strives to provide a broad base for the awareness and appreciation, if not reverence, of mountain biking in Utah while promoting responsible backcountry travel.

SCOPE OF THIS GUIDEBOOK

Initially, the scope of this guidebook was rather simple: gather together the state's "classic" mountain bike routes. About 30 or so came to mind, including Moab's White Rim, Slickrock Bike Trail, and Porcupine Rim; Brian Head's Second Left-Hand Canyon and Twisted Forest; Ogden's Skyline Trail; Salt Lake City's Big Water Trail and Wasatch Crest; Deer Valley at Park City; and Fish

Julie and Bart glide through Albion Basin.

Lake's Mytoge Mountain, to name a handful. But while these all-time greats were pursued, surrounding routes were uncovered and old favorites were rediscovered. Quickly, the true nature of this project began to unfold, or rather, explode. There are far more than a couple dozen great rides throughout Utah; there are literally hundreds from Logan to Monument Valley to St. George, many of which are little known or unknown and are patiently awaiting their moment in the limelight. The outcome is a compilation of Utah's 80 best mountain bike routes, the cream of the crop. Tackle these routes first, then on return visits explore the numberless satellite routes that just missed the cut.

Naturally, these 80 routes vary greatly not only in location but in length, difficulty, condition, trail type, and scenic qualities. Overall, there is something for everyone: rides geared for fat-tire neophytes to the most accomplished bikers; family trips to after-work spins; half-day to whole-day to multi-day excursions; weekend jaunts to week-long vacations; gentle dirt roads, upbeat double-tracks, exacting single-tracks, plus a small sampling of slickrock. A few routes are minutes away from metropolitan areas, while others venture to the state's (if not the nation's) most remote territories. And finally, a good chunk of the routes offer scenery that is not simply inspiring or even breathtaking, but superlative.

So scan through the Table of Contents, then page through the chapters. Read up on a region, location, or set of trails. Pick a ride that is well known or one you've never heard of. Saddle up your trusty steed and prepare to embark on some of the finest mountain biking the state, and the nation, has to offer.

REGIONAL SETTING

Three of the nation's major physiographic provinces converge upon Utah: the Middle Rocky Mountains (Mountainlands), the Colorado Plateau (Canyon Country), and the Basin and Range Province. A fourth region is the Colorado Plateau-Basin and Range Transition Belt (High Plateaus). Consequently, the routes in this guide have been grouped according to their physiographic association.

Northern Utah's Mountainlands extend from Logan's Bear River Range and the Idaho border through the Wasatch Range, which serves as a backdrop for a sprawling metropolis centered around the state's capitol, Salt Lake City. This region also includes the the Uinta Mountains, which stretch from Kamas to Flaming Gorge/Vernal. As can be envisioned from this region's label, rugged peaks coupled with deep, mountain valleys prevail. The abruptness of the Wasatch Range offers a spectacular urban setting for the Salt Lake Valley metropolis, whereas the nearby Uintas are endowed with uncompromised wilderness.

Central Utah's High Plateaus are a band of lofty tablelands arcing through the state's heartland, from where Mountainlands terminates south of Provo to just shy of the state's south-central border with Arizona. This region is alpine in every aspect like northern Utah's mountains, but is characterized by broad, rolling summits offset by long fertile valleys. A necklace of pioneer hamlets envelops the High Plateaus with a quaintness that hallmarks rural Utah.

Southern Utah's Canyon Country engulfs a huge wedge of southeastern Utah plus a west-trending panhandle to the state's absolute southwestern corner. This is Utah's famed redrock country: home to four of the Southwest's acclaimed national parks, backdrops for countless western movies, plus, of course, Moab and its world-renowned Slickrock Bike Trail. The Colorado and Green Rivers, plus their associate tributaries, have exposed a hundred shades of the Colorado Plateau's terra cotta skin. Floating among these desert seas are three alpine islands: the La Sal, Abajo, and Henry Mountains.

SPECIAL ISSUES

To say mountain biking is popular in Utah is like saying the Great Salt Lake is a bit saline. Overall, Utah welcomes mountain bikers to its seemingly endless tracts of open space, and recent statistics show that bikers are, in fact, flocking to the state's mountains and deserts to pursue the liberations that fat-tire cycling provides: In 1993 the Bureau of Land Management (Moab District) recorded over 82,000 rides on the Slickrock Bike Trail—a 63 percent increase over the previous three years; Canyonlands National Park, likewise, tallied 4,246 overnight riders on the White Rim Trail—up by 100 percent from 1989; The Wasatch Range boasts six million year-round visitors—double the number of annual visitors to Zion National Park, and more than that received by either Yellowstone or Grand Canyon National Parks.

It may be quite evident from these imposing figures that Utah's backcountry, especially the mountainlands of the Wasatch Range and canyon country surrounding Moab, may have a saturation point, which is determined (primarily) by the volume of users, environmental impacts caused by these users, plus conflicts within and between user groups. Obviously, to slow what may seem the rapid approach of saturation, one, some, or all of these elemental components must be controlled. In other words, if the allowable number of backcountry users is to remain unrestricted, then the other two elements—environmental impacts and user group conflicts—must be diminished.

Perhaps the most effective way for mountain bikers to thwart future access restrictions is by professing allegiance to trail etiquette, an issue that cannot be overemphasized. Webster defines etiquette as "the forms, manners, and ceremonies established by convention as acceptable or required in social relations . . . " Curiously enough, this applies directly to off-road bicycling. Our every action and interaction with fellow muscle-powered travelers, the environment, and land management agencies is closely watched and scrutinized. Due to the newness and inherent nature of our sport, we bear the heavy burden of continually proving our worthiness as responsible backcountry travelers. If we fall short, the immediate result will be loss of access to our favorite trails and coveted locales, i.e., reaching a self-imposed saturation point.

Leave No Trace, or, "Don't Waste Utah!"

Here are a few specifics on how everyone can help reduce environmental impacts caused by mountain biking and camping (along with other forms of backcountry recreation).

Picking a campsite: Whenever possible, camp at developed campgrounds. Limited services, including water taps, picnic tables, fire pits, tent pads, trash pickup, and outhouses, are worth the nominal fee. If you choose a backcountry site out of necessity or desire, avoid delicate meadows and microbiotic soils;

Slickrock Bike Trail, the world's most popular mountain bike trail.

wooded areas and either slickrock surfaces or sandy areas can better withstand the impact. In both alpine and desert terrain, avoid riparian areas, for the community of water-loving plants along streams is precious to wildlife.

Cooking: Use a gas camp stove whenever possible rather than building a fire ring. Instead of building a new fire ring, use existing rings. Collect only dead or down wood and think small; bonfires are passé. Burn the fire to ashes and douse heavily with water until dead and cold. (National parks prohibit the collection of firewood, even of dead wood that has fallen to the ground.)

Keep a clean campsite: Items such as cans, bottles, and aluminum foil do not burn and their presence in a fire pit may cause subsequent campers to build new pits. Carry plastic bags in your vehicle (grocery bags are great) and pack out all trash if garbage collection is not available.

Washing: Never wash (body, bike, or cooking utensils) in a lake, stream, or desert pothole. The introduction of mud, soaps, sunscreens, bike lubricants, and oils can pollute water sources that are critical for animals. Carry wash water away from the source, then dispose of dirty water in a small hole and cover with dirt. Biodegradable soaps are most effective when rinsed off on land, where soil bacteria can degrade them.

Trash: If you made room in your fanny pack or vehicle to bring stuff in with you, then certainly you have the means to pack it out. Remember, the little

things—candy wrappers, fruit peels, nut shells, pop tops, cigarette butts, etc.—
add up and for the most part are not readily biodegradable. Carry a garbage
bag in your vehicle for camp waste. On the trail a small Ziploc bag can neatly
hold leftovers plus keep packs and panniers mess-free.

Human waste: Bears do it, cows do it, and soon enough you will have to do it.
Use trailhead facilities whenever possible; otherwise, pick a location away from
water sources, trails, and campsites, then dig a small hole (6 to 12 inches in
fertile soil, shallower in desert soils). Tissue paper should be packed out; burning tissue paper is acceptable but can be a fire hazard. Cover the pit with soil,
leaves, and twigs.

Microbiotic soils (formerly cryptogams): Learn to recognize this delicate,
often black, crusty looking complex of desert soil and slow-growing lichens,
mosses, algae, and bacteria. These organisms retain water, fix nutrients, reduce
erosion, and provide a stable base from which higher plants can flourish. A
mature crust may take decades to develop. Avoid stepping on or riding through
patches of microbiotic soils, for they need little to survive other than to be left
alone. These desert soils are essentially *holding the place in place.*

Archaeological and Historical Sites: Evidence of early inhabitants abounds
throughout Utah, and these sites of antiquity add both enlightenment and
curiosity to any mountain bike excursion. Such forms of prehistoric evidence
vary widely from scattered arrowheads and tool fragments to pottery, vessels,
and figurines, to rock art panels and cliff dwellings. Historical sites range from
old homesteads and townsites to relic fortresses and haunting cemeteries. All of
these vestiges are windows into the past and should be preserved for their scientific, cultural, and aesthetic value. Use caution when visiting a site of antiquity.
Avoid touching, scarring, or grasping any remains or rock art panels.
Disturbing, altering, or collecting materials from any dwelling or site is strictly
forbidden. Sites of antiquity, located on federal lands, are protected by law as
provided by the Antiquities Act of 1906. The Archaeological Resources
Protection Act of 1979 considerably strengthens the legal base for protecting
such archaeological resources with criminal penalties of substantial fines
and/or imprisonment. Please preserve these sites for future generations to
admire and study.

Potential Hazards

Health-related problems can result from lack of preparedness, inadequate
physical conditioning, and just plain misfortune. The climate of Utah varies
between extremes: hot, dry deserts to cool, moist forests to cold, breezy tundra.
Some rides begin in one climatic extreme and venture to another.

Lightning: Utah's deserts and mountains are subject to sudden rainstorms
accompanied by lightning. It is not uncommon for a morning's ultramarine sky
to be transformed into savage thunderheads by midafternoon. Midday storms

are most common in July and August. It is best to get an early start and finish your ride by midday.

If you have the misfortune of being caught in a major thunder-boomer, do not panic, but act quickly. Get off ridgetops as fast as possible; avoid lone trees, shallow caves, open areas, and cliff bases. Seek shelter in deeper caves, heavily forested areas, or among big rocks in boulder fields. Separate yourself from your bike, then sit on a small rock with just your feet and buttocks touching the rock and insulating material between (foam pad or pack). Clasp hands around knees. If struck, the lightning may pass around your heart due to the insulation.

Sitting out a storm is a viable option, for in many cases they pass quickly and your ride can be resumed. But think ahead by packing along rain gear. At the very least, carry a plastic garbage bag: poke a few holes for your arms and head and you have a very effective, compact, and inexpensive rain slicker.

Hypothermia: The lowering of the body's core temperature is not just a winter-related health threat. Frigid mountain rains, wind blowing across exposed or wet skin, and lack of food and water can attenuate the onset of hypothermia.

Symptoms of mild hypothermia are feeling deep cold or numbness, shivering, poor coordination, slowing of pace, and slurred speech. As conditions worsen, a person may develop blueness in skin, fingers, or lips; severe fatigue; irrationality and disorientation; and decreased shivering followed by stiffening of muscles.

Treatment for hypothermia includes seeking shelter and warmth. Remove wet clothes and replace with dry clothing or cover with wind-proof materials to prevent increased evaporative heat loss; encourage the ingestion of warm fluids (non-alcoholic) and food; or move at a slow steady pace.

Heat exhaustion: Otherwise known as *hyper*thermia, the body's temperature is elevated due to hot environments and overexertion. Blood vessels in the skin become so dilated that blood to the brain and other vital organs is reduced to inadequate levels.

Symptoms include nausea, dizziness, minor confusion, headache, and mild temperature elevation, and are often accompanied by dehydration. In advanced cases, the victim may not be sweating and skin may be cool to the touch. Cool the victim immediately by seeking shade and shelter, wet the victim and fan vigorously, and have him or her drink cool fluids (non-alcoholic).

Altitude sickness: The rapid ascent to high elevations without acclimating may produce headaches, fatigue, loss of appetite, drowsiness, and apathy—about the same feeling as a good hangover. Treatment includes rest, adequate food and fluids, and pain relievers. Allow a few days to adjust to elevations and then proceed slowly.

Hunting season: Utahns are avid big-game hunters! The lower, drier environments of canyon country are usually safe bets during the autumn hunt; higher grounds are prime deer and elk habitat. Hunters wear neon orange for a reason;

do the same if you insist on biking off-road during late September and October. Avoid opening and closing hunting days.

Mines: Utah has a deep heritage centered about yesteryear's mining activity, in desert and alpine terrain alike. Old mining camps, structures, tunnels, and shafts may spur curiosity but are a form of backcountry roulette. Structures are often in a state of decay and are unstable. Mine tunnels and shafts may contain radioactive gases or low levels of oxygen.

ROUTE TERMINOLOGY

The following terms are used throughout this guidebook to describe a route's configuration:

Out-and-back: This type of route is characterized by riding from the designated trailhead to a distant point, location, town, etc., then returning to the trailhead via the same route by backtracking in the exact opposite direction. Mileage for an out-and-back route is for the total round-trip distance.

Point-to-point: A vehicle shuttle (or similar assistance) is required for this type of configuration, for the route is denoted by riding from the designated trailhead to a distant point, location, town, etc., where the route ends. Total mileage is for the one-way trip from trailhead to end point.

To accomplish a two-vehicle shuttle, all riders (with bikes) congregate at the route's end point first. One vehicle—the pickup vehicle—is left there. All riders (with bikes) travel in the second vehicle, the drop vehicle, to the trailhead. The drop vehicle is left at the trailhead while bikers ride to the end point and the pickup vehicle. The drop vehicle is then retrieved. Do not forget your keys!

Loop: This route configuration is characterized by riding from the designated trailhead to a distant point, location, town, etc., then returning to the trailhead via a different route (or simply the continuation of the same route) without doubling back. You always move forward across new terrain, but return to the starting point when finished. Mileage is for the entire loop from trailhead back to trailhead.

Combination: This type of route may combine two or more of the previously described configurations. For example, a point-to-point route may integrate a scenic loop or out-and-back spur midway through the ride. Likewise, an out-and-back may have a loop at its farthest point. (This configuration looks like a cherry with its stem attached; the stem is the out-and-back, the fruit is the terminus loop.) Or a loop route may have multiple out-and-back spurs and/or loops to the side. Mileage for a combination route is for the total distance to complete the ride.

Introduction

TRAIL DESCRIPTION OUTLINE

Information on each trail in this book begins with a general description that includes length, configuration, scenery, highlights, trail conditions, and difficulty. Additional description is contained in eleven individual categories. The following will help you understand all of the information provided.

Trail name: Trail names are as designated on United States Geological Survey (USGS) or Forest Service or other maps, and/or by local custom.

General location: This category describes where the trail is located in reference to a nearby town or other landmark.

Elevation change: Unless stated otherwise, the figure provided is the total gain and loss of elevation along the trail. In regions where the elevation variation is not extreme, the route is simply described as flat, rolling, or possessing short steep climbs or descents.

Season: This is the best time of year to pedal the route, taking into account trail condition (for example, when it will not be muddy), riding comfort (when the weather is too hot, cold, or wet), and local hunting seasons.

Note: Because the exact opening and closing dates of deer, elk, moose, and antelope seasons often change from year to year, riders should check with the local Fish and Game department, or call a sporting goods store (or any place that sells hunting licenses) in a nearby town before heading out. Wear bright clothes in fall, and don't wear suede jackets while in the saddle. Hunter's-orange tape on the helmet is also a good idea.

Services: This category is of primary importance in guides for paved-road tourers, but is far less crucial to most mountain bike trail descriptions because there are usually no services whatsoever to be found. Authors have noted when water is available on desert or long mountain routes, and have listed the availability of food, lodging, campgrounds, and bike shops. If all these services are present, you will find only the words "All services available in . . ."

Hazards: Special hazards like steep cliffs, great amounts of deadfall, or barbed-wire fences very close to the trail are noted here.

Rescue index: Determining how far one is from help on any particular trail can be difficult due to the backcountry nature of most mountain bike rides. Authors therefore state the proximity of homes or Forest Service outposts, nearby roads where one might hitch a ride, or the likelihood of other bikers being encountered on the trail. Phone numbers of local sheriff departments or hospitals have not been provided because phones are almost never available. If you are able to reach a phone, the local operator will connect you with emergency services.

Land status: This category provides information regarding whether the trail crosses land operated by the Forest Service, Bureau of Land Management, a city, state, or national park, and whether it crosses private land whose owner (at the time the author did the research) has allowed mountain bikers right of passage, and so on.

Note: Authors have been extremely careful to offer only those routes that are open to bikers and are legal to ride. However, because land ownership changes over time, and because the land-use controversy created by mountain bikes still has not completely subsided, it is the duty of each cyclist to look for and to heed signs warning against trail use. Don't expect this book to get you off the hook when you're facing some small-town judge for pedaling past a "Biking Prohibited" sign erected the day before. Look for these signs, read them, and heed the advice. And remember there's always another trail.

Maps: The maps in this book have been produced with great care, and, in conjunction with the trail-following suggestions, will help you stay on course. But as every experienced mountain biker knows, things can get tricky in the backcountry. It is therefore strongly suggested that you avail yourself of the detailed information found in the 7.5 minute series USGS (United States Geological Survey) topographic maps. In some cases, authors have found that specific Forest Service or other maps may be more useful than the USGS quads, and tell how to obtain them.

Finding the trail: Detailed information on how to reach the trailhead and where to park your car is provided here.

Sources of additional information: Here you will find the address and/or phone number of a bike shop, governmental agency, or other source from which trail information can be obtained.

Notes on the trail: This is where you are guided carefully through any portions of the trail that are particularly difficult to follow. The author also may add information about the route that does not fit easily in the other categories. This category will not be present for those rides where the route is easy to follow.

ABBREVIATIONS

The following road-designation abbreviations are used in the America by Mountain Bike series:

CR	County Road
FR	Farm Route
FS	Forest Service road
I-	Interstate
IR	Indian Route
US	United States highway

State highways are designated with the appropriate two-letter state abbreviation, followed by the road number. Example: UT 6 = Utah State Highway 6.

Postal Service two-letter state codes:

AL	Alabama	KS	Kansas
AK	Alaska	KY	Kentucky
AZ	Arizona	LA	Louisiana
AR	Arkansas	ME	Maine
CA	California	MD	Maryland
CO	Colorado	MA	Massachusetts
CT	Connecticut	MI	Michigan
DE	Delaware	MN	Minnesota
DC	District of Columbia	MS	Mississippi
FL	Florida	MO	Missouri
GA	Georgia	MT	Montana
HI	Hawaii	NE	Nebraska
ID	Idaho	NV	Nevada
IL	Illinois	NH	New Hampshire
IN	Indiana	NJ	New Jersey
IA	Iowa	NM	New Mexico
NY	New York	TN	Tennessee
NC	North Carolina	TX	Texas
ND	North Dakota	UT	Utah
OH	Ohio	VT	Vermont
OK	Oklahoma	VA	Virginia
OR	Oregon	WV	West Virginia
PA	Pennsylvania	WA	Washington
RI	Rhode Island	WI	Wisconsin
SC	South Carolina	WY	Wyoming
SD	South Dakota		

TOPOGRAPHIC MAPS

The maps in this book, when used in conjunction with the route directions present in each chapter, will in most instances be sufficient to get you to the trail and keep you on it. However, you will find superior detail and valuable information in the 7.5 minute series United States Geological Survey (USGS) topographic maps. Recognizing how indispensable these are to bikers and hikers alike, many bike shops and sporting goods stores now carry topos of the local area.

But if you're brand new to mountain biking you might be wondering "What's a topographic map?" In short, these differ from standard "flat" maps in that they indicate not only linear distance, but elevation as well. One glance at a "topo" will show you the difference, for "contour lines" are spread across the map like dozens of intricate spider webs. Each contour line represents a particular elevation, and at the base of each topo a particular "contour interval" designation is given. Yes, it sounds confusing if you're new to the lingo, but it truly is a simple and wonderfully helpful system. Keep reading.

Let's assume that the 7.5 minute series topo before us says "Contour Interval 40 feet," that the short trail we'll be pedaling is two inches in length on the map, and that it crosses five contour lines from its beginning to end. What do we know? Well, because the linear scale of this series is 2,000 feet to the inch (roughly 2 3/4 inches representing 1 mile), we know our trail is approximately 4/5 of a mile long (2 inches x 2,000 feet). But we also know we'll be climbing or descending 200 vertical feet (5 contour lines x 40 feet each) over that distance. And the elevation designations written on occasional contour lines will tell us if we're heading up or down.

The authors of this series warn their readers of upcoming terrain, but only a detailed topo gives you the information you need to pinpoint your position exactly on a map, steer yourself toward optional trails and roads nearby, plus let you know at a glance if you'll be pedaling hard to take them. It's a lot of information for a very low cost. In fact, the only drawback with topos is their size—several feet square. I've tried rolling them into tubes, folding them carefully, even cutting them into blocks and photocopying the pieces. Any of these systems is a pain, but no matter how you pack the maps you'll be happy they're along. And you'll be even happier if you pack a compass as well.

In addition to local bike shops and sporting goods stores, you'll find topos at major universities and some public libraries, where you might try photocopying the ones you need to avoid the cost of buying them. But if you want your own and can't find them locally, write to:

USGS Map Sales
Box 25286
Denver, CO 80225

Ask for an index while you're at it, plus a price list and a copy of the booklet *Topographic Maps*. In minutes you'll be reading them like a pro.

A second excellent series of maps available to mountain bikers is that put out by the United States Forest Service. If your trail runs through an area designated as a national forest, look in the phone book (white pages) under the United States Government listings, find the Department of Agriculture heading, and then run you finger down that section until you find the Forest Service. Give them a call and they'll provide the address of the regional Forest Service office, from which you can obtain the appropriate map.

TRAIL ETIQUETTE

Pick up almost any mountain bike magazine these days and you'll find articles and letters to the editor about trail conflict. For example, you'll find hikers' tales of being blindsided by speeding mountain bikers, complaints from mountain bikers about being blamed for trail damage that was really caused by horse or cattle traffic, and cries from bikers about those "kamikaze" riders who through their antics threaten to close even more trails to all of us.

The authors of this series have been very careful to guide you to only those trails that are open to mountain biking (or at least were open at the time of their research), and without exception have warned of the damage done to our sport through injudicious riding. All of us can benefit from glancing over the following International Mountain Bicycling Association (IMBA) Rules of the Trail before saddling up.

1. *Ride on open trails only.* Respect trail and road closures (ask if not sure), avoid possible trespass on private land, obtain permits and authorization as may be required. Federal and State wilderness areas are closed to cycling.

2. *Leave no trace.* Be sensitive to the dirt beneath you. Even on open trails, you should not ride under conditions where you will leave evidence of your passing, such as on certain soils shortly after rain. Observe the different types of soils and trail construction; practice low-impact cycling. This also means staying on the trail and not creating any new ones. Be sure to pack out at least as much as you pack in.

3. *Control your bicycle!* Inattention for even a second can cause disaster. Excessive speed can maim and threaten people; there is no excuse for it!

4. *Always yield the trail.* Make known your approach well in advance. A friendly greeting (or a bell) is considerate and works well; startling someone may cause loss of trail access. Show your respect when passing others by slowing to a walk or even stopping. Anticipate that other trail users may be around corners or in blind spots.

5. *Never spook animals.* All animals are startled by an unannounced approach, a sudden movement, or a loud noise. This can be dangerous for you, for others, and for the animals. Give animals extra room and time to adjust to you. In passing, use special care and follow the directions of horseback riders (ask if uncertain). Running cattle and disturbing wild animals is a serious offense. Leave gates as you found them, or as marked.

6. *Plan ahead.* Know your equipment, your ability, and the area in which you are riding—and prepare accordingly. Be self-sufficient at all times.

Wear a helmet, keep your machine in good condition, and carry necessary supplies for changes in weather or other conditions. A well-executed trip is a satisfaction to you and not a burden or offense to others.

For more information, contact IMBA, P.O. Box 412043, Los Angeles, CA 90041, (818) 792-8830.

HITTING THE TRAIL

Once again, because this is a "where-to," not a "how-to" guide, the following will be brief. If you're a veteran trail rider these suggestions might serve to remind you of something you've forgotten to pack. If you're a newcomer, they might convince you to think twice before hitting the backcountry unprepared.

Water: I've heard the questions dozens of times. "How much is enough? One bottle? Two? Three?! But think of all that extra weight!" Well, one simple physiological fact should convince you to err on the side of excess when it comes to deciding how much water to pack: a human working hard in 90-degree temperature needs approximately ten quarts of fluids every day. Ten quarts. That's two and a half gallons—12 large water bottles, or 16 small ones. And, with water weighing in at approximately eight pounds per gallon, a one-day supply comes to a whopping 20 pounds.

In other words, pack along two or three bottles even for short rides. And make sure you can purify the water found along the trail on longer routes. When writing of those routes where this could be of critical importance, each author has provided information on where water can be found near the trail—if it can be found at all. But drink it untreated and you run the risk of disease. (See *Giardia* in the Glossary.)

One sure way to kill both the bacteria and viruses in water is to boil it for ten minutes, plus one minute more for each 1,000 feet of elevation above sea level. Right. That's just how you want to spend your time on a bike ride. Besides, who wants to carry a stove, or denude the countryside stoking bonfires to boil water?

Luckily, there is a better way. Many riders pack along the effective, inexpensive, and only slightly distasteful tetraglycine hydroperiodide tablets (sold under the names Potable Aqua, Globaline, and Coughlan's, among others). Some invest in portable, lightweight purifiers that filter out the crud. Yes, purifying water with tablets or filters is a bother. But catch a case of Giardia sometime and you'll understand why it's worth the trouble.

Tools: Ever since my first cross-country tour in 1965 I've been kidded about the number of tools I pack on the trail. And so I will exit entirely from this discussion by providing a list compiled by two mechanic (and mountain biker) friends of mine. After all, since they make their livings fixing bikes, and get their kicks by riding them, who could be a better source?

These two suggest the following as an absolute minimum:

tire levers
spare tube and patch kit
air pump
allen wrenches (3, 4, 5, and 6 mm)
six-inch crescent (adjustable-end) wrench
small flat-blade screwdriver
chain rivet tool
spoke wrench

But, while on the trail, personal tool pouches contain these additional items:

channel locks (small)
air gauge
tire valve cap (the metal kind, with a valve-stem remover)
baling wire (ten or so inches, for temporary repairs)
duct tape (small roll for temporary repairs or tire boot)
boot material (small piece of old tire or a large tube patch)
spare chain link
rear derailleur pulley
spare nuts and bolts
paper towel and tube of waterless hand cleaner

First-Aid Kit: My personal kit contains the following, sealed inside double Ziploc bags:

sunscreen
aspirin
butterfly-closure bandages
Band-Aids
gauze compress pads (a half-dozen 4" x 4")
gauze (one roll)
ace bandages or Spenco joint wraps
Benadryl (an antihistamine, in case of allergic reactions)
water purification tablets
Moleskin / Spenco "Second Skin"
hydrogen peroxide, iodine, or Mercurochrome (some kind of antiseptic)
snakebite kit

Final Considerations: The authors of this series have done a good job in suggesting that specific items be packed for certain trails—raingear in particular seasons, a hat and gloves for mountain passes, or shades for desert jaunts. Heed their warnings, and think ahead. Good luck.

Dennis Coello
St. Louis

Northern Utah's Mountainlands

Two of the nation's prominent and unique mountain ranges converge upon northern Utah: the Wasatch Range and Uinta Mountains. The former plays host to one of the Intermountain West's economic and cultural hubs, the latter is a vast mountain wilderness.

Prominent is the Wasatch Range—a 200-mile-long lineament arcing gently from the state's northern border to its heartland. The Wasatch serves as both westernmost limit of the Middle Rocky Mountains and eastern emergence of the Basin and Range Province. Unique is its geologic complexity that is dominated by the razor-sharp Wasatch Fault Line. On a global scale the Wasatch Line, which is synonymous with the Wasatch Front, is deemed one of a kind and incomparable to any other of the Earth's great fractures. The Front's youth (geologically speaking), tremendous vertical displacements, and consequent lack of well-developed foothills make portions of the Wasatch Front some of the world's steepest rising mountains. Foremost Utah geologist William L. Stokes coined the Wasatch "the Backbone of Utah."

From all points west, the Wasatch Front rises abruptly as a seemingly impervious land barrier above the persistent levelness of the Great Salt Lake Valley. Its tallest mountaintops reach 5,000 to 7,000 feet above the valley floor to a maximum elevation of 11,928 feet atop Mount Nebo—monarch of the Wasatch—with an additional two dozen points breaking 11,000 feet. At these elevations, alpine glaciation has been the principal sculptor, shaping lone peaks into horns and ridge lines into serrated arêtes, while scouring out hanging valleys, cirque bowls, and deep U-shaped troughs. Meltwater rivers have notched the mountains' lower canyons into steep-walled conduits, which channel the precious life-giving waters to the valley's fertile farmlands and thirsty inhabitants.

Aesthetically, the Wasatch Range is glorious and beyond compare. Its spectacular silhouette serves as a backdrop for a sprawling metropolis of 1.3 million people (from Logan through Ogden and Salt Lake City to Provo), which accounts for three quarters of the state's population. From certain angles, tall mountain jags appear as though they might topple down upon the valley's populus, who gaze up with undying reverence.

But firm and providing is the Wasatch Range. Frontal canyons offer easy and direct access into the heart of this mountain sanctuary where seven designated Wilderness Areas reside. These outstanding natural areas plus an enormous network of backcountry trails and roads afford a much desired alpine refuge from the confines of urbanization.

At the western foot of the Wasatch Range lies the smooth saline floor of Pleistocene-age Lake Bonneville, now occupied in part by its offspring, Utah

The central Wasatch Range fills the sky with rugged peaks—Wasatch Crest.

Lake and the Great Salt Lake. On this ancient lake bottom coalesce Utah's urban centers, each laid out according to the systematic grid dictated a century and a half ago by Mormon prophet Brigham Young. Opposing the Central Wasatch are the Oquirrh Mountains, which like the Wasatch, are majestic in stature. The dynamic scene of fresh-water lake, land-locked saline sea, metropolitan valley, and confining mountains is strictly unique to northern Utah, and when viewed from up high along a mountain bike route is utterly breathtaking.

Behind the Wasatch, on its east side, lies a string of fertile parks, or back valleys. Logan's Cache Valley, nourished by the Bear and Logan Rivers, is enveloped by lush farmlands, dairy industries, and cheese factories. During the early nineteenth century, mountain men like Jim Bridger and Jed Smith explored this valley and the Bear River Range in search of beaver and plausible routes through the Intermountain West. Laden with a bounty of skins, trappers often had to "cache" their booties, thus the region's name. .

Ogden, Morgan, and Heber valleys harbor equally fertile agricultural parks but each is also a center for water sports. The Ogden River backs up into amoeba-shaped Pineview Reservoir, East Canyon Reservoir fills a small glen above Morgan Valley, and Heber's Jordanelle and Deer Creek reservoirs are fed by Provo River. In the placid surface of each lake is reflected the Wasatch Range's less-vaunted "backside."

Like these valleys, the area once known as Parleys Park lured early settlers from Salt Lake City to pasturelands atop steeply rising Parleys Canyon (through which Interstate 80 now winds). But here in 1868, the rich land produced not only fertile soil but threads of mineral ore. A "silver siren" blared in an era of frenzied mining activity which made Park City one of the West's richest mining districts. Mining moguls found their fortunes in Park City, including the Kearns family of Salt Lake City and George Hearst, father of publishing magnate William Randolph Hearst.

Park City was not exempt from the hardships that plagued similar mining boom towns. Fluctuating ore prices, mining disasters, and the 1898 hotel fire that reduced 75 percent of the town to ashen rubble sustained the vicissitude of fortune-seeking immigrants and the exodus of those left destitute. By the mid-1900s, Park City had slipped into a deep sleep from which similarly devastated mining towns would never awaken. But the same hills that gave life to Park City a century before would lift their souls again with the modern-day boom of alpine skiing. Today with its three resorts and refined turn-of-the-century aura, Park City shares its prominence with the likes of Aspen, Vail, and other elite ski towns.

Equally prominent are the Uinta Mountains (pronounced you-IN-tah), which extend from near Park City 150 miles eastward to Flaming Gorge/Vernal. Utah's tallest peaks reside in the High Uintas Wilderness Area with Kings Peak reaching 13,528 feet. Unique is its physiography, for the Uinta Mountains are the only major east-west trending range in the lower 48 states.

Whereas the Wasatch Range is characterized by a more juvenile assemblage of rough and chaotic glacial terrain, the Uintas expound upon mature glacial topography. During the Pleistocene, the core of the Uintas was blanketed by extensive ice sheets that scoured out broad, flat-bottomed, trough valleys separated by narrow arêtes and gigantic amphitheater cirques. Thousands of lakes left in the glaciers' wakes and the major drainage patterns that evolved make the Uintas both an invaluable watershed and an angler's paradise.

Since volcanic activity and associated mineral resources are generally absent from the Uintas, these mountains have been a great disappointment to the prospector and miner in search of pay dirt. Their bounteous forests, however, have proven attractive to the timber industry, but the range's rugged terrain and hard-to-reach center prevented mass clearing of its woodlands. These combined factors suggest the Uintas have little to offer other than their remoteness and naturalness, two qualities these mountains have in superlative degree.

In today's age of knobby tires, index shifting, and full suspension, all trails justifiably lead to Moab; however, more than a century ago pioneer trails converged upon and radiated from the Wasatch Front, which was labeled "Crossroads of the West."

Spanish friars Dominguez and Escalante were perhaps the first Europeans to venture into northern Utah. Their objective was to explore an overland route between Santa Fe, New Mexico, and missions in Monterey, California—a journey that would skirt the Uinta Mountains and lead into Utah Valley, land of the Timpanogotzis Indians. But their 1776 crusade would never come to fruition.

With supplies exhausted and hardships frequent, they were forced to return to New Mexico, not along their previous route nor by way of familiar terrain in northern Arizona, but through the tortuously incised canyons and harsh terrain of southern Utah's Canyon Country. A 37-foot tall white cross atop Dominguez Hill at the mouth of Spanish Fork Canyon (Provo) marks their passage.

During the early 1800s, mountain men like Jim Bridger, Jed Smith, Peter Skene Ogden, Etienne Provost, and General Ashley would forge additional routes through northern Utah, and in the process they would bestow their names upon many sites throughout the Wasatch and Uintas. Their travels were spurred by rich incentives offered by fur trading companies. Pack trains became common sights, and the annual mountain-man rendezvous on the shore of Bear Lake is reenacted to this day.

While mountain men ventured through northern Utah in search of fur-bearing riches, a group of Easterners persecuted for their religious beliefs sought a "Land of Zion" in the vast West. Lead by Brigham Young, followers of the Latter Day Saints' faith embarked on a historical trek from northern New York through the Midwest and into the Rocky Mountains. Despite glowing reports of California's fruitful lands, Young proclaimed the bleak but visionary Salt Lake Valley as "the right place." Upon this land that nobody else wanted, and even Native Americans seldom inhabited, these determined people would erect their city to God.

These same trails of emigration that led Mormon pioneers to their Promised Land ended their isolation. The short-lived Pony Express would brush by Salt Lake City, a rush for California's gold brought flocks of "Gentiles" (those not of the L.D.S. faith) through the Wasatch Front, and a Golden Spike driven into a first-ever transcontinental railroad heralded Ogden as "Junction City."

As you pedal through Northern Utah's Mountainlands think of its back-country paths not simply as a means to perfect a thrill; instead, envision days long since past when turning wheels were wooden; distances were measured in days, not hours, and trails were replete with life's hardships, not just technical maneuvers.

GREAT WESTERN TRAIL

Joining the ranks of the Pacific Crest, Continental Divide, and Appalachian National Scenic Trails, the newly created Great Western Trail (GWT) has become another of the grandiose north-south recreational routes. Its name alone conjures up visions of the Old West's magic and romance when methods of travel were by foot, horseback, and wagon. This dream unfolds today as the Great Western Trail allows recreational enthusiasts once again to explore the Intermountain West. Included along its path are recreational opportunities for the entire trails community as it passes through areas rich in Western lifestyle and heritage plus some of the most spectacular scenery in the West.

The Great Western Trail traces through the heart of Utah—
Wasatch Crest.

The Great Western Trail (GWT) extends from border to border, connecting
the northern tip of Idaho with the southern end of Arizona, along an estimated
total length of 3,000 miles. En route, the GWT winds through the very center
of Utah while tracing the crests of the Wasatch Range and central High
Plateaus.

The GWT breaks from its fellow long-distance trails in its attempts to
provide access opportunities for both motorized and non-motorized trail users.
In order to accommodate all users, when a certain level of use occurs or
restricted areas are encountered, separate or alternate routes will be provided
within the network of trails, making the GWT a "corridor of diversity." The
overriding principle is "something, somewhere in the corridor for everyone."

Much of the GWT's Utah section is available to mountain bikes. The trail
enters northern Utah in the Bear River Range northeast of Logan. Various trails
and roads connect with the Wasatch Range and trace its crest from Ogden

through Salt Lake City to Provo. Through central Utah, the GWT follows 100-mile-long Skyline Drive atop the Wasatch Plateau and then links Fish Lake Plateau, Thousand Lake and Boulder Mountains, and the Aquarius Plateaus as it winds into south-central Utah. Rounding out the Utah section, the GWT skirts Bryce Canyon National Park via the Paunsagunt Plateau, dives into high deserts that surround Kanab, and travels to the Arizona border. Throughout this guide, those routes that are part of the Great Western Trail or its alternate routes will be highlighted "(GWT)" at the end of the chapter's introduction.

RIDE 1   *BEAVER CREEK / FRANKLIN BASIN*

Spanning the Utah/Idaho border, the Beaver Creek/Franklin Basin loop passes through the rolling backcountry of the Bear River Range. Glistening Beaver Creek tumbles slowly through a narrow valley filled with willows, sage, and wildflowers. Its course is impeded frequently by shallow ponds that pool up behind beaver dams. Spring-fed Franklin Basin harbors the headwaters of the Logan River. Distant views of the Bear River Range's 10,000' highlands contrast with nearby gentle hillsides forested with aspen groves and mixed conifers. A spur road leads to the Pat Hollow Memorial where a C-46 transport plane crashed in 1953, killing its crew and passengers.

This 27-mile loop (counterclockwise) is a great, intermediate-level ride that follows in most part maintained dirt roads. Mountain bike racers will enjoy the route's fast pace, for it makes a good aerobic training ride. (GWT)

General location: Franklin Basin is located about 22 miles up Logan Canyon, near the Beaver Mountain Ski Area.
Elevation change: The trailhead is at the route's lowest elevation at 6,637'. Over the first 14 miles it gains nearly 2,000' to Danish Pass, elevation 8,560'. Thereafter, it is easy pedaling back to Logan Canyon.
Season: May through October. Midsummer riding is very comfortable with daytime highs in the 80s. Wildflowers grow in profusion in the broad valleys and along stream banks. This area may be popular with big game hunters in fall.
Services: Beaver Creek Campground, located 8 miles into the ride, offers developed campsites, outhouses, and water taps; otherwise, there are no services along the route and all surface waters should be purified. Outhouses also are located at the turnoffs for Franklin Basin and Beaver Creek Roads from the Logan Canyon highway.
Hazards: Use caution pedaling up the paved highway through Logan Canyon, for the shoulder is narrow and traffic, especially on weekends, can be heavy.

RIDE 1   *BEAVER CREEK / FRANKLIN BASIN*

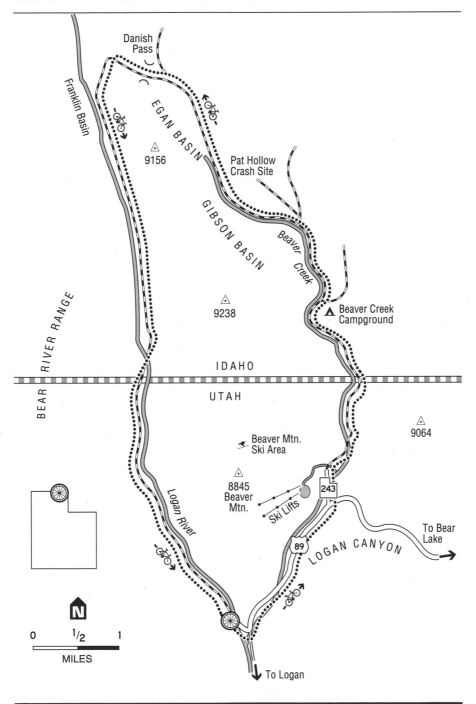

Danish Pass

Franklin Basin

EGAN BASIN

9156

Pat Hollow
Crash Site

GIBSON BASIN

Beaver Creek

9238

Beaver Creek
Campground

BEAR RIVER RANGE

IDAHO

UTAH

9064

Beaver Mtn.
Ski Area

Logan River

8845
Beaver
Mtn.

Ski Lifts

243

To Bear
Lake

89   LOGAN CANYON

N

0   1/2   1

MILES

To Logan

You may also encounter motorists and off-highway vehicles on dirt roads along Beaver Creek and through Franklin Basin.

Rescue index: Motorists are common in Logan Canyon. Recreationists are numerous near the junction of Beaver Creek and Logan Canyon, but less so near the junction of the Franklin Basin Road and Logan Canyon. The farther the route carries you into the backcountry, the less likely you are to encounter others. Logan has medical facilities.

Land status: Wasatch-Cache National Forest.

Maps: USGS 7.5 minute quadrangles: Egan Basin and Tony Grove, Utah.

Finding the trail: Travel east on US 89 (400 North) into Logan Canyon. The signed turnoff for Franklin Basin Road (Forest Service Road 006) is 22.5 miles up Logan Canyon (milepost 397). There are pullouts for parking alongside the dirt road. The turnoff for Beaver Mountain Ski Area (alternative parking and trailhead) is 3 miles farther up the highway.

Sources of additional information:

Wasatch-Cache National Forest
Logan Ranger District
860 North 1200 East
P.O. Box 1433
Logan, Utah 84321
(801) 753-2772

Bridgerland Road and Mountain Bike Trails, Cache-Rich Travel Council (free brochure): (800) 657-5353

Notes on the trail: Although there may be more parking around the Beaver Mountain Ski Area/Beaver Creek turnoff, Franklin Basin Road is the route's preferred starting location. Here, the route ends at its lowest elevation, and pedaling up the paved highway first is an excellent warm-up.

Three miles up Logan Canyon, turn left on UT 243 signed "Beaver Mountain Winter Sports Area." Less than a mile ahead, fork right on an improved dirt road (next to outhouses) signed "Entering Travel Management Area." Shortly ahead the Great Western Trail forks left at a sign for Sink Hollow, FS 110, but stay *right* on the unsigned Beaver Creek Road.

Stream-side forests and thick riparian vegetation line the road as it climbs steadily alongside Beaver Creek. Cross the Utah/Idaho border and then travel out into a broad meadow. Immediately past Beaver Creek Campground, stay left on the main road next to Beaver Creek. Fork left again 2 miles ahead onto FS 415, heading toward Egan Basin. Stay straight/west, rising gently through the narrowing, willow- and wildflower-decked valley and then across open Egan Basin. (Or, tack on 2 miles out-and-back on FS 459 to the Pat Hollow Crash Site. A plaque there tells of a C-46 transport that crashed in 1953 killing its civilian crew and 37 military passengers.)

Danish Pass is marked by a log fence line and a sign reading "Warning, steep, rocky road. Four-wheel-drive only." Do not be deterred. Although the road drops quickly and there are a few obstacles to hop, the descent is fun. Turn left upon entering into expansive Franklin Basin. Shortly ahead, stay left when the road forks and pedal due south. A very subtle pass marks the headwaters of Logan River. The route ends with 8 miles of downhill; some portions are mellow, others swift.

RIDE 2 BEAR LAKE SUMMIT TO BLACKSMITH FORK CANYON

Oftentimes potential mountain bike routes look inviting on a map but fall short, sometimes awfully short, of expectations when attempted. Logan's Great Western Trail mapped out perfectly, which rendered high suspicion. From Bear Lake Summit atop Logan Canyon to Left-Hand Fork of Blacksmith Fork Canyon, the route would join four individual single-tracks with a half-dozen backcountry roads.

When I attempted the route, not only did the Great Western Trail conform to its mapped layout, it soared high above my expectations. Silent forests opened up to commanding views of the Bear River Range, majestic aspens backed miles of rolling jeep roads, wildflowers grew in grand profusion, and single-track varied from free-flowing, serendipitous paths to punishing ascents and exacting downhills. The prize-worthy experience earned Logan's Great Western Trail a high ranking alongside a select number of Utah's decidedly epic mountain bike rides.

This 32-mile point-to-point route is highly demanding, make no bones about it, but one full of reward. You'll encounter a few strenuous climbs, including infamous Ricks Canyon. Both dirt roads and trails vary from silky smooth to technically challenging. Since a lengthy vehicle shuttle is necessary, prudent planning is required. But with some creativity, smaller point-to-point or even loop rides can be constructed. (GWT)

General location: The route begins at the top of Logan Canyon near Bear Lake Summit, located 31 miles east of Logan. It ends in Left-Hand Fork of Blacksmith Fork Canyon, located 10 miles east of the agricultural community of Hyrum (which in turn is about 7 miles south of Logan).

Elevation change: Just shy of Bear Lake Summit the route begins at 7,604´. It concludes in Left-Hand Fork of Blacksmith Fork Canyon, elevation 5,445´. The trip passes in and out of 5 stream canyons for a total elevation *loss* of 6,800´. Consequently, it *gains* a cumulative 4,800´ en route. Nearly half of this elevation (2,100´) is tallied midroute in 3.5-mile-long Ricks Canyon.

Season: This route should be free of snow by mid- to late May, and rideable

RIDE 2 *BEAR LAKE SUMMIT TO BLACKSMITH FORK CANYON*

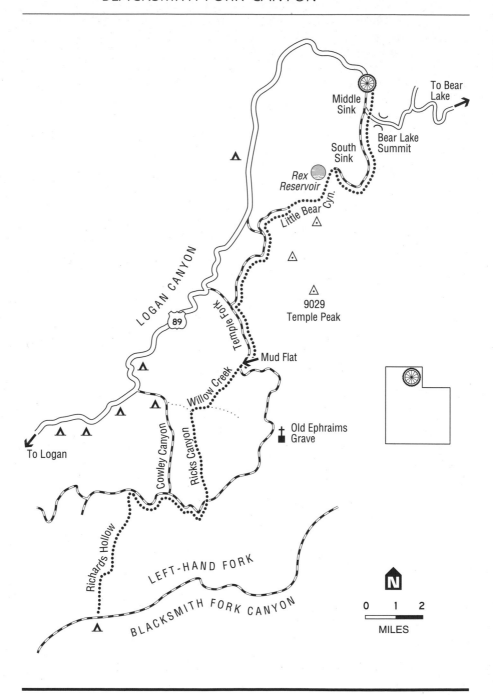

Middle Sink

To Bear Lake

South Sink

Bear Lake Summit

Rex Reservoir

Little Bear Cyn.

LOGAN CANYON

89

Temple Fork

9029 Temple Peak

Mud Flat

Willow Creek

Cowley Canyon

Ricks Canyon

✝ Old Ephraims Grave

To Logan

Richards Hollow

LEFT-HAND FORK

BLACKSMITH FORK CANYON

N

0   1   2
MILES

Ascending Ricks Canyon.

through most of October. Remember, the Logan area boasts cool midsummer temperatures, so early- and late-season biking may be cold. Wildflowers grow in profusion throughout the summer, especially in Ricks Canyon and Richards Hollow.

Services: Logan has all visitor-related services. Logan Canyon hosts several developed Forest Service campgrounds and picnic areas. Along this backcountry route there are no services, and all stream water should be purified. The Friendship Campground (USFS) is located at the route's end in Left-Hand Fork of Blacksmith Fork Canyon, where there are campsites, tables, and outhouses, but *no* water taps.

Hazards: This ride crosses seemingly endless backcountry terrain, so plan to ride all day (6 to 10 hours) plus an additional 2 hours to retrieve shuttle vehicles. Make sure you bring enough supplies and allow yourself plenty of time to complete the ride before dark. Technical difficulty varies from low to high; each downhill section has some highly technical conditions thrown in for good measure.

Rescue index: Recreationists are common midroute in Temple Fork and Right Fork of Logan Canyon as well as at the route's end points. There are a number of "bail outs" that connect with paved roads or well-traveled dirt roads (West Hodges Creek, Temple Fork, Right Fork of Logan Canyon, and Cowley Canyon). Still, shuttle vehicles may be a long distance away. Logan has full medical facilities.

Land status: Wasatch-Cache National Forest.

Maps: USGS 7.5 minute quadrangles: Boulder Mountain, Logan Peak, Temple Peak, and Tony Grove Creek, Utah; and Garden City, Utah-Idaho.

Finding the trail: To reach the trail's end point, travel south from Logan on US 89. Fork left following signs for Hyrum/Providence on UT 165. Turn left/east in Hyrum on UT 101 at a sign for Hardware Ranch. Travel 5 miles up Blacksmith Fork Canyon, then turn left/north on Left-Hand Fork of Blacksmith Fork Canyon road. (This improved dirt and rock road is *unsigned* but is located immediately past milepost 13.) Travel 3.5 miles to the Friendship Campground; Richards Hollow trail (unsigned) is immediately ahead on the road's north side and should be marked with a USFS multi-use trail emblem. Park at the trailhead, campground, or in clearings that line the road.

To get to the route's trailhead, travel east from Logan on US 89 (400 North). Travel 31 miles through Logan Canyon to Bear Lake Summit. The trailhead is an unsigned maintained dirt road (Forest Service Road 055) branching south from the highway immediately west of the "Rich County" sign and about one-half mile prior to Bear Lake Summit and Old Limber Pine picnic area. Take a few minutes to drive to the Bear Lake Overlook for views of turquoise waters that bless Utah's second largest freshwater lake. (Note: In the near future, an official Great Western Trail trailhead will be located at Stump Hollow opposite Beaver Mountain/UT 243.)

Sources of additional information:

Wasatch-Cache National Forest
Logan Ranger District
860 North 1200 East
P.O. Box 1433
Logan, Utah 84321
(801) 753-2772

Notes on the trail: Although this route crosses five topographic quadrangles and incorporates almost a dozen different roads and trails, it unfolds quite clearly once you are out on the trail.

From the route's starting point near Bear Lake Summit, pedal 3 miles south on FS 055 (unsigned) through Middle and South Sink. Turn right/west on FS 173 signed "Little Bear, West Hodges, Peter Sink." Break out of aspen and fir forests, then head north on a dirt road next to a wire fence line. Little Bear Trail (FS 010) cuts off left/west and drops quickly to Rex's Reservoir—a cattle pond. Pedal southward down-valley along a playful single-track to join with Little Bear Creek. The trail traces the canyon's bottom to a junction where Turkey Trail #054 (Great Western Trail) enters from the right/uphill. Ahead, Little Bear Creek trail grades to a double-track that rises gently out of the drainage. From a curve are dramatic overviews of Logan Canyon and the Bear River Range. Coast downhill and fork left for Spawn Trail/GWT. (A right turn descends West Hodges Creek and exits to US 89 in Logan Canyon.)

An ATV trail rises up a half-mile-long, leg-burning climb to a clearing. Veer right and over a knoll to begin the descent to Spawn Creek (watch for 2 wire gates along this technical descent) then down FS 164 to Temple Fork. (To avoid fording Temple Fork, follow the road alongside the stream a short distance.) Rise up Temple Fork road to Hunsaker Corral and then drop down one-half mile to Mud Flat and the head of Willow Creek.

Follow a faint four-wheel-drive road next to some white wooden beehives and through a wire gate. The road immediately narrows to a primitive single-track that parallels Willow Creek on its *east* side. Game and livestock trails branching from the trail may lend to confusion; stay *next* to the creek. Just beyond a broken down log fence line, the trail crosses to the creek's west side. Weave in and out of several side canyons on sometimes technical trail and dip into the creek again. Remember to stay near the creek if game trails tempt you otherwise. Upon reaching the canyon's mouth, descend single-track to Ricks Canyon.

Take a deep breath, for the 3.5-mile, 2,100′ ascent of Ricks Canyon is a serious test of strength and stamina. Dispersed aspen forests and shoulder-high wildflowers make this climb surprisingly gratifying. But the last quarter-mile is a grumbling hike-a-bike that scales the canyon's headwall.

At a T intersection, turn right to descend FS 147 2.6 miles to the clearing atop Cowley Canyon. Continue west and uphill one last time on FS 052. The sustained, 2-mile climb will make already-fatigued quadriceps sizzle. It culminates in a clearing where jeep roads branch in all directions. Take Richards Hollow trail (left/south) and begin the final descent to Left-Hand Fork of Blacksmith Fork Canyon.

This serpentining trail is a dreamy piece of mountain bike heaven: a handlebar-wide path dropping from conifer forests to aspen groves, to a fertile, creek-filled valley. A dozen creek crossings and multiple wildflower "face shots" keep you giggling. Snap back into reality when the canyon narrows, for the trail gets a bit dicey as it drops rapidly into Left-Hand Fork of Blacksmith Fork Canyon. If you've been prudent, the ice cooler will be well-stocked with 6-packs of Old Milwaukee for "it doesn't get any better than this."

RIDE 3 *JARDINE JUNIPER*

The Old Jardine Juniper is a curious sight. Anchored tenaciously above the craggy cliff-lined walls of Logan Canyon, the stoic cedar clings to life—even after 3,000 years! Grossly twisted limbs stretch from its weather-tortured trunk. For the most part the tree appears dead and decaying, except for a small pine needle garland sprouting from its very crown.

You'll enjoy diverse scenery on your way up to the juniper. Wood Camp

RIDE 3 *JARDINE JUNIPER*

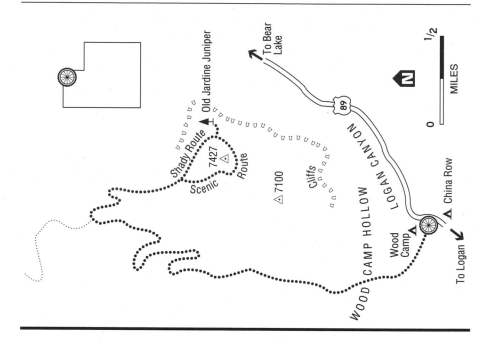

Hollow, through which the trail passes initially, harbors some of the most active avalanche chutes in northern Utah. Steep switchbacks rise to good views of the main ridge of the Bear River Range, including nearby Mount Naomi Wilderness. From the trail's end point are dizzying angles of limestone castles that enclose Logan Canyon.

Although not a long ride, only nine miles out-and-back, the Jardine Juniper trail will challenge intermediate to advanced cyclists. Strong, determined, novice riders may find the route taxing but rewarding. The maintained Forest Service trail is punctuated with loose sediment, gravels, and cobbles. A series of demanding switchbacks rise out of the lower canyon to a high, meadow-lined ridge. The upper trail grades to a narrow furrow that requires attentiveness and may dump even the skilled rider.

Trail information for Jardine Juniper was submitted by Jeff Keller[*] and Robert Gilchrist, Logan, Utah.

---

[*]Jeff Keller, owner of Sunrise Cyclery, knows bikes. They have been his primary means of transportation and recreation for most of his life. In fact he did not own a car until he was 28. Now Jeff is dedicated to providing others with the same two-wheeled pleasures he himself has experienced in the Logan area.

General location: The trailhead is located approximately 10 miles up Logan Canyon at the Wood Camp/Jardine Juniper turnoff.

Elevation change: Wood Camp Campground rests at 5,400′. The trails tops out at 7,200′ just before reaching the Old Jardine Juniper. Along the route's midsection, nearly 1,200′ is gained over 2.5 miles as the trail rises quickly above the main canyon through a series of switchbacks. Total elevation gain is 1,800′.

Season: May through October. During midsummer, the weather is temperate; however, during early and late season the temperatures can be quite cold. This ride offers outstanding spring and fall colors.

Services: No water is available along the route. Wood Camp Campground offers picnic tables, outhouses, and overnight camping but does not have water taps. Several developed USFS campgrounds (with water taps) are located throughout Logan Canyon. Logan provides all visitor services including bike shops.

Hazards: Portions of the trail may prove hazardous to those new to mountain biking, especially upon descending. Watch for loose rock, especially on the steeper switchbacks, and ride cautiously along the narrow, rutted track through the upper meadows. Hiking, instead of biking, the last 200 yards down to the Jardine Juniper is strongly recommended. Since this route is a revered hiking destination, be courteous and yield the trail.

Rescue index: The trail is popular with hikers and mountain bikers. Wood Camp is never more than 4.5 miles away. Motorists frequent Logan Canyon, and Logan has full medical facilities.

Land status: Wasatch-Cache National Forest.

Maps: USGS 7.5 minute quadrangle: Mt. Elmer, Utah.

Finding the trail: Travel east on US 89 (400 North) into Logan Canyon. The Wood Camp/Jardine Juniper turnoff is about 10 miles up canyon between mileposts 384 and 385. Parking is available.

Sources of additional information:

Wasatch-Cache National Forest
Logan Ranger District
860 North 1200 East
P.O. Box 1433
Logan, Utah 84321

(continued from page 22)

Forever a dedicated road cyclist, Jeff was one of the key organizers of the Lo-to-Ja road race (Logan, Utah to Jackson, Wyoming). The famed 200-mile race has grown from a mere nine participants to hundreds. In the early 1980s, mountain bikes caught Jeff's attention. A staunch environmentalist, however, Jeff was concerned with the impact of fat-tire cycling at first, but later realized that mountain bikes can be an environmentally safe means of backcountry travel. "The environment is for us to enjoy, but only if we respect it and care for it."

The "Scenic Route" overlooks cliff-bound Logan Canyon.

(801) 753-2772

Sunrise Cyclery
138 North 100 East
Logan, Utah 84321
(801) 753-3294
Sunrise Cyclery offers the best in top-name mountain, touring, and racing bikes, components, and professional service for today's discriminating rider. Jeff Keller and the folks at Sunrise can outfit your entire family, young and old, with the right bike and accessories.

Bridgerland Road and Mountain Bike Trails, Cache-Rich Travel Council (free brochure): (800) 657-5353

Notes on the trail: Pedal about a half mile up the wide canyon bottom. Avalanche-ravaged Wood Camp Hollow forks to the left; the signed Jardine Juniper trail forks right up a side canyon. Rising through the first set of switchbacks, the trail passes a sign for the Mount Naomi Wilderness (bikes are prohibited). Shortly thereafter, the trail ascends a second set of curves and along a ridge to another signed trail junction. Both route choices encircle the peak overhead and access the Old Jardine Juniper: "Shady Route" circles north through giant aspen groves; "Scenic Route" circles south through open slopes that overlook Logan Canyon and Central Wasatch Range.

RIDE 4 *OLD EPHRAIMS GRAVE*

Old Ephraim was neither settler nor pioneer, but an infamous legend just the same. Ephraim was the last grizzly bear to roam Utah—a giant that ranged this area for many years killing sheep, cattle, and game—and the largest grizzly ever shot in the continental United States. The 1,100-pound beast was as gigantic as the eleven-foot stone monument that marks its 1923 grave site. Its massive skull was first sent to the Smithsonian Institute and then recently transferred to Utah State University in Logan.

The route passes through low, rolling back hills of Utah's northern Wasatch Range (locally termed the Bear River Range). Open meadows painted with alpine grasses and colorful wildflowers blanket scattered forests of aspen and mixed conifers. From the route's high points are grand views of Logan Peak to the west and the Mt. Naomi Wilderness to the north. The serrated Wasatch Range fades into the southern horizon.

This 20-mile loop (counterclockwise) is within the grasp of strong intermediate riders. Two long and drawn out climbs tally up the route's total elevation gain. Although technical difficulty is low to moderate along these backcountry dirt roads, the ride's final descent on narrow, lightly maintained single-track through Willow Creek raises the ante. (GWT)

General location: This route loops around the Right Fork of Logan Canyon, which is located 9 miles east of Logan.

Elevation change: The route begins at 5,400′. Over the first 7 miles, you will gain 2,200′ to the route's high point of 7,600′ near the head of Ricks Canyon. There is a generous descent to Old Ephraim's Grave (6,800′) followed by a 1,000′ climb up Long Hollow. The remainder of the route drops 2,000′ through Willow Creek and back to the trailhead. Total climbing is about 3,400′.

Season: Although snow drapes Logan's high peaks well into June, this route is generally snow-free by mid-May and clear through October. Most characteristic of Logan is its temperate climate. While Salt Lake City's thermometer caps the century mark during midsummer, Logan is typically 10 to 20 degrees cooler. Insect repellant is recommended from May through August.

Services: The quaint college town of Logan has all visitor-related services. Logan Canyon hosts several developed Forest Service campgrounds and picnic areas. The Lodge Campground, located at the trailhead, has water taps and outhouses. There are no services along the route and all surface waters should be purified.

Hazards: No unusual hazards exist along this route. Ruts and loose rocks punctuate the dirt roads. Use caution on the single-track descent of Willow Creek; you'll be facing a wide assortment of technical challenges. (Cattle range in this canyon so watch out for fresh "guacamole" in the trail!) Be prepared for

RIDE 4 *OLD EPHRAIMS GRAVE*

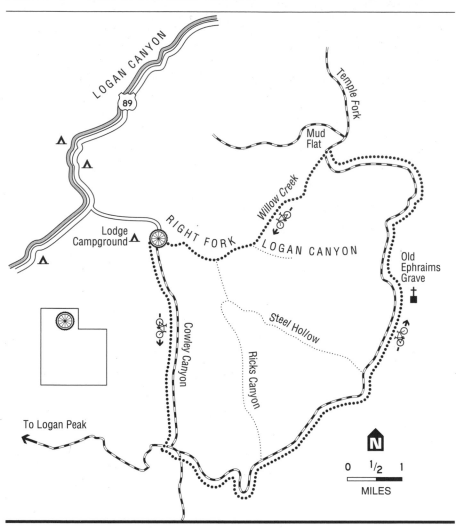

changing weather; afternoon thunderstorms are common.

Rescue index: Portions of the route are well traveled by off-road vehicle users, hikers, and other mountain bikers, but complete solitude is not unusual either. Recreationists are common near the route's beginning (Lodge Campground) and near Mud Flat Spring (head of Willow Creek and Temple Fork canyons). Logan has a hospital.

Land status: Wasatch-Cache National Forest.

Maps: USGS 7.5 minute quadrangles: Boulder Mountain and Temple Peak, Utah; USGS 1:100,000 metric topographic series: Logan, Utah.

The colossal gravestone of Old Ephraim.

Finding the trail: From Logan, follow US 89 (400 North) east into Logan Canyon. Nine miles up the canyon Right-Hand Fork Road turns off unexpectedly to the right between mileposts 383 and 384. (The geologic sign for Fucoidal Quartzite signifies Right-Hand Fork's proximity.) Parking is available near the entrance to the Lodge Campground, located a mile from the highway. You'll begin the ride by following Cowley Canyon Road (Forest Service Road 047) south and uphill.

Sources of additional information:

Wasatch-Cache National Forest
Logan Ranger District
860 North 1200 East
P.O. Box 1433
Logan, Utah 84321
(801) 753-2772

Bridgerland Road and Mountain Bike Trails, Cache-Rich Tourist Council (free brochure): (800) 657-5353

Notes on the trail: Begin by pedaling up Cowley Canyon Road (FS 047) next to a trickling stream. The road climbs consistently at a gentle to moderate grade before breaking out across a broad clearing. To the right, FS 052 provides access to Logan Peak. The route to Ephraims Grave is not the immediate dirt road left, but the next left (FS 147), straight ahead and south about 100 yards. This four-wheel-drive road continues climbing (steeply at times) then flattens for 2 miles of roller-coaster cruising along the heads of Ricks and Steel Canyons and past Marie, Sheep Creek, and Dog Springs. A brisk, winding descent brings you past Old Ephraims Grave before the road bottoms in the Right Fork of Logan Canyon. After nearly 3 miles of sustained climbing up Long Hollow, turn left and uphill at a T junction. Glorious overviews of the Mt. Naomi Wilderness await. A long, fast downhill ends in a grassy meadow at Mud Flat.

Instead of turning right and uphill (to join with the head of Temple Fork Canyon), turn left onto a faded four-wheel-drive road next to some wooden beehives and then go through a wire gate. The road immediately narrows to a primitive single-track that parallels Willow Creek on its *east* side. Game and livestock trails branching from the trail may cause confusion; stay *next* to the creek. Just beyond a broken down log fence line, the trail crosses to the creek's west side. Weave in and out of several side canyons on sometimes technical trail and cross the creek again. Remember to stay near the creek if game trails tempt you otherwise. When you reach the canyon's mouth turn right to descend single-track paralleling the Right Fork and back to the route's beginning.

Advanced cyclists who live by the motto, "Why ride dirt roads when there is single-track?" may opt to ascend Ricks Canyon instead of the sometimes mundane Cowley Canyon Road. From the parking area follow FS 081 (Ricks Trail) east. After about a mile, turn right and through a gate where a sign reads "Ricks Canyon, #127." Ahead is 2.5 miles of prize-worthy but demanding single-track passing through increasingly dense aspen forests and wildflowers that grow to shoulder height. It's a whopping 2,000′ ascent that culminates with one-quarter mile of bike-packing up a precipitous slope that breaches the canyon. After some warranted grumbling, you will celebrate the feat.

RIDE 5   *LOGAN PEAK*

Northern Utah's Wasatch Range boasts a number of classic off-road hillclimbs: Germania Pass at Alta Ski Area (1,800 vertical feet), The Tram at Snowbird (3,000′), Ogden's North Fork Trail to Ben Lomond (4,000′), and Farmington Canyon to Francis Peak (4,900′). But the Grandaddy is the 5,700′ grind to Logan Peak—a painfully pleasurable assault.

RIDE 5 *LOGAN PEAK*

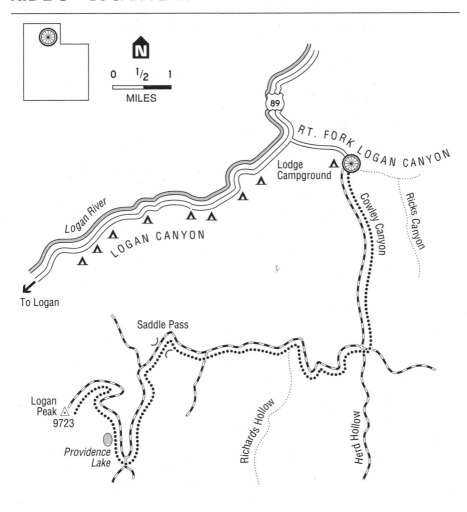

This 28-mile out-and-back route rises along an elevation gradient in which the surrounding forest changes from low-level hardwood brush; to mid-level aspen groves, sagebrush flats, and mixed conifer forests; to alpine old-growth stands of Englemann spruce; and finally to timberline atop Logan Peak. Those who make it to the top will be rewarded with unparalleled views of northern Utah's Bear River Range and Wellsville Mountains, both of which reign over fertile Cache Valley.

Bob enjoys the climb to Logan Peak.

The climb comes in two discernible sections. The first segment to White Bedground Camp is a moderately difficult but sustained ascent mostly on good, hard-packed dirt roads. This is a good out-and-back option for intermediate bikers. The route's second half (reserved for advanced bikers) is a rude assemblage of punishing steps up rough four-wheel-drive roads, climbs that leave you wishing for one smaller granny gear. Early on, the ride is quite enjoyable; nearing the finale the route gets downright ugly—everything a classic hillclimb ought to be. And Logan Peak is destined to be just that—a Utah "classic." Oh yeah, the current record is 1 hour, 45 minutes, 30 seconds.

General location: The Logan Peak Hillclimb begins at the Lodge Campground, located 9 miles up Logan Canyon on the Right Fork Road.
Elevation change: Elevation is the name of the game. Climbing commences at the Lodge Campground, elevation 5,400´. The 1,300´ ascent up Cowley Canyon is a good warm-up. It is followed by sustained climbing to the head of

Richards Hollow and then a relatively mild pull to White Bedground Camp (2,500′ so far). Beyond is a punishing 1,000′ headwall that turns blood-pumped thighs into ground beef. Although the ensuing descent into a back-mountain valley is welcomed, it means more vertical is being tallied: first is an intermittent 460′ teaser, followed by the final 1,100′ soul-searching gut-buster to the apex of Logan Peak (elevation 9,710′). Surprise! The return trip is not all downhill either, for lurking beyond the Providence Lake back-mountain valley is a 700′ muscular meltdown. Congratulations, total climbing is (ugh!) 5,700′. Masseuse, please!

Season: You will have to wait until late spring/early summer for snow to melt off Logan Peak. Since the peak rises to a modest 9,710′, fall cycling will be cold. This route may be popular with big-game hunters during fall.

Services: There is no water along the route. Providence Lake (a generous term) may be dried up by midsummer. Water taps, outhouses, and camping are available at Lodge Campground (the route's starting point) as well as numerous Forest Service campgrounds and picnic areas in Logan Canyon. Logan offers all visitor services.

Hazards: Descending the four-wheel-drive roads off Logan Peak requires attentiveness and acute bike handling skills. Numerous sections are chock-full of loose sediment, gravel, and cobbles, most notably on the steepest grades. The return section from White Bedground Camp to the route's end is an all-out bomber; but watch for vehicular traffic! Be prepared for cool, windy conditions atop Logan Peak, plus the possibility of afternoon rain. Carry a long-sleeve shirt and/or shell.

Rescue index: Logan Peak is no place for a mechanical, physical, or emotional breakdown. Human encounters are less frequent the farther you pedal from the trailhead. Cowley Canyon is popular with motorists on weekends, even up as far as White Bedground Camp. Beyond, you are on your own. Logan has full medical facilities.

Land status: Wasatch-Cache National Forest.

Maps: USGS 7.5 minute quadrangles: Boulder Mountain, Logan Peak, and Temple Peak, Utah.

Finding the trail: From Logan, travel east on US 89 (400 North) into Logan Canyon. Nine miles up the canyon, Right-Hand Fork Road turns off unexpectedly to the right/south between mileposts 383 and 384. (The geologic sign for Fucoidal Quartzite signifies Right-Hand Fork's proximity.) Parking is available near the entrance to the Lodge Campground located a mile from the highway. The ride begins by following Cowley Canyon Road (Forest Service Road 047) south and uphill.

Sources of additional information:

Wasatch-Cache National Forest
Logan Ranger District
860 North 1200 East
P.O. Box 1433
Logan, Utah 84321
(801) 753-2772

Bridgerland Road and Mountain Bike Trails, Cache-Rich Tourist Council
(free brochure): (800) 657-5353.

Notes on the trail: From the Lodge Campground, Cowley Canyon Road
(improved dirt and rock road) offers a good 4-mile warm-up. In the clearing at
the top of the canyon, turn right/west on FS 052 for 3 miles of sustained, aerobic climbing through a corridor of aspen and conifer forests. Take a 2-mile
breather from the junction of FS 052 and Richards Hollow trail to White
Bedground Camp. In the small meadow that signifies White Bedground, an
inviting dirt road leading to Richards Hollow branches left/south. This is the
turnaround point for intermediate cyclists.

If you choose to continue, *now* the climbing begins! Continue toward Logan
Peak on the protracted, rock-strewn, four-wheel-drive road (FS 168) due
west/straight. Not only does the road require brute strength but keen bike
handling skills as well. After 1.5 miles of soul searching, the road reaches a
saddle on a subtle ridge. (Ignore the dirt roads branching north and south.)
Glide over the edge and descend to a junction. Stay left/south and back uphill.
Scenery? Who cares about scenery, just keep those pedals turning. Atop this
small hill, now take a short break to absorb the view. Mixed conifers cover
mountain slopes, meadows are clogged with picture-worthy wildflowers, and a
fortress of banded limestone cliffs towers overhead. That is a false summit, for
Logan Peak resides behind.

Descend to the south again into a back-basin of sorts, ignoring a right-hand
spur that dead-ends at a primitive campsite. After 1 mile, turn right and uphill
on a dirt road marked with a weathered carsonite post. Shortly ahead at a T
junction, stay right and past the dried remains of Providence Lake, which is
more like an ATV velodrome. Two more miles of brutal, four-wheel-drive roads
rise in stairstep fashion to relay towers atop barren Logan Peak.

Views are marvelous: Mt. Naomi Wilderness of the Bear River Range rises to
the north, beyond which is Idaho; the slash in the northern foreground is Logan
Canyon, caged within craggy, quartzite walls; westward are the Wellsville
Mountains; Odgen's Willard and Ben Lomond Peaks head the Wasatch Range,
which disappears into the southern horizon; and below precipitous slopes that
flank Logan Peak sprawls fruitful Cache Valley, through which threads the
convolute meandering belt of the Bear River.

Eat! Replenish those depleted glucose stores in preparation for the dual hill-climb that rises back out from Providence Lake. Then enjoy the 9.5-mile cruise to the route's end.

RIDE 6 *SKYLINE TRAIL*

There are big rides, and then there is Olympic-caliber Skyline Trail. This fat-tire enduro is actually the combination of three closely related single-tracks: Southern Skyline (Pineview), Northern Skyline (North Ogden Pass), and North Fork trails. Each unequivocally defines alpine mountain biking: long, demanding climbs lead to airy ridgelines, quiescent forests and meadows are blanketed with vibrant wildflowers, and single-tracks are nothing less than riveting.

A saturation of top-of-the-world views sets Skyline apart from other alpine routes. Vistas are not simply of mountaintops, although peaks fill the scene like a white-capped sea. Scenic elements include a reservoir-filled valley, stream-nourished farm lands laid out in quilt-like fashion, raw geologic structures exposed with textbook clarity, a reverent metropolis at the foot of godlike mountains, and a great saline lake that is remnant of a once all-encompassing, ice-age predecessor.

Tied together as a 30-mile point-to-point ride, Skyline is reserved for off-road experts, endurance junkies, and "mountain-bike-or-die" hammerheads. If 30 miles sounds wimpy, forego the vehicle shuttle and close the loop with an additional 10 miles of pavement. But strong intermediate cyclists can enjoy Skyline just the same by picking one of the three trailheads (Pineview, North Ogden Pass, or North Fork Park) for great out-and-back routes: Southern Skyline to Lewis Peak is nearly 18 miles round-trip; Northern Skyline and North Fork trails, both of which rise to Ben Lomond, total about 12 miles (round-trip) each. (GWT)

General location: Skyline Trail hovers over Ogden along the crest of the northern Wasatch Range.
Elevation change: Elevation gain comes as 3 sizeable hillclimbs. First is the 3,100′ ascent from the Pineview trailhead (elevation 4,900′) to Lewis Peak (elevation 8,031′). Second is the 2,500′ grind from North Ogden Pass (elevation 6,184′) to the *base* of Ben Lomond (elevation 8,700′). Legs willing, it is another 1,000′ up through highly-technical switchbacks to the very *apex* of 9,712′ Ben Lomond. Total possible elevation gain is 6,600′. Consequently, there is an equal amount of downhill.
Season: Southern Skyline Trail, from Pineview to Lewis Peak, crosses south-facing slopes and melts out by late spring (early May), but the descent into North Ogden Pass may still be snow covered. Likewise, Northern Skyline Trail

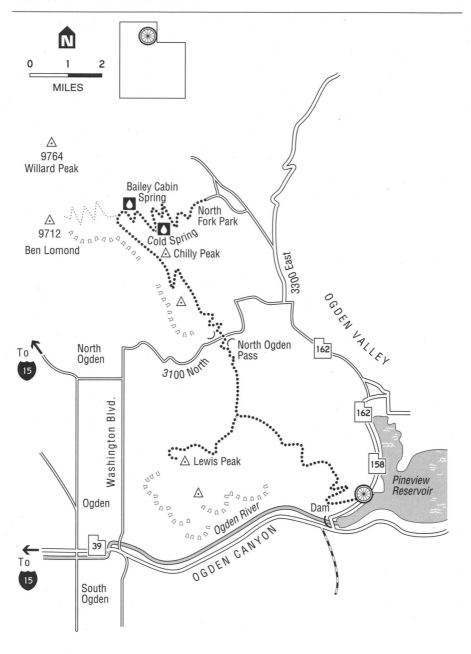

Joe and Chief descend from Ben Lomond Peak.

from North Ogden Pass is a southern exposure and melts out early, but the North Fork Trail may harbor snowdrifts well into June.

Services: All visitor services are found in Ogden, North Odgen, and in Ogden Valley (Pineview Reservoir area), but the latter two do not have bike shops. Rest rooms and water taps are available at the Pineview and North Fork Park trailheads. An outhouse, but *no water tap*, is available at North Ogden Pass. There is no water along the route, except for a small seep at Bailey Cabin Spring atop the North Fork Trail.

Hazards: This grandiose ride will take all the energy you can deliver, and then some. Pack along plenty of high-energy food, three to four large water bottles, and extra clothing. Or travel light and leave a cache of food and water midroute at North Ogden Pass. Consider carrying light-weight raingear; afternoon storms are common. Portions of the trail are highly technical, most notably the descent into North Ogden Pass and portions of North Fork Trail. Be prepared to share the trail, for this multi-use route is very popular. Weekend equestrian traffic is heavy on North Fork Trail.

Rescue index: Because of their multi-use designation, these trails are very popular, especially on weekends and holidays. But do not rely on the assistance of others to compensate for your carelessness or lack of preparedness. Trailheads can be up to 8 miles away. On-trail rescues will be time consuming and difficult. Medical facilities are located in Odgen.

Land status: Wasatch-Cache National Forest.

Maps: USGS 7.5 minute quadrangles: Huntsville and North Ogden, Utah.

Finding the trail: To Pineview trailhead: From Interstate 15, take Exit 347/12th South Street, Ogden Canyon, Recreation Areas. Travel east on UT 39 through Ogden and up Ogden Canyon signed "Recreation Areas." After 5 miles, you'll breach the canyon. Turn left on UT 158 at a sign for Eden, Liberty, and Powder Mountain and cross the Pineview Reservoir dam. A mile ahead is the lakeside parking area. The unobtrusive trailhead marked with a carsonite post with a Great Western Trail emblem is across the highway about 100 yards south next to a dirt road.

To North Ogden Pass trailhead: From I-15, take Exit 352/North Ogden, Plain City, Pleasant View. Drive east on UT 134 for 1 mile. Turn right on US 89 followed immediately by a left on UT 235 (2550 North). Turn left/north on Washington Boulevard (400 East). Just ahead at 2600 North *ignore* signs for North Ogden Pass, for it is a confusing zig-zag route through residential streets. Instead, continue north 1 mile to 3100 North signed "North Ogden Pass." This is a straight shot into the canyon and 3 miles up to the pass/trailhead.

To North Fork Park trailhead: 1) From the Pineview trailhead, travel north on UT 158 (UT 162 on old maps) and through Eden. At the junction for Powder Mountain Ski Area, turn left (should be signed "Old Highway 162"). Come to a T intersection in Liberty after 3 miles. Turn left/west on 4100 North, then right/north at a four-way stop onto 3300 East toward North Fork, Avon. Fork left twice following signs for North Fork Park. Turn left a third time at a sign for horse stalls and camping area. Ahead is a large parking/horse transfer area and a stone monument marking the Ben Lomond Trail. 2) From North Ogden Pass, descend east into Liberty on what becomes 4100 North. At a four-way stop, turn left/north on 3300 East signed "North Fork, Avon." Then proceed as mentioned above.

Sources of additional information:

Wasatch National Forest
Ogden Ranger District
507 25th Street
P.O. Box 1433
Ogden, Utah 84401
(801) 625-5112

Mountain Biking Utah's Wasatch and Uinta Mountains, by Gregg Bromka (Off-Road Publications, Salt Lake City, Utah)

Notes on the trail: Southern Skyline Trail climbs quickly across warm, exposed slopes that support tenacious scrub oak. A fading glimpse of amoeba-shaped Pineview Reservoir, pooled behind the head of Ogden Canyon, is entertaining; this view becomes more impressive with elevation.

The ascent is steady, if not relentless, and offers few breaks. A branch of the Great Western Trail joins from the north after 6.5 miles. Stay left/straight to meet the main ridge just ahead. On the crest, the route to North Odgen Pass is right/north, again signed "Great Western Trail." But the 2.3-mile spur south to Lewis Peak is mandatory, for the mountaintop view of the Great Salt Lake, Ogden metropolis, and Wasatch Front is unsurpassed.

Return from Lewis Peak and pedal north along the ridge. After a mile, fork left at a junction signed "Pineview Res, Lewis Peak," and descend a short distance through a dog-leg that rejoins the ridge. Prepare for the drop to North Ogden Pass. Proceed slowly so you can take in long views of quiltlike farm fields that fill Ogden Valley. Then forget the scenery and hunker down, for the trail dives precipitously through hairpin turns clogged with rocks and root networks.

North Ogden Pass is the decision-making, halfway point. The next 2.5 miles scale 1,000′ through a dozen switchbacks that get progressively more difficult. Angle across the back (east side) of the ridge and then over to its western face. Overwhelming views and slope-hugging trail battle for your attention. (Geologically inquisitive types will spot micro-faults transecting the predominant Wasatch Fault. Together, the exposed Paleozoic sedimentary wedge has been tilted, sliced, thrusted, and transposed.)

An old wooden trail sign marks the base of Ben Lomond. Just looking at the tortuous path rising to its peak brings heavy sighs of desperation. This is unequivocally one of the toughest routes in the Wasatch, so consider parking your rig and taking to foot. Atop Ben Lomond is a plaque explaining the origin of its name, a trail register box, and a vertigo-inducing view along the Wasatch Front.

The route's grand finale is the rollicking descent on the North Fork Trail. From the base of Ben Lomond, head due east into the fir forest, cross a wooden footbridge, and pass Bailey Cabin Spring. Two dozen switchbacks await. Conifers give way to aspens, then oak brush. Portions of the trail are buffed, others choked with rocks. The trail's sheltered midsection is invariably engulfed by thick trailside shrubs and wildflowers. Altogether it is world class.

RIDE 7 *WHEELER CANYON*

Tackling the entire length of Skyline Trail from Pineview Reservoir to North Fork Park may be reserved for the gonzo-abusive types, but for novice bikers, families, or those who have limited time, Wheeler Canyon is the perfect alternative.

Wedged between ledgy limestone cliffs and lightly forested slopes, Wheeler Canyon is a spirited jaunt connecting Ogden Canyon and the Snow Basin access road. A gurgling creek accompanies you along the way while the refrains of songbirds drift from riparian hideaways. And on a warm summer day, nearby Pineview Reservoir offers a cool plunge. The route is also known as Art Nord Drive. A plaque near the top of the canyon bears the inscription: "Named in honor of Arthur George Nord, in grateful recognition of his contributions to the conservation of natural resources."

Wheeler Canyon is a 4-mile out-and back trip—perfect for a little pre-season conditioning. The route is an old dirt road converted to a 10-foot-wide trail of hard-packed dirt with sporadic gravel and imbedded stones. Technical difficulty is low. There are options available for intermediate bikers to extend the ride by several miles by incorporating nearby paved roads. (GWT)

General location: Wheeler Canyon is located 5 miles east of Ogden at the head of Ogden Canyon, near the Pineview Reservoir dam.

Elevation change: The mouth of Wheeler Canyon (parking/trailhead) is at 4,840′. The top of Wheeler Canyon (turnaround point) rises to 5,480′ for a total elevation gain of 640′.

Season: Because of relatively low elevations, Wheeler Canyon may melt out as early as April and remain rideable through the end of October. Midsummer can be very warm. This route is popular with bikers, hikers, and equestrians, especially on weekends and holidays.

Services: There are no services along this route and all surface waters should be purified. There are several cafes and lodges in Ogden Canyon and surrounding Pineview Reservoir. Developed camping is available on the south shore of Pineview Reservoir. Snow Basin Ski Area, located about 4 miles beyond the top of Wheeler Canyon, is not open during the summer, thus no services or water are available. Ogden offers all visitor services, including bike shops.

Hazards: Technical difficulty is generally quite low, but use caution while descending; the route may be littered with gravel and occasional cobbles. Also, be courteous to other trail users by traveling at conservative speeds and yielding the trail.

Rescue index: The route is well traveled on weekends and holidays so encounters with other recreationists are common. At most you are 2 miles from the trailhead. The highway through Ogden Canyon and around the south shore of

RIDE 7 *WHEELER CANYON*

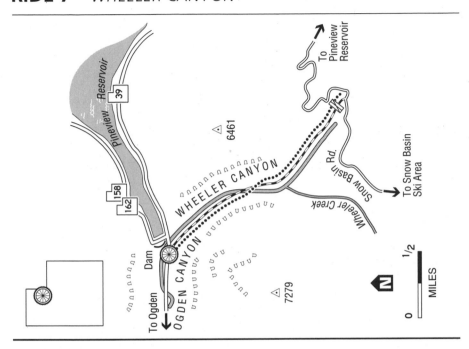

Pineview Reservoir is heavily traveled; telephones can be found at various cafes and lodges. Ogden has medical facilities.

Land status: Wasatch-Cache National Forest.

Maps: USGS 7.5 minute quadrangles: Huntsville and Snow Basin, Utah.

Finding the trail: From Interstate 15, take Exit 347/12th Street, UT 39, Ogden Canyon. Travel 5 miles east on UT 39 and into Ogden Canyon, following signs for Recreation Areas. Immediately *before* the Pineview Reservoir dam the unsigned parking area is to the right/south and alongside the highway. The trail begins at the bottom of the dirt road branching from the parking area.

Sources of additional information:

> Wasatch-Cache National Forest
> Ogden Ranger District
> 507 25th Street, Suite 103
> Ogden, Utah 84401
> (801) 625-5112

> *Mountain Biking Utah's Wasatch and Uinta Mountains,* by Gregg Bromka (Off-Road Publications, Salt Lake City, Utah)

Notes on the trail: Pedal up the canyon 2 miles to the junction with the paved Snow Basin access road. This is the suggested turnaround point for the cruise back down the canyon.

There are a couple of options available to extend this otherwise abbreviated ride. Tack on 8 miles (round-trip) by pedaling the paved road up to Snow Basin Ski Area's main (upper) lodge. The road rises moderately, is lightly traveled, and affords increasingly majestic views of the craggy crown of sovereign Mount Ogden and its court of subservient peaks.

Alternatively, descend the paved road to the shore of Pineview Reservoir and pedal the highway west back to the trailhead near the dam. This 8-mile option (one-way) is full of high-speed sweeping turns, so be aware of vehicular traffic. Overviews of Pineview Reservoir/Ogden Valley (which cliff-entombed Wheeler Canyon cannot afford) are spectacular. The northern Wasatch Range, comprised of Mount Ogden, Lewis Peak, and Ben Lomond, fill the western sky while fertile Ogden Valley sprawls obediently at its feet.

RIDE 8   *FARMINGTON FLATS*

Nestled complacently within the embrace of subtle Bountiful Peak, Farmington Flats is a fine introduction to the joys of fat-tire cycling. This modest alpine basin is peaceful and serene, cloaked with grass meadows and lined with rustling aspen groves. Log and twig dams built by energetic beavers pond a trickling stream into a pearl necklace of reflective pools. Brief views extend both westward across the Great Salt Lake and eastward into fertile Morgan Valley.

Only 5.5 miles long, this loop is well suited for novice and first-time mountain bikers. Improved dirt and four-wheel-drive roads are low in technical difficulty. There is one challenging climb right from the start and a brisk descent at the end, but the majority of the route is quite mellow.

Farmington Flats is also the jump-off point for two intermediate to advanced routes: Skyline Drive rises up to Bountiful Peak; and the Francis Peak Road climbs to the twin air traffic control spheres prominently viewed from the valley below. Both provide powerful vistas of the majestic Wasatch Range and the metropolitan valley it overshadows. These dirt road alternatives are technically easy but cardiac-arresting climbs.

General location: Farmington Flats is found at the head of Farmington Canyon and just behind Bountiful Peak, located 8 miles east of the city of Farmington.

Elevation change: The parking area atop Farmington Canyon is at the route's lowest elevation at 7,230′. It rises to almost 7,600′ while encircling the small

RIDE 8 *FARMINGTON FLATS*

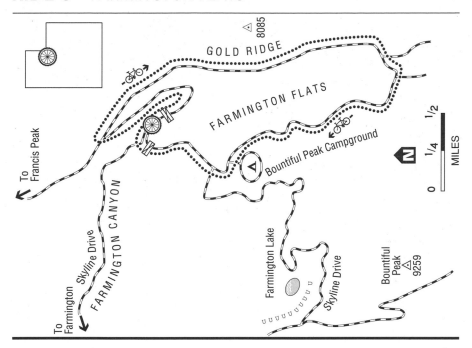

basin. A brisk descent returns you to the trailhead. Total elevation gain is a modest 500´.

Season: Farmington Flats is usually snow-free by early June and rideable throughout October. Midsummer at the Flats is a comforting reprieve from the valley's sweltering heat. Big-game hunters may visit this area during fall.

Services: Farmington offers limited visitor services; Bountiful has all services including bike shops. There are no services along the loop other than USFS Bountiful Peak Campground (water taps available). You'll find a second developed USFS campground at Sunset Campground (5 miles up Farmington Canyon and before the trailhead).

Hazards: Francis Peak Road and Skyline Drive are not technically difficult, but can receive heavy traffic from motorists and off-highway vehicles. The unimproved dirt road looping around the Flats is of low technical difficulty and is traveled less.

Rescue index: Motorists and off-highway vehicles are common on Francis Peak Road and Skyline Drive. The unimproved dirt road that encircles Farmington Flats receives much less use. You are never more than 3 miles from the parking area, and Farmington is 8 miles down canyon. Farmington has a medical clinic.

Bountiful Peak rises above spacious meadows of Farmington Flats.

Land status: Wasatch-Cache National Forest.

Maps: USGS 7.5 minute quadrangle: Bountiful Peak, Utah.

Finding the trail: If traveling north on Interstate 15 (from Salt Lake City), take Exit 326/Farmington. If traveling south on I-15 (from Ogden), take Exit 327/Farmington. Both lead to the same exit ramp. Travel east on Burke Lane to a stop sign. Turn right/south on Main (UT 106), then left/east within one-half mile on 600 North. One block ahead, turn left/north on 100 East, which feeds directly into Farmington Canyon. (Farmington Canyon is improved dirt, gravel, and rock and is suitable for passenger cars.) Eight miles up the canyon is a junction marked by a large brown steel gate. Skyline Drive (where a sign reads "Scenic Backway") forks right; Francis Peak Road is left/straight through the gate. A small pulloff/backcountry campsite at the junction provides limited parking.

Sources of additional information:

Wasatch National Forest
Salt Lake Ranger District
6944 South 3000 East
Salt Lake City, Utah 84121
(801) 943-1794

Mountain Biking Utah's Wasatch and Uinta Mountains, by Gregg Bromka (Off-Road Publications, Salt Lake City, Utah)

Notes on the trail: The ride begins up Francis Peak Road (left/straight and through the brown, steel gate). Skyline Drive (right) is the return route. The improved dirt road rises gently next to the headwaters of Farmington Creek, providing a nice warm-up. Through wedge-shaped Farmington Canyon, Antelope Island floats in the Great Salt Lake's reflective waters. As the road bends north the grade steepens slightly and may test novice riders.

Ahead is a white maintenance building. Turn sharply right/south on an unimproved dirt road to loop around Farmington Flats. (The main road continues north to Francis Peak, 3.5 miles and 2,000 vertical feet away.) After a slight rise, enjoy the effortless cruise around the basin's east side.

On the south end of the Flats, the road bends west and then north for a bit more climbing. (Dirt roads spurring left/south are a good challenge of leg strength and skill level.) Loop past Bountiful Peak Campground and to the junction with Skyline Drive (Scenic Backway). Stay straight/north to complete the loop with a feverish descent to the parking area.

Intermediate to advanced cyclists can extend their day several ways. Tackle the long, sustained climb to Francis Peak, or follow Skyline Drive west past Farmington Lakes and then up to Bountiful Peak. Both vantage points offer overwhelming panoramas of the Great Salt Lake Valley/Wasatch Range assemblage.

But the killer workout begins at the *base* of Farmington Canyon with an 8-mile, 2,700′ climb to the beginning of the Farmington Flats loop. Take a lap around the Flats or knock yourself out with the continued 4.5-mile, 2,300′ grind to Francis Peak. Whew!

RIDE 9   *MILL CREEK TRAIL / MUELLER PARK*

This multi-use trail epitomizes the metro-to-mountains convenience boasted by the Great Salt Lake Valley/Wasatch Mountains transition. Within minutes—literally—the nearby suburban jungle is transformed into a tranquil, backcountry ecosystem of lush riparian growth mixed with hardwoods and mighty conifers. The valley's droning clamor is replaced by spirited sounds of nature, and the odor of urbanization succumbs to the wood's deep, earthy bouquet. Through breaks in the forest cover come good overviews of the Great Salt Lake and the metropolitan valley. And to top it off, pedaling Mill Creek Trail is single-track euphoria.

Mill Creek Trail (coined Mueller Park locally) is a solid intermediate-level, 13-mile out-and-back ride. The maintained Forest Service trail is generally hard-packed dirt, but contains the usual assortment of single-track challenges: intermittent rocky stretches, root networks and water bars, tight but rideable switchbacks, and frequent short, steep climbs. But mostly, the trail is a blissful trip weaving through forested slopes.

RIDE 9 *MILL CREEK TRAIL / MUELLER PARK*

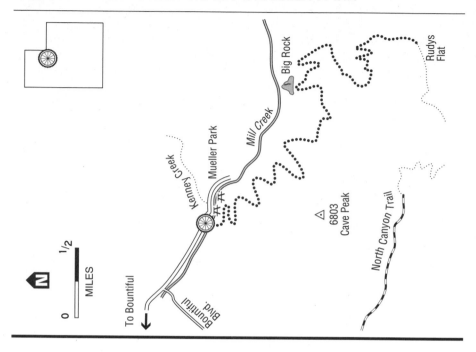

General location: Mueller Park Picnic Ground is located about 2.5 miles east of Bountiful at the mouth of Mill Creek Canyon. (Do not confuse this with the ever-more-popular canyon of the same name in Salt Lake City.)

Elevation change: The Mueller Park Picnic Ground marks the route's trailhead and lowest elevation at 5,250′. Rudy's Flat, the trail's high point and turn-around, rises to 7,160′. Elevation gain is 1,910′.

Season: Because of its lower elevation, this route typically melts out earlier than other Wasatch routes and may be rideable from late April through October. Wildflowers reach their peak earlier in the season as well, usually during May and June. Autumn brings a rich, colorful mixture of hardwoods, aspen, and pine. During midsummer, the trail can be very warm, and afternoon cloud build-up is common.

Services: Picnic tables, water taps, and outhouses are available at the trailhead's Mueller Park Picnic Ground. Overnight camping is not allowed. There is no water available along the route, albeit a handful of trickling springs, which should still be purified. All visitor services, including bike shops, are available in nearby Bountiful.

Hazards: This is a very popular trail among hikers, mountain bikers, equestrians, and motorcyclists alike. Attentiveness is paramount. Anticipate trail users

Laura enjoys an autumn day at Mueller Park.

around blind corners and always *yield the right of way* to others. Control your speed at all times, for trail conditions may change without forewarning. Narrow, wooden footbridges that span creeks and boggy areas are generally in good shape, but these surfaces may be quite slick when wet.

Rescue index: With its growing popularity, solitude is rare on the Mill Creek Trail. Weekends and holidays are especially busy. Residential areas begin at the canyon's mouth, so a phone is nearby. On-trail emergency assistance is difficult.

Land status: Wasatch-Cache National Forest.

Maps: USGS 7.5 minute quadrangle: Fort Douglas, Utah. (This map does not show the route accurately.)

Finding the trail: To access Mueller Park from Interstate 15, take Exit 318/North Salt Lake, Woods Cross. Travel east on 2600 South, then north for 2 miles (2600 South becomes Orchard as it bends north). Turn right/east on 1800 South and travel 2.5 miles directly to Mueller Park Picnic Ground. The trail begins at the wooden bridge spanning Mill Creek. Parking is available.

Sources of additional information:

Wasatch-Cache National Forest
Salt Lake Ranger District
6944 South 3000 East
Salt Lake City, Utah 84121
(801) 943-1794

Mountain Biking Utah's Wasatch and Uinta Mountains, by Gregg Bromka (Off-Road Publications, Salt Lake City, Utah)

Notes on the trail: Immediately after crossing the wooden foot bridge, the trail switchbacks and begins its ascent. Thick stream-side vegetation gives way to a mix of scrub oak, hardwoods, and pine. The trail weaves through numerous side canyons that harbor micro forests of shade-giving aspen and fir. Cross the swath left behind by a newly emplaced natural gas pipeline. Switchback right at Big Rock—the route's halfway point and recommended turnaround for novice cyclists. (For the geologically inquisitive, the marble-white knob is a pegmatite plug—a once molten rock mass that was injected into the surrounding country rock. Its occurrence stems from the Precambrian Farmington Complex immediately north. These contorted metamorphic rocks are a result of the Earth's intense internal heat and pressure. They are dated to be approximately 1.5 billion years old.)

Now, the route steepens and can be moderately technical locally. Aspen, Douglas and subalpine fir, and even spruce forest the hillsides. Rudy's Flat, a small open meadow, marks the top. Return in the opposite direction.

A loop can be constructed by passing west through Rudy's Flat and descending North Canyon. The North Canyon trail is steeper and noticeably more technical than the Mill Creek Trail. The North Canyon trail descends to a rough four-wheel-drive road that parallels the creek, then exits onto pavement in a residential area. Glide downhill, turn right/north on Bountiful Boulevard, pass by the golf course (helmet still on?), then turn right on Mueller Park Road and back to the parking area. Advanced cyclists might like to ride this loop version in reverse by ascending North Canyon first.

RIDE 10 *CITY CREEK CANYON*

The road leading up City Creek Canyon is paved, so it may not qualify as a true off-road route. But the metro-to-canyon experience is so rewarding that City Creek ranks as a local all-time-favorite bike route. Best of all, the canyon is merely one mile from the city's central business district. Within minutes it is possible to trade the frenzied urban atmosphere for a serene mountain environment.

City Creek is a backcountry treasure and its location is an unbeatable asset. An array of riparian brush lines the creek's banks while box elder, cottonwood, pine, oak, and maple overhang the roadway. Springtime wildflowers coat open slopes, and cool shadows are cast by enclosing cliff lines. Songbirds, owls, hawks, squirrels, deer, and even moose inhabit the lush canyon. A dozen roadside picnic sites offer intimate canyon-visitor relations.

RIDE 10   *CITY CREEK CANYON*

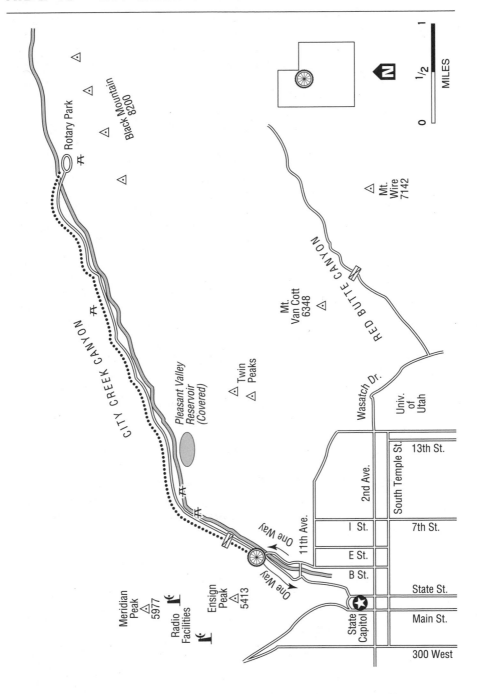

A decade ago, City Creek gained national recognition when swollen spring runoff turned this cascading rivulet into thundering rapids. Fearful of potential flood damage resultant from its uncontrollable flow, Salt Lake City officials transformed the main thoroughfare, State Street, into a temporary overflow canal bound by mile-long sandbag levees. "This is a helluva way to run a desert," declared the late governor Scott Matheson.

City Creek is a joy for novice to advanced cyclists. Ride the entire 12 miles out-and-back, or bite off just a small taste. The lower canyon rises gently; the last two miles is a sustained hillclimb.

General location: City Creek Canyon is located in the foothills directly north of Salt Lake City behind the State Capitol.

Elevation change: The entrance gate to City Creek Canyon is at 4,700′. The 6-mile-long paved road rises to 6,045′. Total climbing is 1,345′. More than half of the total elevation is gained over the last 2 miles from the filtration plant to Rotary Park.

Season: City Creek Canyon is open to year-round recreation, but the bicycling season generally spans from late March through November. The canyon has a specific (and strongly enforced) use policy from Memorial Day through Labor Day. Pedestrian traffic is allowed every day, motorists may enter the canyon on even-numbered days and holidays, and bicycle traffic is *allowed* on odd-numbered days but is *prohibited* on even-numbered days and holidays regardless of odd-even status.

Services: During the summer, water fountains are available at the canyon's entrance gate and about 4 miles up at the filtration plant. The creek itself, like all mountain surface waters, should be purified. Downtown Salt Lake City is 1 mile from the canyon's entrance.

Hazards: Since this is a paved road, hazards are minimal. Scattered gravel, broken pavement, and seasonal potholes may dot the road, especially the upper section. Most importantly, watch for other recreationists. Abide by the rules of the road by staying to the far right and riding in single file. Control your speed when descending, and be very cautious when rounding blind corners. Maintenance vehicles may be present at any time.

Rescue index: Emergency contacts may be made from the guard station at the canyon's entrance and possibly from the filtration plant 4 miles up the canyon. City Creek Canyon is a very popular recreational destination.

Land status: Salt Lake City Public Utilities Department (Watershed Management).

Maps: USGS 7.5 minute quadrangles: Fort Douglas and Salt Lake City North, Utah.

Finding the trail: From Salt Lake City's central business district, travel north on State Street, turn right/east on 2nd Avenue, then left/north on B Street and travel uphill to 11th Avenue. Bonneville Boulevard Loop provides access into City Creek Canyon. This is a one-way road where vehicular traffic is confined

City Creek Canyon—a backcountry sanctuary minutes from downtown Salt Lake City.

to the right lane (outside lane) and must travel east to west (Avenues to Capitol Hill). Recreationists (foot and bike traffic) must use the inside lane but may travel in either direction. The City Creek Canyon road branches from the loop's northern bend and leads a short distance to the gate/parking area.

Sources of additional information:

Salt Lake City Corporation
Public Utilities Department
Watershed Management
1530 South West Temple
Salt Lake City, Utah 84115
(801) 483-6705

City Creek Canyon Reservations
(801) 483-6757

Mountain Biking Utah's Wasatch and Uinta Mountains, by Gregg Bromka (Off-Road Publications, Salt Lake City, Utah)

Notes on the trail: Pedal up the paved canyon road to its end at Rotary Park. The first 2 miles to the cement-topped Pleasant Valley Reservoir are perfect for novice cyclists. Add another 2 miles to the water treatment plant. Beyond, the road rises noticeably steeper to Rotary Park and the road's end. Regardless of the ride's length, the brisk descent is a well-earned reward.

In 1989 the City Creek Master Plan forbade bicycling *off* City Creek Canyon's paved road. To eliminate growing conflicts between user groups and potential erosional problems, the cross country ski trail that parallels the paved road, the dirt road extending from pavement's end at Rotary Park, and *all* trails, routes, and roads descending into the canyon were closed to mountain bikes (regardless of odd-even day status). Bicycling is allowed *solely* on the paved road. Watershed Management officers have the authority to cite and fine violators.

RIDE 11 *BIG WATER TRAIL*

Unequivocally the most popular trail in the Wasatch Range, the Big Water Trail to Dog Lake is without question *the* introduction to Salt Lake City–area mountain biking. When newcomers or first-time mountain bikers ask where to ride, "Dog Lake" is most certainly the response.

Originally maintained for motorcycles (now prohibited), the route has since been quickly adopted by non-consumptive forms of recreation, including hiking and horseback riding. Over the years, mountain bikers have found Big Water to be ideal for knobby tires. The route is void of powerful vistas, punishing climbs, and frightening downhills, but other Wasatch rides offer plenty of that. Big Water is simply an unintimidating cruise through the forest that ends at a small alpine pond worthy of idle time. Along the way, shadows cast by intertwined pines fill darkened corridors; sunlight filters through groves of quaking aspen; trickling creeks nourish a plentitude of trail-side wildflowers. Big Water should *not* be a hurried ride but one on which you can relax and enjoy the trail-side scenery.

This 6.5-mile out-and-back trail may prove challenging for novice cyclists. Although technical difficulty is low, there are a few modest inclines. Even so, ambitious beginners as well as seasoned mountain bikers will find Big Water a small slice of fat-tire heaven.

General location: The Big Water Trail is located at the top of Salt Lake City's Mill Creek Canyon.

Elevation change: The trailhead is at the route's lowest elevation at 7,600′. The trail rises to 8,560′ at the "Dog Lake/Desolation Lake" trail sign just above Dog Lake. Total elevation gain is 960′.

Season: Depending upon winter's snow and spring's thaw, the Big Water Trail typically melts out between late May and mid-June and should be rideable through October. Wildflowers grow in profusion immediately after the snow

RIDE 11 *BIG WATER TRAIL*

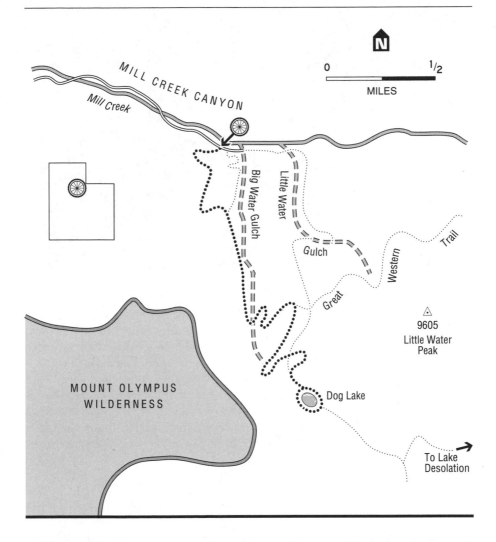

melts and they bloom into August. Autumn colors in Mill Creek Canyon rival those of New England states with a vibrant blend of oak, maple, willow, aspen, and cottonwood. Mill Creek Canyon Road and its trails, particularly the Big Water Trail, receive heavy use on weekends and holidays.

Services: Salt Lake City offers all visitor services, including many top-flight bike shops. Outhouses are available at the trailhead, but there are no water taps. Mill Creek Canyon is lined with numerous developed picnic areas that

Aspen leaves speckle the Big Water Trail.

offer tables, outhouses, and water taps, but overnight camping is prohibited.

Hazards: You will encounter other trail users at any time and on any day, including fellow mountain bikers, equestrians, and hikers. Because of the trail's ease, you'll see families with children and pets frequently. Watch out for them since they, especially toddlers, may not be watching for you. Yield the trail, and ride at a controlled speed so that you can stop *safely* if need be. Big Water should be a fun ride, *not* a fast ride. (Rangers will not hesitate to issue citations for excessive speed or recklessness—or venturing into nearby Mount Olympus Wilderness either.) Watch out for a handful of rocks, log water bars, and tight turns.

Rescue index: You'll rarely be alone on the Big Water Trail because it's so popular. Forest Service rangers do not patrol this and adjacent trails on a regular basis. Emergency assistance can be summoned from the fee station near the canyon's mouth.

Land status: Wasatch-Cache National Forest. Immediately west of Dog Lake is the Mount Olympus Wilderness. Remember, bicycles are prohibited in Wilderness Areas.

Maps: USGS 7.5 minute quadrangle: Mount Aire, Utah. (The Big Water Trail is not shown accurately on this map.)

Finding the trail: Mill Creek Canyon Road begins at 3800 South and Wasatch Boulevard in Salt Lake City. (If traveling Interstate 215 northward, take Exit 4/3900 South; if traveling I-215 southward, take Exit 3/3300 South. In either case, Wasatch Boulevard leads to 3800 South.) Travel 9.5 miles up the canyon's paved road to its end. Two parking areas provide ample space for vehicles. The signed trailhead branches from the lower of the two parking areas. (A fee of $2 per vehicle is collected upon leaving Mill Creek Canyon. There is no fee for foot and bicycle traffic entering the canyon.)

Sources of additional information:

Wasatch-Cache National Forest
Salt Lake Ranger District
6944 South 3000 East
Salt Lake City, Utah 84121
(801) 943-1794

Mountain Biking Utah's Wasatch and Uinta Mountains, by Gregg Bromka (Off-Road Publications, Salt Lake City, Utah)

Notes on the trail: Because of the ever-growing popularity and increased usage of Mill Creek Canyon trails by mountain bikers, the Forest Service has initiated an odd-even day use policy. Mountain bikes are *allowed* on Mill Creek Canyon trails on weekdays and odd-numbered weekend days (Saturday and Sunday). Mountain bikers are *prohibited* from using Mill Creek Canyon trails on even-numbered weekend days. (This includes Big and Little Water trails and Great Western Trail up to the Park West Ski Area saddle.)

Although there are several new trail junctions along the route, the trail is simple to follow. After one-half mile, the Upper Big Water Trail joins from the left. (This is a steeper alternative best traveled by foot.) Cross a wooden footbridge spanning Big Water Gulch and then pedal up into the darkened forest. The Great Western Trail branches left 1.5 miles from the trailhead; Dog Lake is straight ahead. Keep chugging up the trail. The Little Water Trail crosses the Big Water Trail and signifies the top's proximity. (Little Water Trail is half as long and twice as steep as Big Water Trail.) Swing through a tight, right-hand turn and then ride to the signed junction for Dog Lake 0.1 mi., Lake Desolation 2.6 (left), Mount Olympus Wilderness 0.3 (right). Take a lap around Dog Lake (an alpine pond with no outlet) and then return to the trailhead. Although the descent may invite a brisk pace, control your speed. Please, do not jeopardize the continued privilege to pedal the Big Water Trail; ride responsibly and with respect for other trail users.

RIDE 12 *WASATCH CREST*

The Wasatch Crest Trail is one of northern Utah's premier mountain bike routes and recently has been incorporated into the Great Western Trail. Nearly all single-track, the Crest Trail traces the spine of the central Wasatch Range,

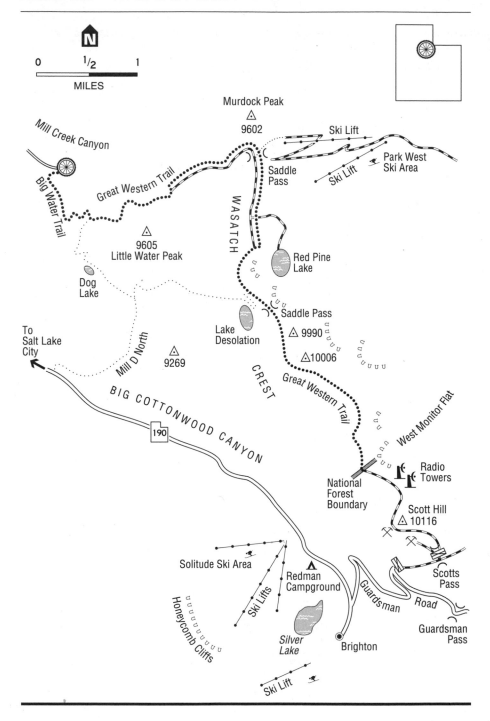

An early evening ride along the Wasatch Crest.

coined "the Backbone of Utah."

Its single-track alone is euphoric. The total backcountry experience is unbeatable. But mostly there are great views of lush alpine basins feeding stream-filled canyons, overpowering views of glacially carved bowls locked in the embrace of chiseled mountaintops, endless views to distant mountain ranges and valleys, somewhat perplexing views of an expansive metropolitan valley resting a mile below, and from selected points there are combined views of all.

Strength, endurance, and polished bike handling skills are prerequisites for this 20-mile out-and-back route. It is generally reserved for strong intermediate and advanced mountain bikers. There are challenging climbs followed by graceful descents, moderately technical conditions, and a generous helping of frolicsome single-track. (GWT)

General location: This section of the Great Western Trail connects the tops of

Brian squeezes through a corridor of crooked aspen.

Mill Creek and Big Cottonwood Canyons.

Elevation change: The Big Water trailhead and parking area is at the route's lowest elevation at 7,600′. The route south of Lake Desolation rises to just shy of 10,000′. But there is an extra 1,000′ of elevation hidden in the undulating ridgeline. Total climbing is in the neighborhood of 3,300′.

Season: The Wasatch Crest is usually rideable from mid-June through most of October. Both cool midsummer temperatures and unpredictable alpine weather justify packing along extra clothing and/or a rain jacket.

Services: Prepare for this ride before leaving the metro-valley; there are no services or potable water along the route. Developed picnic areas lining Mill Creek Canyon have water taps. All visitor services are available in Salt Lake City.

Hazards: The single-track harbors some demanding sections, including loose and imbedded rocks, root networks, and exposure to steep side slopes. None is unusually hazardous. Bedrock exposed in the trail above Lake Desolation warrants dismounting and walking about 100 feet. Most importantly watch for other users; trail traffic may be heavy on weekends and holidays. Always prepare for cool, unpredictable alpine weather.

Rescue index: Along the ridge, you are up to 10 miles or more from a phone and even farther from emergency help. The route is quite popular on weekends and holidays; other times may bring you complete solitude.

Land status: Wasatch-Cache National Forest.

Maps: USGS 7.5 minute quadrangles: Brighton, Mount Aire, and Park West,

Utah. (Portions are incorrectly mapped.)

Finding the trail: The route begins on the Big Water Trail in upper Mill Creek Canyon. Mill Creek Canyon Road begins at 3800 South and Wasatch Boulevard in Salt Lake City. (If traveling Interstate 215 northward, take Exit 4/3900 South, 3300 South; if traveling I-215 southward, take Exit 3/3300 South. In either case, Wasatch Boulevard leads to 3800 South.) Travel 9.5 miles up the canyon's paved road to its end. Two parking areas provide ample space for vehicles. The signed Big Water Trail branches from the lower of the two parking areas. (A fee of $2 per vehicle is collected upon leaving Mill Creek Canyon. There is no fee for foot and bicycle traffic.)

Sources of additional information:

> Wasatch-Cache National Forest
> Salt Lake Ranger District
> 6944 South 3000 East
> Salt Lake City, Utah 84121
> (801) 943-1794
>
> *Mountain Biking Utah's Wasatch and Uinta Mountains,* by Gregg Bromka (Off-Road Publications, Salt Lake City, Utah)

Notes on the trail: Because of the ever-growing popularity and increased usage of Mill Creek Canyon trails by mountain bikers, the Forest Service has initiated an odd-even day use policy. Mountain bikes are *allowed* on Mill Creek Canyon trails on weekdays and odd-numbered weekend days (Saturday and Sunday). Mountain bikes are *prohibited* from Mill Creek Canyon trails on even-numbered weekend days. (This includes Big and Little Water trails and Great Western Trail up to the Park West Ski Area saddle. South of the Park West saddle and along the Wasatch Crest to Big Cottonwood Canyon, the policy does not apply.)

Access to the Wasatch Crest begins 1.5 miles up the Big Water Trail, signed "Great Western Trail" (left). Pass the signed junction for Little Water Trail, then follow the sign for Desolation Lake up to the Park West Ski Area saddle. (This junction is marked by an "odd-even day use" sign.) Turn right/south and ride up the double-track into the pine forest. You'll come upon another overlook of Park West. At a junction with a dirt road that drops east into Red Pine Canyon, continue straight ahead along the ridge. (Red Pine Canyon is private property; recreational access is not allowed without permission.)

The route now reverts to single-track and climbs very aggressively up a short, technical hill where a panorama of the Park City valley and High Uintas awaits. Leave upper Mill Creek Canyon behind and descend to the trail junction above Lake Desolation where a sign reads "Guardsman Road 6" (left); "Desolation Lake .5" (right); "Great Western Trail" (reverse). Stay left/straight and push up and over the red quartzite outcrop to continue the single-track south, high above Lake Desolation. But first enjoy the view of Lake Desolation cupped beneath the ridge line, Gobblers Knob and Raymond Peak due west, and the growing Cottonwood Ridge to the south.

Few single-tracks are better than this as the trail traces the undulating ridge line. About a mile south of Lake Desolation, an overwhelming view of Big Cottonwood Canyon and the central Wasatch may encourage you to break out into the theme song from the movie *The Sound of Music*. Single-track grades back to double-track about 3 miles south of Lake Desolation at a "Leaving Wasatch National Forest" sign. This is the recommended turnaround point since the route now crosses on to private property. (Beyond this point the double-track leads past Scott Hill, then down to Scott's Pass and finally to Guardsman Road, which is a popular but unofficial trailhead. The Forest Service is attempting to establish an official trailhead on Guardsman Road, so contact the Salt Lake Ranger District for current access status.)

RIDE 13 *ALBION BASIN*

Albion Basin is the heart of the central Wasatch Range and birthplace of a glacier. Ten millennia ago, a thick wedge of snow accumulated and compressed into ice, which then began creeping down toward the Great Salt Lake Valley. In turn, smaller glaciers descended from the southern ridge line to join the main trough. The deeply scoured, U-shaped valley of Little Cottonwood Canyon and its elevated, hanging valleys were left in their wake. Rugged peaks that stood above the moving ice were sculpted into a chaotic assemblage of craggy mountaintops—Devil's Castle, Sugarloaf Mountain, Mount Wolverine, and Superior Peak—that now embrace Albion Basin. Twin and Dromedary Peaks, the Pfeifferhorn, and Lone Peak enclose the canyon's length.

A visit to Albion Basin would not be complete without a trip to Secret Lake. This icy glacial pool cupped beneath Devil's Castle makes for an ideal lunch spot or midday siesta. Although the rocky half-mile-long path is not recommended for bikes, it is a pleasant hike. Be sure to pack along a camera and plenty of film; even a rainbow's vivid colors are challenged by Albion's palate of glorious wildflowers.

This route is not one of surmounting lofty mountain passes or battling technical descents into steep-walled valleys. Rather, it is a mild, 6-mile out-and-back tour through a postcard-perfect alpine basin wrapped in mighty peaks. The combination of good dirt roads and gentle to moderate grades make it well suited for novice cyclists and any mountain biker who is an avid "flower-sniffer." Seasoned bikers can always tackle Alta Ski Area's Germania Pass loop—one of northern Utah's classic hillclimbs.

RIDE 13 *ALBION BASIN*

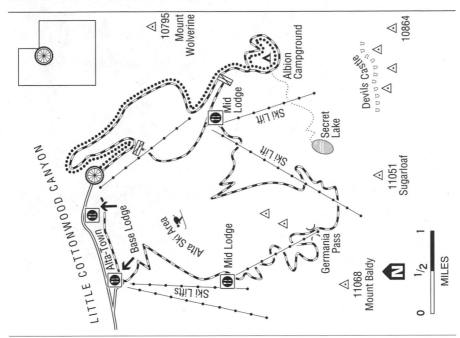

General location: Albion Basin is part of Alta Ski Area, located 20 miles southeast of Salt Lake City at the top of Little Cottonwood Canyon.

Elevation change: The parking area/trailhead is at 8,800´. Albion Campground marks the high point at 9,600´ for a modest 800´ gain.

Season: Albion Basin *usually* melts out by mid-June and is rideable through mid-October, but this is highly dependent on seasonal snowfall, spring thaw, and autumn flurries. (Remember, Alta Ski Area boasts a 100- to 150-inch base during ski season, which does not end until April 30th.) As always, be prepared for cool and unpredictable alpine weather.

There are few locations in the Wasatch Range where wildflowers grow in such plentitude. You can readily identify dozens of species and will note how subtle changes in elevations, slope orientation, and exposure dictate a species' abundance. The Red Butte Garden and Arboretum's wildflower hotline (801) 581-4747 tells when mountain flowers are at their peak.

Services: A snack stand is located at the route's parking area. It offers robust sandwiches, cold drinks, and munchies galore. Along the route, water taps and outhouses are available at the USFS Albion Basin Campground.

Those craving a heartier meal will find an array of continental and interna-

Devils Castle keeps a watchful eye over Secret Lake.

tional cuisines at Snowbird Resort, located 1 mile down canyon. During late summer, Octoberfest, complete with dancing, beer chugging, bratwurst and sauerkraut, and of course revelling oom-pah bands, visits the Plaza.

Lodging is available near Alta and at Snowbird Resort. Mountain bike rentals are available at Snowbird's Activity Center (801) 521-6040.

Hazards: The route is popular with motorists, especially on weekends and holidays, and particularly during the height of midsummer's wildflower show. Pedal to the far right and be prepared to share the road. This is alpine terrain, so cool, quickly changing weather and possible thunderstorms are common.

If exploring Alta's other route (Germania Pass), be aware of resort machinery that may be operating at any time and place, especially up slope.

Rescue index: Albion Basin is a popular mountain retreat from the nearby metropolitan area. Thus, you'll see plenty of motorists, hikers, and other mountain bikers. Telephones are available at lodges near the trailhead. Snowbird Resort (a mile down canyon) has emergency services.

Land status: Wasatch-Cache National Forest. Summer homes dot the basin. Respect the rights of these private property owners by staying on designated roads and trails.

Maps: USGS 7.5 minute quadrangles: Brighton and Dromedary Peak, Utah.

Finding the trail: Little Cottonwood Canyon is the southernmost paved canyon in the Salt Lake section of the Wasatch Range. From Salt Lake City, travel Interstate 215 to Exit 6/6200 South, Ski Areas. Travel southeast to the junction of Wasatch Boulevard and Fort Union Boulevard (7200 South). Continue south on Wasatch Boulevard (UT 210) for Alta/Snowbird. When Wasatch Boulevard forks right for La Caille, stay straight on UT 210, which bends east and into Little Cottonwood Canyon. Alta Ski Area is uphill from Snowbird Resort. The parking area/trailhead is where pavement ends and the dirt/gravel road begins.

Sources of additional information:

Wasatch-Cache National Forest
Salt Lake Ranger District
6944 South 3000 East
Salt Lake City, Utah 84121
(801) 943-1794

Mountain Biking Utah's Wasatch and Uinta Mountains, by Gregg Bromka (Off-Road Publications, Salt Lake City, Utah)

Notes on the trail: Pedal up the dirt and gravel road to the Albion Basin Campground. Take a lap around the campground, and return the opposite way.

To mix in a little excitement to this otherwise undaunting route, follow an optional four-wheel-drive road back to the trailhead. After exiting the campground, turn left/west onto a dirt road and pass around an orange steel gate. Descend toward the base of the Sugarloaf Lift, but not all the way. Turn right/north and descend another jeep road through the basin. This descent is steeper and typically laden with gravel and loose cobbles, so proceed cautiously. The road exits onto the main Albion Basin Road at a gate on a bend. Return to the parking area by coasting down the main road.

Those who prefer a solid workout can tackle the Germania Pass loop, home of the annual Alta Rustler Run mountain bike race. From the parking area, pedal up the Albion Basin Road. But at the first switchback, pass through an orange steel gate and up the rough four-wheel-drive road to the base of Sugarloaf Lift. Now the fun begins—the 1,200′ climb to Germania Pass. The descent through Ballroom Bowl and Collins Gulch is fast and furious. Watch for loose gravel, tight turns, and unannounced drainage ditches crossing the road. Upon dropping to Goldminers Daughter Lodge, pedal the tow rope to the upper parking area. (By the way, during the Rustler Run, expert/pro-class racers do the loop *twice*.)

RIDE 14   *PROVO RIVER PARKWAY*

The Provo River Parkway is well suited for those who like a simple approach to mountain biking—lightly spinning the pedals, coasting a bit, stopping for a

RIDE 14 *PROVO RIVER PARKWAY*

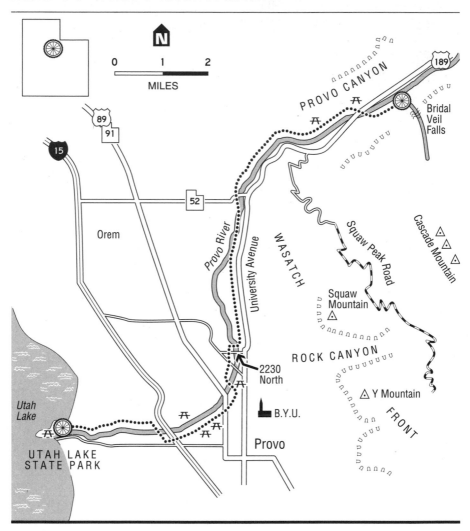

midafternoon siesta next to a stream, or a short jaunt with the family.

The Parkway threads through the heart of Provo connecting Provo Canyon (Bridal Veil Falls) with Utah Lake (State Park). Along the way, the path meanders through nearly a dozen city and county parks and at most times along the banks of placid Provo River, constantly overshadowed by the central Wasatch Range. The Parkway attracts bikers, runners, and walkers of all ages and abilities.

This 13-mile point-to-point route follows a narrow recreational path.

Cascade Mountain is a backdrop to the Provo River Parkway.

Portions are paved while other segments are hard-packed dirt and gravel. The most appealing part of this ride is that you can ride the entire route at once or pursue incremental segments from park to park.

General location: The Provo River Parkway follows the Provo River as it flows out of Provo Canyon through the center of Provo and to the shore of Utah Lake.
Elevation change: Bridal Veil Falls (eastern trailhead) is at 5,120′. Utah Lake State Park (western trailhead) is at 4,500′. Since the grade is nearly imperceptible, the route is enjoyable when you ride in either direction.
Season: You can enjoy the Parkway nearly year-round. Midsummer (July and August) can be very warm with daytime temperatures near 100 degrees. During midwinter, the path may be covered with snow (which can make for a fun day of cross-country ski touring, if you are so inclined).

City and county parks along the route are open from early April through October. The Parkway is very popular on weekends and holidays.
Services: Services abound along the entire length of the parkway because it passes through the center of Provo, plus 10 city and county parks. All parks have water taps and restrooms. Food and snacks can be found at Bridal Veil Falls (eastern trailhead) and at numerous locations along the way. Utah Lake State Park offers developed campgrounds. Provo boasts all visitor services, including bike shops.
Hazards: The Parkway is a narrow, two-lane path (about 8 feet wide) with

recreational traffic flowing in both directions; watch for oncoming recreationists. Bikes should travel in single file since the route is too narrow to ride two abreast safely. At trailheads and where the Parkway crosses roadways, the path may be blocked by gates, entrance labyrinths, or wooden posts that restrict motorized access. These are usually quite visible, but could cause injury if you were to run into them. Yield to vehicular traffic. Finally, this is not a time-trials course; pedal at prudent speeds and with courtesy for other users.

Rescue index: The path is well traveled by recreationists and winds through commercial and residential areas where telephones are easily accesible. Along the last 1.5 miles to the route's western trailhead (Utah Lake State Park), the path passes through farm and ranch lands where residences are more dispersed. Provo has medical facilities.

Land status: Provo City Parks and Recreation.

Maps: A small trail map is available through Provo City Parks and Recreation. See "Sources of additional information."

Finding the trail: To the western trailhead (Utah Lake State Park), take Exit 268/Center Street, UT 114, Utah Lake State Park off Interstate 15. Drive 3 miles west on Center Street/UT 114. Just before Utah Lake State Park's entrance, turn north. The Parkway's trailhead/parking area (unsigned) is shortly ahead on the right.

   To the eastern trailhead (Bridal Veil Falls), from I-15, take Exit 275/8th North (Orem), Provo Canyon, UT 52, US 189. Drive 3.5 miles east toward the Wasatch Mountains and enter Provo Canyon via US 189 North. The signed turnoff for Bridal Veil Falls/Nunns Park is located 3.5 miles up Provo Canyon, between mileposts 10 and 11. Parking is available at the bottom of the exit ramp, north under the highway at Nunns Park, or half a mile ahead at Bridal Veil Falls.

Sources of additional information:

> Provo City Parks and Recreation
> P.O. Box 1849
> Provo, Utah 84603
> (801) 379-6600

Notes on the trail: The following is a summary for the route from Bridal Veil Falls to Utah Lake State Park—eastern to western trailheads. (Note: Mileage markers are posted every half mile alongside the paved path in ascending order beginning at Utah Lake State Park, which is mile 0, and ending at Bridal Veil Falls, which is mile 13. But, mileages noted in the description below were determined by a bicycle computer beginning at Bridal Veil Falls, mile 0, and ending at Utah Lake State Park, mile 13. It is easy to recognize this inverse relationship between mileages noted to those marked alongside the bike path.)

   Ride down Bridal Veil Fall's access road half a mile, then cross under the highway to Nunns Park. Simply follow the Parkway's yellow dashed lines. The next park is Canyon Glen. Along this section, the path parallels Provo River through Provo Canyon beneath towering, craggy cliffs of contorted limestone. The Parkway passes under the highway at the mouth of Provo Canyon (mile 3.5), then heads south alongside US 189 and beneath the shear face of Cascade Mountain. Mount Timpanogos recedes gradually behind and to the north while Provo Peak gains majestic stature. The Parkway has veered away from Provo River but will rejoin its banks after a few miles.

Cross 4800 North, a busy intersection (mile 5) where US 189 becomes University Avenue. You'll reach Wills Pit Stop and Convenience Store at the corner of 3700 North and University Avenue (mile 6). Here the Parkway jogs east a few yards, then parallels the curbside of University Avenue.

At the intersection of University Avenue and 2230 North (mile 7.5), turn right/west and cross Freedom Boulevard. Immediately ahead, leave the sidewalk by veering right at the power/electric substation just *before/east* of Provo River. The path crosses the river via a footbridge, then turns left/south and passes *under* 2230 North.

Now the Parkway rejoins the bank of Provo River, winding idly through a forested canopy as a hard-packed dirt and gravel path. You'll pass a number of city parks, including Exchange Park (mile 9), Riverside Park (mile 9.5), and Wilderness/Paul Rein Parks (mile 10). At mile 11, the path crosses Geneva Road/2050 West.

The last 2 miles parallel Provo River as it meanders through farm and ranch lands. Portions of the path can be sandy. This section affords striking views of the Wasatch Range from Lone Peak (north), through Mount Timpanogos and Provo Peak (central), all the way to Mount Nebo (south).

For incremental segments try the following trailheads and parking areas: Bridal Veil Falls/Nunns Park (3.5 miles up Provo Canyon), mouth of Provo Canyon (junction of UT 52 and US 189, behind the convenience store), Wills Pit Stop (corner University Avenue and 3700 North, park next to white fence), Riverside Plaza (University Parkway and 2230 North), Exchange Park (900 North and 700 West), Riverside Park (1260 West and 600 North), Geneva Road (2050 West and approx. 300 North), Utah Lake State Park (approximately 4000 West on Center Street).

RIDE 15 *SQUAW PEAK ROAD*

Squaw Peak Road reveals some truly exceptional alpine vistas of the southern Wasatch Range. At the beginning, the route supplies two great views: waterfall-infested Provo Canyon and the sky-scraping peaks comprising the Mount Timpanogos Wilderness Area. From midroute there is an inspiring overlook into Rock Canyon. This narrow canyon widens quickly as it rises above Provo,

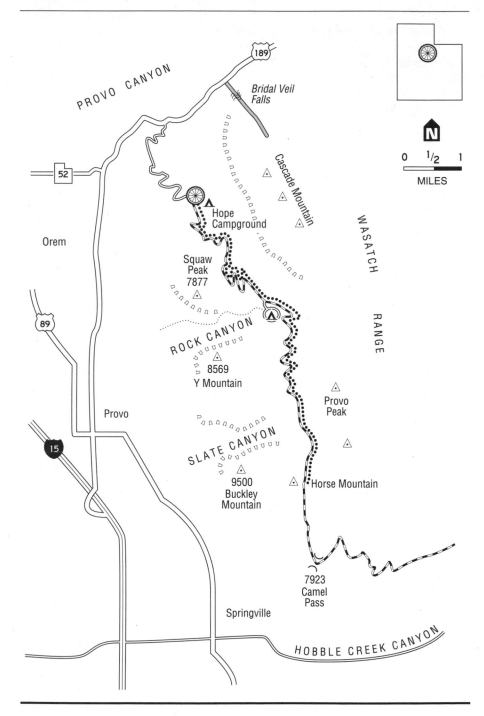

189

PROVO CANYON

Bridal Veil
Falls

Cascade Mountain

52

WASATCH

Hope
Campground

Orem

Squaw
Peak
7877

ROCK CANYON

RANGE

89

8569
Y Mountain

Provo
Peak

Provo

SLATE CANYON

15

9500
Buckley
Mountain

Horse Mountain

N

0   1/2   1

MILES

7923
Camel
Pass

Springville

HOBBLE CREEK CANYON

Provo Peak towers over Squaw Peak Road.

giving way to massive, convoluted cliffs and dark, pine-covered mountaintops. Simultaneously, the western slopes of 11,000′ Provo Peak and bulky Cascade Mountain appear no more than arm's length away and demand attention. Their shadows that fill this hidden alpine valley evoke a feeling of tranquility.

Near the route's end are heart-throbbing angles at the Kolob Basin Overlook. Nearly the entire route from beginning to end is outlined with outstanding aerial perspectives of Utah Valley. Trace the razor-sharp Wasatch Fault as it curves along the base of Spanish Fork Peak and Loafer Mountain en route to the Wasatch's monarch, Mount Nebo.

This 26-mile out-and-back route requires little technical skill; it combines improved dirt and gravel roads with four-wheel-drive roads. But strong legs and lungs will aid in handling the high-altitude ascents. The entire route is for advanced-level cyclists, but intermediate bikers can attempt shortened versions.

Details on the Squaw Peak Road were provided by Ron Lindley,[*] Provo, Utah.

General location: Squaw Peak Road is located high above Provo, between

---

[*]A native of Utah, Ron Lindley has always maintained an undying fascination for the wealth of natural wonders in the Wasatch Mountains and far reaches of southern Utah's canyon country. Up until 1985, he was content with exploring this domain on foot.

Ron Lindley—captain of the Fishlips Mountain Bike Team.

Provo Canyon and Hobble Creek Canyon.
Elevation change: Starting elevation at Hope Campground is 6,700´. The road

---

(continued from page 67)
Then, while hiking near his Provo home, Ron paused to reconsider his sluggish method of travel when a mountain biker danced past him like a nimble mountain goat. Eight years and a dozen mountain bikes later (not that he collects them; he keeps breaking them), Ron has biked nearly every nook and cranny from the Central Wasatch to the Utah/Arizona border, and to nearly every natural hot spring in the intermountain west.

However, frustrated with having to travel to other regions of the state to participate in mountain bike races and disappointed with the lack of local events, Ron co-founded Salamander Promotions (parent of the White Salamander Mountain Bike Squad), which organizes the annual Bike-O-Rama and Tour of Diamond Fork, Utah County's premier mountain bike race and tour. Now Ron is active in promoting mountain biking around the state through other races and tour events.

rises to 7,700′ near the Rock Canyon Overlook, then drops to 7,000′ at Rock Canyon Campground. The route climbs again to its highest point at 8,400′ at Horse Mountain before descending to Camel Pass—the turnaround point at 7,800′. Elevation gain on the way out is 2,400′. Add 1,300′ on the return leg for a total gain of 3,700′.

Season: Squaw Peak Road is rideable from May through October, depending on snow thaw and snowfall.

Services: Water, outhouses, and camping are available at Hope and Rock Canyon campgrounds from May through mid-September. This ride is only a few miles from the Provo-Orem metropolitan area (as the crow flies), where all visitor services, including several bike shops, are available. But you would have to negotiate difficult trails to reach town.

Hazards: Vehicular traffic, especially between Hope and Rock Canyon campgrounds, can be moderate on weekends and holidays. This route is a local favorite for ATVs and four-wheel-drive vehicles, so use caution and be prepared to share the road. Since the road passes through relatively high mountain terrain, cool and cloudy weather can intrude rapidly on a warm, sunny day. Avoid the four-wheel-drive road from Rock Canyon Campground to Kolob Basin Overlook when it's wet because it turns to sticky, claylike mud.

Rescue index: This route is popular with mountain bikers, ATVs, four-wheel-drive vehicles, and weekend sightseers, so help is never far away. Keep in mind that the ride to Provo via Rock Canyon is on a steep descent and the return climb is brutal. (The trailhead is located at the back end of the campground road.)

Land status: Uinta National Forest.

Maps: USGS 7.5 minute quadrangles: Bridal Veil Falls and Springville, Utah; USGS 1:100,000 metric topographic series: Provo, Utah.

Finding the trail: From Interstate 15, take Exit 275/800 North (Orem), Provo Canyon. Travel east on 800 North, then up Provo Canyon on US 189. One and a half miles up the canyon is the signed turnoff for Squaw Peak Road/Forest Service Road 027. Proceed 5 miles up the winding road to the end of the pavement near Hope Campground. Park here (with discretion) and begin pedaling.

Sources of additional information:

Uinta National Forest
Pleasant Grove Ranger District
390 North 100 East
P.O. Box 228
Pleasant Grove, Utah 84062
(801) 785-3563

Mountain Biking Utah's Wasatch and Uinta Mountains, by Gregg Bromka (Off-Road Publications, Salt Lake City, Utah).

Notes on the trail: Pedal 3.5 miles on the improved dirt and gravel road from

Hope Campground up to the Rock Canyon Overlook. Then plunge 1.5 miles to Rock Canyon Campground, twisting through quaking aspen and oak brush while enjoying both the immensity and proximity of the southern Wasatch.

Continue south on FS 027, which is now a four-wheel-drive road. It rises back uphill 4 miles to a pass marked by the Slide Canyon trailhead. Beyond, the rock-studded road contours the flank of Provo Peak 2.8 miles around the head of Slate Canyon to Horse Mountain. This point is noted by outstanding views south down into Kolob Basin and across the Wasatch Front's southern face all the way to Mount Nebo. By now you will have noticed the extensive terracing on the mountain slopes from Provo Peak north to Lightning Peak. This was done in the 1930s by the Civilian Conservation Corps with the intent to control avalanche and erosion problems on these steep slopes.

Turn around here or 2 miles farther downhill at Camel Pass. (At Camel Pass the road turns sharply left and begins a long, jackhammer descent through Pole Heaven and into Left Fork of Hobble Creek.) Enjoy the view, make the climb back to the summit, then get even with the long hill by gliding back down with a huge grin on your face.

RIDE 16 *RIDGE TRAIL 157*

Between the head of Big Cottonwood Canyon and upper American Fork Canyon, the Great Western Trail passes through an alpine region stuffed with mountain beauty; however, this segment of the Great Western is extremely difficult to pursue by mountain bike, to say the least. Those who make the attempt may find themselves walking and back-packing their bikes as much as pedaling. When the Great Western Trail resumes above American Fork Canyon at Pole Line Pass, though, Ridge Trail 157 emerges as the alter ego to the Wasatch Crest.

Like the Wasatch Crest, Ridge Trail 157 is an adventuresome single-track tracing the spine of the Wasatch Range. It boasts scenic splendor equal to that of its northern equivalent, and the terrain is greatly varied. No longer is the Cottonwood Ridge the main attraction, for it has disappeared to the north. The Alpine Ridge, marked by the backsides of Alta and Snowbird combined with the Lone Peak Wilderness, provides stunning visual entertainment. Yet it is multi-faceted Mount Timpanogos (a ridge or arête) sliced and scalloped into multiple hanging valleys and overlapping slopes, that dominates the scene, growing majestically until it clogs the southern skyline.

You'll need a vehicle shuttle to ride Ridge Trail 157, which is a 14-mile, advanced-level, point-to-point route. The route begins with four miles of semi-maintained dirt road, followed by ten miles of sometimes buffed, other times technical single-track. Of course, hard-core bikers can close a loop by adding 9 miles of paved road plus 4.5 miles of dirt road. (GWT)

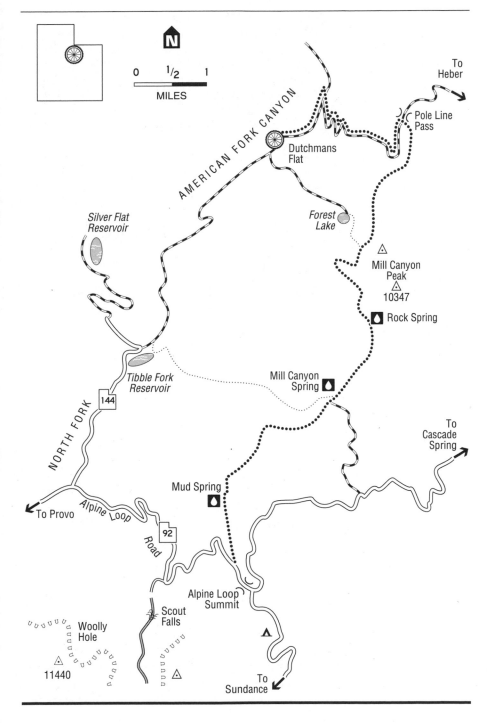

To Heber

AMERICAN FORK CANYON

Pole Line Pass

N

0   1/2   1
MILES

Dutchmans Flat

Silver Flat Reservoir

Forest Lake

Mill Canyon Peak
10347

Rock Spring

Tibble Fork Reservoir

Mill Canyon Spring

144

NORTH FORK

To Cascade Spring

To Provo

Alpine Loop

Mud Spring

92

Road

To Sundance

Alpine Loop Summit

Scout Falls

Woolly Hole

11440

Mountains, mountains, mountains.

General location: Ridge Trail 157 is located above American Fork Canyon, about 25 miles northeast of Provo.

Elevation change: Dutchmans Flat (parking area) rests at 7,600'. The route begins with a 1,350' climb to Pole Line Pass and the trailhead for Ridge Trail 157 (elevation 8,950'). Although the trail's end at the Alpine Scenic Loop Summit drops to 8,060', expect to gain nearly 2,000' en route for total climbing of about 3,300'.

Season: Although most of the trail has good southwest exposure and melts out relatively early in the season, snowdrifts that typically linger on north-facing slopes may limit travel (especially on the ridge extending west from Mill Canyon Peak near mile 7). The route is typically rideable from early June through mid-October.

Services: There are no services on this route. Water is available but should be purified at Rock Spring, located 8 miles into the ride. Forest Service campgrounds and picnic areas in American Fork Canyon offer water taps and outhouses. There is a snack bar at Timpanogos Cave National Monument. All other visitor services are available in the Provo metropolitan area.

Hazards: This trail is maintained on an annual basis, but not necessarily early in the season. The slopes of Mill Canyon Peak are infamous winter avalanche zones. You may encounter downed trees and debris crossing the trail early in the season. Trail 157 is a popular equestrian route, so be prepared to share the trail and yield the right of way.

Rescue index: The number of trail users varies. Recreationists (especially equestrians) are more numerous near the Alpine Scenic Loop trailhead. You'll find fishermen and campers throughout American Fork Canyon and around Tibble Fork Reservoir. Pole Line Pass is more remote. Emergency contacts may be made at Timpanogos Cave National Monument in American Fork Canyon.

Land status: Uinta National Forest.

Maps: USGS 7.5 minute quadrangles: Aspen Grove, Brighton, Dromedary Peak, and Timpanogos Cave, Utah.

Finding the trail: From Interstate 15, take Exit 287/Alpine, Highland. Travel 8 miles east on UT 92, then into American Fork Canyon. Timpanogos Cave National Monument is 2.5 miles up the canyon. Two and a half miles farther is the signed junction for North Fork, UT 144. Leave a drop vehicle near this junction or continue 6.5 miles up the Alpine Scenic Loop to its summit and trail's end where there is designated parking. With the shuttle vehicle, drive 2.6 miles up UT 144 to Tibble Fork Reservoir. On its north side, a semi-improved dirt road leads up the North Fork of American Fork Canyon. (This road is very rough for passenger cars, so use discretion. The road poses no problems for high-clearance vehicles.) After 4.5 miles, a large clearing with numerous back-country campsites marks Dutchmans Flat and the route's recommended starting point.

Sources of additional information:

Uinta National Forest
Pleasant Grove Ranger District
390 North 100 East
P.O. Box 228
Pleasant Grove, Utah 84062
(801) 785-3563

Mountain Biking Utah's Wasatch and Uinta Mountains, by Gregg Bromka (Off-Road Publications, Salt Lake City, Utah)

Notes on the trail: From Dutchmans Flat, pedal 1 mile up the dirt road to a junction. Fork right on Forest Service Road 085 toward Wasatch State Park and Midway and begin the 3-mile, 1,300′, warm-up climb to Pole Line Pass. In this clearing, a sign will direct you to Ridge Trail 157/Great Western Trail to the right/south.

The trail starts out with a little "sand-surfing," then rises up a steep hill before dropping to a junction at Sandy Baker Pass. Pot Hollow Trail 037 and East Ridge Trail 038 branch left/east. Of the two trails up ahead and forking right/southwest, take Ridge Trail 157, the second (upper) trail that stays on the contour. (The lower trail drops west and back toward Dutchmans Flat.)

Let the fun begin! The single-track travels high across the flank of Mill Canyon Peak, weaving through dispersed forests. At times the lush trailside foliage obscures the surrounding views; other times, the open panorama is stunning. Forest Lake appears below next to a graveyard of avalanche-downed trees lying parallel like a box of toothpicks.

Shortly past the "Forest Lake" trail sign, Ridge Trail 157 crosses a talus slope of coarse, angular limestone. Look for wild raspberries growing up slope; yum! The energy boost may aid in tackling the long climb over the ridge ahead.

Awaiting is a megaview of the interior Wasatch Range. The ragged, charcoal-gray crown of Devils Castle, rounded summits of Sugarloaf and Baldy, and Snowbird's Twin Peaks embrace Mineral Fork Basin to the north. Steel-gray cliffs crash down from the Lone Peak Wilderness and pyramid-shaped Box Elder Peak rises to the west. But the physiographic monarch is stately Mount Timpanogos, which commands the southern skyline. Powerful as a battleship crashing through a sea of whitecaps, this awe-inspiring arête overshadows the remainder of the route. At the head of the Giant Staircase's ice-carved valley is the Timpanogos Glacier, just out of sight.

The trail continues through aspen groves and across open, vista-filled slopes. Past Rock Spring there is a mile-long, technically-demanding drop that leads to Mill Canyon Spring. A sign for Mill Canyon Trail 040—a gutsy shortcut down to Tibble Fork Reservoir—is on the right. Ridge Trail 157 continues south, first as a dirt road and then as single-track. The remaining route is roller-coaster style, undulating along the ridge beneath the ever-changing face of Mount Timpanogos. Pass the signed trailhead for Tibble Fork Trail (another demanding bail-out route) and then by the unsigned Mud Spring. After a moderately technical descent, the trail enters into a large meadow. Cross to the south and back into the forest for another gut-busting climb. One mile farther the trail connects with the Alpine Scenic Loop Summit.

RIDE 17 *MONKS HOLLOW*

As members of the muscle-powered family of recreationists, fat-tire cyclists tend to frown upon energy consumptive, exhaust spitting, and deafening ATVs. But one good thing can be said about our axled brethren; they sure can pack down a good trail. Such is the case with Diamond Fork's Monks Hollow Trail. This designated ATV route is ideal for mountain bikes, and the narrow double-track is built for speed.

The generally smooth, packed-dirt trail is the main attraction. But there are some good vistas along the way. Early on, the backsides of Provo Peak and Mount Timpanogos line the distant western skyline. Farther up the trail, Spanish Fork Peak and Loafer Mountain vie for your attention. At the trail's summit, the tri-peaked arête of Mount Nebo breaks the southern horizon.

Monks Hollow is a 15-mile "up-and-back-down" ride. Technical difficulty

RIDE 17   *MONKS HOLLOW*

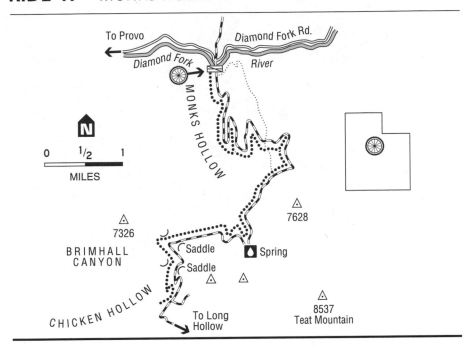

is generally low, and the grade is moderate but steady. The only real limiting factor is keeping a good race pace all the way to the top. This is a great intermediate-level route, but one relished by advanced bikers as well. For hammerheads in training, Monks Hollow is the perfect aerobic hillclimb.

General location: Monks Hollow is located in Diamond Fork, about 25 miles southeast of Provo.

Elevation change: The elevation of the Monks Hollow trailhead is 5,340´. The route rises steadily to 7,280´ on a ridge separating Chicken Hollow from Long Hollow. Total climbing is just shy of 2,000´.

Season: Situated at relatively low elevation and with good exposure, this route may be rideable as early as mid-April and as late as mid-November.

Services: There are no services along this route and all surface waters should be purified. There are two developed USFS campgrounds, Palmyra and Camp Diamond, located a few miles before the trailhead. Both have water taps and outhouses. There are restaurants near the mouth of Spanish Fork Canyon. Provo hosts all visitor services.

Hazards: Monks Hollow is low in technical difficulty overall. Watch for other trail users, particularly fast moving ATVs. If returning to the trailhead via the

A distant view of Mount Nebo from atop Monks Hollow.

optional, high-speed "grassy meadow" route, anticipate an *unannounced,* sharp left-hand turn at the clearing's north end followed by a cobble-infested drop to Diamond Fork.

Rescue index: The farther you pedal from the trailhead the less likely you are to encounter others. ATVs are common on weekends and holidays. Motorists are numerous in Diamond Fork. Emergency contacts might be made from Camp Diamond Campground.

Land status: Uinta National Forest.

Maps: USGS 7.5 minute quadrangles: Billies Mountain and Rays Valley, Utah.

Finding the trail: From Interstate 15, take Exit 261/US 6, Price, Manti. Travel east on US 6 and into Spanish Fork Canyon. Five miles up the canyon, turn left/north at the sign for Palmyra and Diamond campgrounds (between mileposts 183 and 184). Seven and one-half miles up the paved Diamond Fork Road is the unsigned trailhead on the right, marked by a one lane bridge over the river, a green steel gate, and a wooden barn in a clearing. The turnoff is posted as Forest Service Road 072. If the gate is unlocked, parking is plentiful in the meadow; otherwise, there is room alongside the paved road.

Sources of additional information:

> Uinta National Forest
> Spanish Fork Ranger District
> 44 West 400 North
> Spanish Fork, Utah 84660

> (801) 785-3571

Mountain Biking Utah's Wasatch and Uinta Mountains, by Gregg Bromka (Off-Road Publications, Salt Lake City, Utah)

Notes on the trail: Pedal due south one-half mile and then fork left and through a gate signed "Monks Hollow Trail No. 126." Dip through the drainage bottom, and crank up the opposing bank. Turn right and you are on your way up the ATV trail.

Pass through two turns, then take a quick break next to an ATV-bermed embankment to view the "upside-down" tree. After the fourth switchback, the path runs across the head of a grassy meadow. Watch for an unsigned ATV trail crossing the main route at right angles. This is an optional return route to the trailhead—a Mach II, adrenalin-laden blast across the clearing. (If you do take the optional return, pull back the reins at the meadow's north end, for the trail turns sharply left at a cliff's edge. It then drops quickly on a rough, gravel- and rock-strewn road to the barn and parking area.)

Keep chugging uphill. Pass by a spring enclosed by a wooden fence. One mile farther, the trail passes through a saddle on a ridge overlooking Brimhall Canyon. One-half mile beyond, the trail crosses over a second saddle that supplies distant but impressive views south of Mount Nebo. Drop through the whoop-de-doos and up one more hill to a sloping ridge dividing Chicken Hollow from Long Hollow. This is the route's high point/turnaround and is marked by a trail branching left and uphill (dead end). The return descent offers an opportunity to perfect your "YEE-HAs."

RIDE 18 *DIAMOND FORK / STRAWBERRY RIDGE*

Diamond Fork is, by and large, off the beaten path and easily overlooked, but it overflows with adventuresome mountain biking. Tucked neatly behind Provo Peak and the southern Wasatch Range, eye-popping, jaw-dropping scenery is not one its strong attributes. But carry a camera just the same, for there are a handful of photo-worthy angles. More notably, Diamond Fork harbors a surplus of single-track. Its generally seldom-traveled trail network combines well-developed, regularly-maintained paths with primitive routes overgrown with chest-high underbrush. It is this combination of widely varied trails that has led to many highly-memorable Diamond Fork adventures, ones worth duplicating time and again.

The Strawberry Ridge loop is a newfound classic. It incorporates four some-times-forgiving, sometimes-technical single-tracks while encircling a large chunk of the Diamond Fork basin. Trail riding is generally confined to canyon bottoms—splashing through creeks, dodging riparian flora, and slipping along

RIDE 18 *DIAMOND FORK / STRAWBERRY RIDGE*

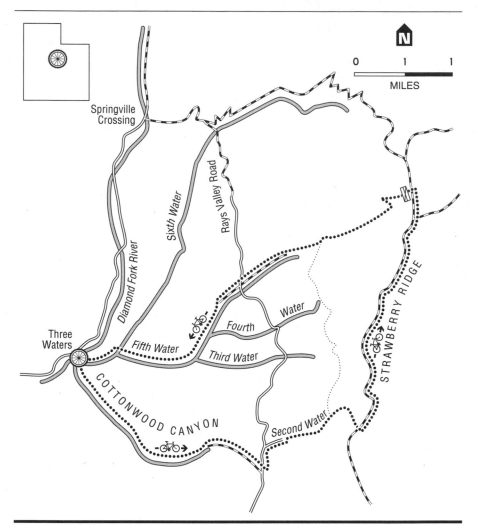

stream banks; however, the midsection along Strawberry Ridge approaches alpine elevations with a dispersed mix of aspen and conifers. From its undulating crest are near-100-mile vistas of the Wasatch Range's less-touted eastern face.

This 24-mile loop is a difficult ride that leads to remote reaches of the backcountry. Strong legs, high endurance, and good handling skills are prerequisite for the sustained climbs and lively descents. If you have a penchant for exploring killer single-track, do not pass up the Diamond Fork/Strawberry Ridge loop. (GWT)

Waterfalls tumble through lower Fifth Water Creek.

General location: Diamond Fork is located about 25 miles southeast of Provo in Spanish Fork Canyon.

Elevation change: The route's parking area/trailhead is also at its lowest elevation at 5,520′. Eight and one-half miles of single-track rise to Strawberry Ridge at 8,400′. The undulating Strawberry Ridge Road gains an additional 900′ before beginning the 10-mile single-track descent back to the parking area. Total climbing for this loop is about 3,800′.

Season: This route is typically rideable from late May through October. Snowdrifts lingering on Strawberry Ridge will be a limiting factor. But while you're patiently awaiting the ridge to melt out, the route's lower sections, Cottonwood Canyon and Fifth Water, are usually dry and rideable by late April/mid-May. This backcountry route is not recommended during deer hunting season, which is the last week in October.

Services: There are no services at the trailhead nor along this route, so self-sufficiency is mandatory. Surface waters should be avoided or purified, for they may be tainted by cattle and natural hot springs. There are 2 developed USFS campgrounds, Palmyra and Camp Diamond, located about 4 miles before the trailhead. Both are fee areas with water taps and outhouses. Restaurants are located at the mouth of Spanish Fork Canyon, 15 miles from the trailhead.

Hazards: Be well prepared for a ride of this length and backcountry nature. Pack along a well-equipped repair kit, plenty of water and food, and appropriate clothing. The route's last 3 miles along the Fifth Water Trail is quite popular, so ride responsibly and be courteous to other trail users. Otherwise, anticipate the usual assortment of single-track obstacles.

Rescue index: The route's last 3 miles along the Fifth Water Trail are frequently visited by hikers, mountain bikers, and fishermen, especially on weekends. But Strawberry Ridge is considered remote. It is nearly 10 miles of single-track from the ridge to the parking area, then 15 miles to a phone, and even farther for medical assistance. Few motorists travel Rays Valley Road, which cuts through the route's midsection.

Land status: Uinta National Forest.

Maps: USGS 7.5 minute quadrangles: Rays Valley, Strawberry Reservoir NW, and Strawberry Reservoir SW, Utah.

Finding the trail: From Interstate 15, take Exit 261/US 6, Price, Manti. Travel east on US 6 into Spanish Fork Canyon. Five miles up the canyon, turn left/north on Forest Service Road 029 (between mileposts 183 and 184) toward Palmyra and Diamond campgrounds. Three Forks parking area is 10 miles up the paved Diamond Fork Road. The turnout accommodates up to a dozen vehicles.

Sources of additional information:

> Uinta National Forest
> Spanish Fork Ranger District
> 44 West 400 North
> Spanish Fork, Utah 84660
> (801) 785-3571

> *Mountain Biking Utah's Wasatch and Uinta Mountains,* by Gregg Bromka (Off-Road Publications, Salt Lake City, Utah).

Notes on the trail: Cross over the wooden footbridge next to the parking area spanning Diamond Fork. Immediately turn right and go over a second footbridge across torrential Sixth Water. Dip through Cottonwood Creek and turn left to begin the loop with 4.5 miles of single-track.

Cottonwood Canyon is both moderately strenuous and moderately technical with a few more demanding sections thrown in for good measure. There are 3 quick water crossings near its beginning that are usually bridged by downed trees or well-placed limbs. You'll encounter Jocks Canyon/Teat Mountain junction after 2.8 miles, followed shortly by "derailleur-bender" boulders. No foot dabs allowed! Ahead, the unmistakable odor of sulphur denotes the presence of natural hot springs. A double water crossing and more climbing precede a wire fence line that bounds a small meadow. On the meadow's east end, connect with a dirt road that leads 1.2 miles up to paved Rays Valley Road.

Turn left/north and up the hill and then travel down into the next drainage. Turn right/east at the sign for Second Water Trail 018, Strawberry Ridge, and Center Trail 009. The dirt road immediately turns to single-track marked with carsonite posts and Great Western Trail decals. After 1.2 deceivingly arduous miles, the trail bends north up canyon and passes a small spring. Roaming cattle can turn the upcoming technical climb into a mile-long hike-a-bike.

Center Trail 009 branches sharply left, but stay straight/right for Indian Spring, Second Water Trail, and Strawberry Ridge to continue climbing on single-track. Upon reaching Strawberry Ridge (marked by a cattle guard and a Great Western decal), turn left onto double-track (FS 135). A half-dozen climbs offset by turbo-charged descents punctuate the undulating ridge. Grand views of the southern Wasatch Range's backside and immense Diamond Fork basin set the western scene.

After 5.5 miles along the ridge, watch for FS 110 (marked by carsonite posts) branching right/east at the bottom of a high-speed hill. Continue straight on FS 135 for half a mile. At the base of the next hill and alongside a wire fence line, keep a sharp lookout for the unsigned Fifth Water Trail branching sharply left/west. Log barriers close the route to motor vehicles greater than 40 inches wide. The trail dodges into conifers and then continues onto an open ridge where it turns sharply left and descends quickly into the head of Fifth Water Creek.

Upper Fifth Water is a combination of overgrown and buffed single-track sailing through dispersed forests and across lush creekside fields. Continue down valley past signs for Second Water Trail/Center Trail (left) and Halls Fork/Center Trail (right). The previous section may have been fun, but the ensuing track is a rage! Single-track turns back to double-track, then connects with paved Rays Valley Road. Cross over and finish off the loop with lower Fifth Water Trail 015, which is signed "Three Forks 5 mi." A handful of technical sections and a couple of wet crossings line the trail. Waterfalls halfway down are worth stopping for. Below, Fifth Water feeds into Sixth Water. The latter, which serves as the outlet of Strawberry Reservoir miles away, boils with turbulent rapids.

One final note: If this route seems like a serious undertaking, do not despair; there is a less daunting 16-mile inner loop that is well suited for intermediate cyclists. Follow Cottonwood Canyon as described. Upon intersecting Rays Valley Road, turn left and pedal north on the huge, paved roller coaster 5.5 miles to the turnoff for the Fifth Water Trail (look for a dirt road and stop sign). Turn left to descend the 5-mile-long single-track back to the parking area.

RIDE 19 *TELEMARK PARK*

Telemark Park is a Park City favorite. Located only a few minutes from town at the base of Deer Valley Resort, it is perfect for a quick, midday workout or early evening spin. The trail system blends dirt roads with double-track and single-track trails, ranging in difficulty from novice to advanced level. Portions of the trail network offer scenic views of Park City and Deer Valley; other sections venture through serene wooded slopes. In past years, Telemark Park has hosted the Utah Fat Tire Festival State Championship and NORBA-GRUNDIG World Cup races.

Telemark Park consists of three main routes that can be tied together for a 7-mile cloverleaf loop: Snow Park Loop (novice level) is a quick, 1.7-mile introduction to Telemark Park and serves as the trail system's main entry point. Combined single- and double-track trails rise with moderate difficulty through a half-dozen switchbacks that test balance and skill level. Trails overlook oak- and aspen-laden slopes, Jordenelle Reservoir, plus the Wasatch Crest rising above Park City.

McKinley Gap Loop (novice/intermediate level) is a 1.1-mile course marked by gradual descents through hairpin switchbacks and gentle climbs on a dirt and gravel road. The route rises above condominium-ringed Deer Valley Meadow.

Spin Cycle Loop (advanced level) is a wild 2.5-mile route that combines highly technical single-track descents with moderately difficult climbs up a dirt road. Highlighting this route is a bobsled-like single-track that twists down a narrow, aspen-filled hollow. When embarking on Spin Cycle, like Disneyland's Space Mountain, "keep your arms and legs inside the ride at all times."

Preserving mountain bike access to Telemark Park and adjoining Park City trails is the aspiration of Jan Wilking and Bicycle Utah,[*] of Park City.

---

[*]Bicycle Utah, Inc. is a non-profit organization whose goal is making Utah the Bicycle Vacation Capitol of America. Hosting perhaps the most diverse cycling terrain in the nation, a unique combination of surrealistic redrock country and stream-fed forests of mountain peaks, Utah guarantees a memorable cycling vacation year-round.

With the support of public and private entities, land management agencies, the Utah Travel Council, and individual Travel Regions, Bicycle Utah has sought to develop and secure access to bike trails and routes. The results have been remarkable with new areas of the state being "discovered" by both mountain and road bike enthusiasts.

Along with the annual Bicycle Utah Vacation Guide, a color brochure highlighting each of Utah's nine travel regions, Bicycle Utah has produced individual guide booklets highlighting road and mountain bike routes for each region. These will be very helpful in guiding people to the most beautiful scenery Utah has to offer.

For a free Bicycle Utah Vacation Guide or information on any of the regional guide booklets, contact Bicycle Utah at the address under "Sources of additional information."

RIDE 19 *TELEMARK PARK*

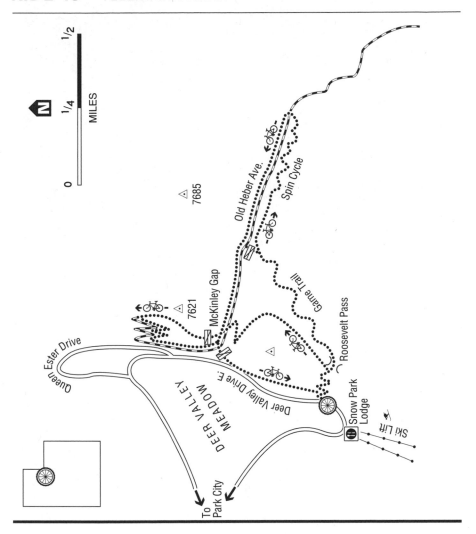

General location: Telemark Park is located 1.5 miles east of Park City at the base of Deer Valley Resort (Snow Park Lodge).

Elevation change: The trailhead near Snow Park Lodge is at 7,280′. Roosevelt Gap rises to 7,413′, for a vertical gain of less than 150′. Spin Cycle drops to 6,840′ leaving a 560′ rise back toward McKinley and Roosevelt gaps. Total gain for a cloverleaf loop is about 700′.

Season: Telemark Park is typically rideable from May through October. This route, along with adjacent Deer Valley, is an excellent destination during autumn's deer hunting season; the land is privately owned and hunting is limited.

Telemark Park is a locals' favorite.

Services: There are no services or water along this route. Nearby Park City offers all visitor-related services, including overnight accommodations, a variety of restaurants and night clubs, and top-notch bike shops.

Hazards: Snow Park Loop is low in technical difficulty, for it follows generally smooth double- and single-track trails. McKinley Gap Loop is moderately technical because of the handful of sharp, switchbacking turns descending off the hillside. Spin Cycle Loop is a highly technical single-track twisting through tightly spaced aspens.

There are several locked steel gates throughout the trail system. All are clearly visible and easily bypassed. You may encounter other trail users, including hikers, equestrians, and fellow mountain bikers. Hikers should yield to horses; bikers should yield to both.

Rescue index: Telemark Park is not patrolled. It is a very popular local bicycling destination, so you'll encounter other trail users. Park City has full medical facilities.

Land status: Telemark Park is privately owned by the Trans-Wasatch Company, Park City, Utah.

Maps: USGS 7.5 minute quadrangle: Park City East, Utah. (This out-of-date topographic map does not show the trail system.)

Finding the trail: From Interstate 80, take Exit 145/Park City, Ski Areas. Travel into Park City on Park Avenue. Turn left onto Deer Valley Drive. After 1 mile, bear left following signs for Deer Valley Ski Resort and Snow Park Lodge. (A right turn leads you to the bottom of Park City's Main Street.) Parking areas are available at Snow Park Lodge.

Sources of additional information:

Telemark Park
c/o Trans-Wasatch Company
P.O. Box 801
Park City, Utah 84060
(801) 649-2545

Bicycle Utah, Inc.
P.O. Box 738
Park City, Utah 84060
(801) 649-5806

Park City Mountain Bike Trails (Bicycle Vacation Guides, Park City, Utah)

Mountain Biking Utah's Wasatch and Uinta Mountains, by Gregg Bromka (Off-Road Publications, Salt Lake City, Utah)

Notes on the trail: In the near future, Telemark Park *may* become a fee-use area where trail users might purchase "passes" on a daily or seasonal basis. Contact Trans-Wasatch Company for Telemark Park's current access status.

Signs posted throughout the area state: "Telemark Park is a privately owned resort and recreational development. Trail conditions may vary and there is no representation that trails are safe or in good repair. Owner reserves the right to close trails at any time, to deny entry to any party, and to eject irresponsible and discourteous parties. Enter and use at your own risk and wear a helmet at all times." When visiting Telemark Park, keep in mind that these trails are made available to public use through the landowner's generosity.

Snow Park Loop: The Snow Park Loop's unsigned trailhead is just northeast of Snow Park Lodge. Cross over Deer Valley Drive and start down the lodge's service road. Within 50´, turn left onto a double-track. Curve left where a faint trail branches toward the lodge, then turn right following a sign for Roosevelt Gap. A half-dozen switchbacks lead to Roosevelt Gap, which is marked with a wooden sign. Turn left onto Loop Trail, a double-track heading north. Travel along the hill's east side and past a picnic table and a steel gate, then curve down to McKinley Gap, also marked with wooden trail signs. Old Heber Avenue (a dirt road) passes through this saddle. Stay left, pass around another steel gate, then gently descend Snow Park Trail back to the trailhead.

McKinley Gap Loop: From McKinley Gap, cross over old Heber Avenue and onto double-track past a sign for McKinley Gap Trail, and past a picnic table. Head north around yet another gate. The double-track narrows and drops through 5 hairpin turns followed by 2 more bends. When you reach the paved road (Queen Esther Drive) turn sharply left to rise back up to McKinley Gap via dirt and gravel Heber Avenue.

Spin Cycle: If confident about your skill level, return to Roosevelt Gap as described above. Staying right, there are 3 choices ahead. The single-track branching right and uphill leads to the Four Point Trail, which accesses Deer Valley's trail system based at Silver Lake Village (a long and difficult hillclimb). The single-track heading straight leads to destinations unknown. Turn left and downhill to enter into Game Trail and then Spin Cycle. After dropping off a steep embankment, the trail banks down Game Trail through looping turns. In less than a mile join with the head of Spin Cycle where a sign reads "Trail, Caution! Experts." (The green gate to the left offers a bail-out onto old Heber Avenue, which rises uphill to McKinley Gap.) Spin Cycle is only one-half mile long, but the grin it produces will be a mile wide. Upon exiting Spin Cycle, turn left and climb dirt and gravel old Heber Avenue directly to McKinley Gap, where you have the option of finishing the ride or starting over again.

RIDE 20 *DEER VALLEY*

Deer Valley has long been recognized as one of the nation's most sophisticated ski areas. Set in an atmosphere of rustic mountain elegance, the resort is renowned for its manicured ski runs, uncompromised hospitality, and gourmet slope-side dining.

Deer Valley has recently emerged as an acclaimed mountain bike destination, blending off-road cycling into its refined, alpine surroundings. In addition to chairlift access to the summit of Bald Mountain (for a nominal fee), Deer Valley boasts an ever-expanding trail network designated specifically for fat tires. The resort's single-track riding is premium. But Deer Valley also serves as a hub for exploring peripheral routes stemming into Park City and the nearby Wasatch Range.

Deer Valley caters to both first-time and advanced mountain bikers, offering routes that cruise gently through the woods and exacting, wide-eyed single-tracks. Presently, over 20 miles of interconnected routes cross Deer Valley's slopes, with additional trails planned for the near future. Mountain bike sales, rentals, and repairs are available at midmountain Silver Lake Village. With advanced reservations instructional clinics and tours can be arranged.

General location: Deer Valley is located in Park City.
Elevation change: The base of Sterling Lift at Silver Lake Village is at 8,100′. The lift's summit atop Bald Mountain is at 9,400′. Elevation change is 1,300′. But Deer Valley is a lesson in downhill cruising. Squeeze in 7 chair rides and you will tally up nearly 10,000′ of elevation.

RIDE 20 *DEER VALLEY*

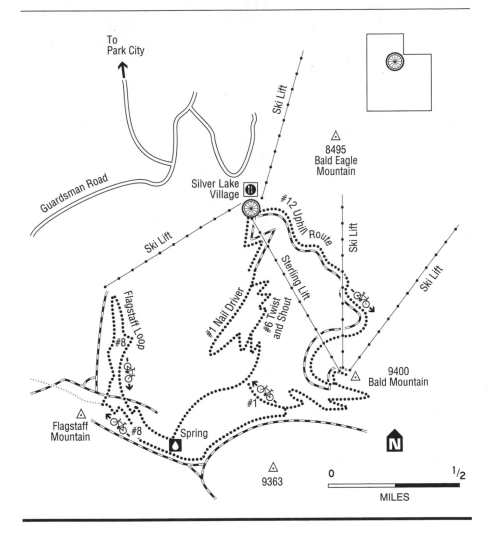

To
Park City

Ski Lift

⚠
8495
Bald Eagle
Mountain

Guardsman Road

Silver Lake
Village

#12 Uphill Route

Ski Lift

Ski Lift

Ski Lift

Sterling Lift

Flagstaff Loop

#8

#1 Nail Driver

#6 Twist
and Shout

9400
⚠ Bald Mountain

#1

⚠
Flagstaff
Mountain

#8

Spring

N

⚠
9363

0   1/2

MILES

Season: Chairlift service operates from mid-June through mid-October. Hours of chairlift access are Wednesday through Sunday 10 A.M. to 5 P.M., weather permitting. Before and after the resort's official season, the trail system is available for use but your own two legs must provide the needed lift.

Services: Lodging, fine dining and casual cafes, bike service, and rentals are available at Silver Lake Village. All visitor-related services are available in nearby Park City as well.

Hazards: Like its meticulously groomed winter ski runs, Deer Valley's mountain bike trail system is well maintained. Even so, with names like Naildriver

Who says getting to the top is tough.

Downhill, GS (as in "giant slalom") Trees, and Twist and Shout, it is fair to assume that these are not idle tours through the park. Be attentive to changing and unannounced trail conditions, in addition to resort-area maintenance and construction. Many routes are characterized by fast descents, hairpin turns, narrow trail, packed and loose sediment, and close trail-side foliage. A helmet must be worn at all times when you're biking the resort's trails, regardless of whether you have a lift ticket or not.

Rescue index: Although the trail system is not patrolled, you are never more than a mile or two from assistance. Lift operators at the base and summit of Sterling Lift have radio communication and are trained in first aid. On-trail emergency assistance is available (but do not send up a distress flare for simple flat tire repair). Park City has full medical facilities.

Land status: Deer Valley is a privately owned and operated resort. Routes leaving the resort's designated trail system enter upon adjacent private lands where recreational access may not be permitted.

Twistin' and shoutin' at Deer Valley.

Maps: *Deer Valley, Utah, Mountain Biking and Hiking Trail Map* (available at Silver Lake Village bike shop, located at the base of Sterling Lift).

Finding the trail: From Interstate 80, take Exit 145/Park City, Ski Areas, UT 224. Travel south and into Park City via Park Avenue. At a stop light, turn left onto Deer Valley Drive. After 1 mile, bear left following signs for Deer Valley Ski Resort. (A right turn leads to the bottom of Park City's Main Street.) Just before you reach Snow Park Lodge, turn right onto Royal Street at a sign for Silver Lake Lodge. Wind uphill following additional signs to Silver Lake Lodge and Village. Underground parking is available, but clearance is too low for most bike-topped cars! Or park at the corner of Royal Street East and Sterling Court.

You can also reach the trail from the top of Park City's Main Street. Turn left on Hillside and immediately right up Ontario Canyon via Guardsman Road/UT 224. Just past the Ontario Mine, where Guardsman Road bends sharply right (at the horse stables), turn left onto Guardsman Connection Road. Shortly uphill, turn right onto Royal Street East and to Silver Lake Village.

Sources of additional information:

Deer Valley Resort
P.O. Box 1525
Park City, Utah 84060
(800) 424-DEER (3337) or (801) 649-1000

Park City Mountain Bike Trails (Bicycle Vacation Guides, Park City, Utah)

Mountain Biking Utah's Wasatch and Uinta Mountains, by Gregg Bromka (Off-Road Publications, Salt Lake City, Utah)

Notes on the trail: Deer Valley boasts up to a dozen designated mountain bike routes crossing the resort, most of which funnel back to the base of Sterling Lift and Silver Lake Village. Novice and first-time cyclists may want to stick to a few selected routes; advanced cyclists may find biking by instinct most rewarding. Here are a few suggestions:

McHenry's Practice Loop (Routes 11 and 12): This novice-level, .7-mile loop is the perfect trail to practice your skills and check out your bike. It combines a mellow dirt road with a short introduction to single-track riding. Start at the base of Sterling Lift and follow resort signs for Wasatch Lift. Fork right onto Route 11, the practice loop; otherwise, stay straight on Route 12, which leads to the base of Mayflower Lift via the dirt road. Return the opposite way to Sterling Lift.

Naildriver Downhill (Route 1): This is Deer Valley's main downhill route— a 3-mile, intermediate-level route dropping from the summit of Bald Mountain to the base of Sterling Lift. It is highlighted by dramatic overviews of the Wasatch Range, including ever-present Mount Timpanogos to the south, Clayton Peak atop Guardsman Pass, and Jupiter Peak capping Park City Ski Area. But vistas quickly become downhill cruising on a wide single-track weaving through aspens and crossing ski runs. There are sections of steep grades and tight turns, so control your speed and be attentive.

From the lift's summit, follow Route 1 off the back of Bald Mountain and through a series of switchbacks into a grassy valley. Take the second right to continue on Route 1 cutting north and downhill through the meadow. Numerous trails cross Naildriver; each is worthy of subsequent exploring. Just shy of 2 miles down, Twist and Shout forks to the right (see below). Drop through Naildriver's switchbacks and onto a flat section where Twist and Shout rejoins from the right. This junction is at the site of the old Naildriver mine, which offers views of Flagstaff Mountain to the west and Park City to the north. More spirited descents wind down to the base of Sterling Lift.

Flagstaff Loop (Route 8): Unlike other downhill routes, this 4-mile, intermediate- to advanced-level single-track stays high on the resort while taking a lap around the flank of Flagstaff Mountain. It combines quick downhills with moderate climbing. A few technical sections require adept handling skills, but these are very short and easy to walk through for those less determined.

Again, begin atop Sterling Lift and descend on the backside of Bald Mountain, following carsonite posts for Route 1. In the grassy saddle, connect with a double-track (Route 8) heading west (just after the turnoff where you would continue on Route 1). Descend on the dirt road staying right. Pedal up Flagstaff Mountain but not all the way to the top. Turn right/north onto single-track to cross the meadow and then travel into aspens along the mountain's eastern flank. There is a challenging set of technical switchbacks rising over milky-white quartzite outcrops and going through a grove of thick fir trees. (A trail branches left that leads to Guardsman Road, on which you can gain access to the Tour de Suds; stay right here.) Upon intersecting a dirt road, cross directly over it and then follow orange trail markers onto more single-track. Reach the top of Red Cloud lift, make a U-turn right, and climb gradually back through the forest. Cross over the previous dirt road again to continue on single-track. The trail enters into a spring-fed meadow posted with a trail map. Bear left to begin descending toward the base, ignoring or exploring peripheral trails. Soon Route 8 joins Naildriver (Route 1), which returns you to the base.

Twist and Shout (Route 6): Twist and Shout (alias Twitch and Pitch) branches from Naildriver Downhill (Route 1) about 1.7 miles from the top of Sterling Lift. This is a quick but thrilling, white-knuckle trail dropping steeply through angular turns and side-swiping trees. Needless to say, this double-black-diamond route is for fearless types who have perfected short radius turns and "hang-your-butt-off-the-back" descending.

Uphill Route: In the *real* world of mountain biking, there is no such thing as a free lunch—you have to earn your downhills. If this is your outlook on life then snub the chairlift and put the hammer down. This route is a 1.7-mile, 1,300′ grind, rising at a relentless 12-percent average grade. There are some good views of Jordenelle Reservoir and western Uinta Mountains along the way, but the beads of sweat dripping from brow to top tube are no doubt more entertaining. Join the pro-circuit if you reach the summit before your buddies who are lounging on the chairlift.

This is only a partial list of Deer Valley's trail network. On your next trip, explore the constantly turning single-tracks of GS Trees (Route 4), Super G Trees (Route 3), or Aspen Slalom (Route 5).

RIDE 21 *TOUR DE SUDS*

The Tour de Suds mountain bike race is a long-standing Park City tradition dating back to 1983, when mountain bikes where true clunkers, many with fewer gears than fingers on hands and near double the weight of today's high-tech breeds. It began as a year-end diversion for 30 or so local road racers—an informal excuse to saddle up their ATBs or cyclocross bikes and spend a day in the dirt, then socialize over a few cold brews. Today, the fall classic is still the

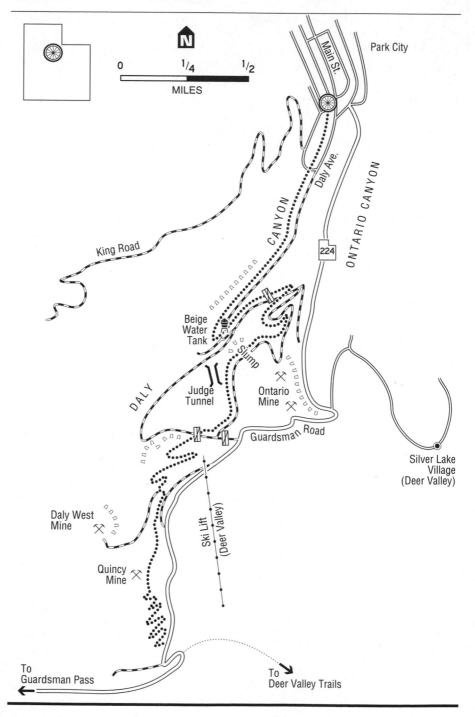

N

0   1/4   1/2

MILES

Park City

Main St.

Daly Ave.

CANYON

ONTARIO CANYON

King Road

224

Beige
Water
Tank

Slump

DALY

Judge
Tunnel

Ontario
Mine

Guardsman Road

Silver Lake
Village
(Deer Valley)

Daly West
Mine

Ski Lift
(Deer Valley)

Quincy
Mine

To
Guardsman Pass

To
Deer Valley Trails

Mountain bike first; drink suds later.

grand finale to a prosperous summer of fat-tire racing and adventures in the surrounding Wasatch Range. And although it draws up to 200 entrants, both devoted racers and admitted non-competitive types, it has maintained its light-hearted, tongue-in-cheek appeal. Boasting an afternoon of post-ride festivities, including good food, fun prizes, best of friends, and plenty of "suds," the Tour de Suds is every bit a social event as it is a timed race.

This ride is full of Park City history, starting with a blend of nineteenth- and twentieth-century architectural themes comprising the facade of Historic Main Street (one of only a few business districts in the country to be named to the National Register of Historic Places). As you pedal up Daly Canyon, you'll see more of this mixture of old and new with many original or replicated turn-of-the-century dwellings. Shortly, the route penetrates the haunting silence of yesteryear's silver boom that literally put Park City, Utah, on the map. The first remnant you'll encounter is Judge Tunnel. Up the canyon is the Daly-West Mine, one of the area's more profitable ventures (but also the mountains' most deadly; in July, 1902, a deep-rooted explosion claimed the lives of 34 miners.) Farther on, the route passes the modernized Ontario Mine and defunct Quincy Mine. In between, the trail cuts across recently expanded Deer Valley Resort, which has contributed to Park City's present-day boom.

This is not a course of breakneck descending or multiple laps through rolling terrain. Hardly. Up is where it's at! The Suds is a near 2,000′ hillclimb over 5 miles (depending on where the starting line is located in town and where the always secretive finish line is up on top.) Presented here, this social tour is a 3.6-mile point-to-point ride that starts right out from the top of Park City's Historic Main Street. The route combines dirt roads with double- and single-track that are always inclined at various grades. Because of the sustained climbing involved (occasionally quite steep), the Tour de Suds is suited for intermediate or stronger bikers. Portions of single-track are technical, winding through tightly spaced aspen and fir trees along a myriad of short-radius turns.

General location: The Tour de Suds begins at the top of Main Street in Park City.

Elevation change: The elevation at the top of Main Street is 7,120′. Sustained climbing rises to 8,800′ at the route's end on Guardsman Road for a total elevation gain of about 1,700′.

Season: Upper portions of the Tour de Suds may harbor snow drifts well into late May and early June. The trail is rideable through October or until snow falls.

Services: All visitor services are found in Park City. There are no additional services along the trail and all surface waters should be purified (or avoided since they drain old mining areas).

Hazards: There are some technically challenging sections along the single-track, especially the series of tight slalomlike turns near the route's summit.

Do not enter into or climb onto any mine buildings or structures. Old shafts or tunnels are unstable and contain low levels of oxygen. Mining areas are private property and posted "No Trespassing." Be mindful of Deer Valley Resort construction and maintenance at all times.

Rescue index: This mountain bike route is a Park City favorite especially on weekends, so you are never far away from assistance. Motorists are common along Guardsman Road at the route's summit. Park City has medical facilities.

Land status: The route crosses private property owned by Deer Valley Resort and United Park City Mines. Unofficial trails stemming from the main Tour de Suds route may not be open to recreational traffic. Please stay on course.

Maps: USGS 7.5 minute quadrangles: Brighton, Heber, Park City East, and Park City West, Utah. (The route is not shown on these out-of-date maps); and *Deer Valley, Utah, Mountain Biking and Hiking Trail Map* (Deer Valley Resort).

Finding the trail: The Tour de Suds begins at the top of Main Street in Park City. A public parking area next to the Wasatch Brew Pub (between Main Street and Swede Alley) makes for a good staging area.

Sources of additional information:

Deer Valley Resort
P.O. Box 1525
Park City, Utah 84060
(800) 424-DEER (3337) or (801) 649-1000

Park City Chamber of Commerce and Visitors Bureau
1910 Prospector Avenue
P.O. Box 1630
Park City, Utah 84060
(801) 649-6100

Park City Mountain Bike Trails (Bicycle Vacation Guides, Park City, Utah)

Mountain Biking Utah's Wasatch and Uinta Mountains, by Gregg Bromka (Off-Road Publications, Salt Lake City, Utah)

Notes on the trail: The Tour de Suds' course has varied widely over the years, but nowadays the accepted route is up Daly Canyon to Guardsman Road. As in the past, the course will no doubt change in the future to accommodate land owners and Deer Valley Resort expansion, construction, or maintenance. (Most changes typically take place near the route's midsection, but the trail should be marked.) This forever-twisting route is difficult to describe, and may seem like a navigational nightmare on your first outing because it is crisscrossed by a network of unofficial trails. (But even if you become disoriented, the trail is so much fun and forests are so glorious that you are bound to have a great ride regardless.)

From the parking lot next to the Wasatch Brew Pub, begin by pedaling up Main Street and continuing uphill on Daly Avenue. After .6 miles, pavement turns to dirt and broken asphalt. Up ahead is a locked gate, but access should be available to the side.

Switchback around the big beige water tank, pass by a road entering from the right (which leads from the Judge Tunnel and Lower Day Canyon), and pedal uphill generally northeastward. Several spools of tram cable and rusted ore carts litter the side of the road. Enter into aspen groves and take a *sharp* right at the blue dumpster and steel posts. Around the curve the road forks; stay right/southwestward on the main road. (You should be on the right/west side of this small ridge.) The road narrows to single-track as it passes through a heap of rusted mine equipment, then switchbacks left followed by a right. (You are now overlooking Ontario Canyon/Guardsman Road to the east and the route is a double-track.) Ignore the first right but take the second right just ahead (immediately beyond the power lines above). Now as the trail swings back to the left it skirts the head of a small landslide with overviews of Lower Daly Canyon, the beige water tank, and Judge Tunnel. You are on track.

Climb uphill gradually for one-half mile. (A dirt road—bailout route to Guardsman Road—enters from the left.) Cross the base of Deer Valley's Northside Express lift. Take the single-track that veers off to the right. It continues a few hundred feet to a red gate. Turn left onto a single-track indicated by an orange trail marker. (The route that continues straight ahead turns to double track, then quickly drops back into Daly Canyon.) The single-track is technical as it weaves through tightly spaced aspen. The trail then pops up onto and intersects a good dirt road marked with a pair of steel posts. (Do not take this road: it leads off course to the mine tailings of the Daly-West Mine.) *Cross* this road and continue on a very short section of single-track that exits immediately onto a second dirt road. Now, turn right.

Pedal up this second dirt road, which rises at a moderate to steep grade. A few hundred yards ahead, fork right onto a single-track. (Look for a tree blaze.) Within a half mile the path passes the old Quincy Mine, distinguished by trail-side tailing piles and wooden ore shoots. Stay left/straight and head back into the fir forest for the culminating switchbacks that are too numerous to count (perhaps two dozen). Pop out onto the graveled Guardsman Road. Return to town via Guardsman Road or retrace the Suds route, provided you have memorized it.

To continue the day's adventure, pedal up Guardsman, round the first left-hand curve, then go to the next right-hand turn. Here, a single-track branches off the road signed "Private Property; Entering Resort Trail System." This lively single-track connects with Deer Valley's Flagstaff Loop (Route 8) just above the technical switchbacks rising over milky-white quartzite outcrops, as described in the Deer Valley chapter (Ride 20). Descend to Silver Lake Village, connect with the Four Points trail, drop into Telemark Park, take a lap through Spin Cycle, and cruise the paved roads back to town for the ultimate Park City loop. A mug of fresh suds awaits at the Brew Pub!

The Tour de Suds mountain bike race is currently promoted by the Park City Mountain Trails Foundation, a non-profit organization whose goal is the preservation and maintenance of Park City–area backcountry trails. For more information, write to Mountain Trails Foundation, P.O. Box 3927, Park City, UT 84060.

RIDE 22   *LITTLE SOUTH FORK OF PROVO RIVER*

Little South Fork is a semi-primitive trail descending the length of a glistening tributary to the Provo River. There are distant but impressive views of the noble Uinta Mountains and proud Wasatch Range. But these short-lived vistas are traded for a valley-confined, single-track experience. The trailhead's rolling, ridge-top pastures give way to creek-fed meadows, opaque forests, and willow-lined stream banks.

Technically, Little South Fork is an 8.5-mile point-to-point, downhill ride that necessitates a vehicle shuttle; but a little vertical gain is good not only for the heart, lungs, and legs, but for the soul as well. Therefore, it is described here as a strong intermediate- to advanced-level, 22-mile loop. The route incorporates paved, improved dirt, and four-wheel-drive roads with a generous helping of lively single-track. Little South Fork may not be splashed on posters or

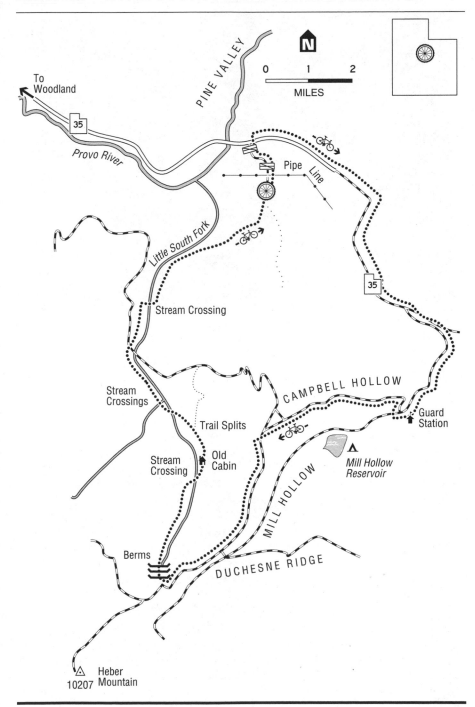

N

0   1   2
MILES

To
Woodland

35

Provo River

PINE VALLEY

Pipe   Line

Little South Fork

Stream Crossing

Stream
Crossings

Trail Splits

Old
Cabin

Stream
Crossing

CAMPBELL HOLLOW

35

Guard
Station

Mill Hollow
Reservoir

MILL HOLLOW

Berms

DUCHESNE RIDGE

10207   Heber
Mountain

Heading down Little South Fork.

touted in mountain bike magazines; it is simply an off-the-beaten-path, single-track adventure.

Route information on the Little South Fork Trail was provided by Charlie Sturgis,[*] Park City, Utah.

General location: Little South Fork Trail is located about 25 miles northeast of Heber.

Elevation change: The junction of UT 35 and Little South Fork's access road is the route's lowest elevation at 7,200′. Paved, improved dirt, and unimproved dirt roads rise to 9,800′ near the single-track's upper trailhead. Adding in a few incremental climbs near the route's end, total elevation gain is about 2,800′.

Season: Little South Fork is well shaded and may not melt out until mid-June. It is typically rideable throughout October, but avoid this route during autumn's deer hunting season.

Services: There are no services along this route and all surface waters should

---

[*]After moving to Park City from Chicago in 1975, Charlie Sturgis became very active in nordic skiing and rock climbing. Later graduating from the University of Utah, his interests shifted to business and retail sales. Today, he blends both business and recreation in Park City. Together with his wife, Kathy, he operates a ski touring center during the winter and White Pine Touring outdoor shop year-round. For more information about White Pine Touring, see "Sources of additional information."

Charlie and Kathy Sturgis of White Pine Touring.

be purified. A developed USFS campground is located at Mill Hollow Reservoir and offers water taps and outhouses. Woodland, the nearest community, does not offer visitor services. Park City and Heber, both equidistant from the trail, offer all visitor services, including bike shops.

Hazards: Little South Fork Trail is a semi-primitive trail and maintained on an irregular basis. Deadfall may be abundant, especially early in the summer before volunteers can clear the route. It is *unsigned* throughout and requires some route-finding skills.

There are several moderately technical sections, and a few are highly technical because of its semi-maintained nature. You will encounter several unbridged stream crossings that require creativity for a dry portage. The last, across the lower stretch of Little South Fork creek, may be knee deep during spring runoff.

Finally, there are Forest Service signs posted in Mill Hollow Canyon: "Bear Frequenting Area."

Rescue index: You won't find many hikers and mountain bikers on Little South

Fork Trail. Equestrians may be more common. Vehicular traffic on UT 35 is sporadic. On weekends and holidays, fishermen and campers visit nearby Mill Hollow Reservoir and Campground. Heber and Park City, each about 25 miles away, have medical facilities.

Land status: Uinta National Forest.

Maps: USGS 7.5 minute quadrangles: Heber Mountain, Soapstone Basin, Wolf Creek Summit, and Woodland, Utah. (Little South Fork Trail is not shown on these maps.)

Finding the trail: From Park City, travel east on UT 248 toward Kamas. In Kamas, turn right/south on UT 35/32. After 2 miles, enter into Francis (flashing stop light) and turn left/east onto Village Way/UT 35 signed "Woodland." Descend through a curve and into the hamlet of Woodland, then travel 6.5 miles to the signed turnoff for Willow Hollow Trail and Little South Fork (right/south). (You'll see this turnoff shortly after you cross the Provo River as it flows through Pine Valley.) The dirt, public access road rises .8 miles to the unsigned trailhead/parking area adjacent to a gas pipeline corridor. Leave all gates as you find them! Passenger cars should use caution over the last .3 miles.

From Heber, travel 4 miles north on US 40/189. Turn right onto US 189 signed "Kamas," and wind around Jordenelle Reservoir. Three miles past its eastern bay, enter into Francis (flashing stop light) and proceed as mentioned above.

Sources of additional information:

Uinta National Forest
Heber Ranger District
2460 South US Hwy 40
P.O. Box 190
Heber City, Utah 84032
(801) 654-0470

White Pine Touring
201 Heber Avenue (the base of Main Street)
Park City, Utah 84060
(801) 649-8710
White Pine Touring actively promotes all forms of responsible outdoor sports, including rock climbing, hiking, ski touring, and mountain biking. During the warm summer months, White Pine hosts weekly mountain bike time trial races plus evening and weekend fat-tire tours in and around Park City. Upon request White Pine will customize and guide you on a wide variety of mountain bike excursions throughout the Wasatch and Uinta Mountains. A professional staff and great service make White Pine Touring Park City's headquarters for all your outdoor endeavors.

Mountain Biking Utah's Wasatch and Uinta Mountains, by Gregg Bromka (Off-Road Publications, Salt Lake City, Utah)

Notes on the trail: From the parking area alongside the gas pipeline corridor, head back to UT 35 and turn right/east. Pedal 4.5 miles on pavement and turn off onto FS 054 signed "Mill Hollow." After a mile, the dirt, gravel, and washboarded road turns up the canyon and rises steadily 1.5 miles to the Mill Hollow Guard Station. Just beyond, turn right onto FS 122 signed "Campbell Hollow, Overflow Camping." This is an alternate route to continuing up Mill Hollow. It is much steeper (gaining the same elevation in about half the distance) but has less traffic and consequently less washboard. As Campbell Hollow levels, stay left at 2 junctions and cruise along the smooth ridge top on FS 052 to a junction signed "FS 096, Heber Mountain, Camp Hollow, Buck Hollow" (straight/west); "FS 052, Campbell Hollow" (reverse/east).

Pedal west toward Heber Mountain. Just short of a mile and at the base of a downhill, look for a wooden post and "Road Closed" sign. This is the discreet Little South Fork trailhead. There are 12 berms awaiting, some worthy of air time. After number 12 the route appears to veer left and uphill. The single-track actually branches right, crosses over one more berm, then heads downhill (look for "dotted i" tree blazes). Now the route is readily apparent.

Cross a creek at a log bridge 1.5 miles down. In the opposing meadow, head downhill to the remains of an old log cabin. The trail continues *due north,* marked with a wooden post supported by a rock pile (not the tempting path rising uphill right/east). The trail veers away from the drainage while crossing meadows cut by small rivulets.

Here comes a tricky junction. Just less than a mile down from the cabin, the trail appears to split (after a small rock garden). The right-hand fork may appear more traveled but is not the main route, although it joins the main route several miles ahead. (Note the etching in an aspen: "Willow Hollow.") As in the Robert Frost poem, take the route less traveled to the left. (There is another hidden etching in an aspen to your left reading "L S X.") Dive into the darkened forest and cross 2 creeks. You'll encounter a third crossing after the woods open. Look for a log post on the creek's west side. Descend through dispersed sapling aspens and sage to a dirt road that crosses Little South Fork.

Here is the second tricky part. *Do not* cross the stream; stay on its west side (contrary to topographic maps). Pedal north (no more than .25 miles) on the dirt road while noticing "dotted i" tree blazes about every 50 feet. Bypass a right turn that leads to a backcountry campsite. Shortly ahead, fork right onto an unsigned trail (there are no more tree blazes along the road). After a mile, the trail splits at a log post. Cross the unbridged stream here. (This may be deep in early spring.) Continue jammin' northward on its east side.

It is a rude surprise, but there is a leg-burning hillclimb awaiting followed by a "banzai" descent. Ride parallel to a wire fence line past a junction signed "Little South Fork" (reverse). Stay next to the fence line and back to the parking area/trailhead.

RIDE 23 *BEAVER CREEK*

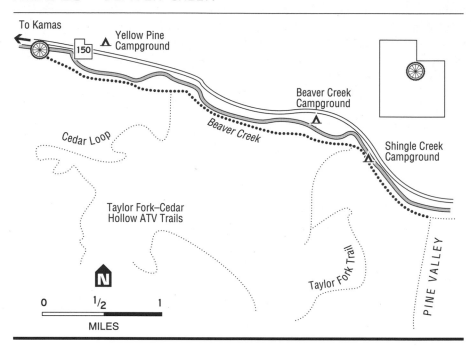

RIDE 23 *BEAVER CREEK*

Punishing climbs, white-knuckle descents, and the pursuit of high-caliber single-track (arguably the purest form of mountain biking) lure many into the world of fat-tire cycling. But for those just starting out or for families with children, something a bit more mellow might be better. For this group, the Beaver Creek Trail offers the perfect introduction.

Beaver Creek is neither dirt road nor single-track. Rather, it is a "megatrack" and part of the Taylor Fork ATV trail system. Sure ATVs tend to be noisy and obtrusive, but they can pack down a fine trail for mountain bikes. The route parallels a gently meandering creek pooled occasionally by beaver dams. On one side lies the creek's willow- and grass-filled floodplain, and on the other rise forested slopes of the lower Uinta Mountains.

The 9.5-mile out-and-back route is ideal for novice mountain bikers of all ages and great fun for families, for it is generally low in technical difficulty. Best of all, it is about as flat as a true off-road ride can be. It is doubtful you will encounter any Lycra-clad, racing types who boast of titanium components and

A beaver pond reflects forested slopes of the Uinta Mountains.

personal bests. Instead, you may pass a few hikers, an ATV or two, or other first-time bikers with their families. There is plenty of room for all. This may not be a solitude-filled wilderness experience, but it is a far cry from Central Park.

General location: Beaver Creek Trail is located 6 miles east of Kamas on the Mirror Lake Highway.

Elevation change: Compared to other Wasatch and Uinta mountain routes, Beaver Creek is flat. The route's western-most trailhead is at the lowest elevation at 7,020´. It rises to 7,600´ at trail's end before dropping to Pine Valley Campground. Total climbing is about 600´.

Season: Beaver Creek is rideable from mid-May through October. The trail and adjacent campgrounds may be very active on weekends and holidays.

Services: There are no services at the trailhead, but the path follows behind 3 developed USFS campgrounds that offer picnic tables, water taps, and outhouses. Most visitor services are found in Kamas, located 6 miles west of the trailhead (no bike shop); otherwise, Park City is the closest full-service town (15 miles west of Kamas).

Hazards: This route is quite tame. For children or first-time mountain bikers, a couple of rocky areas may make bike handling a bit shaky, but these sections are typically very short. Beaver Creek is part of the Taylor Fork ATV area, so watch for motorized traffic.

Rescue index: On weekends and holidays the route's campgrounds are very popular and the Mirror Lake Highway is well traveled. You are never more than a mile or so from assistance. The nearest telephone is at the Beaver Creek Inn, located 3 miles west of the trailhead. Park City, located 15 miles west of Kamas, has a hospital.

Land status: Wasatch-Cache National Forest.

Maps: USGS 7.5 minute quadrangles: Hoyt Peak and Woodland, Utah. (Trailhead is not indicated.) Also, Wasatch-Cache National Forest, Taylor Fork/Cedar Hollow ATV Area (available through Kamas Ranger District).

Finding the trail: From the junction of Main and Center streets in "downtown" Kamas, travel east on the Mirror Lake Highway (UT 150) signed "Scenic Byway, Mirror Lake." At milepost 6 there is a Wasatch National Forest sign on the road's left/north side. The unsigned trailhead, marked with a wooden information board, is directly opposite on the road's south side. A small parking area accommodates a half dozen vehicles.

Sources of additional information:

Wasatch-Cache National Forest
Kamas Ranger District
50 East Center Street
P.O. Box 68
Kamas, Utah 84036
(801) 783-4338

Mountain Biking Utah's Wasatch and Uinta Mountains, by Gregg Bromka (Off-Road Publications, Salt Lake City, Utah)

Notes on the trail: Cross over the wooden footbridge and follow the trail left/east alongside the meandering creek's lush floodplain. There is a moderately steep hill immediately ahead, but it is short in duration and the only one of its kind along the route. (Families with children may want to begin midroute at the Shingle Creek Campground and avoid this more difficult section.)

In just over a mile, a dirt road marked by a green steel gate enters from the left. The trail now becomes the dirt road and bypasses a corral before grading back to the wide ATV trail. After another mile, a short "rock garden" combined with a few ruts will test your handling skills.

You'll come upon a trail information board after 3 miles; it directs ATV users toward "Cedar Loop, rough and rocky" (uphill) or "Beaver Creek, not so tough" (straight). The trail passes through the back of Beaver Creek and Shingle Creek campgrounds. At times the route may seem confusing as it changes from a wide trail to dirt road. Generally stay straight or slightly to the right and along the border between the creek's meadows and the forested hillside. A beaver dam interrupts the gently flowing creek with a reflective pool. Can you find the well-hidden den?

The route begins to descend gently through a rocky section and then appears to end in a small clearing. (Look for a ponderosa pine tree with a split trunk on the north side of the trail.) This is the recommended turnaround point; up ahead the trail descends steeply to Pine Valley Campground and ends anyway. Return in the opposite direction using caution while descending the steep hill near the trailhead.

RIDE 24 *SOAPSTONE BASIN*

Soapstone Basin is a fast-paced, backcountry tour looping around a spacious, meadow-filled valley pocketed with fir and aspen. Although miniature wildflowers cloak this alpine setting, do not expect overwhelming alpine scenery to accompany them. For that you must venture up to the Bluffs where acrophobia-inducing cliffs cascade 2,500´ into the fertile Duchesne River Valley (pronounced doo-shayn´). Across the gorge, peaks of the High Uintas interrupt the horizon. These glaciated mountaintops were not chiseled into serrated ridge lines like those of the central Wasatch Range. Rather, the High Uintas are massive, skeletal domes that open up to broad amphitheaters and long, ice-carved valleys like the Duchesne. Mount Watson, Bald Mountain, Reids and Hayden Peaks hover near 12,000´, but Kings Peak to the far east is the monarch of Utah, reaching over 13,500´.

This 20-mile loop (counterclockwise) is well suited for intermediate bikers. Except for two, more demanding climbs (Soapstone Pass and the Bluffs), the route rolls gently around the basin. For the most part, this is a brisk-paced tour on variably-maintained dirt roads with low technical difficulty.

General location: Soapstone Basin is located about 15 miles east of Kamas and 4 miles south of the Mirror Lake Highway.

Elevation change: The trailhead/parking area near Lambert Hollow is at the route's lowest elevation at 8,570´. The loop begins with a sustained, 1.5-mile, 480´ climb to Soapstone Pass (elevation 9,080´). The route rolls gently across the basin, rising to 9,800´ at its eastern tip. It then drops slowly back to the trailhead. Total climbing for the loop is about 1,320´. If venturing out to the Bluffs overlook (highly recommended) there is one moderately steep, half-mile hill.

Season: The Soapstone Basin Road is usually snow free from late May/early June through October. This route is a very popular one for outdoorsmen during autumn's deer hunting season.

Services: There are no services along this route and all surface waters should be purified. Kamas offers basic visitor services but no bike shop. There are numerous developed USFS campgrounds along the Mirror Lake Highway but none at the trailhead. Backcountry camping is available near the trailhead and along the route, unless posted otherwise.

Hazards: There are no unusual hazards along this loop. Be aware of changing alpine weather; afternoon storms accompanied by lightning are frequent. (Often you are the tallest object in this flattened basin.) Use caution when

RIDE 24   *SOAPSTONE BASIN*

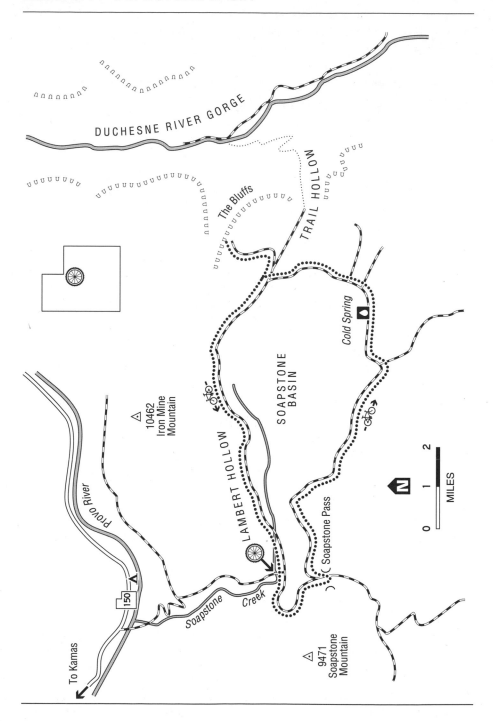

DUCHESNE RIVER GORGE

The Bluffs

TRAIL HOLLOW

Cold Spring

SOAPSTONE BASIN

LAMBERT HOLLOW

10462
Iron Mine
Mountain

Provo River

150

Soapstone Creek

Soapstone Pass

9471
Soapstone
Mountain

To Kamas

N

MILES

0   1   2

A vertigo-inducing view of the Duchesne River valley from the Bluffs.

exploring on and around the Bluffs; the blocky limestone cliffs can be dangerous. Sheep may browse in the basin's meadows.

Rescue index: You may encounter four-wheel-drive and ATV users occasionally. Closer to the Mirror Lake Highway, campers are numerous, but you are still 15 miles from Kamas plus an extra 15 miles from Park City and medical attention.

Land status: Wasatch-Cache National Forest.

Maps: USGS 7.5 minute quadrangles: Soapstone Basin and Iron Mine Mountain, Utah; USGS 1:100,000 metric topographic series: Salt Lake City and Kings Peak, Utah.

Finding the trail: From the center of Kamas, travel 14.5 miles east on Mirror Lake Highway (UT 150). Turn right on Soapstone Basin Road (Forest Service Road 037). This road is a maintained dirt road—passable, but rough for passenger cars in some sections. Drive uphill 2 miles, turn right at the Iron Mine

Lake junction toward Camp Piuta and Wolf Creek Road, continuing on FS 037. Proceed 1 mile to Lambert Hollow and park at your discretion. The loop begins 1 mile south where FS 304 joins FS 037 signed "Wolf Creek, Piuta" (right); "Cold Spring" (left).

Sources of additional information:

Wasatch-Cache National Forest
Kamas Ranger District
50 East Center Street
P.O. Box 68
Kamas, Utah 84036
(801) 783-4338

Mountain Biking Utah's Wasatch and Uinta Mountains, by Gregg Bromka (Off-Road Publications, Salt Lake City, Utah)

Notes on the trail: From the junction of FS 304 and FS 037, pedal right/uphill 1.5 miles to Soapstone Pass signed "Cold Spring 5" (left/east); "Woodland, UT 35, and Wolf Creek" (straight/south). Turn left onto FS 089, a designated ATV route.

It is 4.5 miles to the junction posted "Cold Spring," then another mile to the spring itself on FS 174. Pass by 2 roads branching right and continue on to the junction signed "Trail Hollow Trail." Turn right and slightly downhill, then immediately go left and uphill into the aspens. This four-wheel-drive road leads to the Bluffs overlook and vistas of both 2,500´-deep Duchesne River Gorge and 13,000´-tall High Uinta peaks.

Return to the loop road and enjoy a 6-mile, mostly smooth, but sometimes rocky descent back to the trailhead.

RIDE 25 *RED CLOUD LOOP*

Nowadays, everyone knows Vernal as the heart of Dinosaurland. But beyond "Dino" (which adorns nearly every cafe, motel, and gift shop), Vernal serves as a hub from which radiates a variety of summertime activities. In addition to tourist-oriented Dinosaur National Monument and ever-popular rafting on the Green River, mountain biking is gaining a slow but steady stronghold. Vernal may not have world-class single-track—the trails crossing the Uintas' high country are best suited for boots or horses—but a network of backcountry roads transport fat-tire enthusiasts through a scenic montage that is decidedly northeastern Utah.

Vernal sits in a scorching high desert surrounded by fiery redrock and blowing sand. Yet, nourishing this otherwise parched land are crystalline ribbons of

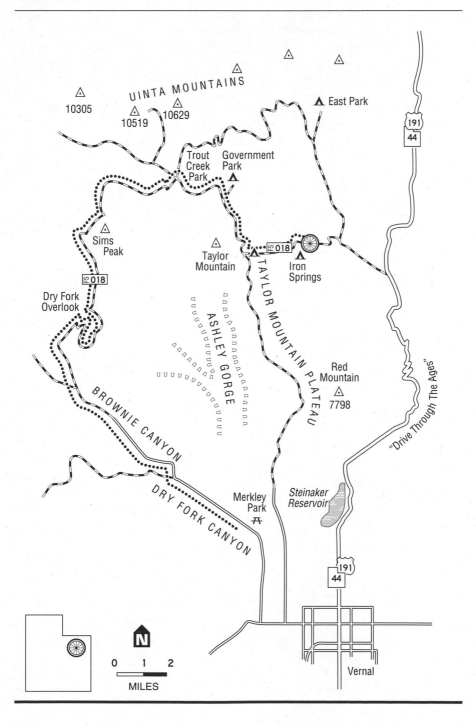

life-giving waters cascading down from the Uinta Mountains' snowcapped peaks. You will travel through these environmental contrasts twice: once on your way to the trailhead on US 191 "Drive through the Ages," where 600 million years of geology are described on signs along the roadside, and again on the bike tour, when you drop from lodgepole mountain slopes into sage-filled valleys pinned between slickrock fortresses.

Contrary to its name, the Red Cloud "Loop" is actually a 40-mile point-to-point ride. The first 30 miles are along maintained dirt roads, the last 10 miles are on pavement. This is an all-day event with several sustained climbs thrown in, but technical difficulty is low. The route is suited for intermediate cyclists with good legs and lungs.

Those who prefer to pack their gear in panniers can turn this into a 70-mile, two- or three-day loop. But a highly developed state of physical and mental conditioning is required for the 20-mile pull from desert to mountains along US 191.

General location: The Red Cloud Loop is located about 23 miles north of Vernal on the southern flank of the eastern Uinta Mountains.

Elevation change: Iron Springs (trailhead) is at 8,600′. The route barely clears 10,000′ near Sims Peak, then drops to 5,990′ in Dry Fork Canyon. The 3,400′ descent through Brownie and Dry Fork Canyons is both exhilarating and highly scenic. Total elevation gain is around 2,500′.

Season: Much of the Red Cloud Loop is strictly alpine. Highest portions may not melt out until June and may be snowbound by early October. Changing alpine weather is common during summer months. Insect repellant is highly recommended.

Services: The developed USFS Iron Springs Campground offers water taps and outhouses. There are no other services along this route. All surface waters (streams and lakes) should be purified. Vernal has all visitor services, including bike shops.

Hazards: Since the route follows improved Forest Service roads, vehicular traffic is common, especially on weekends and holidays. Be prepared to share the road, and use extreme caution when rounding blind corners. There are many brisk, if not furious, downhills. Control your speed and bike attentively.

Rescue index: Campers are numerous at Iron Springs Campground and you may encounter other recreationists along the route. Motorists are common, especially on weekends and holidays. Vernal has full medical facilities.

Land status: Ashley National Forest.

Maps: USGS 7.5 minute quadrangles: Dry Fork, Dyer Mountain, Steinaker Reservoir, and Taylor Mountain, Utah; USGS 1:100,000 metric topographic series: Dutch John and Vernal, Utah.

Finding the trail: Leave a drop vehicle at "Remember the Maine (Merkley) Park." (From Vernal, head north on 500 West and west on 500 North. Turn right at the "Red Cloud Loop" sign and proceed about 4 miles into the mouth of Dry Fork Canyon. Look for an American flag painted high on the sandstone cliffs.) In the shuttle vehicle, drive 20 miles north of Vernal on US 191. Turn left/west on Forest Service Road 018 signed "Red Cloud Loop." Park at the Iron Springs Campground 4 miles ahead.

Sources of additional information:

Ashley National Forest
Vernal Ranger District
355 North Vernal Avenue
Vernal, Utah 84078
(801) 789-1181

Notes on the trail: Follow FS 018 across the southern slopes of the Uinta Mountains down into Dry Fork Canyon. The route is signed "Red Cloud Loop," and portions may be tagged with bike symbols.

From Iron Spring Campground, head west and descend into Big Brush Creek. This part of the ride sets the tone for the rest of the day—a brisk descent followed by a good amount of steady climbing. Pace yourself accordingly. Stay right at the upcoming junction for Red Mountain. Rise through switchbacks and then head north next to Government Creek. Pass by the turnoff for Oaks Park, then turn left/west and continue on FS 018 and cut across the expansive alpine meadows of Government and Trout Creek Parks.

Beyond these meadows, the road follows through a corridor of dense lodgepole pine that hide numerous lakes and ponds. Shadows cast by these pine lances stripe the road with an alpine bar code.

A few miles of gradual climbing around the flank of Sims Peak is followed by big chain ring pedaling. Nearly 22 miles into the tour, the Dry Fork Overlook is worthy of a prolonged rest stop. Marsh Peak hovers above a growing canyon that descends from pine to redrock. A keen eye can trace the road dropping first into Brownie Canyon and then into the head of Dry Fork.

Now let the fun begin! Downhill action is subtle at first but becomes feverish as the road bends north. Watch out for a handful of tight switchbacks dropping into upper Brownie Canyon. Stay left and downhill through Dry Fork Canyon. The air will warm progressively as you pass juniper, pinyon, and sage, which inhabit the high desert. You will swear you have been transported through space and time into southern Utah's Canyonlands, except for the overwhelming presence of the imposing Uintas. Dirt turns to pavement as the sandstone walls widen and lush farm lands fill the canyon floor. File into a pace line and hammer down the paved road or kick back and enjoy the incredibly diverse scene of mountain and desert.

RIDE 26 *CANYON RIM / SWETT RANCH*

"At a distance . . . a brilliant red gorge is seen, the red being surrounded by broad bands of mottled buff and grey at the summit of cliffs, and curving down to the water's edge on the nearer slopes of the mountain. This is where the river enters the mountain range . . . the first canyon we are to explore, or rather, an introductory canyon to a series made by the river . . . We have named it Flaming Gorge," wrote Major John Wesley Powell in 1869. This was the initial leg of Powell's historic expedition down the Green and Colorado Rivers, culminating with the first-ever recorded journey through the mighty Grand Canyon.

With a depth of 1,700′ and width of 4,000′, Red Canyon is an inspiring sight. Its maroon- and rust-colored sandstone cliffs, peppered with pine forests, cascade down to the sinuous aquamarine pool of Flaming Gorge Reservoir. Above rise the rugged slopes of the Uinta Mountains; beyond lie the endless prairie deserts of southern Wyoming. This contrast in scenery is the West's trademark.

In addition to multiple overlooks of Red Canyon, this route ventures to a turn-of-the-century homestead at Swett Ranch. Oscar Swett and his family worked the ranch (claimed in 1909) in pleasant isolation until it was sold in 1968. A graveyard of antiquated horse-drawn plows, a small saw mill, and several log-hewn cabins testify to Swett's penchant for pioneer living, with minimal technological influence. Today the Forest Service-maintained ranch is listed on both the Utah and National Registers of Historic Sites.

The Canyon Rim/Swett Ranch route caters to all ability levels: a five-mile single-track loop is available for novice bikers; a nine-mile out-and-back single-track route is good for strong novice/intermediate riders; and a 16-mile out-and-back/loop combining single- and double-track is suited for strong intermediate/advanced cyclists. All of these routes begin rim-side at the Red Canyon Visitor Center and weave through stately ponderosa and lodgepole pine forests. The first option bypasses a grass-rimmed lake, the second veers from the canyon's edge to cross sage meadows dotted with pines, and the third continues through high chaparrals surrounding the Swett Ranch.

General location: The Canyon Rim/Swett Ranch trail begins at the Red Canyon Visitor Center, located 40 miles north of Vernal.
Elevation change: Red Canyon Visitor Center is at 7,400′. Single-track descends to 7,200′, then rises back up to 7,416′ at the Greendale Rest Area. Total climbing along this out-and-back option is about 400′. If you continue on to the Swett Ranch loop, the route descends to 6,680′ for an additional 740′, moderately strenuous climb back to the Greendale Rest Area. Total climbing for the entire route is about 1,140′.

RIDE 26 *CANYON RIM / SWETT RANCH*

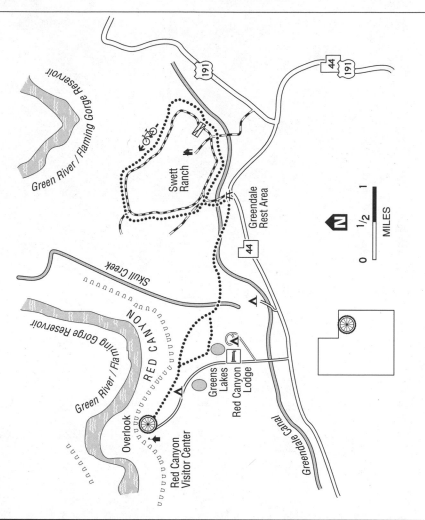

Season: Located on the southern rim of Flaming Gorge, this area has a riding season from late April through October.

Services: The Red Canyon Visitor Center has vending machines, water, and rest rooms. The trail passes 2 developed campgrounds plus the Red Canyon Lodge (about 1.5 miles prior to the trailhead). Red Canyon Lodge has a restaurant, small grocery store, and cabins for rent, plus mountain bike rentals. Farther along the route, there are no services or water (other than an outhouse at the Greendale Rest Area). Other overnight accommodations and visitor

Flaming Gorge as viewed from the Red Canyon Visitor Center.

services can be found at nearby Flaming Gorge Lodge, located on UT 260/US 191 en route to Flaming Gorge Dam. Vernal has all visitor services, including bike shops.

Hazards: You're likely to encounter tourists walking the scenic Rim Trail, so ride cautiously and yield the trail. There are a couple of narrow wooden foot-bridges along the single-track, and trail sections may contain imbedded rock that can make riding unsteady for novice cyclists.

Rescue index: Emergency contacts may be made at the Red Canyon Visitor Center and at Red Canyon Lodge. A volunteer Forest Service ranger is stationed at Swett Ranch. Vernal has medical facilities.

Land status: Ashley National Forest.

Maps: USGS 7.5 minute quadrangles: Dutch John, East Park Reservoir, Flaming Gorge, and Mount Lena, Utah. (Because of the single-track's infancy, these maps do not show that portion of the route.)

Finding the trail: From Vernal, travel north on US 191/UT 44 and ascend the flanks of the eastern Uinta Mountains. Continue on UT 44 3.5 miles past the turnoff for Flaming Gorge Dam/US 191, then turn right at the sign for Red Canyon Recreation Area (between mileposts 3 and 4). The Visitor Center/trail-head is 3 miles north. (The midroute trailhead for Swett Ranch is at the Greendale Rest Area, located 1 mile along UT 44 west of the Flaming Gorge Dam/US 191 turnoff.)

Sources of additional information:

Ashley National Forest
Flaming Gorge Ranger District
P.O. Box 278 (Junction of UT 44 and UT 43)
Manila, Utah 84046
(801) 784-3445

Notes on the trail: Before you begin, you might want to spend some time gazing into Red Canyon and Flaming Gorge Reservoir from the various overlooks along the Visitor Center's paved walkway.

From the parking area, follow the Canyon Rim/Nature Trail (a dirt and gravel path tracing the rim of Red Canyon) southeast. There are numerous junctions with trails leading to Red Canyon and Greens Lake Campgrounds within the first mile. Always follow wooden posts signed "Canyon Rim" or "Rim Trail." Farther portions of the trail are marked with blue diamonds.

After 2 miles, the trail fades south away from the rim and leads to a trail junction signed "Greendale" (left/east); "Greens Lake" (right/west); "Rim" (reverse/north). There are enough blue diamond trail markers here to open a jewelry store! This is a decision point. Novice bikers may opt to loop back to the Visitor Center via East Greens Lake (turn right). Intermediate and advanced cyclists should turn left to continue to the Greendale Rest Area and Swett Ranch loop.

If you decide to continue, take the left and cross over Skull Creek, then the Greendale Canal. At mile 4.6, the trail rises up to the Greendale Rest Area and Overlook along UT 44. This is a good turnaround point for strong novice/intermediate cyclists.

To embark on the Swett Ranch loop, head to the east end of the paved rest area and turn left/north onto Forest Service Road 157. Descend the dirt road about a half mile to a junction of 3 roads. (The left road is signed "Dead End." The middle road, FS 158, is the loop's return road.) Take the right turn, heading east, and pedal to the Swett Ranch. After a mile·or so, turn sharply left to visit historic Swett Ranch one-half mile away. Upon returning to the Swett Ranch junction, veer left about 100 feet ahead to continue the loop. (The right-hand road rises up to US 191.) Follow a carsonite post and blue diamond, then pass through a steel gate.

Some fun downhill cruising awaits. Stay left again, following more carsonite posts. (A right spur branches to a house.) Double-track narrows to single-track and crosses 2 creeks engulfed by a thick grove of aspen.

At a T junction, turn left/south to begin the difficult, 1.5-mile climb back to the Greendale Rest Area, which lives up to this loop's name. (The right/north route is signed "Dead End.") To return to the Visitor Center, simply retrace the original single-track route.

RIDE 27   *DOWD MOUNTAIN*

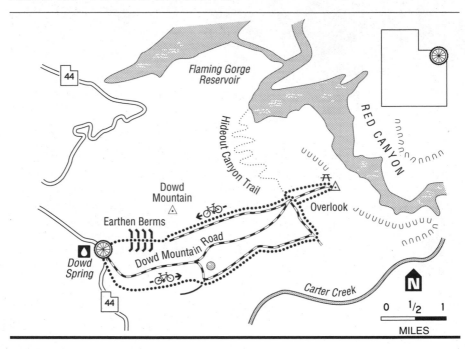

RIDE 27   *DOWD MOUNTAIN*

It is refreshing to hear of a land management agency actively encouraging mountain biking. It is inspirational to learn that the same agency is building and signing trails with mountain bikers in mind. The Flaming Gorge Ranger District of the Ashley National Forest is doing just that. Tucked away on the north slope of the Uinta Mountains are a handful of newly designated mountain bike routes worth pursuing, including Canyon Rim Trail, Elk Park, and Dowd Mountain. In time, Flaming Gorge Country might be known for praiseworthy mountain biking in addition to superb boating and blue-ribbon fishing.

Dowd Mountain is a fine introduction to the area. This undaunting loop passes through dispersed ponderosa and lodgepole pine with good views of the Uinta Mountains' heavily forested slopes, Wyoming prairie lands, and Flaming Gorge Reservoir 1,700′ below. The entire route is well marked with carsonite posts and blue diamonds.

This 10.5-mile loop (counterclockwise) combines 8.5 miles of hard-packed dirt road and double-track with about 2 miles of single-track. Technical diffi-

The Hideout Trail drops from Dowd Mountain to the shoreline of Flaming Gorge.

culty is quite low, except for the last half-mile of abrupt, off-camber whoop-de-doos. Although these earthen berms are fun-loved for those with developed handling skills, they may be unnerving for the less adept. The entire loop is intermediate level, but novice cyclists and families with children can enjoy shortened versions, and advanced bikers can veer off the main loop and dive down the Hideout Canyon Trail to the shore of the reservoir. The return climb is a great workout for racers in training.

General location: Dowd Mountain is located 10 miles north of Flaming Gorge's Red Canyon Visitor Center, which is about 40 miles north of Vernal. (Dowd Mountain is about 14 miles south of Manila.)

Elevation change: The parking area is at the route's lowest elevation at 7,520′. The loop reaches its highest elevation, 8,000′, about a mile from its end near Dowd Mountain. The ride begins with a 400′ climb on single track. Total elevation gain is about 800′.

Season: Dowd Mountain should be rideable from late April through October. Days during midsummer are warm and pleasant, while nights are cool. Afternoon may bring rainstorms accompanied by lightning.

Services: There are no services along this route, nor any sources of water. Picnic tables and an outhouse are available at the Dowd Mountain Overlook. Visitor services (excluding a bike shop) are available at Manila. Food, rustic cabins, developed campgrounds, and limited groceries are available at Red Canyon

Lodge, located near the Red Canyon Visitor Center 10 miles south. Vernal has all visitor services.

Hazards: Overall, the route is low in technical difficulty, *except* for a handful of whoop-de-doos along the route's final descent. (These earthen berms close the old double-track to motor vehicles.) Use caution if you're exploring the overlook's ledgy cliffs.

Rescue index: The Dowd Mountain loop circles around the main dirt road leading to the overlook, which is lightly traveled by motorists. UT 44 (parking area) is well traveled. Emergency contacts can be made in Manila or at Red Canyon Lodge/Visitor Center. Vernal has medical facilities, but is 50 miles away.

Land status: Ashley National Forest.

Maps: USGS 7.5 minute quadrangles: Elk Park, Flaming Gorge, and Manila, Utah. (The main road to the overlook is marked, but this loop ride is not.)

Finding the trail: From Vernal, travel 40 miles north on US 191/UT 44. At the turnoff for Flaming Gorge Dam, continue 14 miles northwest on UT 44 (US 191 forks right/northeast toward the dam). The signed turnoff for Dowd Mountain is located very near milepost 14 on UT 44 and opposite Dowd Spring Picnic Area. (From Manila, travel 14 miles south on UT 44 to the trailhead.)

Sources of additional information:

> Ashley National Forest
> Flaming Gorge Ranger District
> Dutch John Office
> P.O. Box 157
> Dutch John, Utah 84023
> (801) 885-3838

Notes on the trail: There are 2 routes that lead to the overlook: a 9-mile out-and-back along the main dirt road (Forest Service Road 094) or a 10.5-mile loop version. The out-and-back route is easy to follow; the loop tour, however, requires some direction.

Dowd Mountain begins with moderate climbing up a single track, which branches south from the trailhead. Pick an easy gear and enjoy the warm-up. (Families with children may opt to drive to the top of the hill on the dirt road. Then turn right/south on FS 613, just past the cautionary "curves in road" sign.) Where the single-track intersects FS 613, turn right/south and follow blue diamonds that mark the double-track route. About one-half mile past a shallow cattle pond, the double-track splits; fork left/eastward following carsonite posts with blue diamonds. Zig-zag through dispersed lodgepole and ponderosa pine forests underlain by fragrant sage and alpine grasses. Dip through a dry, ledgy gully; pass by a wire-fence enclosure; and turn left at a T junction with a good dirt road. About a mile of gentle, uphill pedaling leads you back to the main overlook road (FS 094). The overlook is .6 miles to the right/east.

Views of Flaming Gorge are incredible. Its sky-blue waters are a haven for boaters and water skiers who slice up the pool with their rippling wakes. Here, the reservoir's sprawling surface narrows before slipping into the head of Red Canyon. Notice that sections of the canyon's far wall are deforested. These slopes were intentionally burned and cleared to provide suitable habitat for transplanted herds of mountain sheep.

Even the layman will notice the area's dramatic geologic complexion. The Uinta Fault, a 100-mile zone of uplift that created the Uinta Mountains, passes through the gorge below. Rock layers have been lifted, tilted, and juxtaposed into a puzzle of wonderful colors and angles. Southern Wyoming—an endless expanse of parched prairielands— is to the north.

From the overlook, hop onto the single-track signed "Dowd Mountain, Hideout Trail." This newly constructed trail skirts the edge of the rounded ridge and passes a rock monument. When you intersect a double-track, turn left and uphill (the Hideout Canyon Trail is to the right and descends to the shore at Flaming Gorge). Beyond the steel gate (and immediately before re-joining with FS 094), turn right/west on the double-track FS 613. A gentle rise to the base of Dowd Mountain precedes the final descent. At first the whoop-de-doos are mellow launch pads that would not prevent a VW Bug from passing, so attack at full throttle. As the hollow narrows, the berms are more authoritative with abrupt faces and off-camber backs. Slip and slide down the gully and back to the parking area.

Okay, so all you hammerheads may be thinking: "Big deal; where is the leg burn, maximum heart rate, my anaerobic threshold?" Tack on an additional 1,700′ of vertical by pursuing the 10-mile, down-and-back-up Hideout Canyon Trail. This old jeep road has its pros and cons: it leads down to Flaming Gorge Reservoir, where a cool plunge awaits; but it is a hot, punishing struggle back out. Sorry, there is no drinking water at the bottom either.

RIDE 28 *ELK PARK*

If you have ever ventured into the core of the Uinta Mountains or driven the Mirror Lake Highway linking Kamas and Evanston, you would have been awe-struck by the grandeur of this mighty range. The High Uintas are marked by 13,000′-plus peaks that thunder above elongated valleys once filled with lumbering rivers of ice, and abrupt slopes that cast indelible shadows into glaciated amphitheaters. Yet, here on the northeastern slope, the range's topographic aspect is more subtle. Peaks are still treeless but roll and undulate along the skyline. Bounteous forests form a thick shawl over the mountains' oblique shoulders.

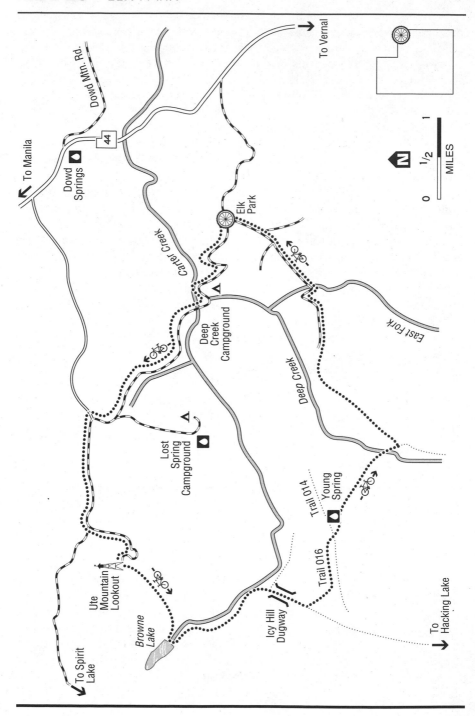

Dean finds Elk Park to his liking.

Much of your time on the Elk Park Trail will be spent bounding through these fragrant forests or pedaling alongside sparkling streams that carry runoff from the snowpack above. For the most part, highland peaks are concealed or filter through a foreground frame of lodgepole pine lances. Occasionally, a canyon widens or woods open to small parks where snowcaps come out of hiding.

You'll have endless, uninterrupted views of the Uinta Mountains and Flaming Gorge Country from the platform of the Ute Mountain Lookout Tower. The Ute Mountain Lookout, built in 1935, was the first of Utah's fire detection towers, and is the only standing tower still in operation. Its 14-foot-square deck rises 50′ above the ground and serves as living quarters for the resident ranger. A part of Utah's cultural heritage, the Ute Mountain Lookout is listed on the National Register of Historic Places.

This 17-mile loop (clockwise) combines good dirt and gravel roads with semi-maintained single-track. Trail riding is characterized by velvety smooth,

The Ute Mountain Lookout.

pine needle- and grass-coated paths; wide, hard-packed dirt ATV trails; and a generous helping of cobble-infested segments that require adept handling skills, balance, and power. A few sections are so rough they are unrideable and necessitate walking and/or carrying your bike short distances. Intermediate cyclists may find this route strenuous, but will no doubt return with a mile-wide grin.

General location: The Elk Park Loop is located in the easternmost Uinta Mountains, 50 miles north of Vernal and 15 miles south of Manila.

Elevation change: The elevation of the route's trailhead at Elk Park is 8,040´. Immediately, the road descends to Deep Creek Campground, the loop's lowest elevation at 7,645´. Sustained climbing rises out of the canyon, then continues to the Ute Mountain Lookout at 8,834´ (the route's high point). After descending along Carter Creek there is 700´ of climbing along the Old Carter Trail to the route's second high point of 8,700´. The loop concludes with mostly downhill pedaling back to the trailhead. Total climbing is about 2,200´.

Season: This section of the Uintas should melt out by late May and be rideable through much of October. Portions of the route may be wet and muddy during spring. Carry insect repellant during summer months. Afternoon clouds may produce chilling rains, at times accompanied by lightning. As its name implies, this backcountry route may not be the wisest choice during autumn's hunting season.

Services: There are no services along this loop. The Deep Creek Campground and Ute Mountain Lookout have outhouses but no water taps. Developed USFS campgrounds are Green Lakes and Canyon Rim, located adjacent to Red Canyon Visitor Center 10 miles away. Red Canyon Lodge (in the same location) offers a restaurant, small grocery store, telephone, cabins, and mountain bike rentals. Visitor information is available at Red Canyon Visitor Center. Additional accommodations are found in Manila and Vernal. Vernal has bike shops.

Hazards: Although this route is brushed out annually by the Forest Service, deadfall may block the trail any time during the year. Distant portions of the loop are considered remote, so travel with appropriate tools, first aid, food, and water. The trail is punctuated with rock-filled, technical sections that require attentiveness and good handling skills. Use caution when pedaling dirt roads leading to the Ute Mountain Lookout, for vehicular traffic is common.

Rescue index: Single-track portions of the Elk Park loop are remote and seldom traveled. Campers are common at Deep Creek Campground, especially on weekends and holidays. The Ute Mountain Lookout is open most daylight hours May through September and has radio communication. Medical facilities are available in Vernal, located 50 miles south.

Land status: Ashley National Forest, Flaming Gorge Ranger District.

Maps: USGS 7.5 minute quadrangles: Elk Park, Jessen Butte, and Leidy Peak, Utah.

Finding the trail: From Vernal, travel north on US 191/ UT 44, up and over the eastern flank of the Uintas. At the junction for Flaming Gorge Dam, fork left/northwest to continue on UT 44 (US 191 forks right and accesses the dam). Eight miles past the turnoff for Red Canyon Recreation Area, turn left onto Forest Service Road 539 (between mileposts 11 and 12) toward Deep Creek. The trailhead and parking area are located 2 miles along the dirt road where a sign reads "Elk Park Trails No 013, 014; Old Carter Trail 4; Summit Park 6.5."

From Manila, the Deep Creek turnoff (FS 539) is 16 miles south on UT 44.

Sources of additional information:

Ashley National Forest
Flaming Gorge Ranger District
P.O. Box 278 (Junction of UT 44
 and UT 43)
Manila, Utah 84046
(801) 784-3445

Vernal Ranger District
355 North Vernal Avenue
Vernal, Utah 84078
(801) 789-1181

Notes on the trail: From the North Park trailhead/parking area, pedal west on the Deep Creek Road and descend feverishly to Deep Creek Campground. Cross Carter Creek and begin a 2.7-mile, moderately strenuous climb out of the stream-filled canyon. There are numerous cliff-side viewpoints worthy of a brief stop and a few photographs. Turn left/west onto FS 221 signed "Spirit Lake, Browne Lake, Sheep Creek Lake." This improved dirt, gravel, and wash-boarded road leads 1.5 miles to a left turn signed "FS 5, Ute Mountain."

Climbing is more aggressive as the dirt road rises from ravaged clearcut zones into thick lodgepole pine and up to the Ute Mountain Lookout. On the tower's south side, connect with the single-track Ute Mountain Trail 005. This spirited path combines smooth, pine needle-coated trail with boulder-infested segments that require finesse and balance. Cross over a broad meadow to the log fence line marking Browne Lake. Parallel the fence south toward the mountains 100 feet or so, then cut back across the lower end of the meadow on single-track. This trail is periodically indistinct, so watch for carsonite posts and trailside trees marked with diamonds and blazes. The path becomes quite obvious and a helluva good time as it follows along glistening Carter Creek.

About a mile along Carter Creek, a double creek crossing is followed by a trail junction where Lost Spring Trail 007 heads east. Stay straight for Young Spring Park. Ahead is a short hike-a-bike up swamped-out and boulder-ridden Icy Hill Dugway. *Shortly* after, turn left/east for Young Spring. (If you continue straight toward Hacking Lake, the trail becomes unbearably steep and wavers far off course.)

A technical hill rising through lodgepole pine precedes a small, grassy park signed "Old Carter Trail 016." Head east across the meadow following carson-ite posts for 016. (Note: Trail 014 also crosses through this meadow *from southwest to northeast;* don't be confused; when the 2 trails intersect, stay to the right on the mountain side of the meadow.) The meadow's eastern edge is marked by Young Spring, a stream that rushes out of the hillside.

Back in the forest, you have 1 mile of power surging, canting and ratcheting, and threading through rock gardens to an obscure junction signed "South Elk Park Trail 013, Elk Park 4 mi" (left); "Old Carter Trail, Summit Park 2.5 mi" (straight); "Young Spring, Browne Lake" (reverse). Turn left to finish the loop with prizeworthy single-track—a combination of a velvety smooth, grass- and pine needle-carpeted trail and good-old-fashioned rock hopping through the aspen-pine forest. Dip into East Fork of Deep Creek and then walk your bike up its unrideable, opposing canyon wall to join with a four-wheel-drive road. In a meadow, turn right followed shortly by a left (marked with a post reading "trails," pointing in reverse) and wind back to the parking area/trailhead.

While in the area, plan a few hours to drive (or half a day to bike) through Sheep Creek Canyon, located north of the Elk Park loop. Sheep Creek is an outdoor geologic classroom where exposed rock formations dating back over 600 million years are a window into the past when lakes, marshes, deserts, and tropical seas covered the land. Many rock layers, originally horizontal when formed, have been tilted to near vertical by the Uinta Fault, which traces the north slope of the Uinta Mountains for nearly 100 miles. Movement along the fault created the nation's only major east-west mountain range.

The Sheep Creek route is marked with roadside signs denoting the various rock layers and their environments of deposition. Obtain the "Wheels of Time" tour guide from the Flaming Gorge Ranger District in Manila, or at either the Vernal Ranger District or Vernal/Dinosaurland Welcome Center in Vernal.

Central Utah's High Plateaus

Central Utah is distinguished by its High Plateaus—a series of lofty, alpine tablelands arcing from the state's heartland to its southwestern reaches. There are eight elevated tracts that comprise the High Plateaus, beginning in the north with the Wasatch Plateau (not to be confused with northern Utah's backbone, the Wasatch Range), then extending southward through the Fish Lake, Awapa, Aquarius, Table Cliff, Sevier, Paunsagunt, and Markagunt Plateaus.

Three of the nation's major physiographic provinces converge upon the High Plateaus: the Colorado Plateau (Utah's Canyon Country) from the south and east, the Middle Rocky Mountains (Northern Utah's Mountainlands) from the north, and the Basin and Range Province from the west. Consequently, the High Plateaus have a combination of attributes characteristic to each of these neighboring regions.

The High Plateaus' southern and eastern margins are largely the products of land stripped away by the erosively insatiable Colorado River and its attendant tributaries. This denudation of the Colorado Plateau, coupled with the High Plateaus' gradual uplift, has created a band of prominent cliffs and terraced slopes that drop from the plateaus' tabletops. Pedal out to the great promontories of Powell Point (Table Cliff Plateau), Pink Cliff (Paunsagunt Plateau), or Strawberry Point (Markagunt Plateau). Beneath each of these cliff points descends a series of colorful terraces that look like massive steps, otherwise known as the Grand Staircase of the Colorado Plateau. Ultimately, this sequence of sedimentary rock units, or stratigraphic section, drops layer after layer across the Utah/Arizona border and into the depths of the Grand Canyon. In the process, more than 100 miles and 500 million years of geologic time are crossed.

The faults and folds that border the High Plateaus' western slopes have dual significance. First, they announce the beginning of the Basin and Range Province, which encompasses western Utah and all of Nevada. Second, they are extensions of northern Utah's great Wasatch Fault, which lifted up the rugged Wasatch Range. Wallace Stegner explains in *Beyond the Hundredth Meridian*, "To the traveler from the east or west . . . the Plateau Province presents difficulties. It is easy to skirt the region, hard to cross it, for from Bear Lake at its northern border to the Vermilion Cliffs along the south, Utah has a spine like a Stegosaurus."

Other recreationists and visitors have long ago uncovered the countless treasures harbored in the High Plateaus: anglers cast many a line into the vitreous waters of Fish Lake in hopes of hooking a Mackinaw lunker; big-game hunters stalk herds of deer and elk that roam endless forests; boaters skim the surface of Joes Valley Reservoir in the Wasatch Plateau; four-wheelers rally to the Tushars and surrounding mountains during the annual Piute ATV Jamboree;

skiers fly down snow-covered slopes at Elk Meadows and Brian Head resorts; hikers venture into the ghostly chasms of the Box Death Hollow Wilderness Area; historians study the cultural significance of Utah's earliest inhabitants at Fremont Indian and Anasazi State Parks; motorists tour Scenic Byways that are rated among the nation's best drives; and sightseers gaze with awe at Capitol Reef's sandstone rotundas from the flank of Boulder Mountain and into the fantasy-filled amphitheaters of both Bryce Canyon and Cedar Breaks. Now mountain bikers are able to discover the abundant riches that await in these alpine hideaways.

Along the plateaus' crests, you will feel suspended between earth and sky. You'll be awed by views of bounteous forests, shimmering lakes, and glistening creeks that nourish flower-speckled meadows. And best of all, you'll enjoy a delightfully cool escape from stifling redrock deserts that bake under a relentless midsummer sun.

CAPTAIN CLARENCE E. DUTTON

Accounts of travelers who ventured into and through the Colorado Plateau during the late eighteenth and early nineteenth centuries abound. Franciscan padres Dominguez and Escalante in 1776 laid the foundation for what would become the Old Spanish Trail; the 1830s trapper Denis Julien incised his name in canyon walls; John C. Fremont led numerous route-finding expeditions in the mid-1800s; railroad crews surveyed corridors for a potential transcontinental route; and dutiful Mormon pioneers proliferated the Church's presence across the territory.

Despite these efforts, the Colorado Plateau, and subsequently half of Utah, remained enshrouded with fables of the unknown. As a master atlas of the western states and territories was being compiled during the mid-1800s, the Four Corners Area was largely left blank or splashed with the word "unexplored."

It was Major John Wesley Powell's famed 1869 exploration of the Green and Colorado Rivers (which ultimately became the first documented voyage through the Grand Canyon) and subsequent second journey in 1871 that are credited for the opening of the Colorado Plateau. His expeditions provided the impetus for a number of government-funded surveys to this remote section of the West.

However, Powell (a geologist by trade) had many interests that steered him away from the surveys he created, including Native American ethnology. Of all the topographers, geographers, anthropologists, and geologists that comprised Powell's crews, none would provide the lasting visionary impact that geologist Captain Clarence E. Dutton did.

Assigned by Powell to map and decipher the geology of Utah's High Plateaus and adjacent Plateau Province (Colorado Plateau), Dutton did so with a liter-

Bryce Canyon National Park is ". . . one mighty ruined colonnade . . . now chained up in a spell of enchantment," C. E. Dutton described more than a century ago.

ary flair that veered far from the exceedingly terse prose that was considered standard presentation of geologic discoveries and discussions. Perhaps this was because Dutton was more than a student of science, but a "omnibiblical" tourist and lover of nature. His superfluous and aesthetic geologic accounts are recited and revered more than a century later, not only by the scientific community but by inquisitive Plateau travelers as well.

Wallace Stegner, in his biography of Powell et al., *Beyond the Hundredth Meridian,* claimed that "Dutton loved a grand view, a sweeping panorama. What [others] loved to paint—the big, spectacular, colorful view—Dutton loved to describe. [And] . . . like a painter . . . his drift was constantly away from the meticulous and toward the suggestive."

Whether you are making your first or fifth mountain bike trip to Utah's High Plateaus or Canyon Country keep an open mind when you're travelling through this bizarre land, as Dutton did when he described the Grand Canyon:

> The lover of nature, whose perceptions have been trained in the Alps, in Italy, Germany, or New England, in the Appalachians or Cordilleras, in Scotland or Colorado, would enter into this strange region with a shock, and dwell there for a time with a sense of oppression, and perhaps horror. Whatsoever things he had learned to regard as beautiful and noble he would seldom or never see . . . . Whatsoever might be bold and striking would at first seem only grotesque. The colors would be the very ones he

had learned to shun as tawdry and bizarre. The tones and shades . . . in which his fancy had always taken special delight, would be the ones which are conspicuously absent. But time would bring a change. . . . outlines which at first seemed harsh and trivial have grace and meaning; forms which seemed grotesque are full of dignity; . . . colors which had been esteemed unrefined, immodest, and glaring, are as expressive, tender, changeful, and capacious of effects as any other. [The Colorado Plateau is] a great invention in modern ideas of scenery . . . whose full appreciation [is] a special culture. . . . if planted upon the plains of Central Europe, would have influenced modern art.

As Stegner notes, these are strange and poetic words for a geologist. It is through Powell's adventures that we feel the power of the Colorado River and its significance in sculpting the Colorado Plateau. But it is with Dutton's eye that we are able to look beyond what is superficial and become utterly spellbound by the bizarre shapes and colors of this unique geologic showcase.

RIDE 29   *SKYLINE DRIVE*

What the White Rim Trail is to Utah's Canyon Country, Skyline Drive is to Utah's plateau country: an epic, multi-day, mountain bike adventure along a famed Utah Scenic Backway. Whereas the White Rim slices through the Colorado Plateau's layer-cake strata of burnished sandstones, Skyline Drive traces the 10,500´ crest of central Utah's Wasatch Plateau, dancing among clouds that scrape the belly of the heavens.

Along Skyline, you will not face chiseled peaks and improbable mountain passes, which characterize northern Utah's formidable Wasatch Range. The summit of the Wasatch Plateau is an open, rolling expanse of virgin tundra meadows pocketed with stands of fir. Graceful, horseshoe-shaped amphitheaters embrace broad, ice-carved valleys and bow to solitary limestone crowns. During the 1880s, Captain Clarence Dutton, John Wesley Powell's protegé, surveyed Utah's high plateaus and described this region: "On the plateaus stand buttes, lone mountains. The buttes are mountain cameos, horizontal strata with escarped sides—they are mountains of circumdenudation."

The classic Skyline Drive adventure is a three- to four-day, 80-mile self- or vehicle-supported tour. Self-supported, the route is restricted to advanced and expert riders who are well versed in alpine, backcountry touring. With vehicle support, cyclists of varying abilities can enjoy the route; but be forewarned. Although Skyline is a hard-packed dirt road with low technical difficulty overall, there are several noteworthy climbs that warrant high-altitude preconditioning. Subsequently, though, each ascent is offset with breakneck descending, culminating with a whopping 20-mile, 4,000´ drop off the plateau. (GWT)

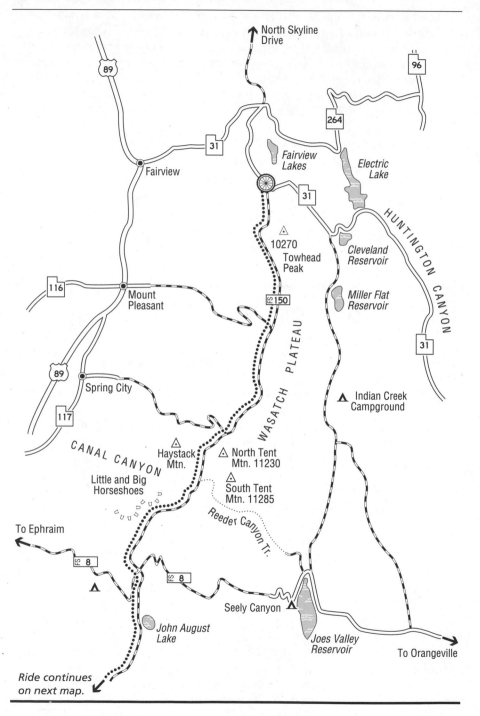

North Skyline Drive

89

96

264

31

Fairview Lakes

Electric Lake

Fairview

31

Towhead Peak
10270

Cleveland Reservoir

HUNTINGTON CANYON

116

Mount Pleasant

FS 150

Miller Flat Reservoir

WASATCH PLATEAU

31

89

Spring City

Indian Creek Campground

117

CANAL CANYON

Haystack Mtn.

North Tent Mtn. 11230

Little and Big Horseshoes

South Tent Mtn. 11285

Reeder Canyon Tr.

To Ephraim

FS 8

FS 8

Seely Canyon

John August Lake

Joes Valley Reservoir

To Orangeville

Ride continues on next map.

CLIMB IT
HIKE IT
FLOAT IT
BIKE IT

AFALCONGUIDE

Whatever you do outside, helps you find a better place to do it. Maps, photos, safety tips, and charts accompany detailed descriptions of state-by-state rock climbing sites, hiking trails, river routes, and mountain biking trails. Falcon also publishes information about many more outdoor activities and nature gift ideas.

For a free catalog of books, maps, recreational guidebooks, and nature gift ideas, please return this card with the following information.

Name _____

Address _____

City _____

State _____ Zip _____

❑ **YES!** I'd like to send a catalog to a friend.

Name _____

Address _____

City _____

State _____ Zip _____

Or call for a **FREE** catalog.

1-800-582-2665

FALCON
P.O. BOX 1718
HELENA,
MONTANA
59624

FALCON™

BUSINESS REPLY MAIL
FIRST-CLASS MAIL PERMIT NO 80 HELENA MT

POSTAGE WILL BE PAID BY ADDRESSEE

FALCON PRESS PUBLISHING CO
PO BOX 1718
HELENA MT 59624-9948

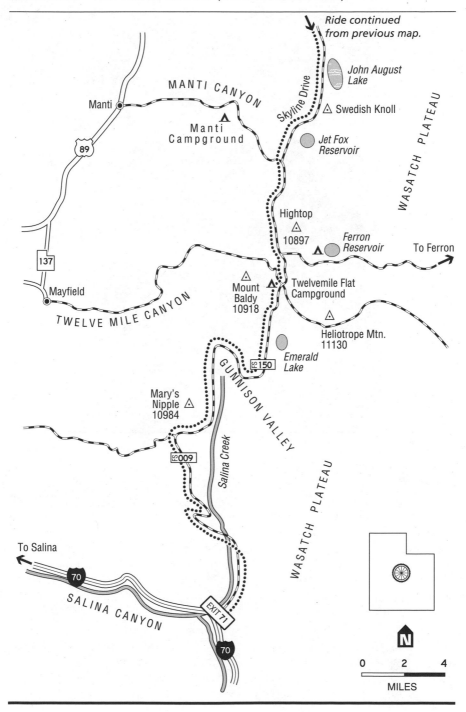

Ride continued from previous map.

MANTI CANYON

John August Lake

Manti

Skyline Drive

△ Swedish Knoll

Manti Campground

Jet Fox Reservoir

89

WASATCH PLATEAU

137

Hightop
△
10897

Ferron Reservoir

To Ferron

Mayfield

Mount Baldy
10918

Twelvemile Flat Campground

TWELVE MILE CANYON

△ Heliotrope Mtn.
11130

FR 150

Emerald Lake

GUNNISON VALLEY

Mary's Nipple △
10984

Salina Creek

FR 009

WASATCH PLATEAU

To Salina

70

EXIT 71

SALINA CANYON

70

N

0   2   4
MILES

Emerald Lake.

General location: Skyline Drive and the Wasatch Plateau are located in the center of Utah, neatly packaged between US 6 to the north (Spanish Fork Canyon) and Interstate 70 to the south.

Elevation change: Skyline Drive begins at 9,700′ (at the junction with UT 31), then undulates to 10,987′ at High Top (45 miles into the ride). The route peaks again at 10,780′ above Blue Lake before beginning its famed 20-mile descent to I-70, resting at 6,660′. Although net elevation change along the plateau's rolling crest appears slight, total climbing approaches 5,000′; total descending is nearly double.

Season: Skyline Drive has a relatively short biking season, from late June/early July through late September. Evenings will be crisp, perhaps near freezing; midday temperatures may reach 70 to 80 degrees. Because of the high elevation, summer's midday rains may bring high winds, radical drops in temperature, and possibly hail. Carry a rain shell.

As the warmth of midsummer intensifies so does a pallet of brilliant wild-flowers. Aster, lupine, bluebell, alpine paintbrush, penstemon, wild rose, geraniums, mule ear, and skyrockets populate open meadows, painting the plateau with a rainbow of vibrant colors.

Services: There are no services along this route. There are developed campgrounds at Ferron Reservoir and Twelvemile Flat (each nearly 50 miles into the ride). Water is restricted to a few springs, small reservoirs, and irrigation ditches; all should be purified because there is sheepherding in the area. Rustic cabins and limited provisions are available at Ferron Reservoir's Skyhaven Lodge, but inquire first.

The towns lining Sanpete Valley (west) and Castle Valley (east) offer basic visitor services, including lodging, food, and gasoline; but there are no bike shops. More extensive services and bike shops are located in Price, Provo, and Richfield. All are several hours away by vehicle. A hospital is located in Mount Pleasant (Sanpete Valley).

Hazards: Skyline Drive itself poses no significant hazards for mountain bike travel; however, chassis-deep mud holes after recent rains and/or lingering snowdrifts (notorious near the Horseshoes and High Top) may hinder support vehicles. Although bikes may be portaged around these obstacles, vehicles may have to descend off the plateau along variably maintained dirt roads and then re-ascend the next canyon.

Route conditions vary from smooth, hard-packed dirt and gravel when dry to greasy, potter's clay when wet. A high-clearance vehicle equipped with four-wheel-drive is recommended for support and should be stocked with emergency equipment, including a good spare tire, shovel, tow rope, "handy-man" jack, and perhaps a few sturdy wooden planks.

Prepare for cool days and cold nights; bring sunscreen and carry more than adequate water supplies.

Rescue index: Motorists, recreationists, and campers are common near the Skyline Drive trailhead, in Manti Canyon, at Joes Valley Reservoir, and at Ferron Reservoir. Along the route's remote midsection, however, you'll see few travelers other than occasional ranchers. Towns located in Sanpete Valley (west) are often 20 miles and several bike hours from Skyline Drive; those located in Castle Valley (east) are much farther.

Emergency assistance *may* be summoned from the cafe/boat dock or nearby Olsen Ranger Station (both at Joes Valley Reservoir) and perhaps Skyhaven Lodge (Ferron Reservoir). Mount Pleasant (Sanpete Valley) has a hospital; Manti, Ephraim, Salina (all in Sanpete Valley), and Castle Dale (Castle Valley) have medical clinics.

Land status: Manti–La Sal and Fish Lake National Forests.

Maps: USGS 1:100,000 metric topographic series: Manti, Nephi, and Salina, Utah; Manti–La Sal National Forest Travel Map (Sanpete, Ferron, and Price Ranger Districts) and Fish Lake National Forest Travel Map.

Finding the trail: Skyline Drive begins where UT 31 crosses the crest of the

Wasatch Plateau, about 15 miles east of Fairview (Sanpete Valley) or 35 miles northwest of Huntington (Castle Valley). Access is also provided by UT 96 and UT 264 via the town of Scofield and Scofield Reservoir. Skyline Drive is marked as Forest Service Road 150/Great Western Trail. The route ends at I-70 (Exit 71), located 35 miles east of Salina. A lengthy vehicle shuttle is required. Park at your discretion.

Sources of additional information:

Manti–La Sal National Forest
599 West Price Drive
Price, Utah 84501
(801) 637-2817

Fish Lake National Forest
115 East 900 North
Richfield, Utah 84701
(801) 896-9233

Skyhaven Lodge (Ferron Reservoir)
(801) 835-5342

Mountain Biking Utah's Canyon and Plateau Country, by Gregg Bromka (Off-Road Publications, Salt Lake City, Utah)

Notes on the trail: Skyline Drive begins with a modest climb around Towhead Peak followed by a generous descent spiced with a few ruts, mud holes, and scattered rocks across the head of Rolfson Canyon. These conditions are the general fare for the next 75 miles as you rise and descend the gigantic roller coaster.

Early on, road conditions are good and the ride progresses rapidly. Here, the Wasatch Plateau's crest is quite narrow with sharp, craggy canyons plunging west, countered by broad, shallow bowls opening to the east. As the route progresses, the plateau widens, canyons lengthen, and escarped buttes cap the summit.

After 8 miles, FS 37 branches right and descends to Mount Pleasant. Two miles ahead, under the power lines, the road, which is primarily clay based, can get messy when wet.

Around mile 18, FS 036 cuts off and drops to Spring City. Beyond is the domed assemblage of North and South Tent Peaks, 2 of the plateau's tallest at 11,230′ and 11,285′, respectively. The road winds around their western flanks pinned between precipitous limestone cliffs and steep headwalls of Canal Canyon.

Big and Little Horseshoe, 2 ice-cut scallops stamped into the plateau's side, will soon come into view. Along with Mary's Nipple to the south, the Horseshoes are the Wasatch Plateau's most pronounced landforms, easily visible throughout Sanpete Valley. There is a long, grinding hill to the crest of the Horseshoes, followed by one of Skyline's great descents, a 4-mile, all-out bomber.

As the downhill flattens, UT 29/FS 8 crosses Skyline. It descends left/east to Joes Valley Reservoir and right/west to Ephraim. You are 30 miles in with 50 to go. Pass by Snow Lake and Jet Fox Reservoir for gradual climbing all the way up to High Top, elevation 10,897′ and signed "Highest Point on Skyline Drive." Break out the cameras to record the event.

Just beyond, a decision awaits: descend off Skyline Drive to Ferron Reservoir or continue straight to Twelvemile Flat; you can camp at either place. (If you chose Ferron Reservoir, remember there is a 900′ climb to rejoin Skyline. But a bed and roof overhead at one of Skyhaven's rustic cabins may be worth it.)

Huge meadows mark Twelvemile Flat. Pass through the log fence line and bear right to continue on Skyline beneath the barren flanks of Mount Baldy. The valley opening up to the east marks the dendritic headwaters of Muddy Creek. This stream dives into the San Rafael Swell 50 miles away, disappearing into the darkened sandstone narrows of the Chutes (an adventuresome hike).

There is one more difficult climb past Emerald Lake; then breathe a sigh of relief, for you have beaten Skyline. Except for a couple of uphill teasers, 20 miles of some rough and some smooth cruising await. The beacon of the Wasatch Plateau, Mary's Nipple (Musinia Peak), guides you across grass-covered Gunnison Valley and down Salina Creek to I-70. (On the south flank of Mary's Nipple, Skyline continues as FS 009; the Great Western Trail branches right to destinations unknown.) Say farewell to the tundra, fir, and aspen of the plateau's crest and welcome the scrub oak, sage, and cacti of the Sonoran high desert.

RIDE 30 *PETES HOLE*

You won't find many mountain bikers in this part of the state for obvious reasons: it is remote and generally unknown. Ask someone where Joes Valley Reservoir is, or the Wasatch Plateau for that matter, and the likely response will be a quizzical look and a shrug of the shoulders. Perhaps that is good. Many people don't know that the Wasatch Plateau, located bull's-eye in the center of the state, hosts an untapped wealth of recreational opportunities. Most people don't realize that this section of the Wasatch Plateau is blessed with a gorgeous reservoir lying within an entrenched valley, overshadowed by 10,000′ plateaus, or that fields of luxuriant grasses blended with pastel wildflowers blanket thick forests, or that a handful of glistening ponds are cupped gently beneath rugged slopes. Even more people don't realize that there are outstanding mountain bike adventures waiting to be discovered. Petes Hole loop is an adventure that incorporates all of these Wasatch Plateau attributes, plus it boasts one of the finest single-tracks between the Wasatch Front and Brian Head.

This 28-mile loop (counterclockwise) incorporates improved dirt roads with fast-paced double-track and 7 miles of serendipitous single-track. It is an advanced-level ride because of the sustained climbing and semi-maintained single-track sections that are moderately technical. Intermediate cyclists who

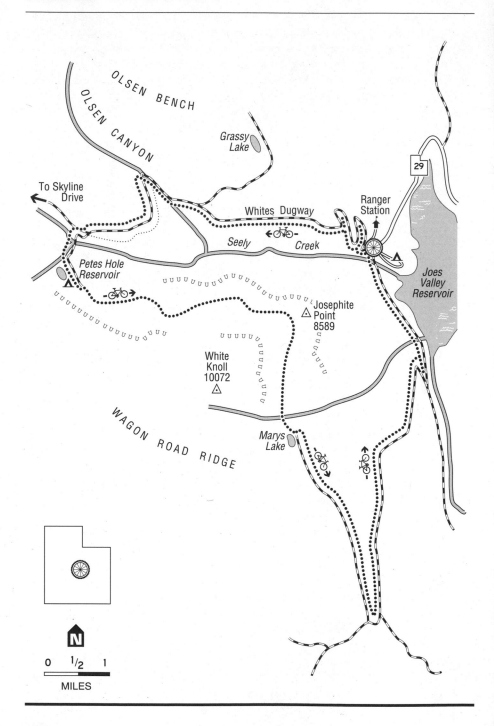

OLSEN BENCH

OLSEN CANYON

Grassy Lake

To Skyline Drive

Whites Dugway

Ranger Station

29

Seely Creek

Petes Hole Reservoir

Joes Valley Reservoir

Josephite Point 8589

White Knoll 10072

WAGON ROAD RIDGE

Marys Lake

N

0   1/2   1

MILES

Single-track and breezy meadows highlight the Petes Hole loop.

still feel fresh upon reaching Petes Hole should consider tackling the rest of the loop; the exhilaration you feel throughout the day offsets exhaustion you suffer at trail's end. (GWT)

General location: Petes Hole is located near Joes Valley Reservoir in the heart of the Wasatch Plateau, located 40 miles south and west of Price.

Elevation change: The parking area/trailhead at Joes Valley Reservoir is at 7,000′. Commencing the route is a 1,400′ climb through Whites Dugway. The route's high point is at 9,000′, which is just beyond Petes Hole Reservoir and south of Josephite Point. Concluding the route is a raucous 1,700′ descent back to the reservoir's shore. Total elevation gain is 3,000′.

Season: This section of the Wasatch Plateau should melt out by mid-June and be rideable through mid-October. During midsummer, daytime temperatures are pleasant (80s) and nights can be crisp (40s). Be alert to changing alpine weather; afternoon storms are common. Wildflowers grow in profusion from late spring through summer, and fall colors are spectacular.

Services: Limited services (food, some camping supplies, and perhaps gasoline) are available at the boat-ramp cafe near the trailhead (west side of Joes Valley Reservoir) and across the reservoir at a second cafe. Meat and potatoes are generally the cuisine. A developed USFS campground is also located at the trailhead. There are no other services along this route and all surface waters should be purified. (A primitive campground/picnic area is located at Petes Hole but does not have water taps.) Extended services are available in Castle

Dale/Orangeville, located 15 miles from the reservoir. The closest bike shops are in Price.

Hazards: Much of the single-track along this route exists in a semi-maintained condition. Thus, expect the usual fare of trail-related obstacles, including deadfall, unbridged creeks, and swampy areas, plus scattered rocks and tree-root networks. You may encounter sporadic vehicular traffic on dirt roads. This route is not recommended when it's wet. Afternoon thunderstorms are common.

Rescue index: Joes Valley Reservoir is popular with boaters, campers, and fishermen. Recreationists can also be found at Petes Hole Reservoir. Dirt roads are irregularly traveled and the single-track sees few users. A telephone can be found at the boat dock (if the cafe is open), across the lake at a second cafe, or at the Forest Service Ranger Station near the campground. A medical clinic is located in Castle Dale. Price has a hospital.

Land status: Manti–La Sal National Forest.

Maps: USGS 7.5 minute quadrangles: Danish Knoll, Ferron Canyon, Joes Valley Reservoir, Utah. (Single-track is not mapped.)

Finding the trail: From Price, travel 26 miles south on UT 10. Turn west on UT 29 for Orangeville and Joes Valley Reservoir. In the center of town, turn right and follow signs for Joes Valley Reservoir, which is located 15 miles up "twisting" Straight Canyon. Travel around to the reservoir's west side where the boat ramp and USFS campground are located. Day-use parking is available.

From I-70, take Exit 89 and travel about 40 miles north on UT 10. Connect with UT 57, which leads to UT 29 in Orangeville. Follow signs for Joes Valley Reservoir as mentioned above.

Sources of additional information:

> Manti–La Sal National Forest
> Ferron Ranger District
> 98 South State
> P.O. Box 310
> Ferron, Utah 84523
> (801) 384-2372

> *Mountain Biking Utah's Canyon and Plateau Country,* by Gregg Bromka (Off-Road Publications, Salt Lake City, Utah)

Notes on the trail: From the day-use parking area or campground, pedal west on UT 29/Forest Service Road 008, which is now a hard-packed dirt road. The route commences with a good warm-up in the way of a 5-mile, moderately steep pull through Whites Dugway; a series of switchbacks rising quickly above the reservoir. The route parallels Seely Creek, a deep V-notched canyon marred by avalanches. Across the canyon, the first prominent break in the eastern slope is Josephite Point. In an hour or two you will be there, looking back here.

Juniper and pinyon flirt with ponderosa, all of which gradually succumb to aspen and mixed fir. You'll pass the junction for Grassy Lake after 5.5 miles.

About 1.4 miles beyond the junction, FS 008 turns sharply left as it wraps through Olsen Canyon. After you take the left, you can take the elusive trail (marked as the Great Western Trail) branching left off the road's embankment. (This is an exciting double-track, narrowing to single-track, weaving through dense forests and past an old cabin. It is 2 or 3 miles to a road junction; turn left and rise up to Petes Hole Reservoir.) Or, if you miss the single-track turnoff, just continue up the main dirt road, turn left for Thistle Flat/Beaver Dams, descend, then rise up to Petes Hole—a good lunch stop.

Pedal around to the reservoir's south side and to the signed trailhead for Josephite Point Trail. Let the fun begin! This semi-maintained path crosses breezy meadows lying beneath layered cliffs; passes small reservoirs and beaver-dammed ponds; dips through a number of creek-filled gullies; threads through dense, fragrant forests; and mingles with fields of succulent grasses sprinkled with wildflowers. When the trail bends south at Josephite Point, hike out toward the slope for good views of Joes Valley Reservoir and the sunken valley it occupies.

Single-track continues southward through more fields and forests with one gut-busting climb. At Marys Lake, the route proceeds south as a double-track for 4 miles to a T junction. Turn left and downhill, then left again, now heading north. A long, paint-shaker downhill drops quickly back to the valley floor. A left turn and 2 miles of easy pedaling return you to the boat ramp, where a cool plunge in the reservoir awaits.

RIDE 31 *U M PASS*

Alias the whoop-de-doo trail, U M Pass is highlighted by an old jeep road-turned-single-track trail loaded with air-worthy earthen berms. Your bike will buck like a bronco trying to toss you from its saddle. But hold on tight and ride it out. The rest of the tour ventures up one meadow-filled valley and down another.

U M Pass is not lacking in scenic charm either. This is central Utah's plateau country, a continuous platform of high, level ground broken by deep, broad valleys. The loop begins in Sevenmile Valley, winding alongside a blue-ribbon creek cloaked with hummocky meadows. The Fish Lake High Top's Sevenmile Cirques and opposing Mounts Terrill and Marvine neatly package the valley with glacial escarpments. U M Valley is equally tranquil. Expansive sage and grass fields are wedged between mountains of lofty but subtle aspect. As the route concludes, Johnson Valley Reservoir reflects its aspen-rimmed shore and elevated plateau tops.

This 19-mile, intermediate-level loop follows mainly good dirt roads and a few miles of gentle pavement at the end. Dirt roads are generally low in techni-

RIDE 31 *U M PASS*

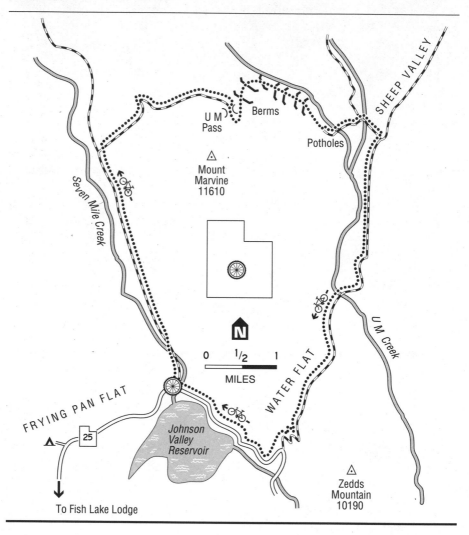

cal difficulty and the climb to U M Pass is the loop's only significant chore. But the single-track descending from U M Pass requires good handling skills, especially a keen sense of fore and aft weight distribution coupled with prudent braking.

General location: The U M Pass loop is located just north of Fish Lake and Johnson Valley Reservoir. Fish Lake is located between Richfield and Capitol Reef National Park in central Utah.

Camaraderie is found during the Fish Lake in the Fall Mountain Bike Rally.

Elevation change: The parking area/trailhead near Johnson Valley Reservoir is at 8,820′. U M Pass rises at a moderately difficult grade to 10,700′. The descent through U M Valley drops to 8,900′. There are 2 small climbs before you return to the trailhead. Total elevation gain is 2,100′.

Season: Snow can linger well into May and even June and return by mid-October. Midsummer days are temperate; nights are crisp. Wildflowers in Sevenmile Valley are showy during July and August, but autumnal colors are some of the best in the state. The area is popular with hunters during mid- to late October.

Services: There are no services along this route. The parking area has an outhouse but no water taps. All surface waters should be purified. Bowery Haven, Fish Lake Lodge, and Lakeside Resort (all located south of the parking area along the paved road) offer restaurants/cafes, lodging, limited groceries and supplies, and pay showers. Bowery Haven and Lakeside Resort have gasoline. Numerous developed USFS campgrounds line Fish Lake's western shore. There are no bike shops in the area.

Hazards: The descent from U M Pass warrants caution. The jeep road-turned-single-track is loaded with earthen berms that prevent vehicular traffic. Although these catapulting ramps are the route's main attractions, they deserve respect. Look before you leap! You may encounter vehicular traffic along the paved highway and along the dirt road leading up Sevenmile Valley.

Rescue index: Motorists are common on the return leg along the paved road.

Fishermen work the banks of Sevenmile Creek along the route's initial portion. U M Pass and upper U M Valley receive few visitors.

Telephones are located at Bowery Haven, Fish Lake Lodge, and Lakeside Resort. A Forest Service ranger station is located across the road from Fish Lake Lodge. Richfield has a hospital.

Land status: Fish Lake National Forest.

Maps: USGS 7.5 minute quadrangles: Fish Lake, Forsyth Reservoir, Hilgard Mountain, and Mount Terrill, Utah.

Finding the trail: The trailhead (Piute Parking Area) is about 8 miles north of Fish Lake Lodge. From Interstate 70 (west), take Exit 48/Sigurd and travel south on UT 24 toward Capitol Reef National Park. After 33 miles, turn left/east on UT 25. Fish Lake Lodge is 8 miles ahead.

From I-70 (east), take Exit 89 or Exit 85/Rest Area and then travel south on UT 72. Two miles south of the National Forest boundary and Forsyth Reservoir, turn right/west on UT 25. The trailhead (Piute Parking Area) is on the northwest side of Johnson Valley Reservoir, just beyond the junction of UT 25 and Sevenmile Creek Road.

From the south (Capitol Reef National Park/Torrey), travel west and then north on UT 24. About 17 miles north of Loa, turn right on UT 25. Fish Lake is 8 miles ahead.

Sources of additional information:

Fish Lake National Forest
Loa Ranger District
150 Main
Loa, Utah 84747
(801) 836-2811

Fish Lake Lodge
(801) 836-2700

Mountain Biking Utah's Canyon and Plateau Country, by Gregg Bromka (Off-Road Publications, Salt Lake City, Utah)

Notes on the trail: From the parking area, pedal north, then turn immediately left onto Forest Service Road 640 signed "Sevenmile Creek, Gooseberry." Initially, the rising dirt and gravel road will get the heart pumping. As it breaks out across broad, hummocky meadows that engulf the meandering creek, it becomes an idle ramble. After 4 miles, turn right/east onto an unsigned four-wheel-drive road (FS 042) next to a USFS information board. Begin the 1.7-mile, 1,000′ climb to U M Pass.

Groves of aspen quiver in cool midday breezes. Across the valley, the crest of the Fish Lake Hightop is stamped with a succession of coalescing glacial imprints, called Sevenmile Cirques. Mount Marvine, with its craggy cockscomb ridge, creates the southern gate to U M Pass; the subtle stature of Mount Terrill rises to the north.

At U M Pass, the road bends south and ends. Locate the gate in the log and wire fence line, but first enjoy the view east of sky, mountain, and valley. You'll see Hilgard Mountain, an inclined plateau of sorts across the valley.

Now lower your seat and securely fasten your brain bucket. At first, the trail drops quickly and the berms are quite large. Check your weight distribution and hang your butt off the back if needed. Feather the brakes—not too much pressure on the front. As the trail flattens the bumps are smaller and allow for a little air to gather between ground and tires. But keep things in perspective; you are not trying to jump the Snake River like Evel Knievel.

Keep an eye on the trail as it wavers through the Potholes; it may become faint and confusing. Splash through U M Creek and then a larger water trap signed "Black Flat." Keep pedaling eastward back into aspens and over a small ridge. Turn right on the U M Valley road (FS 015) and ramble down the valley's length. After cresting and then banking down a rough hill at the valley's southern end, turn right on pavement to wind around Johnson Valley Reservoir and back to the parking area.

RIDE 32 *MYTOGE MOUNTAIN*

Mytoge Mountain is regarded as the classic Fish Lake–area ride and is the featured tour of the Fish Lake in the Fall Mountain Bike Festival held annually in early September. The laid-back but well-catered event attracts hundreds of fat-tire enthusiasts to the aquamarine waters of Utah's mountain jewel. Three days of guided tours lead through pristine forests, across stream-cut meadows, and to lofty viewpoints of shimmering lakes and sweeping panoramas of the surrounding high plateaus.

By all means bring a fishing pole, for trophy-size Mackinaw and rainbow trout lurk in Fish Lake's frigid, spring-fed waters. They say there was a day when fish were so plentiful that wagon drivers had to clear them from the creek crossings, else the horses' hoofs would churn them up onto the creek banks by the score. Perhaps fish are not as abundant today, but anglers still cast their lines feverishly in hopes of landing that illusive 36-pound lunker, which stands as an all-time record catch.

The Mytoge Mountain loop is 25 miles long (16 miles of dirt road and single-track and 9 miles of relatively flat pavement). It is geared toward strong intermediate bikers. Dirt roads are both maintained and four-wheel-drive varieties, and single-track is playful to highly technical.

General location: Fish Lake is located about 40 miles southeast of Richfield (and Interstate 70) or about 45 miles northwest of Capitol Reef National Park. Mytoge Mountain forms the basaltic cliffs that hover above Fish Lake's eastern shore.

RIDE 32 *MYTOGE MOUNTAIN*

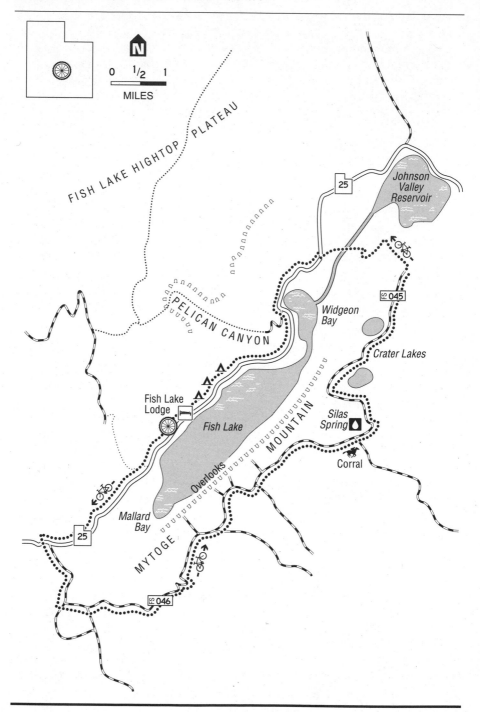

Fish Lake—the jewel of Utah's High Plateaus.

Elevation change: Fish Lake Lodge (trailhead and lowest elevation) rests at 8,850′. The route climbs to 9,900′ atop Mytoge Mountain at the third Fish Lake overlook. (En route is an arduous 1.5-mile, 800′ pull to reach the top of Mytoge Mountain.) Total vertical gain approaches 2,800′.

Season: Snow can linger well into May and even June and return by mid-October. Midsummer days are temperate; nights are crisp. Although terribly inviting for a post-ride plunge, Fish Lake is cold—if not numbing. The area is popular with hunters during mid- to late October.

Services: Fish Lake Resort (one of the great rough-cut timber lodges of the west) offers dining, a small convenience store, a gift shop, and showers. Overnight accommodations range from rustic, one-room cabins to multi-family lodges. Additional cabins, cafes, showers, and gasoline are found at Lakeside Resort and Bowery Haven, located south and north of Fish Lake Lodge, respectively. There are numerous developed USFS campgrounds along the lake's western shore. There are no bike shops at Fish Lake.

Hazards: Most of the route lacks significant hazards. Motorists and lumbering RVs are common on the paved road, but not so on dirt roads. Use caution when exploring the mountain's cliffs. Most importantly, the descent off Mytoge Mountain is a steep, boulder-studded, highly technical single-track. Know your limits. Although the most experienced riders may be able to clear the multiple obstacles, dismounting and walking the steepest, most intimidating sections is recommended (not only to ensure your safety but to minimize trail erosion).

Rescue index: You'll encounter motorists along the initial and concluding paved road. Telephones are located at Bowery Haven, Fish Lake Lodge, and Lakeside Resort. Once you're into the heart of the ride, however, human contact may be uncommon to nonexistent. A Forest Service ranger station is located across the road from Fish Lake Lodge. Richfield has a hospital.

Land status: Fish Lake National Forest.

Maps: USGS 7.5 minute quadrangles: Abes Knoll, Burrville, Loa, and Fish Lake, Utah.

Finding the trail: From the west on I-70 (Richfield), take Exit 48/Sigurd and travel south on UT 24 toward Capitol Reef National Park. After 33 miles, turn left/east on UT 25. Fish Lake Lodge is 8 miles ahead.

From the east on I-70 (Green River), take Exit 89 or Exit 85/Rest Area and travel south on UT 72. Two miles south of the National Forest boundary and Forsyth Reservoir, turn right/west on UT 25 and continue to Fish Lake Lodge 25 miles away.

From the south (Capitol Reef National Park area), travel west and then north on UT 24. About 17 miles north of Loa, turn right on UT 25. Fish Lake is 8 miles ahead.

Sources of additional information:

Fish Lake National Forest
Loa Ranger District
150 Main
Loa, Utah 84747
(801) 836-2811

Fish Lake Lodge
(801) 836-2700

Mountain Biking Utah's Canyon and Plateau Country, by Gregg Bromka (Off-Road Publications, Salt Lake City, Utah)

Notes on the trail: From Fish Lake Lodge, pedal south on UT 25 about 3.7 miles, then turn left on Forest Service Road 046 (Mytoge Mountain Road). Descend slightly and rise up to a log fence line. Bear left, continuing on FS 046. Roll through open fields of fragrant sage, then weave through stands of quaking aspen past Cabin and Dog Springs. A cattle guard and forest boundary mark the beginning of the unyielding grind to Mytoge Mountain's rolling summit.

The turnoff for the first, easily missed but highly scenic overlook is at the bottom of the descent after gaining the plateau's top. (Across the lake-filled valley rises the High Top Plateau, the tallest of central Utah's tabletops at 11,600'. Guarding the valley's northern reach is the bony spine of Mount Marvine.) Over the next 5 miles are 3 more spurs accessing equally spectacular overlooks of lake, valley, and mountain. (The third overlook is positioned directly opposite Fish Lake Lodge with views up glacially scoured Pelican

Canyon. To the east are vistas of lava-capped Thousand Lake Mountain rising above fertile Fremont Valley.)

A riotous downhill drops to Silas Spring and a log corral. Turn left onto FS 045 where "Crater Lakes" is painted on a roadside boulder for more climbing. Quietly wrap around the twin depressions bound by skeletal basalt knobs, and keep an eye out for foraging deer. Beyond North Crater Lake, the four-wheel-drive road rises up through aspens, then narrows to a single-track of sorts. Angle across a small clearing to the fence line and carsonite post that announce the technical plunge off Mytoge.

When you reach Porcupine Draw, the trail may be faint. Turn left and head south along the sage-filled valley, following carsonite posts. Look for the route rising into the aspens to the right. After a series of whoop-de-doos, cross Lake Creek (no bridge) and rise up to the parking area for Crater Lakes Trail. A popsicle or cold beverage awaits on the lodge's airy back porch 5 miles away.

RIDE 33 *RICHFIELD HOGSBACK*

The Richfield Hogsback is not the most scenic route in Utah (one only a geologist could love), nor is it the best trail riding experience (no pine needle-coated single-track or slickrock). Even so, it is a local favorite because it's close to town and it provides both a great workout and testing ground for honing a repertoire of technical skills. There is plenty of rock-hopping, blasting through sand traps, and leaping off dry stream embankments—and that's only on the way up. When you descend, anticipation, quick reflexes, and fast shifting make the difference between clearing a technical stunt with polished flair and the proverbial "twitch and pitch."

The loop's first leg affords uninterrupted views of Signal, Monroe, and Marysvale Peaks bordering fertile Sevier River Valley, plus distant vistas of the 12,000′ Tushar Mountains due south. Flat Canyon boasts an interesting play of sullen colors of gray, tan, light purple, and green volcanic pyroclastic rocks interlayered with blond and orange sandstones. These formations erode into badlands-style topography that creates dreary and desolate, if not dreadful, overtones and an impending feeling that an ambush is around each concealed bend.

This 14-mile loop is within the grasp of intermediate cyclists. It combines easy cruising on dirt and gravel roads with sandy, rock-studded ATV paths. Culminating the loop is a bobsled-like downhill full of "crash-and-burn" potential. Prerequisite are good handling skills plus true and split-second assessment of those skills.

RIDE 33 *RICHFIELD HOGSBACK*

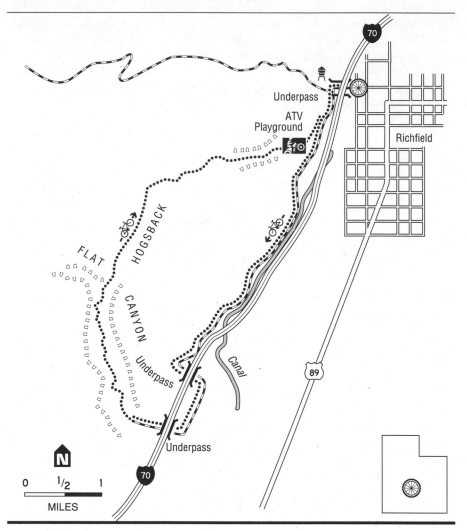

General location: The Hogsback forms the varicolored hills and ridges directly west of Richfield, located in central Utah.

Elevation change: The trailhead elevation at Lions Park is 5,400′. The route's first 5.5 miles is nearly level to the mouth of Flat Canyon. Flat Canyon rises up to the Hogsback at 6,200′. Rapid descending returns you to the trailhead. Total elevation gain is approximately 800′.

Season: The Hogsback can melt out early, perhaps mid-April, and is rideable well into late fall. Riding this route midday during summer is very warm. This route isn't recommended if it's wet; it can get pretty messy.

Services: Aside from water fountains and rest rooms at the trailhead, there are no services or additional water along this route. Richfield offers all visitor services, but lacks a full-service bike shop. (Some bike-related supplies are found at the local Honda motorcycle shop.)

Hazards: This low-lying, warm environment may attract snakes. Use caution when descending the bobsled-like trail from the Hogsback's summit; many sections are very steep and loaded with unannounced obstacles that will require technical maneuvers. Route-finding skills and a good sense of direction (or at least a sense of humor) are recommended, for the route is unsigned and occasionally difficult to follow.

Rescue index: The trail begins at Lions Park on the west side of town, which is usually quite active. You may encounter a few trail users once you're into the ride. You are never more than 3 or 4 miles from residential areas. Richfield has a hospital.

Land status: Bureau of Land Management, Richfield District, Fish Lake National Forest.

Maps: USGS 7.5 minute quadrangles: Anabella, Elsinore, Richfield, and White Pine Peak, Utah. (These maps do not show the route or Interstate 70.)

Finding the trail: The route begins at Lions Park, located at 400 North and 600 West. There is ample parking available.

Sources of additional information:

Bureau of Land Management
Richfield District
Sevier River Resource Area
180 North 100 East
Richfield, Utah 84701
(801) 896-8228

Fish Lake National Forest
Richfield Ranger District
115 East 900 North
Richfield, Utah 84701
(801) 896-9233

Notes on the trail: From Lions Park, pedal one-half block south, turn right/west on 300 South and pass under I-70, then turn immediately left/south onto the dirt frontage road after a cattle guard.

The frontage road grades between maintained dirt and gravel to a double-track of compacted sand, paralleling the west side of I-70. To the right/west are low-lying clay and sandstone hills that serve as an ATV playground. The power lines and a small earthen dam mark the route's return off the Hogsback.

After a mile there is an underpass tunnel to the left/east that crosses beneath I-70; continue straight and alongside a canal for the next 3 miles. As the double-track dips down away from the canal, turn left and pass under I-70 to its east side via a cement tunnel/culvert.

Keep pedaling south on another improved dirt and gravel frontage road. After 1.3 miles, swing through another cement tunnel/culvert back to I-70's west side and pass under power lines. Bear right next to bullet-ridden vintage autos and into the barren and bleak mouth of Flat Canyon.

The route is now a narrow double-track/ATV trail of sorts, following the generally dry wash bottom of the canyon. Most of the time, the trail is in the gully's bottom or jumping out to crosscut meandering bends. Depending on the amount of spring runoff and ATV traffic, the path can be moderately to highly technical (locally) due to stream boulders, sand traps, and washouts. And if you get completely frustrated, stop, pick apart the polygonal mud cracks, then try to reassemble nature's jigsaw puzzle.

The trail jumps out of the wash bottom 2.7 miles from the canyon's mouth. There are no signs, no carsonite posts or rock cairns, or prominent landmarks; you will swear you are lost. Veer eastward and cut across a small grassy clearing. The route follows a rutted four-wheel-drive road angling up a calico-striped hill to the top of a crusty mud ridge. Dip into a second grass clearing followed by a dry tributary. Still heading generally northward, the trail becomes a readily identifiable ATV track rising up through juniper and pinyon.

The Hogsback's summit is denoted by good overlooks of Richfield and the Sevier River Valley, with the backdrop of the Fish Lake Hightop. Hunker down and drop into the first chute. Never assume the trail is flat and smooth beyond what you can see. Anticipate, or you may be rudely awakened. When taken with speed, a few steep plunges redline the "crash and burn" meter.

Nearing the route's bottom there are hints of respectable scenery as the trail traces the edge of a sandstone-bound canyon. Drop down one last rock-infested slope to the earthen retaining dam and into the ATV playground. Test your climbing ability on the huge ant hills or follow the pseudo-ATV circuit course over berms and jumps. (Do you still have the resiliency of your pre-teen years, when you and your friends spent hours in similar back lots seeing who could pedal the fastest, skid the farthest, catch the most air, or crash the best? And if you bent the monkey bars on your purple stingray, you simply bent them back again.) Angle northwest under the power lines, then parallel I-70 to finish off the loop.

RIDE 34 *KIMBERLY ROAD*

Not many people know much about the Tushar Mountains. Perhaps that is understandable; perhaps that is good. The Tushars' presence is peripheral, if not subliminal as you cruise past the wayside town of Beaver on Interstate 15. From afar the Tushars rise sluggishly through subtle contours to seemingly submissive heights. A snowcapped peak or two hover above timberline, and a shadow-filled canyon creases a slope; but all are too distant and ill-defined to spark real curiosity. But dare to venture into the canyons that pierce the

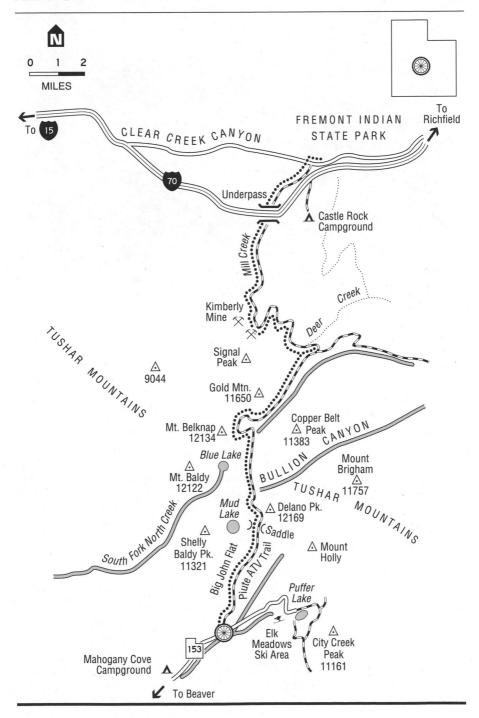

N

0   1   2
MILES

To 15

CLEAR CREEK CANYON

70

FREMONT INDIAN
STATE PARK

To
Richfield

Underpass

Mill Creek

Castle Rock
Campground

Kimberly
Mine

Deer

Creek

Signal
Peak

9044

Gold Mtn.
11650

Mt. Belknap
12134

Copper Belt
Peak
11383

BULLION

CANYON

TUSHAR   MOUNTAINS

Blue Lake

Mt. Baldy
12122

Mount
Brigham
11757

TUSHAR

MOUNTAINS

South Fork North Creek

*Mud
Lake*

Shelly
Baldy Pk.
11321

Big John Flat

Piute ATV Trail

Delano Pk.
12169

Saddle

Mount
Holly

*Puffer
Lake*

153

Elk
Meadows
Ski Area

City Creek
Peak
11161

Mahogany Cove
Campground

To Beaver

Mount Belknap blocks the horizon.

Tushars' interior and you will find your preconceptions pleasantly erred. The Tushars are home to the state's third tallest peaks (a height just shy of that of the Uintas and La Sals). They harbor large populations of elk, are draped with pristine forests and alpine meadows, are rich in history and lore, and even host a quaint ski resort. To those who patiently pursue their elusive trails and backways, the Tushars offer great reward.

The Kimberly Road, which ventures over the Tushars, qualifies as a soon-to-be Utah classic. This is a route that goes somewhere, and crosses a mind-blowing ensemble of terrain in the process. The majority of the route is decidedly alpine, reaching an elevation of 11,500′. (That makes it the highest route in this guidebook!) Glistening streams tumble through virgin tundra meadows, while these meadows bow to confident peaks. The route brushes by Mounts Baldy, Belknap, Brigham, and the Tushars' patriarch, Delano Peak, which soars to a deceptive height of 12,169′. Along the route, notice the defunct Kimberly Mine, which is a window into the massif's colorful but short-lived mining heritage. When you reach Fremont Indian State Park at the end of the route, take some time to visit the museum and to hike the nature trails there and learn a little about an ancient culture.

This 32-mile point-to-point ride is reserved for advanced cyclists well-versed in remote, backcountry exploration. Elevations gained (and elevations attained) require strong legs and high altitude acclimation. The route follows good four-wheel-drive roads that are generally low in technical difficulty. Once you have "made the grade" (twice), an endless downhill completes the tour. The entire route is part of the Piute ATV trail.

General location: The Tushar Mountains form the predominant massif east of Beaver. The Kimberly Road connects Beaver Canyon/UT 153 with Interstate 70 near Fremont Indian State Park.

Elevation change: The tour's starting point in Beaver Canyon is at 8,620'. Eight miles into the ride, the road reaches its highest elevation of 11,500', followed by a considerable descent to an intermediate low elevation of 8,740' at Deer Creek. A second long and tedious climb rises 1,260' to Winkler Point (elevation 10,000'). The route culminates with a 12-mile, break-neck descent to Fremont Indian State Park at 5,800'. Total elevation gain is 4,140'; total elevation loss is 7,000'.

Season: Because of high elevations, this route has a relatively short biking season restricted to early July through September. Since elevation changes are extreme (high of 11,300'; low of 5,800'), the climatic variation will be extreme as well. Pack extra clothing in the shuttle vehicle and re-assess the weather upon reaching the trailhead. Rain at high elevation will be frigid and there are no reasonable bail-out routes. Be aware of current weather patterns. Prudent planning is essential.

Steel gates restrict vehicular access to the route's highest portions until snow melts out. While these gates will not impede bike travel, they will hamper any vehicle support or rescues.

Services: There are no services along this route and all surface waters should be purified. The town of Beaver offers all visitor services, but does not have a bike shop. A developed campground is operated by Fremont Indian State Park and is located a few miles from the Visitor Center. Developed USFS campgrounds are located in Beaver Canyon.

Hazards: Overall, the Kimberly Road is low in technical difficulty. Portions descend rapidly and are coated with ball-bearing-like gravels that make steering a challenge, especially the descent from the old Kimberly Mine toward I-70. Be respectful of suddenly changing alpine weather. Morning sun may turn to boiling thunderheads by afternoon, accompanied by winds, sharp drops in temperature, and chilling rain mixed with hail.

Rescue index: Motorists are frequent in Beaver Canyon. Campers are common in Big John Flat, especially on weekends and holidays. Between Big John Flat and Fremont Indian State Park, contacts with others will be minimal at best. A phone can be found at Fremont Indian State Park. All portions of the route are accessible by high clearance/four-wheel-drive vehicles. Beaver has a medical clinic.

Land status: Fish Lake National Forest.

Maps: USGS 7.5 minute quadrangles: Marysvale Canyon, Mount Belknap, Mount Brigham, Shelly Baldy Peak, and Trail Mountain, Utah; USGS 1:100,000 metric topographic series: Beaver and Richfield, Utah.

Finding the trail: First, you must leave a vehicle at or near Fremont Indian State Park, located 23 miles west of Richfield on I-70 and 17 miles east of I-15/Exit 132. Parking is available at the park, but note that the parking lot's gate is locked when the Visitor Center closes (usually about 5 P.M.). Otherwise, leave a vehicle near the park's campground, located on the south side of I-70 about a mile up the gravel road.

In your shuttle vehicle, drive 17 miles west on I-70 to its junction with I-15. Drive south on I-15 and take Exit 112/Beaver. Drive to the center of town and turn left/east on UT 153 at the sign for Elk Meadows and Beaver Canyon. Drive 16.5 miles up UT 153 to the signed turnoff (left/north) for Big John Flat/Forest Service Road 123. Park at your discretion.

Sources of additional information:

Fish Lake National Forest
Beaver Ranger District
190 North 100 East
P.O. Box E
Beaver, Utah 84713
(801) 438-2436

Notes on the trail: After a 3-mile warm-up, a sign welcomes you to Big John Flat, elevation 9,954′. While skirting this glorious meadow, you will be introduced to Tushars' high peaks. From afar, Shelly Baldy's smoothly contoured slopes seem to welcome explorations by foot, but its savage talus of angular volcanic scree is a hiker's lament. Delano Peak to the east, on the other hand, has managed to cloak much of its graceful slopes with a carpet of tundra grasses.

Quickly, the path begins to ascend with little regard for those lacking aerobic stamina. Stay right where the road splits on the east side of the basin, then pass by the trailhead for Skyline National Recreational Trail. A protracted grade announces Mud Lake (a generous name) and the commencement of the final switchbacks rising to the basin's divide.

At the divide you are greeted by a dynamic mountain scene: stream-fed basins drop in all directions and barren, conical peaks swarm the ultramarine skies. A big payoff awaits in the order of an 8-mile, roaring descent around the flanks of Mount Belknap and Gold Mountain while you remain high above luxuriant Big Meadow. Just stay on the main road signed "Piute ATV Trail 01."

Upon reaching the Beaver Creek road junction, turn left for Piute ATV, Kimberly, I-70 and into the alpine jungle that engulfs Deer Creek. Hopefully you are still fresh, for a strenuous hillclimb awaits. Pick a granny gear and start chugging.

Take a break at Winkler Point (named in honor of Ernest Winkler, who had an illustrious career with the Forest Service from 1923-1936). Savor this last great viewpoint of the San Pitch Mountains and Wasatch Plateau to the north and flanks of the Tushars elsewhere, for in a moment's time you will be concentrating squarely on the road before your front wheel.

You'll be descending briskly as you pass through and beyond Upper and Lower Kimberly mine sites. (From 1899 to 1908, the townsite rang with activity as thousands of miners extracted gold from the wily volcanic country rock. But like most boom towns, prosperity faded as the pay dirt ran thin.) Search for dilapidated cabins, mine structures, and vacant foundations lining the road and hiding in the forest. You may even catch a glimpse of the sad skeleton of the Annie Laurie Mill.

Cross Mill Creek and continue the rampage. Note the peculiar conical hoodoos that line the slopes above the drainage. Pass under the span of I-70 and follow the frontage road back toward Fremont Indian State Park.

Those with an interest in geology will notice that the Tushars differ greatly from Utah's other mountain ranges. Northern Utah's Wasatch and Uintas Mountains are primarily faulted and folded sedimentary rock layers; southern Utah's La Sal, Henry, and Abajo Mountains are uplifted magma chambers; and the surrounding High Plateaus are mountain tables. The Tushars have a more "eruptive" history.

The Tushars are the remains of a collapsed caldera—a massive volcanic vent—whose fiery, molten deposits of lava, ash, and pyroclastic flows covered a broad area. Some events were violent, like the eruption of Mount St. Helens; others were thick, slow flowing rivers of magma. Volcanic rocks tend to be quite drab in color, but because of weathering and oxidation of numerous minerals, many of the Tushars' high peaks are streaked with yellow, orange/brown, light green, and pale violet.

RIDE 35 *SKYLINE NATIONAL RECREATION TRAIL*

Like much of the highlands south of the Wasatch Range and Uinta Mountains, the Tushars are one of Utah's alpine hideaways—seldom visited and largely unknown. Ardent skiers may be familiar with the quaint resort of Elk Meadows, and big-game hunters might know of a good camp spot or two, but the Tushars have successfully eluded the fevered quest of mountain bikers.

The majority of the Tushars' backcountry trails can shred even the most seasoned mountain biker since they are more suited for sturdy pack horses. Skyline National Recreation Trail, on the other hand, is a serendipitous find. Keep in mind that this is no place for flatlanders; Skyline is a tough ride. Its semi-maintained tread demands advanced-level handling skills, its long climbs require firm quads, and its high elevations strangle the lungs of those not acclimated.

Skyline Trail crosses terrain that is alpine in every aspect, where groves of subalpine fir and quaking aspen flirt with tundra meadows and treeless peaks;

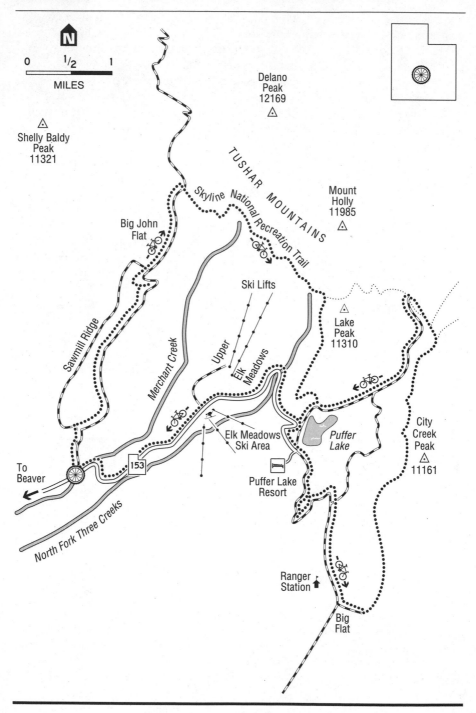

N

0   1/2   1

MILES

Shelly Baldy
Peak
11321

Delano
Peak
12169

TUSHAR MOUNTAINS

Mount
Holly
11985

Big John
Flat

Skyline National Recreation Trail

Sawmill Ridge

Merchant Creek

Ski Lifts

Upper

Elk
Meadows

Lake
Peak
11310

Elk Meadows
Ski Area

Puffer
Lake

City
Creek
Peak
11161

To
Beaver

153

Puffer Lake
Resort

North Fork Three Creeks

Ranger
Station

Big
Flat

Daydreaming in the Tushar Mountains.

where sparkling creeks tumble down from winter's snowfields to merge with blue-ribbon hatcheries; and where distant views extend across southwestern Utah into Nevada's Basin and Range Province.

This 27-mile, figure eight-shaped loop combines pavement with improved dirt roads and single-track. It is the route's single-track that dictates an advanced-level difficulty rating. Skyline is a periodically maintained path, but portions may exist in a semi-primitive state primarily because of low use. You will encounter sustained climbs, protracted slopes, sharp descents, rock gardens and talus slopes, and segments of trail that are hard to see. Although less fervent bikers may shun Skyline N.R.T. for a more leisurely tour, those with greater resolve will likely add this route to their list of all-time favorites.

General location: The Skyline National Recreation Trail is located 20 miles east of Beaver in the Tushar Mountains and is centered around Puffer Lake.
Elevation change: The recommended starting point in Beaver Canyon is at the route's lowest elevation at 8,620′. A 2,220′ climb "highlights" the first 5.5 miles. The Delano Peak section of single-track travels across the flanks of Mount Holly at about 10,800′. A midroute descent to Puffer Lake drops to 9,660′. The second section of single-track tops out at 10,720′ near City Creek Peak. Total elevation gain is nearly 4,400′.
Season: High elevations mean snow may linger well into June and return by mid-October. Expect mild daytime temperatures and cold nights during summer. Since the Tushars are the first major landmass encountered by east-

bound weather systems crossing Utah's western desert, afternoon clouds accompanied by thunderstorms are common. This route is not recommended in fall during hunting season.

Services: Food and beverages *may* be available midroute at Puffer Lake Resort, but in years past supplies were very limited. (There is a pool table, though.) A water tap is at the Big Flat Ranger Station, located along UT 153 a few miles south of Puffer Lake. All surface waters should be purified.

Puffer Lake Resort offers rustic cabins and a semideveloped (private) campground at Puffer Lake. Developed USFS campgrounds are located in Beaver Canyon and backcountry camping is allowed in the National Forest, unless otherwise posted. Overnight lodging (but no dining) is available at Elk Meadows Ski Area; inquire first. Elk Meadows' upper lodge (old Mount Holly) may be open for light lunches. Beaver offers all visitor services, except a bike shop.

Hazards: Although Skyline is a developed and maintained trail, several portions are technical and rough because of loose cobbles, talus, and narrow tread. There are several steep descents that require good judgement and sharp climbs that may require walking. You might encounter equestrians, especially near Mount Holly lodge. Please yield the trail.

Part of the route follows UT 153, which is paved up to Puffer Lake and hard-packed dirt beyond. Be aware of vehicular traffic and changing road conditions, especially on the fast, paved descent past Elk Meadows.

Rescue index: Motorists are common along UT 153. Campers, fishermen, and recreationists frequent Puffer Lake, Big John Flat, and Big Flat. Emergency contacts can be made at Elk Meadows and perhaps at both Upper Elk Meadows (Mount Holly Lodge) and Puffer Lake Resort. Beaver has a medical clinic.

Land status: Fish Lake National Forest.

Maps: USGS 7.5 minute quadrangles: Delano Peak and Shelly Baldy Peak, Utah. (Portions of the single-track are not shown accurately.)

Finding the trail: From Interstate 15, take either Exit 109 or Exit 112; both are for Beaver. In the center of town, travel east on UT 153 toward Elk Meadows, Puffer Lake, and Beaver Canyon. Drive 16.5 miles up Beaver Canyon to the signed turn off for Big John Flat, Forest Service Road 123. Park at your discretion. Alternatively, park midroute at Puffer Lake, located an additional 5 miles up UT 153.

Sources of additional information:

Fish Lake National Forest
Beaver Ranger District
190 North 100 East
P.O. Box E
Beaver, Utah 84713
(801) 438-2436

Notes on the trail: After a sustained 3.5-mile warm-up, a sign welcomes you to Big John Flat, elevation 9,954′. Pedal around the meadow's perimeter staying right when the road splits, following Piute ATV trail markers. A short but demanding climb brings you to the signed trailhead for Puffer Lake/Delano Trail and Skyline National Recreation Trail 225.

The closed jeep road (but open to bikes) rises steeply to a small ridge (tree blazes mark the route), then turns eastward to cross the head of Merchant Creek basin. Delano Peak is the monarch of the Tushars, capping 12,169′. Travel across Delano's treeless flanks on the sometimes highly technical trail. Push up and over a small ridge of talus cobbles, then across the flank of Mount Holly. Lake Peak comes into full view after you cross a small nose extending from the south face of Mount Holly. Ahead is a trail junction signed "Big Flat" (straight), "Big John Flat" (reverse), "Puffer Lake Trail 175" (sharp right). Turn right on the Puffer Lake Trail and start descending, but not too far! (Ignore any trails that drop into the North Fork of Three Creeks basin.) After a turn or two, the trail continues eastward across the head of the basin directly toward Lake Peak; aim for the conifers midslope. (If you descend to a pioneer cabin deep within the basin, you have gone too far downhill.)

The well-defined Lake Peak segment of the trail continues through a darkened tunnel of conifers on a mat of crunchy pine needles. Descend steep switchbacks through aspens to the shore of Puffer Lake, then to UT 153.

If you have had enough adventure for the day, simply ride the paved highway 5 miles back to your vehicle. Otherwise, head up UT 153 (dirt and gravel). You'll reach the Big Flat Ranger Station after 3 miles. Take a left turn toward Skyline National Recreation Trail. Pedal around the northern perimeter of Big Flat to a wooden staging ramp for horses. The trail is signed "Big John Flat 8.3 mi" (left/north). This section is moderately technical and semi-primitive. Watch for tree blazes and other trail indicators.

After 2 miles, the path crosses a knob of bedrock. This is a fine rest stop that boasts powerful views of the Tushars' regal high peaks. Single-track wraps around City Creek Peak, then descends through angular switchbacks to a saddle that appears to have been clear cut. The trail can be elusive. Head due north across the saddle and push up an ugly slope back into the forest. You'll pass a trail sign reading "Bears Hole, Cottonwood."

There are 2 trail junctions over the next half mile; stay left and along the subtle ridge. As the trail crosses over to the ridge's west side, it splits again (that's the third time). Stay right and descend gradually past a sign for Big Johns and into a meadow at the base of Mount Holly.

Skyline Trail proper continues west and up to a saddle between Lake Peak and Mount Holly. This section is difficult to follow and full of dismounts, so descend left/south on FS 642. Control your speed; the descent is fast! After a mile, intersect Cullen Creek Road (FS 129) and stay right for Puffer Lake. Upon connecting with UT 153 again, turn right, chug up one last hill (make it burn!), then take delight in a full-blown, screaming descent past Elk Meadows on the paved highway. (Stay attentive to vehicular traffic and variable road conditions). The tight **S** turns announce the approaching turnoff for Big John Flat and your vehicle.

RIDE 36   *VELVET RIDGE*

If your travels take you to Capitol Reef National Park, spend a couple of hours on Velvet Ridge; this is a fun little ride. Just west of Torrey, gateway to Capitol Reef National Park, Velvet Ridge is the band of low cliffs capped with hummocky, calico-striped hills that line the north side of the Fremont River valley. Erosion has etched the cliff's face into a succession of striated columns that are as pronounced as those that support the Parthenon. But unlike the marble-white pillars of the Greek temple, these are composed of maroon and chocolate brown mudstones ribboned with creamy-tan stringers. The smooth, velvety knolls atop the cliffs are streaked with contrasting hues of gray, blue-green, and purple as their bentonite-rich clays weather.

This tour takes you along the top of the columnar cliffs and past the smooth, clay hills that cap them. From the main route, two short spurs lead to viewpoints of the peaceful valley below and of Capitol Reef's sandstone rotundas in the distant east. Towering above Velvet Ridge is Thousand Lake Mountain. Colorful sandstone cliffs ring the mountain's lower flank; its forested crest is a flat cap of black basaltic lava. On Velvet Ridge, the spectrum of color is as wide as a rainbow.

This 14-mile loop (clockwise) is perfect for intermediate cyclists and well within the grasp of strong novice bikers. Technical difficulty along the route's jeep roads is generally low, except for localized sand traps and a smattering of rocks. The short but quick climb up onto Velvet Ridge is the route's most arduous task and may force some to take their bikes for a little stroll. (GWT)

General location: The Velvet Ridge loop is located immediately west of Torrey on the north side of the Fremont River Valley.
Elevation change: The route's trailhead is in Torrey and at the ride's lowest elevation at 6,850′. The trail rises to just shy of 7,400′ atop Velvet Ridge. Including a few undulations atop the ridge, total climbing is about 700′.
Season: Because of low elevation and good southern exposure, Velvet Ridge could be rideable by late March/early April and throughout fall until mid-November. Don't attempt this route after recent precipitation. The wet clay will turn the knobbiest of tires into smooth cement doughnuts. The Catch-22 is that after prolonged dry spells, the clay breaks down to powdery silt—but at least you can pedal through the silt.

RIDE 36 *VELVET RIDGE*

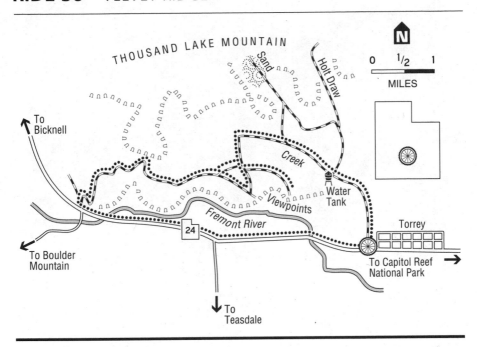

Services: There are no services along this route and all surface waters should be purified. Torrey offers most visitor services, including lodging, dining, limited groceries, and gasoline. There is no bike shop. Similar services are available in nearby Bicknell and Loa.

Hazards: A network of interconnected dirt roads on Velvet Ridge may lead to some confusion, but the main route is marked with signs and carsonite posts. Again, avoid this route after recent rains. Use caution when seeking the perfect viewpoint from the cliff's rim.

Rescue index: There's a good chance you'll experience complete solitude on Velvet Ridge. You'll never be more than 4 miles from the highway, and Torrey is nearby.

Land status: Fish Lake National Forest.

Maps: USGS 7.5 minute quadrangles: Bicknell and Torrey, Utah.

Finding the trail: You can start this ride anywhere in Torrey; otherwise, travel west out of Torrey one-half mile and turn right/north on Sand Creek Road. Less than a mile up the hard-packed dirt road there is a Great Western Trail information board and limited parking.

Velvet Ridge lines the fertile Fremont River Valley.

Sources of additional information:

Fish Lake National Forest
Loa Ranger District
138 South Main
Loa, Utah 84747
(801) 836-2811

Notes on the trail: From Torrey, pedal west on UT 24. Within a half mile, a dirt road signed "Sand Creek, Sulphur Creek" branches right. This is the loop's return route, so continue west on the highway. After 5 miles, the road bends north toward Bicknell. (On the left/south side of the highway, the Boulder Mountain access road signed "Wildlife Viewing Area" branches south.) Just after this junction (note the power lines overhead), turn right/north on a dirt road that splits immediately. Take the rougher road to the right, climbing a sandy and bouldery hill. (The left/lower road leads to an electrical substation.) This short climb is moderately steep with deep ruts and a generous amount of boulders—a good workout for advanced cyclists and a challenge for novice/intermediate cyclists.

Once you're on top of the ridge, the going is easy, punctuated with a few rolling hills. Keep an eye out for pebbles of basalt, silica, and petrified wood; they make great paper weights!

About 3 miles out on the ridge, a wooden post points right/south for the trail, followed by a second USFS post signed "Highway 24" (reverse), "Sand Creek" (left), "Scenic Point" (right). Fork right and after a half mile teeter at cliff's edge above the lusciously fertile Fremont River Valley.

Return to the last junction where you'll see a sign for Scenic Point and follow the road to the right/north. Shortly ahead you can take the spur that goes right/east and leads to an equally splendid overlook; otherwise, head north at a sign reading "Sand Creek Trail" toward Thousand Lake Mountain. There is some sand surfing ahead as the road begins descending. Turn right/east at a junction where a sign reads "Velvet Ridge," then stay right again and head generally southeast. (Either of these roads entering from the left will lead up to Sand Creek.)

Downhill cruising marks the remainder of the loop. (A good thing, because sand traps would be dreadful in a reverse direction.) Splash through Sand Creek, pass a sign for Holt Canyon and Great Western Trail, then cross Sand Creek a second time. A small climb takes you past a yellow water tank, then it is easy cruising on hard-packed Sand Creek Road back to the paved highway.

RIDE 37 *BOULDER TOP / BEHANIN CREEK*

Boulder Mountain's Bowns Point is a sublime viewpoint that ranks high among Utah's mountain bike power spots. From the high rim on Boulder all of southeastern Utah and parts of northern Arizona fill the horizon. More than a century ago, geologist C. E. Dutton surveyed Utah's high plateau country. His sensitive description of the Aquarius Plateau (viewed no doubt from Bowns Point) is worth paraphrasing.

The Aquarius should be described in blank verse and illustrated upon canvas. From numberless lofty standpoints we have seen it afar off . . . nearer to it . . . its mellow blue changes day to day to dark somber gray, and its dull, expressionless ramparts grow upward into walls of majestic proportions and sublime import.

When the broad platform is gained the story of "Jack and the beanstalk," the finding of a strange and beautiful country somewhere up in the region of the clouds, no longer seems incongruous.

The view to the south and southeast [Escalante River and Circle Cliffs] is dismal and suggestive of the terrible. It is a maze of cliffs and terraces lined off with stratifications, of crumbling buttes, red and white domes, rock platforms gashed with profound cañons, burning plains barren even of sage—all glowing with bright color and flooded with blazing sunlight. Everything visible tells of ruin and decay. It is the extreme of desolation, the blankest solitude, a superlative desert.

RIDE 37 *BOULDER TOP / BEHANIN CREEK*

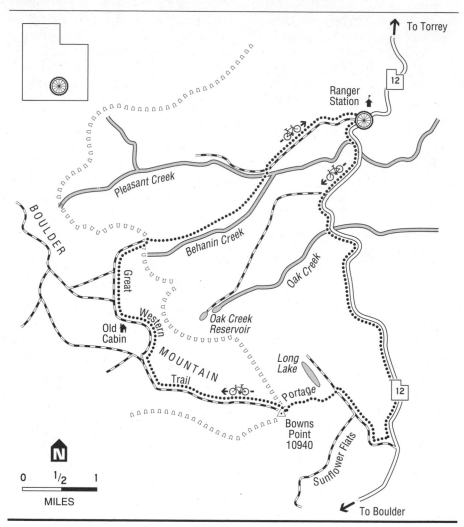

This region is home to one of the largest mountain lion populations in the state plus herds of deer and elk. Look for remnants of past logging activity along the route, including an old cabin.

This 25-mile loop (clockwise) is reserved for advanced cyclists who thrive on backcountry adventure, have a good sense of direction, and view a mountain bike as a convertible backpack with two wheels. Single-track leading up onto Boulder Mountain is beyond the limit of guidebook terms "steep" and "technical." The descent off Boulder is equally brow-raising.

The panorama from atop Bowns Point is unparalleled, but
first you have to get there.

Information on the Boulder Top/Behanin Creek route was provided by Kevin
James,* Salt Lake City, Utah. (GWT)

General location: Boulder Mountain is located in south-central Utah, directly
west of Capitol Reef National Park.
Elevation change: The route's parking area on UT 12 is at 8,645´. The highway

---

*Kevin and Jill James have always loved the outdoors and dreamed of making a living
in the recreation industry amidst Utah's wealth of natural resources. Their dream came
true after one chilly mountain evening in the backcountry and a slight miscommunica-
tion that left Jill and Kevin without the basic necessities to cook a single meal. You see,
they both realized how wonderful a backcountry trip would be if someone else were to
plan the itinerary, load the gear, and cater to their needs so they could relax and enjoy

climbs moderately to its summit at Roundup Flat, elevation 9,591´. Climbing Boulder Mountain (elevation 10,940´) entails about a mile of highly technical boulder hopping combined with pushing, dragging, and shouldering your bike 900´ up the formidable volcanic rim. The wild descent along Behanin Creek drops 2,000´ to the route's beginning. Total climbing is 2,300´.

Season: Because of relatively high elevations, snowpack limits the route's opening to late May. It remains rideable through October. Midsummer brings daily thunderstorms. This area is popular with hunters during the fall.

Services: No services exist along this route or nearby. Water may be obtained from a number of developed USFS campgrounds along UT 12. All surface waters should be purified. Food, lodging, and gasoline are available in Torrey 30 miles to the north or at the outpost of Boulder Town 10 miles to the south along UT 12.

Hazards: Although part of this route is integrated into the Great Western Trail, much of it exists in a primitive state. Sections of single-track, both ascending and descending Boulder Mountain, are clogged with loose cobbles and boulders that make for highly technical riding. Be aware of deadfall early in the season. Afternoon rains are commonly accompanied by lightning.

Rescue index: Emergency assistance *may* be summoned from the Wildcat Ranger Station—when it is manned. Motorists are common along the paved highway, but the bulk of the route is considered remote in terms of organized help. The closest medical clinic is in Bicknell, about 40 miles north.

Land status: Dixie National Forest.

Maps: USGS 7.5 minute quadrangles: Deer Creek Lakes and Lower Bowns Reservoir, Utah.

Finding the trail: From Torrey (located west of Capitol Reef National Park), travel 30 miles south on UT 12, up Boulder Mountain, to the Wildcat Ranger Station. Backcountry parking can be found just south of the ranger station on Forest Service Road 247 (Pleasant Creek) or at nearby USFS campgrounds.

Sources of additional information:

Dixie National Forest
Teasdale Ranger District
138 East Main
P.O. Box 99
Teasdale, Utah 84773
(801) 425-3702

(continued from page 165)
their natural surroundings! So, they created Utah Outback, a guided mountain bike tour company exploring central and southern Utah.

No longer organizing and guiding mountain bike tours, Kevin has taken up the pen to compile *The Mountain Biker's Guide to the Northern Rockies*. Part of the America by Mountain Bike Series, Kevin's Northern Rockies guide presents the best mountain bike routes in Montana, Wyoming, and Idaho.

Notes on the trail: A good map, the knowledge to interpret it, and a sense of direction are prerequisite for traveling this route. If things go as planned you should find yourself back at the trailhead in about 5 hours.

From the Wildcat Ranger Station, pedal south along the highway about 6 miles to Roundup Flat. Turn right/west on FS 554 signed "Sunflower Flats, Steep Lake, Bowns Point Trail." Within a half mile, fork right at an unsigned junction. Continue about a mile through a few meadows to a trail sign for Bowns Point, Great Western Trail on the left. The trail is often indistinct so follow the carsonite posts across the meadows and into the forest. Once in the trees, the route is somewhat identifiable. It is nearly 900′ of steep uphill single-track through dense stands of subalpine fir and spruce to the top of Boulder. The lower section is highly technical and the last half mile is a vertical portage (reminiscent of Moab's improbable portage up Jacob's Ladder to Amasa Back) over a boulder-clogged trail. Once atop Boulder, walk out to the very brink of Bowns Point for an overlook that rivals the best in the state.

Because Bowns Point does not receive a lot of traffic, the trail can be elusive. This is where a map and the ability to read it comes in handy. One landmark you may pass is an old cabin that was the site of a sawmill. If you miss this, do not worry, there are several other possible routes that take you around the cabin. If you follow Great Western Trail markers, you are heading in the right direction.

About 5 miles across the plateau, there are some turnoffs to the right. Here, the route may be difficult to follow because of all the old logging roads. Look for tree blazes marking the trail. The route takes you to the edge of Boulder Mountain at the head of Behanin Creek. Trace Pleasant Creek drainage as it drops below you, cutting its way through the uplifted backbone of Capitol Reef toward the desert badlands beyond.

The single-track you'll encounter next begins with a frightening descent down narrow, winding switchbacks. After a short time, the path will take you into some enjoyable, moderately technical trail riding. Sections of steep riding are tempered by glades of aspen and open meadows with views of the desert below. The single-track ends at the four-wheel-drive road at Pleasant Creek. From here, the road is an adrenalin-laden blast to the highway and route's end.

RIDE 38 *POWELL POINT*

The salient of Powell Point is as distinct as the nineteenth-century geologist and western explorer it was named after. From any point on the southern plateaus, the truncated tableland of Powell Point maintains a stately presence. It is more than a lofty vantage point, though. It is a throne from which Nature might appraise the land it has so brilliantly sculpted.

RIDE 38 *POWELL POINT*

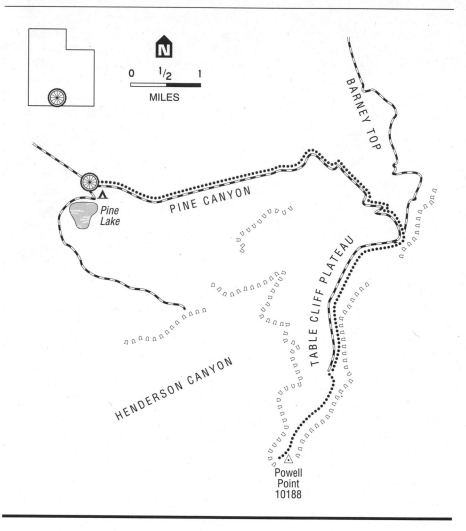

Far to the east lie the canyons of the Escalante, which disappear behind the razor sharp edge of the Kaiparowits Plateau's Straight Cliffs. To the south sprawl the furrowed efforts of the Paria River, where ashen gullies coalesce into notched canyons, which in turn deepen to constricted sandstone hallways. Off to the west and at an elevation equal to Powell Point, Bryce Canyon National Park, is a white-, orange-, and strawberry-hued frieze breaking from the forested rim of the Paunsagunt Plateau. The Wasatch Formation, which comprises Bryce Canyon, is the very same rock unit that lends striking color and

The Wasatch Formation fortifies Powell Point.

peculiar erosional shapes to the Pink Cliffs, Sunset Cliffs, Strawberry Point, and Cedar Breaks National Monument, the latter being more than 50 miles away. The Wasatch also forms the brightly colored colonnades that fortify the citadel of Powell Point, one of the greatest power spots in southern Utah.

This 21-mile out-and-back ride caters to strong intermediate and advanced riders since it begins with a 2,000′ hillclimb. Fat-tire neophytes should not dismay, for this ascent can be conquered by transporting your bike in a high-clearance vehicle. With this approach, the Powell Point trail proper ambles 9 miles (out-and-back) along the crest of the Table Cliff Plateau by way of double-track and a mile of tantalizing single-track.

General location: Powell Point is located 30 miles northeast of Bryce Canyon National Park in south-central Utah.
Elevation change: The elevation of the parking area at Pine Lake Campground is 8,200′. The Table Cliff Plateau rises to 10,110′ for a direct 1,910′ climb. The Powell Point trail proper rises another 140′ to a high elevation of 10,250′. Total climbing out-and-back to Powell Point proper is merely 500′. Total elevation gain from the Pine Lake trailhead is 2,400′.
Season: This high plateau receives a considerable amount of snow during winter. It should melt out by mid- to late June and be rideable throughout September and into October. Midsummer daytime temperatures are mild (70s and 80s) and nights are quite cool (40s or colder). Changing alpine weather is common and Powell Point is usually quite breezy. Consider carrying extra clothing.

Services: The developed USFS Pine Valley Campground (parking area) has water taps and outhouses. There are no other services along the route. Backcountry camping is allowed in the National Forest unless otherwise posted. Lodging, dining, gasoline, and curios shopping are available near the Bryce Canyon junction. Mountain bike rentals are available at Old Bryce Town across from Ruby's Inn, located at the entrance to Bryce Canyon National Park. Medical facilities are available in Panguitch.

Hazards: Use caution when scouting viewpoints from the tip of Powell Point; the friable limestone crumbles easily. Any fall could prove fatal. Otherwise, there are no unusual hazards along the route. Be prepared for changing alpine weather.

Rescue index: Campers, fishermen, and other recreationists frequent Pine Valley Reservoir and Campground. The Powell Point trail is not heavily traveled. Emergency contacts can be made from gas stations, motels, and cafes at the Bryce Canyon junction (State Highways 12 and 63). Panguitch has medical facilities.

Land status: Dixie National Forest.

Maps: USGS 7.5 minute quadrangles: Griffin Point, Pine Lake, Sweetwater Creek, and Upper Valley, Utah.

Finding the trail: From the Bryce Canyon Junction (UT 12 and UT 63), travel north on UT 22 signed "Antimony, Pine Lake." After 4 miles, pavement turns to hard-packed gravel. Seven miles thereafter, turn right/east onto Forest Service Road 132 signed "Pine Lake, Table Cliff Plateau." You'll reach Pine Lake Reservoir and Campground after 5.5 miles along this well-maintained dirt and gravel road. Park at your discretion at or near the campground.

Sources of additional information:

> Dixie National Forest
> Powell Ranger District
> 225 East Center
> P.O. Box 80
> Panguitch, Utah 84759
> (801) 676-8815

Notes on the trail: From the Pine Lake Campground, pedal up FS 132 for Barney Top and Table Cliff Plateau. Juniper and pinyon, followed by limber and ponderosa pine, then aspen and fir, line slopes underlaid with pastel shades of white, yellow, orange, and pink. A few hoodoo-lined escarpments hint of the visual wonders that await you at the trail's terminus.

The 6-mile climb to the top of the Table Cliff Plateau steepens progressively and is difficult. When you reach the plateau's narrow crest, the road turns sharply northward. The Powell Point trail (double-track) branches south at this bend. It should be marked with a carsonite post with an ATV decal.

But before heading out to Powell Point, take in the staggering overview eastward across southern Utah. The Table Cliff Plateau blends with the Aquarius

Plateau to the north. Their sheer slopes drop into Upper Valley then across the blazing deserts cut by the Escalante River and its attendant washes. The Henry Mountains float above the redrock lineament of the Waterpocket Fold, which runs the length of Capitol Reef National Park.

The playful double-track leading to Powell Point crosses the broad, flat-topped mountain through a fragrant corridor of fir and aspen. Periodically, the plateau's crest pinches to a narrow backbone that affords more astounding views eastward across vast emptiness. After 3.5 miles, the double-track ends at a trailhead sign that announces the beginning of single-track. Even though the single-track is irregularly maintained, and much too short, it is great fun and the location is unbeatable.

There is one sharp ascent before the path meanders to its precipitous terminus. (In 1880, geologist C. E. Dutton poetically described the abutment of Powell Point as representing " . . . the aspect of a vast Acropolis crowned with a Parthenon.") This is indeed a heavenly perch. Turn around and head back the way you came.

RIDE 39 *CASTO CANYON*

Bryce Canyon National Park is not a canyon at all but a band of salmon-colored cliffs that break sharply from the forested Paunsagunt Plateau. The Paiute Indians call it "Unka - timpe - wa - wince - pock - itch," which translates: "red rocks standing like men in a bowl."

The amphitheaters of Bryce Canyon are lined with delicately shaped rock formations that conjure up scores of fanciful images: obelisks, steeples, and temples; needles and sentinels; castle walls and windows overseen by monks and robed priests; minarets, gables, pagodas, and even platoons of Turkish soldiers in pantaloons. There is Thor's Hammer, Hunter and Rabbit, and the Hat Shop; the Silent City's Wall Street, the Cathedral, and China Wall; and trails named Fairyland, Queen's Garden, and Peekaboo. Bryce Canyon blends an architectural balance of intricacy and dazzling color beyond comprehension.

If only mountain bikes were allowed through Bryce Canyon, what a dream ride it would be. But attempt that sort of stunt and you will be counting bricks lining your cell inside the town poky. There is an alternative: Casto Canyon— a miniaturized version of Bryce Canyon—beckons fat tires. Casto boasts much of the phantasmagoria of Bryce Canyon, and all can be seen from a playful single-track that snakes along the wash's dry creekbed.

The Casto Canyon ride is a 10-mile out-and-back route geared for strong novice to intermediate cyclists. The alternative is a sensational 20-mile loop (for intermediate- to advanced-level riders) that combines Casto's single-track with four-wheel-drive and paved roads.

RIDE 39 *CASTO CANYON*

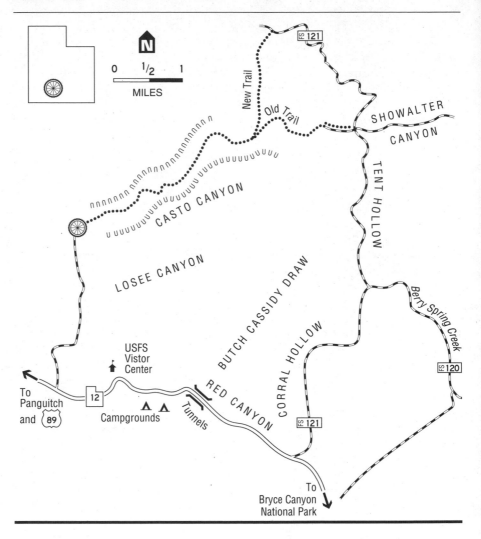

General location: Casto Canyon is located equidistant between Panguitch and Bryce Canyon National Park in south-central Utah, just north of UT 12 as it passes through Red Canyon.

Elevation change: The mouth of Casto Canyon is very close to the route's lowest elevation at 7,000′. The top of Casto Canyon rises to 7,880′, for an elevation gain of 880′. The loop version continues beyond Casto Canyon to an elevation of 8,350′ atop Tent Hollow. Total elevation gain for the loop is approximately 1,550′.

Casto Canyon—a miniaturized Bryce Canyon National
Park.

Season: Despite all the redrock surrounding this area, Casto Canyon is hardly
a desert, but rather low alpine terrain. Daytime temperatures during midsummer are temperate (70s and 80s) and nights are cool (40s). This route may be
rideable as early as April and as late as October.

Services: There are no services in Casto Canyon, nor any drinking water.
(There is a pit toilet at the trailhead/parking area.) Water may be found at the
Red Canyon Visitor Center and at USFS campgrounds in Red Canyon, both on
UT 12. Lodging, dining, and gift shops are available along UT 12 on both ends
of Red Canyon. Panguitch offers all visitor services, but no bike shop.
Mountain bike rentals are available at Old Bryce Town (across the road from
Ruby's Inn near the entrance to Bryce Canyon National Park).

Hazards: The single-track through Casto Canyon is irregularly maintained. It
frequently crosses the bouldery dry wash bottom, which can be moderately to
highly technical. These portions are easy to walk through. Use extreme caution

if looping to UT 12 and descending through Red Canyon. Red Canyon's overwhelming scenery may not only distract your attention, but the attention of the many passing motorists as well. Use caution when you're traveling through 2 very short tunnels along the paved highway.

Rescue index: You may be alone on the trail in Casto Canyon during weekdays, but you may be sharing the trail with a few ATVs and equestrians on weekends and holidays. Motorists are numerous along UT 12 through Red Canyon. Emergency assistance may be summoned from the USFS Red Canyon Visitor Center. Panguitch, located about 10 miles west, has medical facilities.

Land status: Dixie National Forest.

Maps: USGS 7.5 minute quadrangles: Casto Canyon and Wilson Peak, Utah. (The trail through Casto Canyon is not shown.)

Finding the trail: From the junction of US 89 and UT 12 (6 miles south of Panguitch), travel east on UT 12 toward Bryce Canyon National Park. At milepost 2 on UT 12, a good dirt road marked by a wooden corral branches left/north. This is the 3-mile access road to Casto Canyon's trailhead/parking area.

From the east, pass the Bryce Canyon National Park turnoff (junction of UT 12 and UT 63) and continue west on UT 12. Pass through Red Canyon. Less than a half mile west of Red Canyon (noted by a Dixie National Forest sign), turn right at milepost 2, which is marked by a wooden corral. This hard-packed dirt and gravel road is the 3-mile access to Casto Canyon.

Sources of additional information:

Dixie National Forest
Powell Ranger District
225 East Center
P.O. Box 80
Panguitch, Utah 84759
(801) 676-8815

Notes on the trail: From the parking area at the mouth of Casto Canyon, pedal east into the canyon. Immediately, the route is engulfed by a fantasyland of white, pink, and orange hoodoos and peppered with limber and ponderosa pine. Periodically, the trail crosses the (usually) dry wash bottom. Scattered boulders and soft sand will test the abilities of even hard-core bikers. (These sections are nearly impossible to maintain due to yearly snowmelt and heavy rains that surge through the canyon.)

Note: In years past, the route through Casto Canyon was simply a narrow cattle path that actually heightened the experience. The Forest Service has since constructed a wider path suitable for ATVs. The new ATV route turns northward (about 3.5 miles up Casto) and heads up toward Barney Cove and connects with Forest Service Road 121. This route is rough and unforgiving. Keep an eye out for where this ATV trail turns north and rises out of Casto Canyon. You may want to continue east, up Casto, on the old cattle path.

If you're riding out-and-back through Casto Canyon, simply turn around when you desire (usually after about 5 miles) and enjoy the varied perspective upon descending. If you're pursuing the optional 20-mile loop, ignore the new ATV trail that forks northward out of the main canyon toward Barney Cove (about 3.5 miles from the trailhead). Instead, continue straight up Casto Canyon on the old cattle trail. After about a mile or so, the path intersects with FS 121, which is signed "Limekiln Canyon, Sanford Canyon" (left/north); "Showalter Canyon" (straight/east). Turn right/south and ascend the steep, mile-long double-track up Tent Hollow. A junction beyond the hill's crest is signed "Utah Hwy 12, Berry Spring Creek, FS 120" (left/east); "Corral Hollow, Cabin Hollow, FS 121" (right/south). Follow Corral Hollow/FS 121 to UT 12.

When you reach UT 12, turn right/west and coast through radiant Red Canyon. The USFS Visitor Center offers a few short hiking trails that mingle with hoodoo-lined cliffs. (You will also find a soft drink vending machine and water fountain.) Less than half a mile west of Red Canyon (noted by a Dixie National Forest sign), turn right/north at milepost 2 (next to a corral) and pedal 3 miles north back to Casto Canyon.

RIDE 40 *SUNSET CLIFFS*

It would be a grave injustice if you did not visit Bryce Canyon National Park while you're in this area. But after hovering like a vulture for a parking space and then sightseeing and hiking with the masses, pursue your mountain biking a few miles west in Tropic Valley along the Sunset Cliffs Loop. Here you'll be sharing your views with sparrows overhead and yielding the trail to foraging deer. Pack along a fishing pole, for Tropic Reservoir is worthy of a line.

Like Bryce Canyon, the Sunset Cliffs are a luminescent band of escarpments weathered into curious shapes that stir the imagination. But unlike Bryce, whose glory is heightened with a rising sun, the Sunset Cliffs are set aglow when the sun wanes in the western sky. Upon rising up to and then descending from the cliffs, scan the ponderosa pine forests for miniature Bryce Canyon exposures.

This 16-mile loop (counterclockwise) is a great intermediate-level ride. Dirt roads of low technical difficulty make up the entire route. The rise to Sunset Cliffs comes in stair-step fashion with short breathers offsetting moderately difficult pulses. The descent back to the valley swoops you through the forest like a super GS ski run.

General location: Tropic Reservoir, where this loop originates, is located 2 miles west of Bryce Canyon National Park as the crow flies, but closer to 15

RIDE 40 *SUNSET CLIFFS*

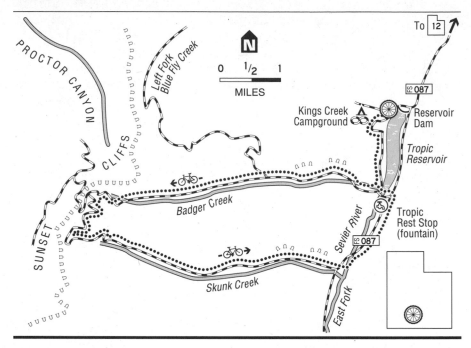

miles by vehicle.

Elevation change: Tropic Reservoir rests at 7,835´. The route climbs to 9,250´ atop Sunset Cliffs and then drops back to the reservoir. Total elevation gain is around 1,400´.

Season: The route is rideable from late April through October. Despite the redrock nature of the surrounding terrain, the Paunsagunt Plateau is decidedly alpine. Midsummer daytime temperatures are moderate (80s) and nights are very cool (40s). Early and late season will be mild during the day and near freezing at night. This area may be popular with big-game hunters during October.

Services: A developed USFS campground is located at Tropic Reservoir (Kings Creek). Water taps are available. There are no other services along this route and all surface waters should be purified. Lodging, dining, and curios shopping are found along State Highway 12. Panguitch offers all visitor services but no bike shop. Mountain bike rentals may be found at Old Bryce Town, located across from Ruby's Inn at the entrance to Bryce Canyon National Park.

Hazards: The route follows dirt roads that are generally low in technical difficulty. Use caution if exploring along the rim of Sunset Cliffs; the friable limestone substrate crumbles easily.

Rescue index: Campers, fishermen, and other recreationists are common around Tropic Reservoir. Few motorists travel this backcountry route, though.

Sunset Cliffs break away from the forested Paunsagunt Plateau.

At most you are 8 miles from the campground. Panguitch, located 24 miles from Tropic Reservoir, has medical facilities.

Land status: Dixie National Forest.

Maps: USGS 7.5 minute quadrangle: Tropic Reservoir, Utah.

Finding the trail: From the west (Panguitch), travel east on UT 12 from its junction with US 89. Pass through Red Canyon. About 10 miles from US 89, turn right/south on Forest Service Road 087 (between mileposts 10 and 11) signed "Tropic Reservoir." Travel 8 miles south on the maintained dirt and gravel road to the reservoir's dam. Turn right/west toward Kings Creek Campground, cross the dam, and park in the boat ramp/day-use parking area or at the nearby campground.

Sources of additional information:

Dixie National Forest
Powell Ranger District
225 East Center
P.O. Box 80
Panguitch, Utah 84759
(801) 676-8815

Notes on the trail: From the reservoir's boat ramp/day-use parking area, pedal south past the entrance to Kings Creek Campground, then continue along the west frontage road for about a mile to the reservoir's southern tip. Turn right on FS 109 and up Badger Creek. Within a half mile, the road splits. Bear right and cross over the luxuriant grass-filled valley. Keep an eye out for deer and elk in the morning or early evening. Surrealistic banded escarpments of white, gold, and orange hoodoos poke through pockets of ponderosa pine underlaid with glossy manzanita.

Two miles up Badger Creek valley, the road splits again. Stay left on FS 233 signed "Skunk Creek, Proctor Canyon". Climbing comes in stairstep fashion as the valley succumbs to pine, aspen, and fir. Stay left/south at a junction signed "Proctor Canyon, Hatch" (right); "East Fork" (left).

A mile or so ahead, the road curves precariously close to the cliff's edge. This is a good locale to park the bike and hike out along the Sunset Cliffs' rim. The Paunsagunt Plateau is rimmed by a band of brilliant color—Bryce Canyon on the east and Sunset Cliffs on the west. Water and wind have carved the soft, crumbly limestone into fanciful displays of spires, pinnacles, and small castles. If you hike a short distance north along the rim's edge you'll see a natural arch just below you. Making this splendid scene complete would be a huge bowl of vanilla ice cream swirled with orange sherbet.

The gently arcing double-track you'll be traveling next is a super giant slalom course designed for fat tires. Feather your brakes lightly while leaning into the turns. Feel the tire's side knobs grip. Then bank to the other side. As the forest begins to open let gravity take over, but keep one eye scanning the hillsides for more hoodoos. The incredibly lush area around Lower Skunk Creek is just where deer and elk might forage.

Take a left onto the main East Fork road and pedal 1.5 miles north. Just past the Tropic Water Stop (fountain), turn left on FS 109 toward Badger Creek. Circle around the reservoir and follow its western frontage road back to the campground/boat ramp.

RIDE 41   *PINK CLIFFS*

The Pink Cliffs (which encompass Bryce Canyon, Sunset Cliffs, Strawberry Point, and Cedar Breaks) constitute the topmost rung of the Grand Staircase. Here, the northwestern margin of the Colorado Plateau is characterized by a great series of sheer, stationary cliffs that descend through relatively flat terraces like stairs. Pink Cliffs, Gray Cliffs, White Cliffs, and Vermillion Cliffs—the names of which only begin to describe the variation of color and form in each succession—extend south across the Arizona border, eventually stepping into the depths of the Grand Canyon. Geologic time spanning over a half billion years from the Tertiary Period (atop the colorful plateaus) to the Precambrian Era (in the core of the Grand Canyon) is represented here.

In addition to views that extend to the horizon that this ride affords, the route

RIDE 41 *PINK CLIFFS*

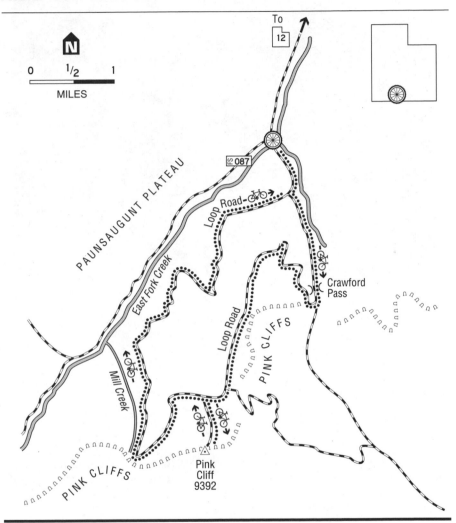

takes the biker to precipices and amphitheaters that are the visual equivalent to those in Bryce Canyon National Park. But these banks of imagination-stirring hoodoos can be enjoyed in complete solitude. John Wesley Powell and crew enjoyed this same vantage point when surveying southern Utah during the late 1870s. A century-old triangulation point of weather logs at the brink of the Pink Cliffs is a remnant of their visit.

This 15-mile loop (clockwise) follows good four-wheel-drive roads throughout. Technical difficulty is generally low, but a few sections may be rutted or

Storm clouds gather over the Pink Cliffs.

contain loose gravel and cobbles. Climbing is moderately difficult, and the tour culminates with plenty of easy cruising through elk-inhabited forests. This route is well suited for intermediate cyclists. (GWT)

General location: Pink Cliffs proper is located at the very southern tip of the Paunsagunt Plateau in south-central Utah (35 miles southeast of Panguitch).

Elevation change: The parking area/trailhead is at the lowest elevation at 8,155′. The route rises to 9,375′ at Pink Cliffs. Total elevation gain is about 1,500′.

Season: Despite the tour's strong redrock overtone, the Paunsagunt Plateau resides in the montane and subalpine life zones. This route should be rideable from May through September. Midsummer daytime temperatures are mild (70s and 80s) and nights are cool (40s). Expect changing alpine weather; afternoon thunderstorms are common. The area may be popular with big-game hunters during late September and October.

Services: There are no services along this route and all surface waters should be purified. The USFS Podunk Guard Station does not have public drinking water and is not always manned. Developed camping is available at Kings Creek Campground at Tropic Reservoir. Backcountry camping is allowed in the National Forest, unless otherwise posted. Lodging, dining, and curios shopping are available along UT 12. Panguitch offers all visitor services but no bike shop. Mountain bike rentals may be found at Old Bryce Town, located across from Ruby's Inn at the entrance to Bryce Canyon National Park.

Hazards: This route follows four-wheel-drive roads that are only occasionally rutted and rough. Use extreme caution when exploring the cliffs' rims; the friable limestone crumbles easily. Use discretion when biking during hunting season—wear lots of bright orange. Be aware of changing alpine weather; dirt roads may become impassable when wet.

Rescue index: This route is relatively remote. At its farthest point, you will be 8 miles from your vehicle and 18 miles from UT 12 and a phone. Panguitch has medical facilities (16 miles from the junction of UT 12 and Tropic Reservoir Road).

Land status: Dixie National Forest.

Maps: USGS 7.5 minute quadrangle: Podunk Creek, Utah. (Portions of the loop are not shown.)

Finding the trail: The route is located at the southern end of the Tropic Reservoir Road/East Fork of the Sevier River (Forest Service Road 087).

From the west (Panguitch), travel east 10 miles on UT 12 from its junction with US 89. Between mileposts 10 and 11 (at Loggers Inn), turn right/south on FS 087 toward Tropic Reservoir. From the east (Bryce Canyon National Park), travel west 3 miles on UT 12 from the Bryce junction (UT 12 and UT 63). Between mileposts 10 and 11 (at Loggers Inn), turn left/south on FS 087 toward Tropic Reservoir.

Tropic Reservoir Road is improved dirt and gravel, suitable for passenger cars. After 7 miles, pass by Tropic Reservoir and Kings Creek Campground. Continue south 8 miles to a Y junction signed "Podunk Creek, Bryce Canyon Boundary 3 miles, FS 099" (left); "Podunk Guard Station 1 mile, Robertson Canyon 8 miles, FS 087" (right). Stay right on FS 087. Park (at your discretion) 1.5 miles south of the Guard Station at a junction signed "Crawford Creek, Meadow Canyon" (left); "Robertson Canyon, FS 087" (right).

Sources of additional information:

Dixie National Forest
Powell Ranger District
225 East Center
P.O. Box 80
Panguitch, Utah 84759
(801) 676-8815

Notes on the trail: From the parking area, pedal southeast toward Crawford Creek and Meadow Canyon. After .7 miles, FS 215 joins sharply from the right. (This is the loop's return route.) Stay straight for Crawford Pass and Meadow Canyon. The road rises gently to a yellow cattle guard. Turn right/south on FS 203 signed "Loop Road, Pink Cliffs." This hard-packed dirt road is suitable for high-clearance vehicles and rises at a moderately difficult grade, but it is low in technical difficulty.

As the road bends south and descends, it winds within a few feet of the Pink

Cliffs, which are drenched in white, orange, and pink. Take a short hike uphill along the cliff's rim. You will be rewarded by your own private Bryce Canyon–style amphitheater.

At the upcoming Y junction, stay right on FS 215. (FS 203 forks left and descends considerably.) Shortly, FS 215 continues straight, but *turn left* at the sign for Pink Cliff (no FS number). This cobble-filled double-track rises steadily through the pine forest, then enters into a grassy meadow atop a knoll. Branch left onto a discreet ATV trail. It may appear to dead end within a few hundred feet but actually continues to the right/south for .2 miles. It ends at the brink of yet another of southern Utah's "power spots." The large triangle made of interlocked logs is one of John W. Powell's historical triangulation points.

Stop a moment to take in the 270-degree view. The plateau's crimson cliffs descend to a terrace, which in turn steps through successive cliffs and platforms all the way into Arizona. Navajo Mountain's unmistakable hump straddles the 2 states. At its foot lies Glen Canyon, where the Colorado River was dammed to create Lake Powell. The Paria River carves up the land to the east and Powell Point oversees the entire ensemble.

Return to the previous junction signed "Pink Cliff" and turn left onto FS 215. The road descends briskly high above Mill Creek valley and turns sharply right just before the cliff's edge again. Now it parallels the valley northward. You'll be doing nearly 5 miles of big-gear cruising through incredibly lush forests before rejoining Crawford Creek road at the Mill Hollow Loop sign. The parking area is less than a mile to the left/west.

RIDE 42 *SIDNEY PEAKS / SECOND LEFT-HAND CANYON*

Dubbed the "Vertical Mile," Sidney Peaks/Second Left-Hand Canyon is a downhiller's delight. This route begins at the very crest of the Markagunt Plateau at 11,307´ Brian Head Peak, with infinite views in every direction. The horizon is bound by Wheeler Peak in Nevada, Mount Trumball in Arizona, Powell Point on the Aquarius Plateau, and Mounts Baldy and Belknap in the Tushar Mountains. The middle ground is flooded with profuse forests broken by tundra meadows. But the blazing amphitheater of Cedar Breaks National Monument will seize your attention. After you descend through miles of dense forests, these same vermillion cliffs reappear as towers, castles, and curious hoodoos near the route's end.

You'll be crossing a wide spectrum of vegetative zones on this route: treeless alpine tundra gives way to subalpine forests of fir, aspen, and mixed pine; these forests become chaparrals of juniper and pinyon, then finally sage and cacti of the high desert. The route culminates near Parowan, southern Utah's oldest

RIDE 42 *SIDNEY PEAKS /*
SECOND LEFT-HAND CANYON

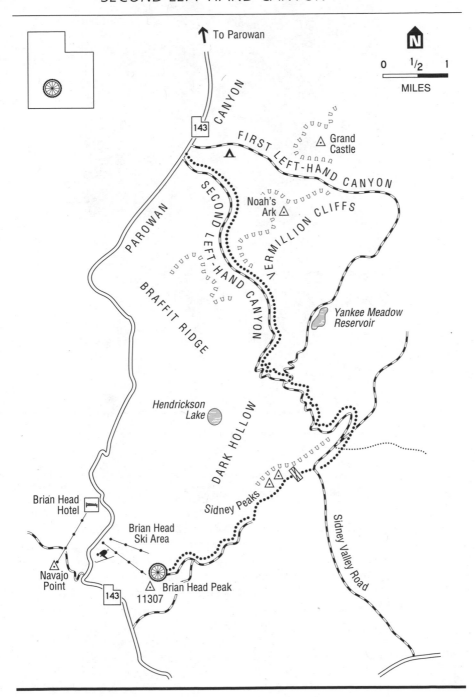

To Parowan

N

0   1/2   1
MILES

143

CANYON

FIRST LEFT-HAND CANYON

Grand
Castle

PAROWAN

SECOND LEFT-HAND CANYON

Noah's
Ark

VERMILLION CLIFFS

BRAFFIT RIDGE

Yankee Meadow
Reservoir

Hendrickson
Lake

DARK HOLLOW

Sidney Peaks

Sidney Valley Road

Brian Head
Hotel

Brian Head
Ski Area

Navajo
Point

143

Brian Head Peak
11307

The Vertical Mile drops from the alpine tundra to a
hoodoo-lined redrock canyon.

town.

This 16-mile point-to-point ride follows primarily four-wheel-drive roads
with a mile or two of single-track. (Tack on three more miles of pavement if
you're coasting all the way down to Parowan.) There is trivial climbing along
Sidney Peaks ridge. Strong forearms (or frequent stops) are necessary to handle
sustained braking down long hills. Second Left-Hand Canyon is well suited for
intermediate cyclists. Several bike shops at Brian Head offer shuttle service.

Trail data for Sidney Peaks/Second Left-Hand Canyon was provided by Bill
Murphy,[*] Brian Head, Utah.

---

[*]Bill Murphy, "the Man of the Mountain," and Dean Reader, former General Manager
of the Brian Head Hotel, former Vice President of Planning and Development at Brian
Head Resort, and current Director of the Utah Travel Council, have taken pride in
promoting Brian Head, not only as an outstanding alpine and nordic ski center but as
an emerging world-class mountain biking destination.

Bill Murphy (left) and Dean Reader.

General location: This route begins at the top of Brian Head Peak and descends northward, ending near Parowan.

Elevation change: Brian Head Peak marks the route's highest point at 11,307′. A few rolling hills punctuate the Sidney Peaks ridge line with elevation gains of less than 300′. The route then begins descending, and descending, for nearly 15 miles until it reaches Parowan, which rests at 6,000′.

Season: When Canyonlands and Utah's high deserts begin to boil by mid-June, take off for Brian Head. Midsummer days on the Markagunt Plateau are temperate and nights are very cool. This route should melt out by mid- to late June and be rideable throughout September. A rainbow of wildflowers, which bloom throughout the summer months, compete with bounteous forests and brilliant redrock escarpments.

Services: There are no services along this route and all water should be purified. Both Parowan and the town of Brian Head offer lodging, dining, limited groceries, and gasoline. Developed campgrounds are located at Cedar Breaks National Monument and in Parowan Canyon about 10 miles below Brian Head. The Brian Head Cross Country Ski and Bike Shop offers bike rentals, sales and repairs, and shuttle services. Cedar City offers all visitor-related services.

Hazards: Brakes should be in perfect working order. Deadfall may cover the trail along the Sidney Peaks single-track and in Second Left-Hand Canyon.

Also, watch for washouts and sections of loose gravel. You'll encounter few motorists in Second Left-Hand Canyon. Be sure to bring sunscreen. Afternoon rainstorms are common, so carry appropriate clothing.

Rescue index: This ride is relatively remote, but most sections are accessible by high-clearance or four-wheel-drive vehicles. Emergency assistance can be obtained in Brian Head or Parowan. Fishermen and campers frequent Yankee Meadow Reservoir, which is near the route's midsection.

Land status: Dixie National Forest.

Maps: USGS 7.5 minute quadrangles: Brian Head and Parowan, Utah. (Single-track across Sidney Peaks ridge is not shown.)

Finding the trail: This route requires a vehicle shuttle. Leave one vehicle at the bottom of Second Left-Hand Canyon (marked only by a stop sign), located about 4 miles from Parowan on UT 143. (Second Left-Hand Canyon is a quarter mile uphill from First Left-Hand Canyon, which is signed "Vermillion Castle, Yankee Meadow.") Alternatively, park in Parowan at the town park and pool.

In the shuttle vehicle, drive up UT 143 and through Brian Head. Two miles past Brian Head, turn left/north on the Brian Head Peak Road. After 2.3 miles, the gravel road bends sharply left/west. The double-track branching right/north is the route to Sidney Peaks. But park atop Brian Head Peak; the views are exceptional.

Sources of additional information:

> Dixie National Forest
> Cedar City Ranger District
> 82 North 100 East
> P.O. Box 627
> Cedar City, Utah 84721-0627
> (801) 865-3200

> Brian Head Cross Country Ski and Bike Shop
> (Brian Head Hotel)
> P.O. Box 190065
> Brian Head, Utah 84719-0065
> (801) 677-2012
> Great snow, the most sun, and the best scenery lured Bill Murphy to
> Brian Head in 1978 where he first operated his cross-country ski shop out
> of his cabin's tiny living room. Now expanded and relocated to the Brian
> Head Hotel, the Brian Head Cross Country Ski and Bike Shop offers
> quality nordic ski touring and mountain biking rentals, equipment sales,
> and uncompromised service. Guided mountain bike tours and shuttles are
> available upon request.

Notes on the trail: Before you start your ride, you'll want to spend lots of time atop Brian Head Peak, one of southwestern Utah's great viewpoints. You'll be looking down into Cedar Break National Monument, which interrupts forests and meadows with vermillion luminosity.

Begin your ride by pedaling back downhill less than 1 mile to where the road bends sharply. Fork left/north on a rock-studded double-track (Sidney Peak Road). Pass the Dark Hollow trailhead after a mile and continue straight on Sidney Valley Trail.

One-half mile ahead, the road begins to fade and the Sidney Peaks single-track, which is marked with rock cairns, forks left. Dodge into sporadic forests and cross a wire fence line. Rugged cliffs break from the high valley to afford grand overlooks of forests and redrock escarpments through which Second Left-Hand Canyon funnels. The ultramarine pool within the basin is Yankee Meadow Reservoir. The Hurricane Cliffs border Parowan Valley and Little Salt Lake, all a vertical mile below. Beyond are the Escalante Desert, the Wah Wah Mountains, and Nevada. Dive through the pine forests once more to connect with the Sidney Valley Road.

A half mile north, the Sidney Valley road dives off the ridge and begins the endless descent toward Parowan. Four miles down, fork left on Forest Service Road 048 signed "Parowan." Note the gradually changing environment and warmer climate. Switchbacks announce the drop into Second Left-Hand Canyon proper and its moss-encrusted creek. Scenic value increases dramatically as redrock hoodoos poke through stands of ponderosa pine. Total immersion into this vermillion fantasyland soon follows.

Completing the excursion is a saturating splash through Second Left-Hand Creek. The creek is 6 to 12 inches deep, but the bottom is paved with cement, so it is rideable at full speed. If venturing down to Parowan on the highway, first take a 2-mile spur up First Left-Hand Canyon to view and hike around the Vermillion Castle, Noah's Ark, and the Grand Castle. Then continue down to Parowan for a cool plunge in the town pool.

RIDE 43 *HENDRICKSON LAKE*

Over the past few years, Brian Head has emerged as one of southern Utah's premier mountain bike venues. Delightfully cool temperatures, lush groves of aspen and pine, stunning redrock canyons, and wildflowers that cozy up to the trail beckon mountain bikers to explore this high plateau locale.

It was the Hendrickson Lake loop that convinced this author, as well as an ever-growing contingent of serenity-seeking urbanites, that Brian Head is in fact a mountain bike destination worth returning to time and time again. This path lacks the dramatic, eye-popping vistas you'll come across on nearby routes, but the trail-riding experience will satisfy even the most impassioned single-track devotee. The route spans luxuriant meadows rimmed by aspen and fir, then threads through placid forests. Along the way, a short spur leads to

RIDE 43 *HENDRICKSON LAKE*

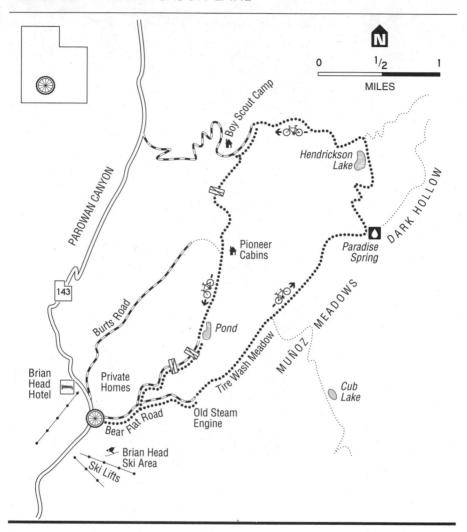

Hendrickson Lake, which mirrors an often indigo-saturated sky. If your time to visit Brian Head is limited, place Hendrickson Lake near the top of your "must-do" list.

This 10-mile loop (counterclockwise) captures the essence of Brian Head's fat-tire offerings. Five miles of lively single-track are combined with good dirt roads and variably technical double-track. There is one short, demanding hill midroute that may require walking, but does not warrant anxiety. This is a great intermediate-level route.

Lake-shore reflections.

General location: The Hendrickson Lake loop begins and ends in the town of Brian Head.

Elevation change: This loop begins in town at an elevation of 9,656´. It rises to 10,100´ at Steam Engine Meadow, then gradually descends to 9,200´ near the Boy Scout camp. The route culminates with intermittent climbing back up to about 9,800´. Total climbing is about 1,100´.

Season: Brian Head should melt out during June and be rideable throughout September and into October, weather permitting. The midsummer climate is mild, with temperatures in the 70s and 80s during the day, 30s and 40s at night. Afternoon rainstorms are common. Use liberal amounts of sunscreen.

Services: There are services at the route's trailhead, but not along the trail itself. Lodging, dining, groceries, gasoline, and bike shops are available at Brian Head. Bike rentals are also available from various shops. Developed campgrounds are located in Parowan Canyon (10 miles below Brian Head) and at

Cedar Breaks National Monument (about 10 miles south of town).

Hazards: You can expect the usual assortment of single-track obstacles to negotiate along this route, including root networks, loose rocks and gravel, narrow tread, deadfall, and large boulders. None of these should deter any rider; in fact, they add to the route's overall level of enjoyment. Be aware of other trail users, especially young scouts near the camp.

Rescue index: This is a popular route, especially on weekends. Emergency assistance may be summoned from the trailhead at Brian Head. Assistance *may* be sought at the Boy Scout camp, when it is in session. At most, you are 5 miles from the trailhead.

Land status: Dixie National Forest. Private property borders portions of the route, so please stay on designated trails and dirt roads.

Maps: USGS 7.5 minute quadrangle: Brian Head, Utah. (This map does not show the entire trail. Brian Head Cross Country Ski and Bike Shop sells the USGS Brian Head quadrangle, which shows all local trails accurately mapped.)

Finding the trail: The route begins at the corner of UT 143 and Bear Flat Road in the center of town (at Cosmo's). Parking is available at Brian Head Hotel, the Ski Area, or the town mall.

Sources of additional information:

Dixie National Forest
Cedar City Ranger District
82 North 100 East
P.O. Box 627
Cedar City, Utah 84721-0627
(801) 865-3200

Brian Head Cross Country Ski
 and Bike Shop
(Brian Head Hotel)
P.O. Box 190065
Brian Head, Utah 84719-0065
(801) 677-2012 / (800) SKI-BIKE

Notes on the trail: The route begins with a rude little hillclimb up Bear Flat Road—a more than adequate warm-up. One-half mile up, the dirt road splits. Bear right and enter into Steam Engine Meadow and ride to the old turbine's rusted out hull. In days past, long before the skiing industry took over, logging and timber sustained the local economy.

Keep an eye out for the trail; the many roads in this area may confuse you. From the old steam engine, turn left/north and pedal about 50 feet. Locate a wooden post next to a row of sapling fir trees. Take a sharp right, then left onto a double-track heading northward. Shortly ahead, the double-track grades to a wide single-track (marked with arrows). A fragrant bouquet of wildflowers blankets the thick forest.

After a mile or so, the path crosses Tire Wash and Muñoz Meadows. If the trail fades beneath a carpet of grass and wildflowers, just stay on a straight course directly down the length of the field. Once back in the forest, the path is well worn.

Soon after, you'll be on one of the best single-tracks in all of southern Utah. Large boulders scattered in the trail, root networks, log bars, dips, and twists make this part of the ride especially exciting. (In autumn the shimmering colors of the leaves make this a woodland sanctuary of unsurpassed serenity.)

About 2.5 miles from the old steam engine, an old wooden sign nailed to an aspen signifies the left turn (uphill) toward Hendrickson Lake. (If you continue straight toward Paradise Spring, you'll be heading toward Second Left-Hand Canyon.) The route levels, but this slalom course is made for fat tires. Take a short break at Hendrickson Lake.

In another mile you'll come to a signed trail junction on the north end of the Boy Scout camp. Turn left/south on a double-track along the perimeter of the clearing. After a few hundred yards, turn left again and rise back into the forest. (If you ride to the camp's main lodge, you have gone too far.) A silver steel gate announces "agony" hill—100 yards of hellish gravel, cobbles, and boulders strewn across a respectably steep grade. Lots of power and refined balanced are essential.

Enter into a meadow and cut straight across (south) on the faint double-track. Hidden uphill and to your left are 2 dilapidated pioneer cabins. Once back in the forest, you'll traverse a rock-infested road past a small pond, then break out into another clearing marked with a broken wooden fence. Stay straight to pass through a steel gate. After you go through a second steel gate, turn left onto a dirt road (note a "9" posted overhead in an aspen) and pass by private cabins. There is a four-way junction just ahead; turn left and up a small hill on a well-used double-track. Upon intersecting Bear Flat Road, turn right and drop into town.

RIDE 44 *RIGHT FORK OF BUNKER CREEK*

Like Second Left-Hand Canyon, downhill elation is the name of the game along Right Fork of Bunker Creek. But this time you are seduced by some fine single-track along the way. Powerful overlooks inaugurate the route. From Brian Head Peak, all of southwestern Utah, plus portions of adjoining states, are visible. Yet nothing is more absorbing than the delicately carved escarpment of the Great Red Amphitheater—Cedar Breaks National Monument. Terraced cliffs, convolute ridges, and castles rimmed with hoodoos break from stately forests and plunge into Ashdown Gorge.

Along Sidney Peaks ridge, the view of Parowan Canyon's endless forests interspersed with salmon-hued pinnacles is compelling; for an eternal moment your thoughts of dancing along a tantalizing single-track are erased. Bunker Creek's two-wheeled fanfare is equally captivating. Both views and trail riding are fantastic. And there will be plenty of time to think about the day's attractions while you sip a cold drink, comfortably propped on the Panguitch Lake General Store's airy porch.

This 16-mile point-to-point ride is perfect for intermediate cyclists and for

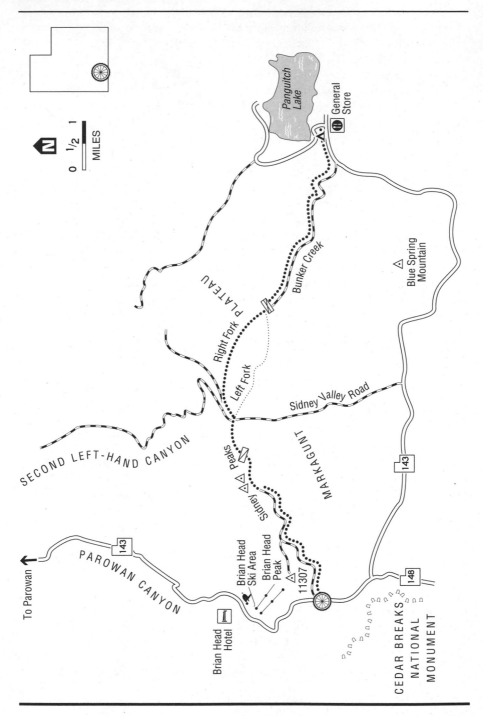

Brian Head offers the best single-track in southern Utah.

strong novice bikers who are attentive and use good judgement. The route begins with a short segment of maintained gravel road to Brian Head Peak, followed by double-track and single-track across Sidney Peaks ridge. Right Fork of Bunker Creek is three miles of moderately technical single-track that ends with several miles of fast-paced cruising on good dirt roads.

General location: The Right Fork of Bunker Creek trail descends east from Brian Head Peak/Sidney Peaks ridge to UT 143 near the south shore of Panguitch Lake.

Elevation change: The parking area at the base of the Brian Head Peak road is at 10,420´. The Peak road rises to 11,000´ at the turnoff for Sidney Peaks ridge. (Add on 300 vertical feet plus an extra mile to take in the views atop Brian Head Peak, elevation 11,307´). Sidney Peaks ridge undulates gently to the Right Fork of Bunker Creek trailhead at 10,445´. The trail then descends to an elevation of 8,400´. Total elevation gain is about 800´; total descent is close to 2,600´.

Season: Snow fields may linger on Sidney Peaks ridge through mid-June. The route is rideable through September and into October, weather permitting. The midsummer climate around Brian Head is mild, with temperatures in the 70s and 80s during the day and 30s and 40s at night. Afternoon rainstorms are common. Use liberal amounts of sunscreen.

Services: There are no services along this route other than at the trail's end. (The Panguitch General Store offers limited groceries and gasoline.) Lodging, dining, groceries, gasoline, and bike shops are available at Brian Head. Brian Head Cross Country Ski and Bike Shop and other local bike shops offer shuttle services. Developed campgrounds are located at Panguitch Lake (across from Panguitch Lake General Store) and at Cedar Breaks National Monument.

Hazards: The Right Fork of Bunker Creek single-track is moderately technical in some sections and requires both attentiveness and good handling skills. The trail is not regularly maintained and may contain obstacles including deadfall, narrow tread, loose rocks, root networks, boggy areas, and steep descents—the usual assortment of trail challenges. Use caution when pedaling the short stretch of paved highway from the trail's end to the Panguitch Lake General Store.

Rescue index: This route is growing in popularity. You may encounter other trail users on weekends, but you may be alone on the trails midweek. Motorists are common on UT 143 at the trailhead and trailend parking areas. You can summon emergency assistance from Brian Head and the Panguitch Lake General Store. Cedar City and Panguitch have medical facilities.

Land status: Dixie National Forest.

Maps: USGS 7.5 minute quadrangles: Brian Head and Panguitch Lake, Utah. (Portions of the route are not mapped.)

Finding the trail: Leave a vehicle at the Panguitch Lake General Store (but get permission from the storekeeper first). The store is located on the south side of Panguitch Lake, about 20 miles south of Panguitch on UT 143, or 17 miles east of Cedar Breaks National Monument and Brian Head via UT 143.

In the shuttle vehicle, drive 15 miles west on UT 143 to the Brian Head Peak road. Parking is available near the junction (at Mammoth Summit).

Sources of additional information:

Dixie National Forest
Cedar City Ranger District
82 North 100 East
P.O. Box 627
Cedar City, Utah 84721-0627
(801) 865-3200

Notes on the trail: From the parking area, pedal 2.3 miles up the Brian Head Peak road to where it bends sharply left/south. Branch right/north onto the rock-studded double-track Sidney Peaks road. (The extra mile to the left to the top of Brian Head Peak is well worth the effort, for its scenic value is unsurpassed.) On the main route, pass the Dark Hollow trailhead after a mile and continue straight on Sidney Valley Trail.

One-half mile ahead, the road begins to fade and the Sidney Valley singletrack forks left where it is marked with rock cairns. Dodge into sporadic forests and cross a wire fence line. Rugged cliffs break from the high valley to afford grand overlooks of lush forests and redrock escarpments through which Second Left-Hand Canyon funnels. The ultramarine pool within the basin is Yankee Meadow Reservoir. The Hurricane Cliffs border Parowan Valley and Little Salt Lake, all a vertical mile below. Beyond are the Escalante Desert, the Wah Wah Mountains, and Nevada. Dive through the pine forests once more to connect with the Sidney Valley Road.

Hop onto the Sidney Valley Road (improved dirt) and pedal north, but not more than a couple hundred yards. (If the road begins descending quickly over the ridge and westward, back up; otherwise, you will end up on the wrong side of the mountain in Parowan.) Look for a carsonite post on the right marked "040." This single-track cuts across a tundra meadow. Watch for tree blazes and rock cairns marking the often faint path. When the trail breaks out onto a four-wheel-drive road, turn right onto the road, then *immediately* left (100 feet or so) to continue on the single-track. From here the trail is readily identifiable and provokes mile-wide grins.

Unfortunately, the single-track lasts a mere 3 miles. Pass through a green steel gate signed "Right Fork Bunker Creek 040, Sidney Valley Road," and continue down valley on a double-track. A handful of earthen berms are worthy of air time and there will be a whole lot of whooping and hollering going on.

After 1.5 miles, the double-track takes a dogleg left and rises uphill moderately. Double-track grades to a good dirt road winding down through aspens and across creek-fed meadows. A short climb puts you onto the paved highway. Turn left and cruise a half mile down to the General Store where cold brews and ice cream await.

RIDE 45 *TWISTED FOREST*

The name Twisted Forest evokes childhood fairy tales of country folk put under villainous spells to spend eternity in foreboding woodlands. This Twisted Forest, on the contrary, is open, sunny, brightly colored, and welcomes curious travelers. Twisted it is, though, for these hillsides harbor large communities of bristlecone pines, one of the Earth's oldest living species. These tenacious conifers have been known to live for more than 2,000 years. With tangled roots that sprawl across the crumbly limestone, contorted limbs curled into spirals, and sprouts of pine garlands, they appear feeble and arthritic. But they are sturdy and stoic.

RIDE 45 *TWISTED FOREST*

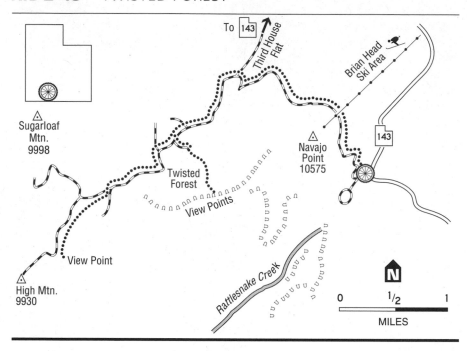

The ride described in this chapter follows a trail leading up to the Twisted Forest. You'll have to hike through the forest itself, though. Bikes are restricted from the Twisted Forest because its lightly vegetated slopes are quite fragile. But the walking is easy and you can venture where you please. A mile's effort takes you to a rim that opposes the striking amphitheater of Cedar Breaks National Monument. Cedar Breaks is a young, compact Bryce Canyon, but every bit as spellbinding. Its salmon-hued cliffs are terraced with battalions of lance-bearing sentinels parading along castle walls capped with spires. The cliffs "break" away from pine forests and funnel to luxuriant meadows below—a veritable intaglio of stunning color and form. Save this route for sunset.

This 9-mile out-and-back route is a good novice/intermediate-level ride. You'll be riding on dirt roads throughout, which vary from smooth hard-packed dirt to moderately technical double-track. The mile-long climb back to the route's parking area is the greatest challenge and may test the ability of novice riders.

General location: The route to the Twisted Forest begins about a mile south of Brian Head Ski Area.

Elevation change: The Sugarloaf Mountain Road trailhead/parking area is at

The setting sun illuminates Cedar Breaks National Monument.

10,000′. A short climb around Navajo Point rises to 10,240′. Thereafter, the route generally descends to the Twisted Forest trailhead at 9,640′. The hardest climb is the return up the Sugarloaf Road back toward the parking area—a 500′ gain in about 1.5 miles. Total climbing is about 900′.

Season: This area should be free of snow by mid-June and rideable throughout September and possibly October. Part of the allure of Brian Head is that midsummer daytime temperatures are temperate (70s and 80s) and nights are crisp (30s and 40s). Wildflowers typically bloom during late spring and last throughout the summer.

Services: There are no services along the route nor any drinking water. Lodging, dining, limited groceries, and gasoline, as well as bike shops (and bike rentals), are available at Brian Head. All other visitor services are available in Cedar City, and most are in Parowan. Developed camping is located at Cedar Breaks National Monument and in Parowan Canyon 10 miles below Brian Head.

Hazards: The route is generally low in technical difficulty. When hiking through the Twisted Forest to catch rim-side views of Cedar Breaks National Monument, use extreme caution along the cliff's edge. The limestone substrate crumbles easily.

Rescue index: Emergency assistance can be summoned from the town of Brian Head, located about a mile down UT 143 from the trailhead/parking area. Cedar City has medical facilities.

Land status: Dixie National Forest and Brian Head Ski Area.

Maps: USGS 7.5 minute quadrangles: Brian Head and Flanigan Arch, Utah.
Finding the trail: From the main lodge at Brian Head Ski Area, drive (or pedal) less than a mile up UT 143. Where the road bends left (before the sharp rise toward Brian Head Peak), Sugarloaf Mountain Road (signed) branches to the right. Park at your discretion.

Sources of additional information:

Dixie National Forest
Cedar City Ranger District
82 North 100 East
P.O. Box 0627
Cedar City, Utah 84721
(801) 865-3200

Brian Head Cross Country Ski
  and Bike Shop
(Brian Head Hotel)
P.O. Box 190065
Brian Head, Utah 84719-0065
(801) 677-2012

Notes on the trail: From the parking area (at the turnoff onto Sugarloaf Mountain Road), follow the four-wheel-drive road to the right and travel up and around Navajo Point. As you cross ski runs and pass under lifts, there are good views of Brian Head (town and resort). Descend about a mile to a junction with a second dirt road and turn left. (Note the sign for a scenic overlook overhead.) After another mile, turn left again at a sign for Twisted Forest Trailhead. The trailhead is not far from here. Park (lock or stash) your bikes and take to foot.

The trail through the Twisted Forest is primitive to nonexistent and unmarked. For the most part you hike where you want across open, Creamsicle-colored hills and through dispersed communities of bristlecone pines. It is easy to become disoriented, so make note of specific landmarks (groups of trees, outcrops in gullies, or other prominent points) to facilitate your return. The rim is less than a mile from the trailhead in a south/southeast direction; you will know when to stop!

RIDE 46   *VIRGIN RIVER RIM TRAIL*

The Virgin River Rim Trail is one of the newest trails on the Dixie National Forest. Constructed during the summer of 1993, some sections are still having final touches applied. This visionary trail provides some of the most spectacular scenery in southern Utah's plateau country, for it follows the rim of the luminous Pink Cliffs. There are overlooks that rival those of Bryce Canyon National Park with intimate views into red limestone amphitheaters filled with spires, castles, and hoodoos. To the distant south rises the sandstone gallery of Zion National Park. The Virgin River, which dissects the park with its famed Narrows of Zion Canyon, finds its headwaters beneath the Rim Trail. Pack along your camera, for photographic opportunities abound.

In addition to overwhelming vistas you'll enjoy, the route winds through

RIDE 46 *VIRGIN RIVER RIM TRAIL*

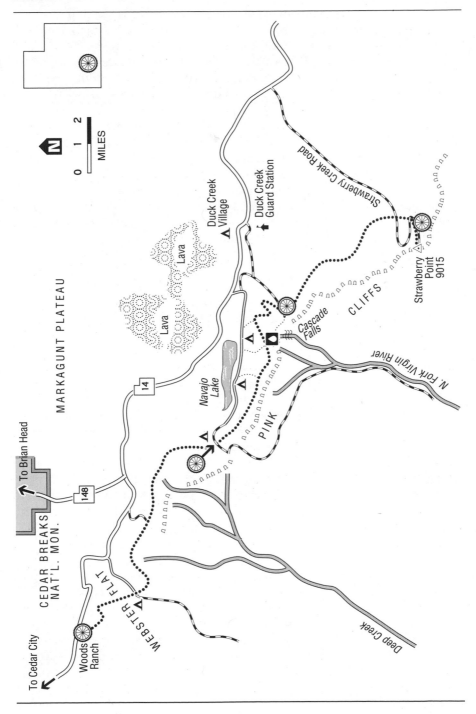

MARKAGUNT PLATEAU

N

0 1 2
MILES

To Brian Head

CEDAR BREAKS
NAT'L. MON.

148

To Cedar City

Woods
Ranch

WEBSTER FLAT

14

Navajo
Lake

Lava

Lava

Lava

Duck Creek
Village

Duck Creek
Guard Station

Strawberry Creek Road

Cascade
Falls

CLIFFS

PINK

Strawberry
Point
9015

N. Fork Virgin River

Deep Creek

fragrant pine and fir forests mixed with aspens, cuts across wildflower-blan-keted alpine meadows, and passes the shore of ultramarine Navajo Lake. Even bristlecone pines, Nature's oldest living trees, are found along the way. A short side hike leads to Cascade Falls where a creek gushes from a cave in the face of the cliff. This waterfall is both the actual headwaters of the Virgin River and subterranean outlet of Navajo Lake, which lacks drainage by surface streams.

The entire 36-mile point-to-point single-track is reserved for advanced cyclists who are acclimated to high altitudes. Much of the route is low to moderate in technical difficulty and grades have been held generally to 8 percent or less. Still, there are long, demanding climbs to be conquered, some over a mile in length. This should not scare off intermediate or even novice bikers; numerous connecting trails that stem to campgrounds and other trail-heads along Navajo Lake create several optional routes of 5 to 15 miles. This well-planned, highly scenic trail offers opportunities for all ability levels.

Trail information was provided by the Dixie National Forest, Cedar City Ranger District.

General location: The Virgin River Rim Trail is centered around Navajo Lake, which is located 30 miles east of Cedar City on UT 14.

Elevation change: The trail has a mean elevation of 9,300′. Highest elevations reach near 10,000′; Woods Ranch (western trailhead) is at the lowest elevation at 7,800′.

Season: The trail should be rideable from early June through October, although snow may linger near Navajo Lake well into late June. Midsummer daytime temperatures are mild (70s and 80s) and nights can drop to near freez-ing. Colorful displays of both springtime wildflowers and fall foliage are excep-tional.

Services: Water taps are available along the route a short distance off the trail at the Te-ah and Webster Flat campgrounds. No other services are available along the route. Additional campgrounds (with water taps) and the Navajo Lake Lodge are accessible only via spurs extending off the main trail. There are numerous USFS campgrounds at Navajo Lake and along UT 14; backcountry camping is allowed unless otherwise posted. Limited services are available at Duck Creek, east of Navajo Lake. Cedar City offers all visitor services, includ-ing medical facilities. All surface waters should be purified.

Hazards: This route follows along a natural fault, which is responsible for providing the spectacular views, so there are cliffs and steep drop-offs near the trail. The trail is generally free of hazards, but some switchbacks can be tricky. You may encounter livestock in the spring and fall.

Rescue index: Portions of the trail, especially near Navajo Lake, are well trav-eled by others. Other sections offer complete solitude. Emergency assistance may be summoned from the Navajo Lake Lodge and Duck Creek Village. Cedar City has medical facilities.

Land status: Dixie National Forest.

Maps: USGS 7.5 minute quadrangles: Navajo Lake, Straight Canyon, Strawberry Point, and Webster Flat, Utah. (Because of the trail's infancy, it is not shown on these maps.)

Finding the trail: You can reach the Strawberry Point trailhead by traveling 38 miles east of Cedar City on UT 14 and then 7 miles south on the Strawberry Creek Road (Forest Service Road 058). The Cascade Falls trailhead is located 28 miles east of Cedar City on UT 14, then 5 miles south on the Navajo Lake and Cascade Falls Roads. The Te-ah trailhead is located 28 miles east of Cedar City on UT 14. Turn south on UT 14 for Navajo Lake and travel to the lake's eastern end. You'll reach Woods Ranch trailhead 10 miles east of Cedar City by turning south off of UT 14. All trailheads are accessible by passenger cars.

Sources of additional information:

Dixie National Forest
Cedar City Ranger District
P.O. Box 627
Cedar City, Utah 84721
(801) 865-3200

Note: A small trail guide to the Virgin River Rim Trail will be available in the near future from the Cedar City Ranger District.

Notes on the trail: From the Strawberry Point trailhead, the first 2 miles are generally downhill through pine forests. The trail crosses a large meadow and the Strawberry Creek Road. Afterward, the path begins a long but gentle climb to the top of a plateau covered with ponderosa pines. Travel northwest along this plateau and you'll come to one of the route's most spectacular viewpoints—a deep amphitheater lined with spires and hoodoos. The trail follows the rim offering views southward across the Virgin River headwaters and eastward to Powell Point 50 miles away. A steep descent off the plateau is followed by more scenic views from the Lars Fork Overlook.

More climbing takes you up along the rim with fine overviews of Zion National Park in the distance. Another descent drops to the Cascade Falls trailhead. Park your bike and hike on the three-quarter-mile foot trail, which is closed to bikes, to the natural subterranean outlet of Navajo Lake.

Back on the bike trail, you'll encounter a strenuous, 1-mile climb through multiple switchbacks that lead back up to the rim and across the level plateau. Zion's towering rock cathedrals in the distance grow more impressive. You'll encounter the Spruces Trail 4.5 miles from the Cascade Falls trailhead. This spur leads half a mile down to the campground on the shore of Navajo Lake. You'll cross additional side trails, which in turn lead to respective campgrounds lining Navajo Lake. (This section of the trail is quite gentle and provides excellent options for novice to intermediate bikers.)

Descending off the plateau, the route crosses the Navajo Lake road and follows a dirt road northwest while skirting past the Te-ah campground.

Follow this dirt road one-quarter mile, then fork right and continue on the trail. (Watch for a trail sign.) The next 7.5 miles rise gently uphill but well beneath the rim of Gooseberry Point. You will pass through spruce and fir interspersed with aspen and alpine meadows. Wildlife abounds, and sightings of deer, wild turkey, and other species can be expected. After this 7.5 miles, you'll encounter a dirt road. Turn right and follow it uphill about half a mile; then branch off to the west and continue on the trail. After a short distance, intersect and cross over the Webster Flat road and climb up past Lundell Springs. About a mile past the springs, the trail joins yet another dirt road. Webster Flat campground is to the left, but turn right onto the dirt road and complete the route with a 1,000′ descent to Wood's Ranch—the Rim Trail's western trailhead.

Southern Utah's Canyon Country

Utah's Canyon Country lies within the northwest sector of the greater Colorado Plateau and is defined by classic "redrock" terrain. It is easy for the mountain biker to succumb to the obvious when venturing into Canyon Country by making a beeline to Moab—mountain bike mecca, and arguably, center of the universe. There is good reason for such haste since the area has been widely acclaimed, offers endless services, and is a veritable utopia for fat tires. By all means, experience the hyperactivity of Moab, but do not overlook Canyon Country's other multitudinous offerings of open space and endless adventures.

Southern Utah is home to numerous world-renowned national parks, including Arches, Canyonlands, Capitol Reef, and Zion, plus Natural Bridges National Monument, Monument Valley Navajo Tribal Park, and Glen Canyon National Recreation Area. All have something to offer the mountain biker, either in the way of scenic roads that venture through these parks' interiors or backcountry routes located just beyond their boundaries.

Some national parks are becoming less revered as sanctuaries of solitude, though. For those seeking intimate relations between self, bike, and nature, Canyon Country is well suited. One of the region's less celebrated treasures is the San Rafael Swell. This kidney-shaped uplift located just west of Green River is national-park caliber indeed. San Rafael Swell is neatly bisected by Interstate 70, so you might assume it to be easy prey for concessionaires and the RV crowds they attract. On the contrary; despite easy (but often elusive) access, the Swell has remained remote, rugged, and a desert biker's haven. With a little perseverance, and the assistance of a good guidebook, you will experience redrock pageantry thought only to exist in the Moab area.

The same can be said for the remainder of Canyon Country's outback. If your penchant is gazing at the Milky Way's twinkling swath, swigging coffee sweetened with sand, and awakening to a sunrise intensified by the burnt umber walls it rebounds off, Canyon Country will quickly draw you deeper into its embrace.

Despite the all-encompassing nature of this region's red rocks, there are three alpine retreats worth seeking for midsummer refuge: the La Sal, Abajo, and Henry Mountains. Each beckons the desert biker with the promise of cool breezes and fragrant forests.

Finally, if winter-long powder skiing has become mundane, car-top down to St. George where off-season biking is always pleasant. You can even squeeze in a round or two of golf.

There are many opportunities to study ancient Indian cultures in southeastern Utah, particularly the Anasazi and Fremont Indians who inhabited central and southeastern Utah, roughly between A.D. 500 and 1300. The Anasazi, who

Canyon Country—an ensemble of desert, mountains, and sky.

occupied the Four Corners Area, first lived in underground pit houses during what is called the Basketmaker period. As the culture developed into the Pueblo period, life became centered around small villages. The Anasazi began building elaborate stone structures confined to cliffs and alcoves, some the size of castles. As a more sedentary life evolved, the Anasazi became skilled artisans, began to cultivate and store crops, and produced ornamented pottery. The kiva, an underground chamber believed to be a ceremonial room, is a symbol of Anasazi culture.

The Fremont Indians roamed widely throughout central Utah, inhabiting both desert and mountainous areas. Not much is known about the Fremont Indians since they were considered nomadic hunters and gatherers rather than a developed sedentary tribe. They lived in small villages and occupied pit houses, like the early Anasazi, but moved their villages seasonally or to seek more productive grounds. The Fremont were also craftsmen who produced primitive baskets and clay figurines. In addition, the Fremont adorned the desert's walls with imagination-stirring rock art. Mysteriously, though, both the Anasazi and Fremont cultures disappeared around A.D. 1300, arguably the result of climatic changes and subsequent unfavorable living conditions, or of the hostile encroachment of neighboring tribes.

Mesa Verde National Park is unequivocally the most famous and spectacular display of Anasazi masonry, but the scattered ruins at Hovenweep National Monument are especially haunting. Edge of the Cedars, Anasazi, and Fremont Indian State Parks offer modern museums and displays with interpretive trails.

Newspaper Rock Historical Monument is a veritable tabloid of prehistoric and modern headlines etched into stone.

As informative and spectacular as these parks are, there is immeasurable enchantment in spying prehistoric vestiges during a backcountry bike ride: A small granary perched precariously in a cliff alcove, a broken arrowhead or pottery shard, or a curious arrangement of rough-cut rocks that outline a dwelling are all windows into a clouded past.

Rock art is particularly captivating and has been subject to considerable interpretive efforts at scientific, cultural, and aesthetic levels. Whimsical images depict the cultures' routine activities and relay messages with religious and spiritual undertones. A single bighorn sheep or spiral on a tilted boulder is every bit as compelling as panels composed of shamanistic humanoids and elaborate hunting scenes.

Please remember that prehistoric ruins, remains, and rock art displays are delicate, irreplaceable, and protected by law (see "Special Issues," page xix). Even the best intentioned visitor can cause irreparable damage with a gentle touch. Take away with you only their lasting emotional and visual impact while allowing future visitors to experience the same.

SLICKROCK

Slickrock is not simply the evocative tag given to the world's most highly touted mountain bike trail, nor is it a riding surface that is restricted to that specific locale or any particular rock formation; rather, "It's more like the whole country is slickrock, even where it's crumbling away," Edward Abbey explained in his book *Slickrock*.

Slickrock gained its name from early settlers whose metal-shod horses found the smooth, barren sandstone slick to cross. But in the realm of mountain biking it is exactly the opposite; this naturally abrasive surface is about as "slick" as sandpaper and soft as concrete. Arguably, this unique riding medium allows a mountain bike its fullest expression but at the same time is absolutely unforgiving. Slickrock may intimidate the first-time or tentative biker because it can hold the bike at angles that seem to defy gravity. But if you accept and then master its apparent distemper, you might profess—as did Moabite Todd Campbell, who wrote the book on the stuff—that the two-wheeled experience is "the most fun you can have with your clothes on."

To gain an appreciation for slickrock—its rough-to-the-touch surface and its boundless extent—it helps to have a basic understanding of the geologic processes that formed and exposed these rocks for us to enjoy. Geologic history can confound many people because it involves events that took place over millions of years.

Slickrock Bizarrerie.

In a nutshell, the geologic complexity of the Colorado Plateau (inclusive of Canyon Country) is based on huge volumes of sediments derived from various sources and deposited under various environmental conditions, followed by tectonic-related uplift and subsequent down-cutting by erosional forces. Sounds a bit complicated, doesn't it? Still, like chapters in a book lying flat on your desk, the sequence of these layers, or stratigraphic section, can be read even by the untrained eye. Of course, keep in mind that pages and whole chapters are often missing due to lapses in deposition or long periods of erosion, and that the entire book has been bent, broken, cut up, and deeply grooved in some places. But it is this chapter-by-chapter progression that gives Canyon Country its trademark "layer cake" appearance.

The geologic history of the Colorado Plateau (including Utah's Canyon Country) dates back about 550 million years, when a primordial sea encroached up the Four Corners Area, covering the continent's Precambrian crystalline core with mud and limestones. These ancient strata are visible only in the absolute bottom of the Grand Canyon. (If time is money, and one year equals a dollar, then the geologic value of modern man's existence is equivalent to a meager $35,000, a mere pittance compared to the Colorado Plateau's "financial age.")

From the Cambrian Period to the Tertiary Period (a span of 500 million years) the environment of the relatively low-lying Colorado Plateau varied from shallow seas with shoreline tidal flats, to thin freshwater lakes fed by rivers, to basins of blowing and drifting sand dunes. The products of these environmental episodes are the terra cotta rocks that can be seen throughout southwestern Utah. Throughout this great time span, plate tectonics (the movement of the Earth's crust) would uplift and fold areas of Canyon Country. But it would not be until the very last page in this book of geologic history, the late Tertiary Period, that erosively voracious rivers, like the Colorado, would carve the landscape into the the deep canyons and curious shapes we see today.

Of all the sedimentary rock layers deposited across the Colorado Plateau, perhaps the most extensive and easily recognized is the Glen Canyon Group. (A "group" is a stratigraphic sequence of two or more rock units, or formations, that are closely related in composition and origin of deposition.) The Glen Canyon Group consists of three layers of sandstone formations: Wingate, Kayenta, and Navajo—oldest (bottom) to youngest (top), respectively. Specifically, the sequence spans the interface of the Triassic and Jurassic Periods roughly 210 million years ago. As a whole, the Glen Canyon Group represents an environmental episode occurring when vast deserts and dune fields swept across the Colorado Plateau. William L. Stokes notes in *Geology of Utah* that some geologists half-jokingly refer to these strata as the "Great Sand Pile."

Glen Canyon is partially submerged in Lake Powell, but you'll be able to see rocks representative of the Glen Canyon Group that spread from Zion through Capitol Reef and Canyonlands National Parks to Moab. The Glen Canyon Group is largely responsible for the colossal vertical walls, overhanging alcoves, fins, towers, and domes that are the hallmark of Canyon Country.

The reddish orange Wingate Sandstone forms sheer walls, mesa peninsulas, or island spires. This homogeneous sandstone has a desert-dune origin. The Kayenta, which lies atop the Wingate, typically forms steep, broken terraces and varies in color from red to purple to brown layered with grey. A mixture of sandstone and shale, the Kayenta originated from slow-flowing rivers. Finally, the Navajo Sandstone (resting on the Kayenta) produces sheer cliffs or massive towers as well, but ones usually capped with hummocky domes, fins, and rounded humps. The trademark of the Navajo is its near-white color and gigantic, sweeping crossbeds, indicative of desert sand dunes.

Where is the Glen Canyon Group best displayed? Good exposures include the San Rafael Reef; Moab Rim and the Portal of the Colorado River (Moab); Amasa Back, Poison Spider Mesa, and the Slickrock Bike Trail (the latter rolls over the Navajo Sandstone); the looming walls above the White Rim Trail and beneath Panorama Point off Canyonlands National Park; the Waterpocket Fold of Capitol Reef National Park; the canyons of the Escalante River; and, of course, Checkerboard Mesa and the majestic towers of Zion National Park.

This colorful sequence is just the beginning of a rewarding process of paging through the varied chapters that comprise Canyon Country's geologic history. Expand your geologic awareness both up and down strata by comparing the different rock structures of Arches National Park with those of the Canyonlands' Needles District, and in turn, with those of Monument Valley. Once you get the hang of it, "slickrock" will take on a whole new meaning.

RIDE 47   *GORDON CREEK / PINNACLE PEAK*

The combination of cedar flats, deep gorges, and sweeping desert vistas makes the Gordon Creek/Pinnacle Peak route a good introduction to riding in Utah's Castle Country. The route winds up from sagebrush flats into stands of pinyon pine and juniper. It traverses the eastern benches of the Manti Mountains and crosses several deep gorges cut by Gordon Creek. Riders will pass directly under one of the country's largest railroad bridges—a massive structure built to transport coal out of several of the area's mines. Although many of the coal mines are now defunct, a few are operating and you can still see trains crossing the bridge.

You'll want to explore the intriguing human history of the area while you ride. Several Indian rock art panels, including pictographs (paintings on rock) and petroglyphs (a form of rock art created by chipping off oxidized sandstone surfaces to expose the lighter underlayers), are within easy walking distance of the route. The route also roughly retraces the reputed escape trail used by Butch Cassidy and Elza Lay after their infamous robbery of the Castle Gate payroll in 1897.

This 28-mile loop (clockwise) begins in Price and is well suited for intermediate riders. Because of its low elevation, it also makes for a good early season ride. The route follows a variety of surface types from paved roads to improved dirt and gravel roads to double-track, but most of it can be easily navigated on a bike. The descent into Gordon Creek gorge will challenge even hard-core riders. Novice cyclists can shorten the ride by driving to where the pavement turns to dirt, then biking out and back to the railroad bridge. Information for Gordon Creek/Pinnacle Peak was provided by Kevin Christopherson and the Wild Bunch, Price, Utah.

General location: The Gordon Creek/Pinnacle Peak loop is located in the canyon and bench region 5 miles west of Price.
Elevation change: Price, the route's starting location, is at 5,600′. Dirt roads rise to 6,470′ at the railroad junction. More ups and downs as the route crosses the drainage add to the overall elevation gain. Total climbing is about 1,300′.
Season: The best time to ride this route is spring (April through June) and fall (September through October). During midsummer, the route can be very warm.
Services: There are no services or drinking water along the route. All visitor services, including bike shops, are located in Price.
Hazards: Cyclists should avoid the railroad tracks because coal trains still run the rails. There are 2 wire gates that are occasionally closed along the route. Both are located on a downhill section and may surprise you, so be attentive. You'll encounter vehicular traffic along paved roads. Be alert to truck traffic on Consumers Road.

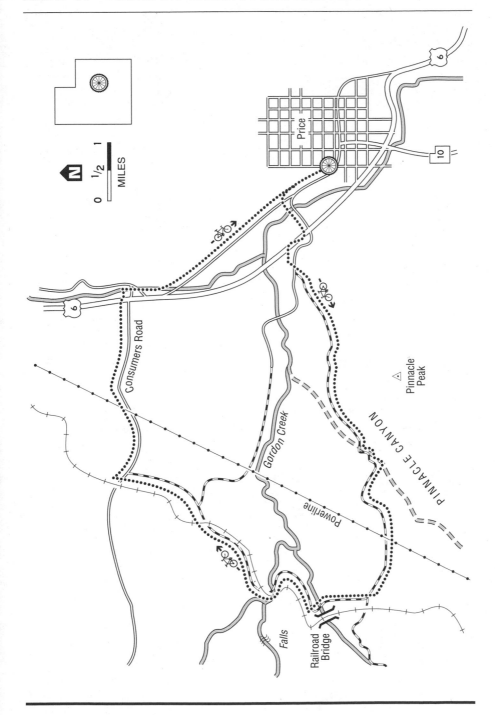

Rescue index: You could be as far as 15 miles from help at the route's farthest point. The route is passable by high-clearance vehicles if a rescue is necessary. Price has a hospital.

Land status: Bureau of Land Management, Price River Resource Area.

Maps: USGS 7.5 minute quadrangles: Helper, Pinnacle Peak, Price, and Standardville, Utah.

Finding the trail: There is no official trailhead since the loop simply follows backcountry roads in Carbon County. A good starting location might be near Exit 241/North Price off US 6. Park at your discretion.

Sources of additional information:

Bureau of Land Management
Moab District
Price River Resource Area
900 North 7th East
Price, Utah 84501
(801) 637-4584

Castle Country Travel Council
P.O. Box 1037
Price, Utah 84501
(801) 637-2788

Wild Bunch (Mountain Bike Club)
384 North 700 East
Price, Utah 84501
Kevin Christopherson has long been active enjoying and promoting outdoor recreation. He has joined forces with Dan (Sparky) Bittick and several of their friends to form the Wild Bunch—a loose-knit group of people who have come together to share experiences and promote mountain biking. They are active on Bureau of Land Management trail committees, in festival organization, and in race promotion. To get more information on tours, festivals, or simply getting together for a group ride in the area, contact Kevin and the Wild Bunch.

Notes on the trail: From Exit 241/North Price, travel west out of town on Westwood Boulevard past Days Inn until you come to a stop sign. Go straight through the intersection. The road will wind northwest about a mile through a residential section and through a 4-way stop. Stay on Westwood Boulevard, which eventually becomes Gordon Creek Road. Just after this residential area and at the top of a small hill, there is another 4-way stop. Turn left/west, staying on Gordon Creek Road. About a mile up this road, go left/south onto Pinnacle Peak Road.

Pinnacle Peak Road ventures up through Pinnacle Canyon, so named for the large rock monument that rises 600′ above the valley floor (to the left/south). Rising out of Pinnacle Canyon is the tour's most strenuous part—a long, slow climb over about a half mile. The road then climbs gradually to Porphyry Bench. Stay on the main road until you come to the railroad tracks.

Just before you reach the tracks, turn right/north on a double-track that more or less follows the railroad tracks. Along this double-track, the riding becomes more technical and interesting. Wind in and out of the trees, and up and down several washes, until you come to Gordon Creek gorge (after about 2 miles) and the expansive railroad bridge crossing the canyon. The road drops down to the stream. Be careful! This is a technical section requiring advanced bike handling skills; otherwise, enjoy the short *walk* down.

Plan on spending some time exploring inside the gorge, where you'll find Indian rock art displays worth seeing. About one-half mile down stream along a bench on the south side of the canyon, there is a pictograph of an 18-inch-tall humanoid figure called "the headhunter." When you see it you will know how it got its name. If you follow the bench on the north side about 200 yards below the bridge, you'll find a petroglyph panel depicting a hunting scene. There are also waterfalls up and downstream from the bridge.

The double-track climbs out of the gorge and roughly follows the railroad tracks north for another 4 miles until it reaches a paved road (Consumers Road). Turn right/east and follow the pavement 3 miles back to US 6. Consumers Road was built for coal trucks. Be aware that coal trucks often travel along here in pairs. At US 6, turn right/south and follow the road 5 miles back to Price, staying to the far right on the shoulder.

There are many side roads branching from the main route that are worth exploring. Some lead out to scenic overlooks, others follow technically difficult paths down rocky canyons. If you wish to expand the distance of this ride or increase the difficulty, these side roads are the ticket.

History buffs will enjoy visiting the Mining and Railroad Museum in Helper or the Museum of Natural History in Price. You may want to read *The Wild Bunch at Robbers Roost*, by Pearl Baker, which describes the "outlaw history" in the Price area.

RIDE 48 *NINE MILE CANYON*

Nine Mile Canyon is considerably longer than its name implies. Its creek runs over 40 miles, beginning northeast of Price and emptying into the Green River at the head of Desolation Canyon. On its way, the creek penetrates the arid and austere Book Cliffs, one of the largest de facto wilderness areas in the continental United States.

There are many places that are the scenic equal of Nine Mile Canyon, with its sagebrush and banded red cliffs, but few rival its archaeological richness. This is the spot where the Fremont Indians, a relative of the Anasazi, were first identified and described. With more than 10,000 estimated sites, the canyon contains the largest concentration of Indian rock art in North America. But, you have to look closely to find it.

RIDE 48 *NINE MILE CANYON*

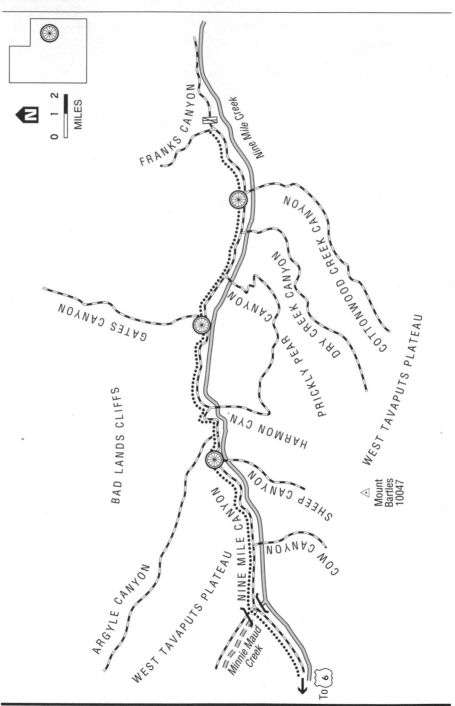

MILES
0 1 2

N

FRANKS CANYON

Nine Mile Creek

COTTONWOOD CREEK CANYON

DRY CREEK CANYON

PRICKLY PEAR CREEK CANYON

GATES CANYON

WEST TAVAPUTS PLATEAU

BAD LANDS CLIFFS

HARMON CYN.

△ Mount
Bartles
10047

SHEEP CANYON

COW CANYON

NINE MILE CANYON

WEST TAVAPUTS PLATEAU

ARGYLE CANYON

Minnie Maud Creek

To 6

Terraced plateaus enclose Nine Mile Canyon.

Petroglyphs, a form of rock art created by chipping off oxidized sandstone surfaces to expose the lighter underlayers, occur as individual displays and complex panels. You'll see images of owls, coyotes, bighorn sheep, and mystical horned beings etched into rock surfaces. Be sure to have a pair of binoculars handy to spot the small ruins atop the cliffs along the road.

The Nine Mile Canyon out-and-back ride, which follows a graded dirt road, requires little technical ability and modest conditioning. Depending on the weather, the road can be as smooth as glass, washboarded, or extremely rutted, gumbo-like mud. With a flexible length of up to 55 miles out-and-back, the route caters to both novice and advanced mountain bikers.

This chapter on Nine Mile Canyon was submitted by Steve Howe,[*] Salt Lake City, Utah.

---

[*]To say Steve Howe is an outdoor enthusiast is an understatement. Former editor of the *Sports Guide,* a magazine of outdoor recreation, fitness, and travel for the intermountain west, Steve is presently the southwestern field editor for *Backpacker Magazine.*

Steve spends the majority of his professional time with a pack on his back, hiking through the western states' most breathtaking terrain. Likewise, his spare time is spent in the field with camera in hand, tracking wildlife and framing scenery throughout Utah and the West. And, of course, Steve manages to squeeze in an occasional mountain bike, white-water, or ski-touring adventure, just for balance.

One of many mysterious messages left by the ancient Fremont Indians.

General location: Nine Mile Canyon is located about 25 miles east of Price and about 20 miles north of US 6 in Wellington.

Elevation change: The elevation of Sheep Canyon (roughly Nine Mile Canyon's beginning) is 6,200′. Over the main road's 27-mile length, it descends gradually to 5,150′ for a total elevation loss of about 1,050′. Side loops onto the surrounding plateaus require steep climbs of approximately 2,000′.

Season: Nine Mile Canyon is at its best whenever it is dry. However, the area can be quite hot during July and August. Black flies can be nasty in May and early June. Spring is a good choice, but autumn is even better.

Services: Services, what services? Water can be filtered from Nine Mile Creek, but Wellington is the last outpost for drinking water and, more importantly, beer, ice, and junk food. There are some good, cheap motels and restaurants along the highway in Wellington. Beyond that it's sticksville. Backcountry camping is available up the passable side canyons. Avoid camping at ruins or near rock art panels; these places have been vandalized in the past.

Hazards: The area can be hot in summer so bring an adequate water supply. Traveling Nine Mile road is not recommended when it's wet, because the clay-based road can turn instantly to potter's slip. The remote network of optional side routes, which are dead dry and utterly deserted, can be confusing. But don't be daunted; these trails are worth exploring. Be sure to take a map, compass, repair kit, knowledge, food, and way more water than you expect to drink . . . or you'll end up as buzzard meat.

Steve Howe.

Rescue index: Anyone who finds his/her way into Nine Mile Canyon will realize how remote this area is. Emergency help might be available at the various ranches lining the canyon's bottom, but serious medical attention is at least an hour from where you park, and perhaps days away from the side loops. Be careful! You're on your own.

Land status: Bureau of Land Management, Price River Resource Area. Private lands border much of the Nine Mile Canyon road, but the main road and most side canyon roads are on public land. Abide by the posted signs.

Maps: USGS 7.5 minute quadrangles: Cowboy Bench, Currant Canyon, Minnie Maud Creek West, Pine Canyon, Pinnacle Canyon, and Wood Canyon, Utah; USGS 1:100,000 metric topographic series: Price, Utah.

Finding the trail: A BLM sign, located 8 miles south of Price and 3 miles east of Wellington on the north side of US 6, marks the beginning of a 45-minute drive along asphalt and eventually along a dirt road. The road climbs Soldier Creek drainage into pinyon- and juniper-covered canyons. You will pass the

Soldier Creek Mine, a corrugated tin building on your left. Soon afterward, the road descends slightly into Nine Mile Canyon and across the bridge spanning Minnie Maud Creek.

Sources of additional information:

Bureau of Land Management
Moab District
Price River Resource Area
900 North 7th East
Price, Utah 84501
(801) 637-4584

Castle Country Travel Council
P.O. Box 1037
Price, Utah 84501
(801) 637-2788

Nine Mile Canyon, A Guide, by Castle Country Travel Council, Price, Utah

Notes on the trail: There are no enticing turnoffs between the Soldier Creek Mine and the main Nine Mile drainage, but you may swear you're lost anyway. The first signed turnoff within Nine Mile Canyon is Sheep Canyon, more than 27 miles from US 6. Keep an eye out for the small sign that sits to the right of the road.

Sheep Canyon is a good starting point since it also offers a short, easy ride to an excellent petroglyph panel. But that leaves a 50-mile out-and-back ride to take in all of Nine Mile Canyon. An alternate parking area/trailhead is Gate Canyon, located about 9 miles beyond Sheep Canyon. This leaves about a 30-mile out-and-back. Drive down the canyon even farther to Dry or Cottonwood Canyons for shorter options.

If you're lucky, you might spot some of the wildlife in the area, which is home to black bear, cougar, elk, mule deer, coyote, wolverine, and bobcat. You're most likely to encounter them at dawn or at dusk, but you'll see tracks at all hours. Remember: be a polite guest; just because you're not in a Park or Wilderness Area doesn't mean you can trash the place.

The broad valley of Nine Mile Creek also supports cattle grazing and hay fields. The main operation is at the historic Nutter Ranch, located at the outlet of Gate Canyon. (Preston Nutter was the first stockman to run cattle into eastern Utah in the late 1870s. The extensive working ranch still harbors an original hand-hewn log tavern complete with packed dirt floor, hitching post, and newspaper clippings from the shootouts that occurred there in the 1890s.)

For the more physically ambitious, excellent side trips are available up Cow Canyon, Sheep Canyon, Argyle Creek, Cottonwood, Franks, and particularly the Harmon-to-Prickly Pear Canyon Loop. The road surfaces vary, but Harmon-to-Prickly is an excellent endeavor for advanced riders who are well versed in technical riding.

Harmon Canyon is steep and rocky. Its 2,000′ climb deposits you on top of the West Tavaputs Plateau, where you'll have excellent views of the Badlands Cliffs to the northeast. A flat road network takes you past the "Interplanetary

Airstrip" (so called on topographical maps) and down the steep, bouldery switchbacks of Prickly Pear Canyon.

One final and important note: In accordance with the Antiquities Act of 1906 and the Archaeological Resources Protection Act of 1979, it is illegal to disturb or deface any archaeological site or to remove artifacts. Enforcement is by substantial fines and/or imprisonment.

RIDE 49 *BUCKHORN WASH / WEDGE OVERLOOK*

The San Rafael Swell, a kidney-shaped uplift in east-central Utah, is graced with a wealth of scenic splendors and Canyon Country attributes thought to be exclusive to Utah's famed national parks. But unlike these national "parking lots," as Edward Abbey has referred to them, the San Rafael Swell sees far fewer visitors, thus enabling it to retain its primitive beauty. A member of Captain John W. Gunnison's government-lead survey that took place over a century ago saw the region as "an absolutely sterile country . . . not even a wolf could make a living." Today, we can't get enough of this desert sanctuary.

The Buckhorn Wash/Wedge Overlook route is a fine introduction to the San Rafael Swell. From lithified sentinels—Bottleneck, Window Blind, and Assembly Hall Peaks—that reign over the San Rafael River, you will venture into the redrock gash of Buckhorn Wash. Along the way, the canyon's enclosing cliffs are topped with sandstone domes; above the domes are more cliffs. Buttes rest atop buttes; dark alcoves hide in high ledges, and rock ceilings arch overhead. Pecked and painted on the canyon's walls are vestiges of the Fremont Indians, earlier visitors who inhabited this desert region 1,000 years ago. As mysterious as the reason for the Fremont Indians' disappearance are the indecipherable messages in their bizarre rock art.

The head of Buckhorn Wash succumbs to vast desert prairies. A distant peppering of juniper will be your only companion as you pedal across this bleak and painfully desolate area. If you persevere, however, you will be duly rewarded when, without much warning at all, the Earth opens up to a yawning chasm of incomprehensible size and fantastic form. This is the Wedge Overlook; beneath you drops the San Rafael River Gorge (coined "Utah's Little Grand Canyon"). Earlier in the day when you were beside the river's bridge, the San Rafael was a fair stream; "rim-rocked" at the Wedge Overlook, the river apears to be no more than a twisted thread. Quietly appreciate one of the Colorado Plateau's sublime viewpoints.

This 35-mile out-and-back route is actually the combination of two individual tours. Buckhorn Wash is 22 miles round-trip, and the Wedge Overlook is about 12 miles round-trip. Together, the entire route is intermediate/advanced level; individually, each is novice/intermediate level. The entire tour travels

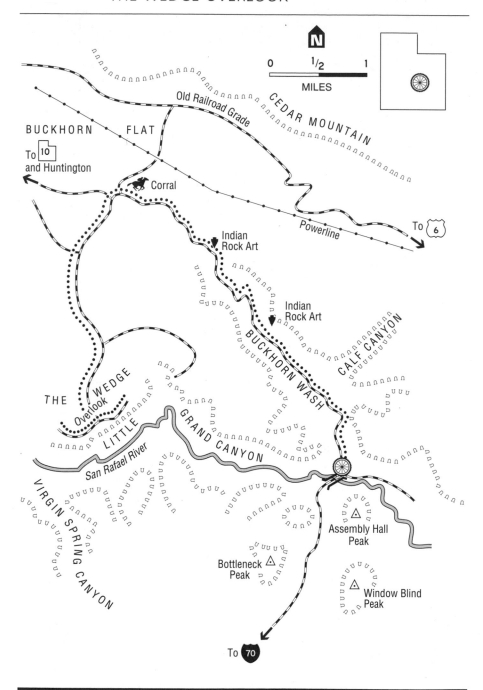

The San Rafael River Gorge—Utah's "Little Grand Canyon."

improved dirt roads marked by gentle grades, some washboarding, and negligible technical difficulty. Allow yourself all day to complete the trip; there is plenty of sightseeing and peripheral exploring to do.

General location: The San Rafael Swell is located in central Utah about 15 miles west of Green River. Buckhorn Wash and the Wedge Overlook are both in the northern Swell, 20 miles north of Interstate 70.

Elevation change: The San Rafael River at the mouth of Buckhorn Wash is at the route's lowest elevation at 5,100′. The top of Buckhorn Wash is 5,600′, a mere 500′ gain. Extending the ride to the Wedge Overlook entails an additional 700′ to 6,283′. Total vertical gain from the river to the overlook is about 1,200′.

Season: Spring (March through May) and fall (September through mid-November) are the best times to visit the San Rafael Swell. Midsummer is *very* warm and insects can be bothersome, especially near water sources. Rain may make dirt roads impassable. Blooming desert flowers peak by late April. Fall is surprisingly striking when golden hues of cottonwoods, willows, and tamarisks compliment the fiery tones of surrounding sandstones.

Services: There are no services along this route or within an hour's drive of the trailhead. A primitive BLM campground (more popular with cattle than campers) is located at the San Rafael River Bridge. It offers tables and outhouses, but no water taps. Backcountry camping is allowed throughout the Swell, unless posted otherwise. Huntington and Castle Dale (both located west in Castle Valley) offer most visitor services, including limited lodging, cafes, and gasoline. The closest bike shop is in Price.

Hazards: Dirt roads are suitable for passenger cars and aren't technically difficult for bicycles. Since this is a desert environment, carry plenty of water both on your bike and in your vehicle. All surface waters should be purified.

Buckhorn Wash is the main thoroughfare through the northern San Rafael Swell, so expect to see some vehicular traffic. ATVs and off-road vehicles visit the area, especially on weekends and holidays. Use caution rounding blind corners and be ready to share the road.

Rescue index: The San Rafael Swell is a popular spot for recreationists and sightseeing motorists, so you're likely to encounter others. You are a minimum of 30 miles from emergency contacts (Castle Dale and Huntington) and about 50 miles from a hospital (Price).

Land status: Bureau of Land Management, San Rafael Resource Area.

Maps: USGS 7.5 minute quadrangles: Bob Hill Knob, Bottleneck Peak, Buckhorn Reservoir, and Sids Mountain, Utah; USGS 1:100,000 metric topographic series: Huntington and San Rafael Desert, Utah.

Finding the trail: One of San Rafael Swell's assets is that it is easily accesible. From Green River, travel about 30 miles west on I-70 to Exit 129/Ranch Exit. Head north on the dirt road 21 miles to the bridge over the San Rafael River. The campground and adjacent areas along the river provide ample parking and a good base camp. Begin pedaling northwest on the main road up Buckhorn Wash.

From Price, head south on UT 10, pass through Huntington, then continue 7.5 miles toward Castle Dale. Look for an old wooden corral next to a dirt road (between mileposts 40 and 39) marked with a BLM sign reading "Buckhorn Wash, Wedge Overlook." You'll encounter the Wedge Overlook road after about 13 miles. Two miles farther is the turnoff for Buckhorn Wash. Drive down Buckhorn Wash to reach the San Rafael River.

Sources of additional information:

Bureau of Land Management
Price River Resource Area
900 North 7th East
Price, Utah 84501
(801) 637-4584

Castle Country Travel Council
P.O. Box 1037
Price, Utah 84501
(801) 637-2788

Mountain Biking Utah's Canyon and Plateau Country, by Gregg Bromka (Off-Road Publications, Salt Lake City, Utah)

Notes on the trail: From the San Rafael River bridge, pedal up the main dirt road into the mouth of Buckhorn Wash. Immediately, precipitous sandstone walls lock the canyon in an open embrace. After 2 miles, Calf Canyon enters from the right. Its four-wheel-drive road, although tempting, is just one big sand box.

Up canyon another 2 miles are the Buckhorn Indian Writings. Although faded and abhorrently vandalized, the assemblage of winged anthropomorphs (humanoids), coiled serpents, and indecipherable pictographs (paintings on rock) are worthy of long, pensive study and many photographs.

At the cattle guard (7.5 miles up canyon), park and walk the path toward the northern cliffs, where you'll find another fine rock art panel of petroglyphs, this time of box-shaped deer and what look like big horn sheep, stick figures, rows of dots, and linked humanoids.

Two miles past the cattle guard, the head of the canyon rises up to meet broad desert prairies. At the road junction, fork left/west toward Huntington/Castle Dale/UT 10. Shortly ahead, as the road bends right, fork left again onto an unsigned dirt road that rises over shallow hills. After 1.5 miles of gentle climbing, turn left on the main Wedge Overlook road (improved dirt and gravel). You'll pedal across 4.5 miles of moonscape terrain to one of the Colorado Plateau's more dramatic overlooks. You will know when to stop!

RIDE 50 *BLACK DRAGON CANYON*

As its name suggests, the San Rafael Swell (pronounced san ra-fel´) is neither a mountain nor a plateau, but a prominent bulge resembling an inverted bowl. From an aerial perspective the kidney-shaped Swell is a geologic blister on the face of the Earth. Most stunning is the San Rafael's eastern border marked by a formidable, sawtooth ridge of protracted strata that juts abruptly from the surrounding desert plains. The "Reef" as it is called is not a cliff or a straight crest-line, ". . . but a row of cusps like a battery of shark's teeth on a large scale," described by C. E. Dutton in the 1880s. Seemingly impenetrable from afar, the Reef is actually breached by sinuous canyons, or "narrows." Some of these slots constrict to less than shoulder width and block all but a mere sliver of sky above.

The Black Dragon Canyon ride is a trip through one of the Reef's corridors of sandstone. The route begins up high in the Swell's Sinbad Country where low rising mesas mingle with high desert prairies. Soon after, the route is drawn toward the Reef's menacing cusps and is then engulfed by Black Dragon Canyon. Although this passage does not pinch to claustrophobic widths, it is bound by colossal walls and overhanging alcoves. Indian rock art panels, including the elusive "black dragon" pictograph itself, adorn the canyon. In a cave along the way, you'll see handprints and drawings that look like necklaces, plus what looks like might have been a primitive means of accounting, scrawled on the walls.

This 16-mile point-to-point ride is well suited for intermediate cyclists and for strong novice bikers who have an understanding of basic technical skills. The entire route follows dirt roads of improved and four-wheel-drive varieties.

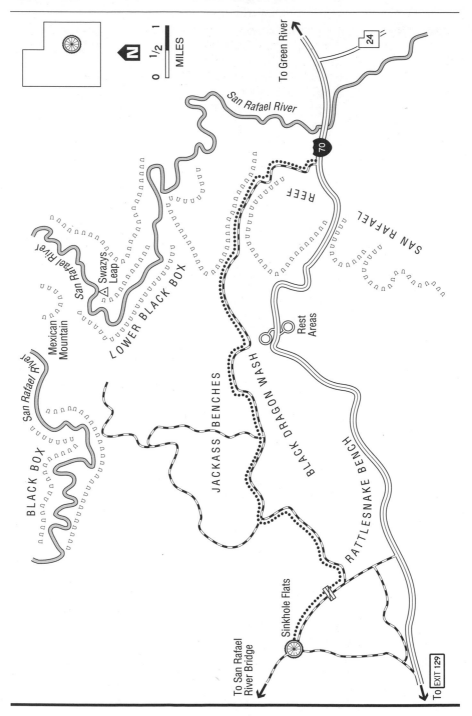

A wall of inclined cusps comprises the San Rafael Reef.

Sections are punctuated with loose cobbles and ledgy bedrock. Periodically, the canyon's dry wash bottom can mire even the knobbiest of tires. But dismounting and walking a short distance gives you a chance to crane your neck skyward to appreciate the streaks of blackened desert varnish that quench the blazing hallway.

General location: The San Rafael Swell is located in central Utah about 15 miles west of Green River. Black Dragon Canyon is just north of Interstate 70.
Elevation change: The route's trailhead at Sinkhole Flats is very near the highest elevation of the route at 6,480′. The route is downhill all the way to the mouth of Black Dragon Canyon at 4,360′, for an elevation loss of 2,120′.
Season: Spring (March through May) and fall (September through mid-November) are the best times to visit the San Rafael Swell. Midsummer is *very* warm and insects can be bothersome, especially near water sources. Rain may make dirt roads impassable. Blooming desert flowers peak by late April.
Services: There are no services along this route, nor is there any drinking water. Backcountry camping is allowed throughout the San Rafael Swell, unless otherwise posted. Remember, if you pack it in, pack it out. Green River, located 15 miles from the trail's end, offers all visitor services, but does not have a bike shop.
Hazards: Since this is a desert environment, carry plenty of water both on your bike and in your vehicle. Four-wheel-drive roads vary from smooth and fast to rough and slow. If you're exploring the slickrock at the canyon's mouth, there

are no dashed lines to indicate a main route as there are on Moab's Slickrock Trail. This is strictly freestyle biking. Use extreme caution near cliff edges.

Rescue index: The San Rafael Swell is getting more and more popular with recreationists. But you aren't likely to encounter others along the route's initial portion. Near the bottom of Black Dragon Canyon, you may encounter recreationists and sightseers, especially on weekends and holidays. Green River, located 15 miles east of the route's end, has a medical clinic.

Land status: Bureau of Land Management, San Rafael Resource Area.

Maps: USGS 7.5 minute quadrangles: Drowned Hole Draw and Spotted Wolf Canyon, Utah. (Neither shows the route.)

Finding the trail: From Green River, travel west on I-70 past Exit 147 for UT 24, Hanksville, and Capitol Reef. Between mileposts 145 and 144, look for an unsigned dirt road branching right/north off the interstate (about a half mile west after you cross over the San Rafael River). Pass through the wire gate (close it behind you) and park at your discretion. Black Dragon Canyon is about a mile down the dirt road (may or may not be suitable for passenger cars).

In your shuttle vehicle, drive west on I-70 through Spotted Wolf Canyon and take Exit 129/Ranch Exit. Travel north on the dirt and gravel road for 6 miles and park near the signed turnoff for Sinkhole Flats/Jackass Benches.

Sources of additional information:

Bureau of Land Management
Price River Resource Area
900 North 7th East
Price, Utah 84501
(801) 637-4584

Castle Country Travel Council
P.O. Box 1037
Price, Utah 84501
(801) 637-2788

Mountain Biking Utah's Canyon and Plateau Country, by Gregg Bromka (Off-Road Publications, Salt Lake City, Utah)

Notes on the trail: From the parking area near a sign for Sinkhole Flats/Jackass Benches, pedal eastward on the double-track 1.2 miles to a wire gate. Go through the gate, then turn left/east and descend across Rattlesnake Flat and past Rattlesnake Reservoir, which is usually dry. After 2.5 miles of descending, fork right at a well-defined but unsigned junction of dirt roads. The low platform of Jackass Benches rises immediately to the north. Full-throttle cruising leads 1.5 miles to the next, less evident junction. Turn right onto a four-wheel-drive road that may be marked with a rock cairn. (If you were to continue on the main road, it bends north and rises through a notch between mesa tops.)

You'll continue to descend quite fast, so watch out for ruts, gravel, and both loose and imbedded cobbles. The road drops into the wash bottom about the same time the sheer cliffs of the Reef engulf the scene. Now the route follows the sand and gravel wash bottom as it slices through the Reef. You'll want to do some sightseeing through here, so slow your pace down a bit. Look for the "Counter Cave" and go inside. The Fremont-age pictographs here consist of a series of dots combined with what look like necklaces and handprints. The hard-to-find Black Dragon pictograph is also nearby.

When you have reached the other side of the Reef, look for a short spur leading left/north to the base of a slickrock ramp. Freestyle rockin' will lead you to the very summit of the Reef, which affords vertigo-inducing views into the gut of Black Dragon.

If you loathe vehicle shuttles (or if one simply is not available), you can ride this route as a loop. But that, however, entails pounding out about 7 miles of unyielding 6-percent grades along the interstate. You'll have to contend with traffic as well, but there are few stretches of the nation's highways that are more scenic.

To do the loop, from the mouth of Black Dragon Canyon pedal west on I-70 through Spotted Wolf Canyon. The grades are steep but the play of reds, browns, and burnt orange reflecting off the protracted sandstones is spectacular. Pass the view areas and keep chugging.

Less than half a mile *west* of milepost 135, turn right/north onto a double-track. You'll then pass a sign reading "Limited Highway Access." Bear right on the good dirt road ahead, then right at the next junction to join with the main route that descends to Jackass Benches. (This last junction, located just beyond the wire gate about a mile from Sinkhole Flats, is the same one noted in the description of the point-to-point ride.)

RIDE 51 *TEMPLE MOUNTAIN*

Temple Mountain is a hub of recreational activity, from mountain biking to "narrows" hiking to exploring mining ruins. Beacon of the southern San Rafael Swell, the tower-capped mountain received its name from its resemblance to the Mormon temples found in Manti and Salt Lake City. In the past, the Temple drew to it a strong following of worshippers—but not a religious-minded congregation.

The atomic age of the 1940s and 1950s heralded a flurry of activity to the Colorado Plateau and desert southwest. Temple Mountain was the focus of much attention when prospectors and mining magnates alike scurried about Utah's Canyon Country in search of uranium and other radioactive minerals. Its maroon, gray, and chalk-white banded slopes were honeycombed with tunnels and shafts while a sizeable mining community prospered. Many found quick fortunes while others periled in financial ruin. Its life span was short, but Temple Mountain's boom days are evident in abandoned mining camps and numerous defunct mine workings that litter the district.

This 10-mile loop (clockwise) is well suited for intermediate cyclists. Pedaling around Temple Mountain and plowing through sand traps in North

RIDE 51 *TEMPLE MOUNTAIN*

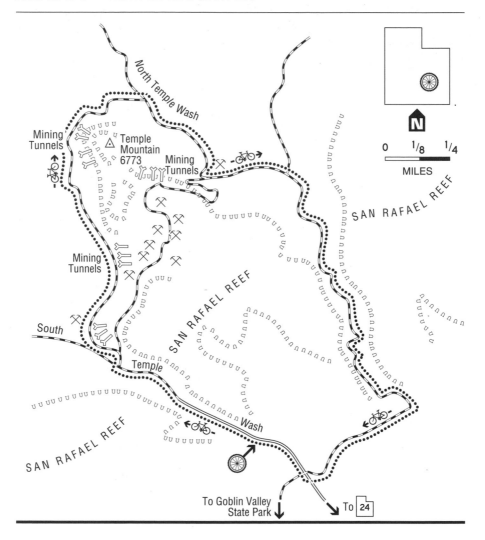

Temple Wash require some strength, but the route's four-wheel-drive roads are generally low in technical difficulty.

General location: The San Rafael Swell is located in central Utah about 15 miles west of Green River. Temple Mountain is about 30 miles south of Interstate 70 on the southeastern border of the San Rafael Swell.

Elevation change: The route's trailhead/parking area is at the lowest elevation at 5,320′. On the northwest flank of Temple Mountain, the route rises to 6,200′, for total climbing of 880′.

An abandoned mining camp haunts Temple Mountain.

Season: Spring (March through May) and fall (September through October) are the best times to visit the San Rafael Swell. Midsummer is very warm and insects can be bothersome, especially near water sources. Rain may make dirt roads impassable. The Temple Mountain/Goblin Valley State Park area is very popular during weekends and holidays, especially during spring.

Services: There are no services along this route. Backcountry camping is allowed throughout the San Rafael Swell, unless otherwise posted. Goblin Valley State Park, located 7 miles south of Temple Mountain via washboarded dirt and gravel roads, offers developed camping—including showers! But you must pay an entrance fee, even if you wish only to use the rest rooms or stock up on water.

Hazards: Since this is a desert environment, carry plenty of water both on your bike and in your vehicle. Dirt roads are low to moderate in technical difficulty. Because of the unstable conditions and threat of cave-ins and collapsing mine structures, venturing into any mine portal or shaft is very dangerous. Also, low oxygen levels may exist as well as radon "daughters" (a colorless, odorless, and potentially lethal radioactive gas that tends to accumulate in old uranium mines, usually near their entrances).

Rescue index: You are likely to encounter sightseers near the trailhead, but less so as the route winds around Temple Mountain. There is a park ranger (and radio communication) at Goblin Valley State Park, located about 7 miles south of the parking area/trailhead. Green River, located about 45 miles northeast of Temple Mountain, has a medical clinic.

Land status: Bureau of Land Management, San Rafael Resource Area.
Maps: USGS 7.5 minute quadrangle: Temple Mountain, Utah.
Finding the trail: From Green River, travel 12 miles west on Interstate 70 to Exit 147 for UT 24, Hanksville, and Capitol Reef. Head 25 miles south on UT 24. At milepost 137 and the sign for Goblin Valley/Temple Mountain, turn right/west and drive 5 miles on the paved road to the Goblin Valley turnoff. Continue straight/west on the South Temple Wash road for half a mile and park in the large clearing just before you enter the Reef, or anywhere else at your discretion.

From Hanksville, travel about 20 miles north on UT 24 to milepost 137. Turn left/west and proceed as described above.

Sources of additional information:

Bureau of Land Management
San Rafael Resource Area
900 North 7th East
Price, Utah 84501
(801) 637-4584

Castle Country Travel Council
P.O. Box 1037
Price, Utah 84501
(801) 637-2788

Mountain Biking Utah's Canyon and Plateau Country, by Gregg Bromka (Off-Road Publications, Salt Lake City, Utah)

Notes on the trail: From the parking area/trailhead, pedal west on the South Temple Wash road as it slices through the inclined San Rafael Reef. The canyon's walls reveal classic exposures of the Triassic/Jurassic-age Glen Canyon Group (see the section entitled "Slickrock," p. 205). This prominent trio of sandstones is visible throughout Canyon Country and forms many of the colorful features that typify the southwest. The Navajo Sandstone (easily recognized by its off-white color, sweeping crossbeds, and hummocky surface) comprises the outer face of the Reef. Beneath the Navajo, the Kayenta Formation forms alternating orange and brown ledges. At the base of the sequence, the reddish-orange Wingate Sandstone makes up the sheer cliffs that line the inside of the Reef.

Stop in about a half mile and look for pictographs of anthropomorphs (humanoids) and box-shaped animals on the right/north side of the canyon. One-half mile after the paved road turns to dirt, you'll breach the Reef. Beyond is Sinbad Country, a barren and bleak wasteland of varicolored terraces etched in low relief. Temple Mountain now comes into clear view, wrapped in a shawl of purple and white. Turn right/north onto a four-wheel-drive road that passes a few abandoned mining camps. The road angles around the western flank of Temple Mountain, rising gently at first and then more steeply past dozens of deserted mine tunnels and structures.

On the northwest edge of the mountain, the road appears to dead-end. Back up a few feet and turn right/east onto another four-wheel-drive road that descends around the mountain's north side. Stay on the main road past more mining camps. Sinbad Country recedes as the sandy road drops into North Temple Wash, a narrow canyon that cuts through the Reef again. Your imagination will run wild when you're greeted by the weighty presence of hollow eyes, ghoulish shapes, and melting figures that hide in this phantasmagoric sandstone hallway.

When you have passed through the Reef completely, turn right/south on a dirt road that parallels the face of the Reef and leads back to the parking area in South Temple Wash.

Allow an extra day to romp on foot among battalions of gremlin soldiers, mushroom heads, and other oddly-shaped hoodoos in the bizarre fantasyland of Goblin Valley State Park. You can hike through any of the many narrows (slot canyons) that penetrate the Reef, including Chute, Crack, Little Wild Horse, and Bells Canyons. Since these canyons are included in the Crack Canyon Wilderness Study Area, bike traffic is strongly discouraged.

RIDE 52 *TANTALUS FLATS*

Capitol Reef National Park is decidedly the focus of the Tantalus Flats tour. The Park's collection of uplifted and inclined sandstones played in colors of white, gold, and reddish orange; profound canyons that elude sunshine; and rotundas of lithified sand dunes are scenic treasures that would place this route high on any list boasting Utah's best off-road rides. But, elevating this route one step closer to mountain bike utopia is the *approach* to Capitol Reef National Park.

The tour begins high on the flanks of Boulder Mountain, where cool breezes filter through tightly spaced aspen and fir; where icy creeks tumble in bouldery, moss-encrusted channels; and where glaciation has cut the plateau's top into a series of arcuate recesses and promontories. Boulder Mountain is by definition alpine terrain, but from the mountainside trailhead, Boulder's lush forests dissipate quickly into a peppering of juniper, pinyon, and sagebrush mixed with small, grassy parks as elevation drops. Pulsating through heat vapors rising from the distant desert floor awaits Capitol Reef, marked by the Waterpocket Fold's unwavering lineation. By midday, you will drop from alpine to desert country, then follow the length of the Fold beneath its skeletal sandstone strata exposed in bold relief.

This point-to-point trip requires a vehicle shuttle. Depending on where you leave your pick-up vehicle, at the Visitor Center or the end of the paved Scenic Drive, it is a 30-mile, intermediate-level or 20-mile, strong novice-level ride, respectively. Twenty miles of dirt roads and double-track (varying from hard-packed dirt to loose stones and cobbles to mixed sand and gravel) drop from Boulder Mountain through Capitol Reef. The paved Scenic Drive leads ten miles back to the Visitor Center. The route is not technically difficult, except for

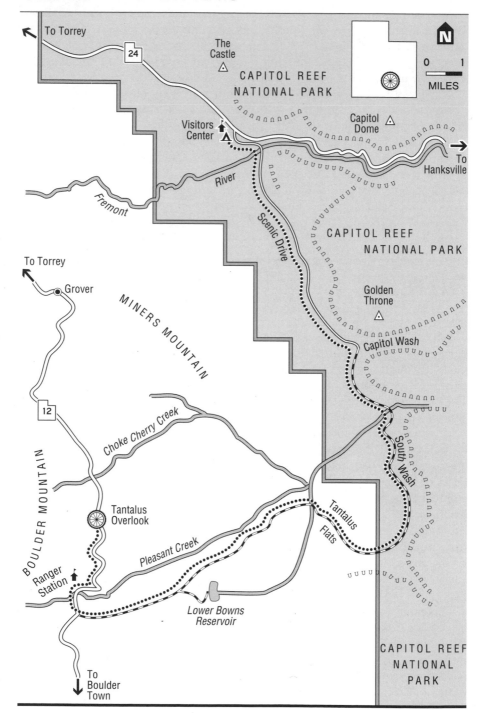

Near route's end along the Scenic Drive.

a few sections that are moderately so. Of course, those who scoff at vehicle shuttles can tackle the entire 60-mile loop. Rest assured, day's end will bring weary bones and a great "feeling" of accomplishment.

General location: Located in south-central Utah, Tantalus Flats begins up on the eastern flank of Boulder Mountain and then drops through the midsection of Capitol Reef National Park.

Elevation change: The parking area/trailhead is at the route's highest elevation at 8,750′. The route's lowest elevation is at its end at the Visitor Center, elevation 5,400′. For the most part, this is a downhill ride, but there is some climbing involved: a 450′ rise from Tantalus Flats to the National Park boundary, plus 550′ of incremental climbing along the Scenic Drive. Total ascending is about 1,000′; total descending is closer to 4,000′.

Season: This route has a fairly long season beginning in early spring (March) and extending through fall (late October). Midsummer will be very warm along the final leg in Capitol Reef, but temperate on Boulder Mountain. Conversely, early and late season bring pleasant weather to Capitol Reef's desert and frigid temperatures on Boulder Mountain.

Services: There are no services along this route. Lower Bowns Reservoir has a campground but there are no water taps. Water can be found (but will have to be purified) at both Tantalus Creek and farther along at Pleasant Creek. Developed USFS campgrounds are located along UT 12 on Boulder Mountain. Capitol Reef National Park has developed campgrounds as well. Torrey offers most visitor services, including lodging, dining, limited groceries, gasoline, and minor vehicle services, but does not have a bike shop.

Hazards: Use caution when pedaling along UT 12 on Boulder Mountain and the Scenic Drive in Capitol Reef; motorists are common. Along the off-road section, you will encounter sand traps, some of which you'll have to walk through, plus loose cobbles and pavement bedrock. Two water crossings are encountered, first at Tantalus Creek and second at Pleasant Creek. Both may be hub deep, but rideable, *except* during heavy spring runoff or flash floods.

Rescue index: Motorists are common along UT 12 on Boulder Mountain and along the Scenic Drive in Capitol Reef. Fishermen and campers are attracted to Lower Bowns Reservoir. But the route's midsection (Tantalus Flats through South Wash) is remote and you'll see few travelers. You can get emergency assistance from Torrey and the park's Visitor Center.

Land status: Dixie National Forest; Capitol Reef National Park.

Maps: USGS 7.5 minute quadrangles: Bear Canyon, Fruita, Golden Throne, Grover, and Lower Bowns Reservoir, Utah.

Finding the trail: Leave a vehicle at Capitol Reef's Visitor Center. In the shuttle vehicle, travel 10 miles west on UT 24 to Torrey. Turn left/south onto UT 12 and begin the steep ascent up Boulder Mountain. Drive 14 miles to the Tantalus Overlook, located between mileposts 110 and 109. (For more information, see Ward J. Roylance's *Tour of the Waterpocket Fold* available at the Visitor Center.) Park and embark.

Sources of additional information:

National Park Service
Superintendent
Capitol Reef National Park
Torrey, Utah 84775
(801) 425-3791

Dixie National Forest
Teasdale Ranger District
138 East Main
P.O. Box 99
Teasdale, Utah 84773
(801) 425-3702

Notes on the trail: Do not be hasty in your departure, because the scenic pandemonium that unfolds before you warrants pensive study. During the 1880s, geologist Captain Clarence E. Dutton explored these high plateaus and described the scene:

Perhaps the most striking part of the picture is the middle ground, where the great Water Pocket fold turns up the truncated beds of the [Triassic] and [Jurassic] . . . great gashes cut across the fold or perpendicular to the face of the outcrop [carving] the stratum into colossal crags and domes.

Directly east of us, beyond the domes of the flexure, rise the Henry Mountains. Among innumerable flat crest-lines, terminating in walls, they rise up grandly into peaks of Alpine form and grace like a modern cathedral among catacombs—the gothic order of architecture contrasting with the elephantine.

From the Tantalus Overlook, pedal 2 miles south on UT 12 to the Wildcat Ranger Station, then another half a mile to the signed turnoff for Lower Bowns Reservoir. Turn left and descend Forest Service Road 181—an improved dirt and gravel road. Ecosystems change rapidly from the Subalpine Life Zone (aspen and fir) to Montane (ponderosa and mixed pine) to Upper Sonoran/high desert (juniper, pinyon, and sage).

After 4 miles of easy cruising, fork left on FS 168 signed "Tantalus 5." (The right fork leads to Lower Bowns Reservoir, a haven for waterfowl.) About a mile ahead, veer left for Jorgensen Flat. This stretch descends gradually, is sometimes sandy, sometimes rocky, and sometimes hard-packed and smooth.

To your left through the juniper and pinyon, the gape of Pleasant Creek Canyon appears, widening quickly between sandstone walls baked to brilliant hues of orange and brown. Take a side trip down the rough spur to Pleasant Creek. The creek has eroded numerous bathtub-sized potholes into the sandstone-lined streambed. Each pothole has its own pour-over that is inviting on a warm summer day.

The main route descends to Tantalus Creek, where similar sun-drenched walls enclose micro-parks of tall grasses. Splash through the creek and continue eastward through the flats on a sandy double-track. The climbing becomes more aggressive as the route crosses the park boundary and rises up to a subtle pass.

Spend some time here to absorb the contrasting environment. Forested Boulder Mountain has long since receded, and grass meadows, bound by glowing sandstone mesas, lie behind. Up ahead, the Waterpocket Fold reaches far north; it will be your companion for the remaining 15 miles. Peeking through canyons that are notched into this colossal stone barrier, the Henry Mountain's 12,000′ summits shyly reveal themselves.

For the geologically inquisitive, the Waterpocket Fold is the monoclinical flexure (one-sided "fold") that gives rise to the multitude of cliff faces topped with beehive domes. Tanks (erosional depressions) that form in the sandstone hold "pockets" of water after a rain and give life to many of the desert's creatures. The Fold has created a 100-mile-long "reef"—a ridge of rock that is a land barrier. Pioneers who ventured into this region noted that many of the rock domes capping the reef resembled the rotunda on the U.S. Capitol building. Capitol Dome, which is located east of the Visitor Center, is so called because it is the best example of this type of formation.

Sections of the descent from this pass can be technical because of loose cobbles and ledgy outcroppings. Once in South Wash, the four-wheel-drive road serpentines along the dry wash bottom. Even without outstanding desert scenery, this luge-style run would be worth the trip.

When you reach Pleasant Creek, which is rideable most of the time, you can either hit it full bore and unreconnoitered or cross it cautiously after a little scouting. Either way, you'll get wet.

Three more miles of dirt road bring you to the Scenic Drive at Capitol Gorge, where 10 miles of paved cycling complete the day's tour.

RIDE 53 *MOUNT ELLEN*

The Henry Mountains were the last major mountain range to be explored and named in the lower 48 states. These mountain islands floating on the Colorado Plateau were named after Professor Joseph Henry of the Smithsonian Institute. He was an active supporter of the John Wesley Powell expeditions, which explored the Colorado River and surrounding areas in the late 1800s.

The Henrys are also home to the only free-roaming and huntable herd of American bison in the lower 48 states. In 1941, 18 head of the once-threatened species were transplanted from Yellowstone National Park to the Henry Mountains area. Today over 200 buffalo roam the western lower benches in the winter and higher elevations during summer. Seeing them up close is rare, but tremendously rewarding.

Like the La Sal and Abajo Mountains, the Henrys are would-be volcanoes whose insides did not quite reach the surface. Semi-molten rock from deep beneath the Earth's crust pushed upward but was thwarted by a massive pile of sedimentary rock. Unable to breach the surface, the magma domed the overlying rock layers and spread laterally between them, forming laccolithic intrusions. As they stand today, the Henry Mountains represent the core of the magma chamber after the capping rocks have been eroded away. Evidence of these once overlying layers are the arched sedimentary units lapping against the mountains' flanks.

This 20-mile loop (counterclockwise) is an instant Utah classic, but one that requires strong legs, and lungs acclimated to high altitudes. Although technical difficulty is low on these periodically-maintained dirt roads, the route is advanced level based on two punishing climbs: one at the very beginning of the loop and one at the end. You'll find that the chance to explore this rugged and intriguingly isolated massif, however, is well worth the effort.

General location: The Mount Ellen loop encircles the northernmost massif of the Henry Mountains and is located 21 miles south of Hanksville.

Elevation change: Lonesome Beaver Campground (trailhead) shares the route's lowest elevation with Bromide Canyon/Crescent Creek at 8,200'. Bull Creek Pass, which separates North and South Summit Ridge of Mount Ellen, rises to 10,485'. There are 3 substantial ascents along this loop: the first 2 are the back-to-back hillclimbs from Lonesome Beaver to Wickiup Pass and Wickiup to Bull Creek Pass (2,285' of vertical in 4 miles); the third is from

RIDE 53 *MOUNT ELLEN*

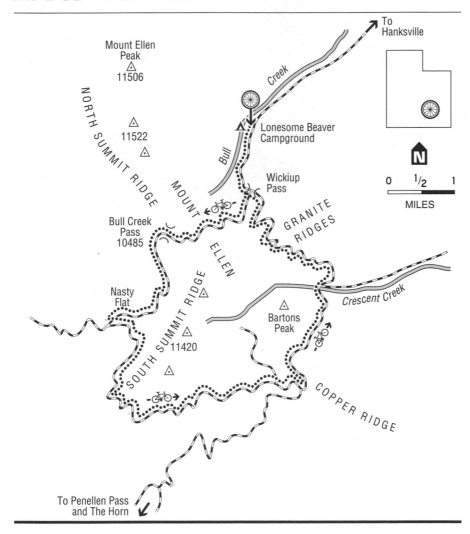

To Hanksville

Mount Ellen
Peak
△
11506

NORTH SUMMIT RIDGE

△
11522

△

MOUNT

Creek

Bull

Lonesome Beaver
Campground

Wickiup
Pass

GRANITE
RIDGES

Bull Creek
Pass
10485

Nasty
Flat

ELLEN

SOUTH SUMMIT RIDGE

△
11420

△

Bartons
Peak

△

Crescent Creek

COPPER RIDGE

To Penellen Pass
and The Horn

N

0   1/2   1
MILES

Crescent Creek back up to Wickiup Pass near the ride's conclusion (1,040′ in 1 mile). Total elevation gain is close to 4,400′.

Season: Although most of the Henry Mountains melt out by May or June, notorious snowdrifts may block Wickiup and Bull Creek Passes throughout June and possibly into July (depending on spring thaw). The route should be rideable through September and into October. These mountains are lightly forested and provide little shade from the afternoon sun, so apply sunscreen liberally. Midday temperatures are warm and nights are pleasantly cool. Afternoon thunderstorms are common and can be severe.

On reconnaissance in the Henrys.

Services: Lonesome Beaver is a developed BLM campground with 10 sites complete with tables, outhouses, and water taps. But no other source of potable water is available along the route and all surface waters should be purified. (Many creeks drain mining areas and may be tainted with heavy minerals.) Hanksville offers limited services, including lodging (very basic, no frills motels), food, and gasoline. Green River has a medical clinic.

Hazards: Although this route is generally low in technical difficulty, the sensible biker will ride well equipped with repair tools; this area is quite remote. Obtain a current weather forecast. At these elevations when the weather turns foul, it can be downright merciless and lightning can be intense.

Rescue index: This area is quite remote. Campers at Lonesome Beaver and backcountry motorists are rare. It is 20 miles of slow-going travel on dirt roads from Lonesome Beaver Campground to Hanksville and then 60 miles to Green River and medical attention. A BLM office is located in Hanksville.

Land status: Bureau of Land Management, Henry Mountain Resource Area.

Maps: USGS 7.5 minute quadrangle: Mount Ellen, Utah; USGS 1:100,000 metric topographic series: Hanksville, Utah.

Finding the trail: From Hanksville, at the junction of UT 24 and 100 North Street, turn south on 100 East next to the Post Office, where a sign reads "Lonesome Beaver 21." This road is hard-packed dirt and sand and provides good cruising for 12 miles to a signed junction near a homestead. As you continue straight/south, the road becomes progressively rougher. Clearance is not a problem, but the abundance of imbedded gravels and stones test both your patience and car's suspension. Passenger cars may be stymied 8 miles ahead at a double creek crossing. A primitive campground is 1 mile beyond the creeks. Lonesome Beaver is just a half mile farther, but coarse gravels and angular cobbles may make the primitive campground an inviting parking area.

Sources of additional information:

Bureau of Land Management
Henry Mountain Resource Area
P.O. Box 99
Hanksville, Utah 84734
(801) 542-3461

Notes on the trail: From Lonesome Beaver Campground, the route begins immediately with an unforgiving hillclimb to multi-signed Wickiup Pass, followed by a second gradual uphill grind to Bull Creek Pass. The route rises through mixed forests to open tundra meadows.

A rewarding deviation at Bull Creek Pass is the short hike out along Mount Ellen's North Summit Ridge, where you are treated to endless views across southern and central Utah: the domed San Rafael Swell; the Blue Hills badlands and Factory Butte; Capitol Reef and the Waterpocket Fold; high plateaus of Aquarius, Thousand Lake, and Fish Lake; wastelands and convoluted redrock of Canyonlands' Maze District; and distant views of sister mountain islands of the Abajos and La Sals.

Just a morsel of descending will tease you because there is one more small but grumble-inducing climb beyond Bull Creek Pass. Thereafter, it is a screaming downhill ride to Nasty Flat, which is marked by a small patch of wind-whipped aspen huddled amidst a grassy meadow and a junction signed "McMillon Spring, UT 24." Turn sharply left/eastward to continue the loop on a gentle contour around the southwestern flank of South Summit Ridge.

When you are at the loop's southern tip, you can see how Mount Ellen is separated from its spouse, Mount Pennell, by the spacious void of Pennellen Pass. The Horn, a muscular but topographically insignificant hump cuddled in the pass, is the igneous offspring produced by these parental massifs.

The road continues eastward around South Summit Ridge, winding into lightly forested drainages that crease the mountain's massive flank, then back out across open ridges that extend from its main crest. A number of ramps will keep the thighs well pumped and lungs fully expanded. There are 2 road junctions on the mountain's southeastern point. The first is a spur that angles northward up into Bromide Basin. Stay straight/east for some rapid descending to the second junction signed "Copper Ridge." Turn left/north to swing around the mountain's eastern front.

There are huge overviews of desert and hopelessly deserted wilderness that extend *ad infinitum* from the base of the Henrys. The Dirty Devil, Green, and Colorado Rivers, backed by intermittently voracious tributaries, have indiscriminately consumed this bleak and unproductive terrain. The parts that are more resistant to erosion remain as an impossible-to-reconnoiter sandstone labyrinth.

The descent into Crescent Creek precedes the final gut-busting assault back up to Wickiup Pass. Sorry, but there are no flowery superlatives to smooth over this otherwise grueling ascent. Forget the scenery and stop conversing. Concentrate on "power breathing" and pedaling in smooth circles to take advantage of every muscle group. Remember, if you're pedaling, you're not walking! It is only a mile and a half up to Wickiup Pass. (If you still feel fresh, place bets on who can make it the farthest up the angular double-track rising due south from Wickiup Pass's directional signs.) Finish the loop with a palm-bruising, but vengeful, descent to Lonesome Beaver.

RIDE 54   WOLVERINE ROAD

The Wolverine Road takes you into the colorful past of prehistoric southern Utah. The route leads to the Wolverine Petrified Wood Natural Area. More than 200 million years ago these trees were buried under a protective layer of soil. While buried, the wood dissolved and was replaced by a silica material. Through erosion, these "hardwoods" have been liberated from the shaley substrate.

Much of Wolverine's allure is the journey to it via the Boulder to Bull Frog Road (commonly referred to as the Burr Trail). The approach begins high on the cool alpine slopes of flat-topped Boulder Mountain. You'll dive into a quickly changing realm of slickrock beehives and checkerboard mesas. The road pursues the sun-drenched crease of Long Canyon, a postcard-perfect corridor encased by luminous Wingate palisades, to the brink of the Circle Cliffs. The Cliffs, which stand in bold relief, ring a terminally forsaken but decidedly pristine desert basin. It is through this vanishing segment of the West's romantically wild terrain that the route passes.

This 36-mile loop (counterclockwise) follows good four-wheel-drive roads that periodically receive the blade of a plow. Upbeat downhills highlight the first third of the route, followed by a middle segment of moderate climbing that seems endless. The loop culminates with easy cruising along the recently paved Burr Trail. The entire loop is advanced-level. Energetic novice and intermediate cyclists may opt for the 18-mile out-and-back ride to the Wolverine Petrified Wood Area.

General location: The Wolverine Road lies between the southern portion of Capitol Reef National Park and Boulder Town and swings south off the Burr Trail.

Elevation change: The Wolverine Road's western junction with the Burr Trail

RIDE 54 *WOLVERINE ROAD*

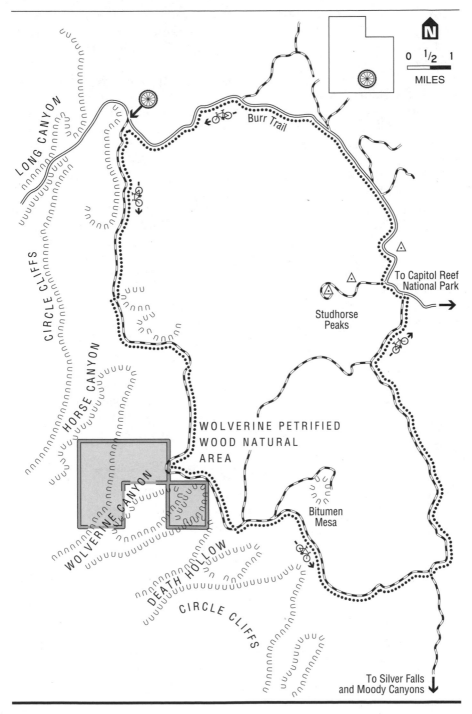

N

0   1/2   1
MILES

Burr Trail

LONG CANYON

CIRCLE CLIFFS

HORSE CANYON

WOLVERINE CANYON

WOLVERINE PETRIFIED
WOOD NATURAL
AREA

DEATH HOLLOW

CIRCLE CLIFFS

Studhorse
Peaks

To Capitol Reef
National Park

Bitumen
Mesa

To Silver Falls
and Moody Canyons

(starting point) is at 5,880'. The road descends gently to 5,400' at the Wolverine Petrified Wood Natural Area. Thereafter, the route oscillates up to 6,800' at the Wolverine Road's eastern junction with the Burr Trail. Total elevation gain is about 2,800'.

Season: This route is best enjoyed during spring (April through June) and fall (September through October). Midsummer is very warm and insects are annoying. This route does not pass any reliable water sources, so carry 2 to 3 oversized bottles. Rainstorms may make portions of the route impassable and may flood otherwise dry creekbeds.

Services: This route is reserved for self-sustained, backcountry camper types. There are no services within 20 miles of the trailhead. And at that, Boulder Town offers bare-bones visitor amenities—2 or 3 eating establishments, very limited groceries, and gasoline—usually. Beyond Boulder, it is nearly 50 miles north to Torrey or south to Escalante, both of which are one-horse towns. There is a semi-developed BLM campground at Deer Creek, located 6 miles east of Boulder Town. (The area hosts a half dozen tent sites with tables and an outhouse but no water taps. Water from the nearby creek should be purified.)

Hazards: Lack of preparedness is the greatest potential hazard. This route is remote, dry, and desolate, so carry plenty of water, food, and appropriate repair tools. Rain may turn portions of hard-packed road into viscous, claylike mud. Downpours may cause dry creekbeds to fill with some water, but should not make them impassable.

Rescue index: With the recent paving of Burr Trail, tourist traffic has increased between Boulder Town and points east (Capitol Reef and Lake Powell's Bull Frog Marina). Even so, you won't see many motorists. Solitude is the norm along the Wolverine Road, except for a visitor or two at the Petrified Wood Natural Area. A phone can be found in Boulder Town, but emergency assistance will come from Torrey or Escalante.

Land status: Bureau of Land Management, Escalante Resource Area.

Maps: USGS 7.5 minute quadrangles: Bitter Creek Divide, Bitumen Mesa, Lamp Stand, and Wagon Box Mesa, Utah.

Finding the trail: From Boulder Town and UT 12, travel east on the Boulder–Bull Frog Scenic Backway (the Burr Trail). Drop into "The Gulch" (an Outstanding Natural Area), then up through scenic Long Canyon. Descend from the top of Long Canyon 1.7 miles to the junction with the Wolverine Road. You'll find a sign for Boulder 19 and Burr Trail 17 *behind* a juniper. Park at your discretion.

Sources of additional information:

Bureau of Land Management
Escalante Resource Area
P.O. Box 225
Escalante, Utah 84726
(801) 826-4291

The Burr Trail slips into Long Canyon.

Notes on the trail: From the western junction of the Wolverine Road and Burr Trail, pedal south on the good four-wheel-drive road. The road is hard-packed sand and clay and descends gently, so the pace is brisk. After 4 miles, the road dips through a (usually) dry creekbed coated with thick sand and gravel. A mile farther, hop through another gulch marked with a BLM sign for Horse Canyon. Float through intermittent sand, gravel, and gulches for 4 more miles to a junction sign that reads "Wolverine Petrified Wood Area." There is a small parking area up ahead to the right. Lock, tether, or stash your trusty steed and take to foot.

Inside the fence line, there is a trail (of sorts) that leads through sage and cactus deserts, over knolls, into dry washes, and across sandy wastes. Hoof out about a mile or so staying generally in or close to the (somewhat) prominent creekbed. Your destination is the band of spreading slopes that flare out like calico skirts below the rust-orange cliffs to the west. These smoothly weathered humps of grey, tan, maroon, and chocolate-brown claystone host the silicified timber.

Small pieces of petrified wood are scattered about. You'll find cracked but aligned segments of partial limbs and whole logs. Stumps and severed trunks form perfect stools, ottomans, and end tables; other pieces are simply rough-cut wheels from Fred Flintstone's Stone Age car. *Note: collecting petrified wood is prohibited.* Besides, a fist-sized specimen will quickly defeat the purpose of your several hundred dollars' worth of titanium add-ons. And, of course, a feather-light bike takes precedence over whimsical paper weights.

Back to the signed junction, head east on the main road to continue the loop. Three miles ahead, pass a wooden corral, then stay straight when a spur branches left/north. Big chainring cruising precedes several miles of gradual but sustained climbing to Moody Road, where you turn left at a sign for Burr Trail Road. The right turn is signed "Silver Falls and Moody Canyons." You'll reach the paved Burr Trail after 8 endless miles of soul searching across a pictureless land of dust and scrub.

The Burr Trail was one of Utah's great backcountry roadways that lead through this stark but pristine desert landscape. In recent years the Burr developed into a battleground between environmentalists, land managers, and county commissioners. The heated debate centered on whether the Burr Trail should remain a four-wheel-drive dirt road or upgraded to boat-towing RV standards. After hearings, appeals, and quick court actions, the Burr met its demise and was "improved," but only after a few incidences of attempted sabotage, no doubt encouraged by Edward Abbey's novel *The Monkey Wrench Gang*.

Even a staunch environmentalist will welcome the shoddy chip and seal that now coats the road, though, for the past laborious miles can leave you feeling "bonked." The remaining 10 miles is easy cruising, and the complex scenery of desert growth, redrock palisades, and distant forested plateaus is overwhelming.

Be sure to stop at Anasazi State Park before or after you ride. Located on the north end of Boulder Town (which is less than a stone's throw from the south end of Boulder Town), the park is a place to explore the habitation and cultural significance of the "Ancient Ones." You'll find exhibits, murals, and a wealth of literature inside the small museum there. Outside, a short, self-guided tour takes you through the partially excavated village.

RIDE 55 *FIFTYMILE BENCH*

As you drive out the Hole in the Rock Road from Escalante, two features are readily apparent. To the east the Escalante Desert is a despairing wasteland of desert scrub and cacti, drift sand, and sun-baked slickrock. Features of discernible relief only periodically interrupt the general levelness. But if you attempt traveling toward the center of this tableland your progress will be impeded by hundred- or thousand-foot drops from an unforeseen canyon's edge. To the west are two superimposed cliff lines extending as far as the eye can see. The upper tier is a ruler-straight escarpment, hence named the Straight Cliffs of the Kaiparowits Plateau. The lower platform is a succession of cusps jutting out from a common bench. Fifty miles to the south, the Escalante Desert and the lower and upper terraces converge. The first row of cliffs has been tagged Fiftymile Bench.

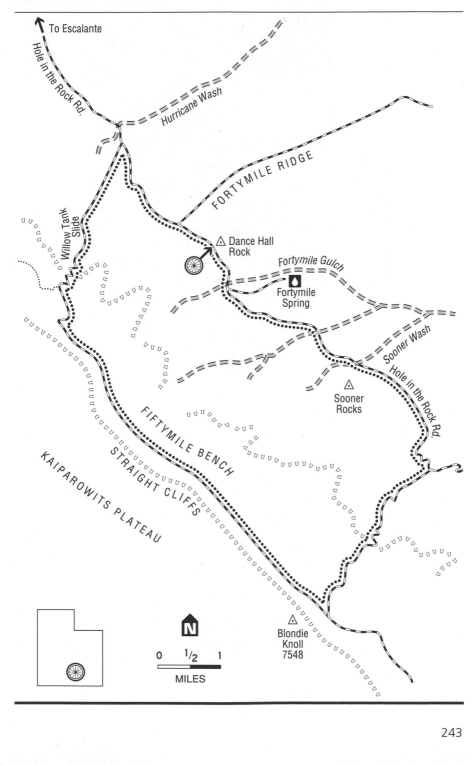

To Escalante

Hole in the Rock Rd.

Hurricane Wash

FORTYMILE RIDGE

Willow Tank Slide

△ Dance Hall Rock

Fortymile Gulch

Fortymile Spring

Sooner Wash

Hole in the Rock Rd.

△ Sooner Rocks

FIFTYMILE BENCH

STRAIGHT CLIFFS

KAIPAROWITS PLATEAU

N

0 1/2 1

MILES

△ Blondie Knoll 7548

The Escalante Desert extends *ad infinitum* beneath Fiftymile Bench.

From atop Fiftymile Bench, you'll gain a true perspective of the lay of the land. The lower badlands are characterized by a profusion of inverted topography. The meandering lines of darkness you see are shadow-filled canyons etched into the desert's face. These narrow slots feed into deep hallways, which in turn join widened corridors. Corridors fuse with the Escalante River gorge, which ultimately joins with flooded Glen Canyon of the Colorado River.

This 27-mile loop (clockwise) not only provides a unique scenic experience, it makes for a great early season training ride. It combines mile upon mile of flat ground to dial in your cadence with dozens of short interval bursts out of deep gullies. Best of all, there is a sustained 4-mile, heart-pumping, leg-searing, 2,000′ climb thrown in for good measure. Most of the route is low in technical difficulty, but a mile-long descent of boulder bashing will test the fearless and adept biker.

General location: This segment of the Hole in the Rock Road begins at Dance Hall Rock, located about 42 miles southeast of Escalante.

Elevation change: Dance Hall Rock is at 4,600´. The Hole in the Rock Road dips through numerous steep-walled gulches that tally elevation gain quickly. But you'll gain the most elevation during the direct, 2,000´ ascent of Fiftymile Bench that rises to 6,500´. Total climbing exceeds 3,200´.

Season: This region of southern Utah is best enjoyed during spring (March through most of June) and fall (September through mid-November). Midsummer can be stiflingly hot and insects are a nuisance.

Services: There are no services along this route nor are there any reliable water sources. Escalante offers most visitor services, including lodging, food, groceries, and gasoline. Backcountry camping is allowed along the Hole in the Rock Road, unless otherwise posted. Escalante has an outdoor shop that may offer bike-related supplies but no true mountain bike accessories.

Hazards: This route is dry, dusty, and desolate. Carry plenty of water, food, and appropriate tools. Use a liberal amount of sunscreen. The Hole in the Rock Road dips through steep-walled gulches, so use caution when descending around blind corners.

Be careful on the descent off Fiftymile Bench, which requires stalwart bike handling. It is a wide-eyed, white-knuckle freefall along a deeply rutted, rock-clogged, four-wheel-drive road. (You'll lose 1,000 feet of elevation over the next mile.)

Violent afternoon cloudbursts may produce flash floods that can make sections of the Hole in the Rock Road impassable. High clearance and four-wheel-drive vehicles have an obvious advantage.

Rescue index: The farther you venture from Escalante on the Hole in the Rock Road, the less frequently you will encounter others. You'll rarely encounter four-wheel-drive vehicles and ATVs on Fiftymile Bench. Escalante has medical facilities but is located 42 teeth-chattering, washboarded miles and several hours away from the trailhead at Dance Hall Rock.

Land status: Bureau of Land Management, Escalante Resource Area.

Maps: USGS 7.5 minute quadrangles: Big Hollow Wash, Blackburn Canyon, and Sooner Bench, Utah.

Finding the trail: The Hole in the Rock Road branches south from UT 12 about 5 miles east of Escalante (near milepost 65). Dance Hall Rock is located 37 miles down the regularly-maintained sand and dirt road. The first 5 to 10 miles are smooth and suitable for near-highway speeds. Beyond, the road can have the most severe, devilish washboarded surface imaginable. Whether you travel this section at 5 mph or 50 mph, your teeth will chatter and bolts will rattle.

Sources of additional information:

Bureau of Land Management
Escalante Resource Area
P.O. Box 225
Escalante, Utah 84726
(801) 826-4291

Notes on the trail: This route begins at Dance Hall Rock, a solitary hump of sandstone that doubled as an outdoor amphitheater during the 1879 Mormon pioneer trek to Hole in the Rock.

From the "Hall," follow the Hole in the Rock Road 3.6 miles south to Sooner Wash and Sooner Rocks, then travel another 2.8 miles to the signed Fiftymile Bench Road. Turn right/west to begin the 2,000′ ascent. The road begins as soft but bladed sand and gravel. Gradually the road angles upward more steeply. With elevation, the road's quality deteriorates for vehicular access but actually improves for mountain bikes.

This is a great hillclimb: unyielding but not relentless, demanding but not agonizing. It does require well-conditioned legs and bellows for lungs. You'll reach a false summit a half mile beyond a steel gate. The true summit awaits another 1.5 miles ahead and is marked by a T junction.

Turn right/north at the T junction on a double-track that passes through juniper, pinyon, and mixed pine, plus a few aspen sheltered in recessed canyons. During springtime, purple lupine bloom with profusion on the Bench. The Straight Cliffs rise another 1,000′ immediately overhead. For the next 7 miles, the Bench road maintains a nearly level grade with short, interval-training surges mixed in.

Pass a wooden corral and a small pasture. A few miles beyond, the road begins to descend. A mile into the downhill you'll reach a junction at the head of Willow Tank Slide Canyon. This is a good time to lower your seat, cinch down the helmet, and secure all belongings; the plunge off Fiftymile Bench is wicked. Forearms will burn, back will ache, and brakes will smoke.

Once you're off Fiftymile Bench, you'll travel on 2 miles of soft, sandy double-track to the Hole in the Rock Road, followed by a mile of persistent washboarded surface back to Dance Hall Rock.

RIDE 56   *HOLE IN THE ROCK*

To extend its boundaries and promote its principles, the Mormon Church decided to establish a settlement in the Four Corners Area. During October of 1879, families, their livestock, and 80 wagons left the comforts of Escalante on a historic migration across Utah's southeastern desert. The chosen route would

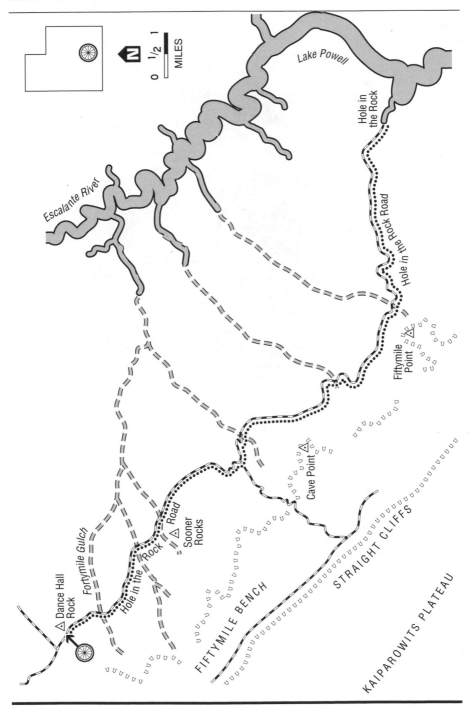

An aerial view of Lake Powell from the Hole in the Rock.

require an unfathomable descent from the rim of the Colorado River Gorge down through the precipitous passageway called the Hole in the Rock.

Crossing the inhospitable Escalante Desert was the travelers' first challenge. But midway to the Hole in the Rock, the pioneers found temporary solace at the natural sandstone amphitheater of Dance Hall Rock. Here, music, song, and merriment erased the hardships they had endured and kept momentarily at bay anxious thoughts of the Hole.

Before the migrants could descend to and then cross the Colorado River, the passageway through the Hole had to be forged. Courageous blasting crews were lowered in rope-tethered barrels to drill holes in the rock for powder charges; rock was chiseled to open the notch to wagon width; and a platform road of log, brush, rock, and gravel was tacked along a ledge to prevent wagon wheels from slipping over and pulling rig and team into a perilous plunge.

The travelers, along with wagons and livestock, made their way 1,000´ down the Hole in the Rock to the Colorado River, where a hand-hewn ferry awaited to carry them across. Their midwinter trek then continued across equally god-forsaken lands where additional hardships were faced and conquered. After what was expected to be a six-week journey, which turned into a six-month expedition, the weary migrants settled in what is known today as Bluff. Surprisingly not a soul, wagon, or animal was lost.

This 37-mile out-and-back ride follows good four-wheel-drive roads of low technical difficulty over its first 13 miles. The midsection traverses a sandy double-track punctuated by sandstone bedrock that can be moderately technical. This is an advanced-level ride, but with a high-clearance vehicle intermediate riders can shorten the route by driving to Sooner Rocks or Fiftymile Point. Beyond Fiftymile Point, four-wheel-drive is prerequisite to reach the Hole in the Rock.

General location: This segment of the Hole in the Rock Road begins at Dance Hall Rock, located about 42 miles southeast of Escalante.
Elevation change: The elevation of Dance Hall Rock is 4,600′. The Hole in the Rock Road ends above Lake Powell at 4,400′. Along the route, the road dips through dozens of steep-walled, dry drainages. Total elevation gain out-and-back approaches 2,800′.
Season: This region of southern Utah is best enjoyed during spring (March through most of June) and fall (September through mid-November). Midsummer can be stiflingly hot and insects a nuisance.
Services: There are no services along this route nor are there any reliable water sources. Water can be purified out of Lake Powell but it lies at the bottom of a 1,000′ scramble down through the Hole. Escalante offers most visitor services, including lodging, food, groceries, gasoline, and private campgrounds. The town has an outdoor shop that may offer bike-related supplies but not true mountain bike accessories.
Hazards: This route is dry, dusty, and desolate. Carry plenty of water, food, and appropriate tools. Use a liberal amount of sunscreen. The first half of the route follows improved four-wheel-drive roads that dip through steep-walled gulches. Use caution when descending around blind corners. The second half of the route follows a rough road punctuated by pavement bedrock.

Use extreme caution when exploring in and around the cliff-bound gash of the Hole in the Rock. A fall could be fatal.

Violent afternoon cloudbursts may produce flash floods that can make sections of the Hole in the Rock Road impassable. High clearance and four-wheel-drive vehicles have an obvious advantage.
Rescue index: The farther you venture from Escalante on the Hole in the Rock Road, the less frequently you will encounter others. Visitors with four-wheel-drive may venture all the way out to the Hole in the Rock, but they are sporadic even on weekends and holidays. Escalante has medical facilities but is located 42 teeth-chattering, washboarded miles and several hours away from the trailhead at Dance Hall Rock.

Land status: Bureau of Land Management, Escalante Resource Area; Glen Canyon National Recreation Area. (*Note:* Bicycling off designated roads is prohibited in the Glen Canyon N.R.A.; i.e., no slickrock exploring!)

Maps: USGS 7.5 minute quadrangles: Davis Gulch and Sooner Bench, Utah.

Finding the trail: The Hole in the Rock Road branches south from UT 12 about 5 miles east of Escalante (near mile post 65). Dance Hall Rock is located 37 miles down the regularly-maintained sand and dirt road. The first 5 to 10 miles are smooth and suitable for near-highway speeds. Beyond, the road can have the most severe, devilish, washboarded surface imaginable. Whether you travel this section at 5 mph or 50 mph, your teeth will chatter and bolts will rattle.

Sources of additional information:

Bureau of Land Management
Escalante Resource Area
P.O. Box 225
Escalante, Utah 84726
(801) 826-4291

Notes on the trail: From Dance Hall Rock, pedal southeast on the Hole in the Rock Road. The Straight Cliffs of the Kaiparowits Plateau hover to the west; an endless expanse of burnt, glowing slickrock extends to the east. Portions of the road are smooth, others are washboarded. You'll dip into and struggle out of numerous dry washes that cross the road a couple of times. After 4 miles, you'll pass Sooner Wash and Sooner Rocks (sandstone domes floating in the parched desert).

Cross the Glen Canyon Recreation Area boundary. You'll reach Fiftymile Point at the 13-mile mark. The road now grades to four-wheel-drive as it drops off a shallow bench and turns eastward. The symmetrical hump of Navajo Mountain, which marks the Utah/Arizona border, comes into full view. It is 6 miles of double-track and broken bedrock to the road's end and a visitor registration box.

If you scramble down the Hole in the Rock, you can take a cool swim in Lake Powell. On your way, notice the drill holes, chiseled steps, and deep scars that were scratched by wagon wheels a century ago. Hike up onto neighboring sandstone exposures and enjoy inspiring overlooks of Glen Canyon and Lake Powell. With your new and enlightened perspectives of this bleak but priceless land, the return ride to Dance Hall Rock won't seem so long.

RIDE 57 *GOOSEBERRY MESA*

Biking off-road within Zion National Park is forbidden, but after you stroll through this divine gallery of rock towers, weeping alcoves, and sunlight-eluding canyons, you can pedal outside the Park's boundary to Gooseberry Mesa.

RIDE 57 *GOOSEBERRY MESA*

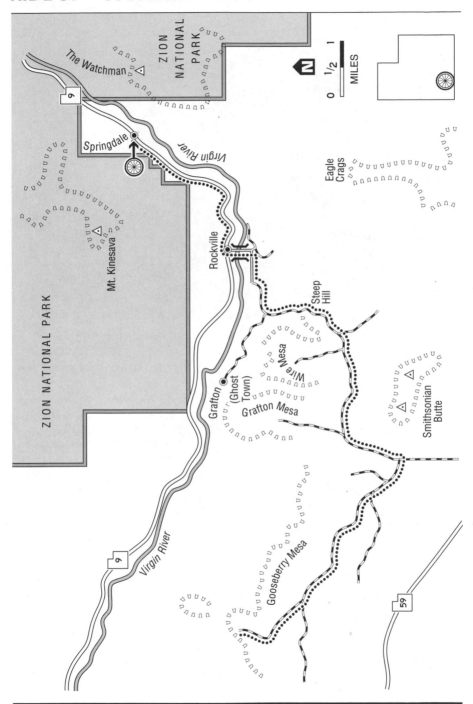

Zion National Park's Towers of the Virgin as a backdrop for Gooseberry Mesa.

This ride offers you an opportunity to pedal free from RV-clogged roads and tourist-saturated trails to points where solitude rings with deafening silence.

Colossal sandstone monuments and shadow-filled gorges frame Zion Canyon from numerous locales along this tour. From the route's terminus, Gooseberry Point overlooks the scenic complexity of the Virgin River corridor. Temples of the Virgin rise as sacred shrines and the Kolob Canyons blaze in the setting sun. There are fault-bound mesas separated by deep valleys and vermillion escarpments carved up into fanciful convolutions and cockscomb-like ridges. The nearby Pine Valley Mountains Wilderness Area interrupts the arid motif with a swollen alpine acclivity.

This 30-mile out-and-back ride follows hard-packed dirt and gravel roads along with a few miles of pavement. Technical difficulty is low throughout and the pedaling is easy, *except* for a mile-long, agonizing grade rising from the Virgin River valley up onto the surrounding mesas. This protracted climb will test even the most conditioned cyclist and gives the route an intermediate- to advance-level rating. But, novice cyclists can enjoy the route simply by thumbing their noses at the gut-wrenching hill and car-topping to Gooseberry Mesa. This option leaves a 10-mile, flat-as-a-pancake, round-trip tour atop the mesa.

General location: Gooseberry Mesa proper is located about 10 miles southwest of Springdale, which is the western gateway to Zion National Park.
Elevation change: Springdale rests at an elevation of 3,900′. The Gooseberry

Mesa road hovers at 5,000′. Elevation gain to *access* Gooseberry Mesa is 1,200′. Elevation gain out-and-back *along* the mesa is merely 400′.

Season: Utah's Dixie boasts fine off-season biking, with early spring (March through May) and late fall (September through November) being the best times of the year. Midsummer will be very warm.

Services: All visitor services, including a bike shop, can be found in Springdale at the west entrance to Zion National Park. Developed campgrounds are located in Springdale and in Zion National Park. Backcountry camping is available en route to Gooseberry Mesa on public BLM lands.

Hazards: Way out on Gooseberry Mesa, the route is seldom traveled and low in technical difficulty. Use caution pedaling the paved highway out of Springdale; you'll be traveling with motorists, including vacationers in lumbering RVs. Control your speed when you descend the steep dirt road rising out of Rockville toward Smithsonian Butte and Gooseberry Mesa. Watch for sporadic vehicular traffic on this dirt road all the way out to Gooseberry Mesa.

Rescue index: Motorists frequent the paved highway leaving Springdale. Traffic is sporadic on the dirt road leading to Gooseberry Mesa. Out on the mesa itself, there is plenty of solitude, except for a cattle rancher or two. Emergency assistance (and a medical clinic) can be found in Springdale. The route's farthest point is 15 miles from Springdale.

Land status: Bureau of Land Management, Dixie Resource Area.

Maps: USGS 7.5 minute quadrangles: Little Creek Mountain, Smithsonian Butte, Springdale West, and Virgin, Utah; USGS 1:100,000 metric topographic series: St. George, Utah.

Finding the trail: From Interstate 15, take Exit 27/UT 17 (if traveling southward from Cedar City) or Exit 16/UT 9 (if traveling northward from St. George) and head about 25 miles to Springdale and Zion National Park. Park at your discretion in Springdale. (The route actually branches south from UT 9 in the center of Rockville, located 3 miles west of Springdale; but Springdale makes for a good starting location.)

Sources of additional information:

Bureau of Land Management
Cedar City District
Dixie Resource Area
225 North Bluff
St. George, Utah 84770
(801) 673-4654

Zion Canyon Cycling Co.
998 1/2 Zion Park Boulevard
Springdale, Utah 84767
(801) 772-3929

Notes on the trail: From Springdale, pedal 3 miles west along UT 9 to Rockville. Turn left/south on Bridge Road, and cross over the Virgin River. Bear right toward Grafton and Highway 59, continuing on pavement that soon turns to maintained dirt and gravel. At the cattle guard, fork left/south on the Smithsonian Butte National Backcountry Highway where a sign reads "Highway 59, 7 miles" (the BLM sign also points to Grafton to the right/west).

The hard-packed dirt road rises gently at first, then angles very steeply for a strenuous, mile-long hillclimb. Thereafter, the road rolls 3.5 miles around the base of Smithsonian Butte to the signed junction for Gooseberry Mesa.

The improved-dirt Gooseberry road heads west out across the mesa on a fairly level keel. Vegetation varies from juniper and pinyon with a ponderosa pine or two, to sagebrush and a variety of cacti. After 3 miles, cross over a cattle guard. Shortly ahead, the road splits. Stay right and pass a relict windmill. In another 1.5 miles you'll reach the end of the road at the mesa's edge.

Another fine novice-level ride the entire family can enjoy is the short 7-mile out-and-back ride to the ghost town of Grafton. Begin in Rockville and follow the directions to Gooseberry Mesa described above. Shortly after pavement turns to dirt, turn right on a dirt/gravel road signed "Grafton, 2 miles." The road hugs vermillion cliffs that descend from mesas above, while paralleling lush farm fields that border the Virgin River.

You may recognize some of the dilapidated buildings from the famous bicycle scene in the movie *Butch Cassidy and the Sundance Kid*. Although established in what may seem an idyllic stream-filled valley, this nineteenth-century Mormon hamlet succumbed to marauding Indians, crop-killing droughts, floods, insects, and life-threatening epidemics. All that remains are 2 ranch buildings, a small cemetery, and the town schoolhouse, whose belfry is still intact but has been silenced for nearly a century.

RIDE 58   *SILVER REEF*

The Silver Reef tour travels along a broad bench of juniper, pinyon, and ponderosa pine that separates the Pine Valley Mountains from deep, redrock canyons. The route affords scenic vistas of sandstone temples and majestic peaks of distant Zion National Park, including the Guardian Angels and Towers of the Virgin. Stop occasionally, especially at the route's higher points, to catch over-the-shoulder glimpses of this famed gallery of sculpted rock.

Overhead, rugged slopes of the Pine Valley Mountains Wilderness Area contrast with checkerboard swirls etched into sandstone canyons. Toward the route's end, looming red cliffs above Warner Valley and the cultivated fields east of Washington are in view. The final descent to St. George is highlighted by miles of rock-hopping, from juniper and pinyon communities to sagebrush country to steaming desert prairies.

This 26-mile point-to-point tour follows a combination of maintained dirt/gravel roads and good four-wheel-drive roads. The last four miles are paved. On numerous occasions, the route crosses drainages and side canyons that are usually dry, but during spring runoff or after heavy rains may be flowing. Rain may also turn otherwise firm road base into viscous, clayey mud. The

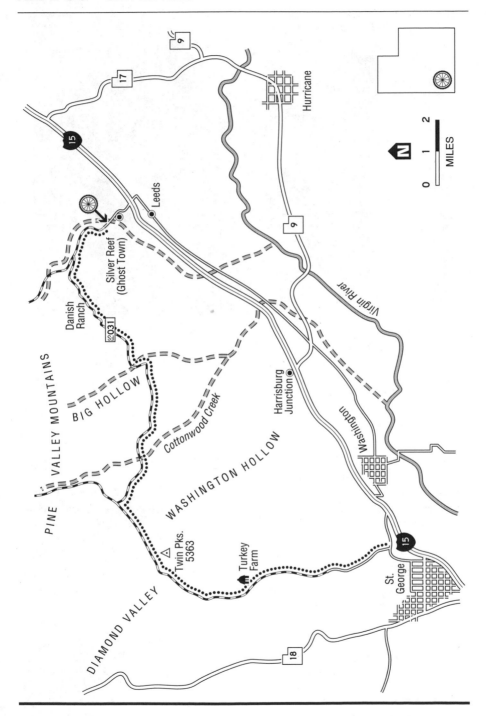

A distant view of Zion National Park from the Silver Reef route.

terrain is marked by rolling hills, moderate to difficult climbs that require stamina, and lengthy descents. Technical difficulty is low to moderate. Overall, the
route is suitable for strong intermediate to advanced cyclists.

Details for the Silver Reef chapter were provided by Kent B. McDonald and
Mark McLaughlin,[*] St. George, Utah.

General location: The Silver Reef tour begins 15 miles northeast of St. George
and traverses the southern flank of the Pine Valley Mountains.
Elevation change: From Silver Reef, elevation 3,900′, the ride begins with a
strenuous 1,200′ hillclimb. Afterward, the road crosses several ridges that separate drainages and caps 5,300′ about midroute. You'll finish the route with a
long descent to St. George, elevation 2,500′. Total elevation gain is about 2,700′.
Season: The St. George area (coined "Utah's Dixie") is noted for superb off-
season mountain biking. Spring, fall, and most of winter are quite pleasant, but
midsummer can be terribly hot with daytime temperatures consistently above
100 degrees. Start this route at daybreak during summer.

---

[*]Mark McLaughlin, owner of Bicycles Unlimited, and Kent McDonald, one of his
most loyal customers, have developed a strong camaraderie through bicycling both the
paved and backcountry routes around St. George. A native to Utah, Kent grew up in
the pastoral setting of Heber Valley in northern Utah. He relocated to St. George,
where he has been a physician for 15 years.

Services: There are no services along this route, nor any drinking water. This area can be very warm, so carry ample water supplies. St. George offers all visitor services, including bike shops. Developed campgrounds are available at Quail Creek Reservoir (BLM), located 12 miles northeast of St. George, and at Oak Creek (USFS), located in the Pine Valley Mountains 8 miles above Silver Reef.

Hazards: If you're riding during midsummer, expect daytime temperatures to exceed 100 degrees. Carry extra water and apply sunscreen liberally. Start your ride at dawn to avoid the hottest part of the day. The route is generally low in technical difficulty. Dry creeks may flow during spring runoff and after heavy rains. Wet weather may turn firm road into viscous, claylike mud—the type that eats derailleurs. Use caution riding with vehicular traffic on paved roads at the route's end.

Rescue index: Expect complete solitude on weekdays. On weekends or holidays, you may have to share the road with a few passing vehicles or with ranchers. For all practical purposes, emergency assistance will have to be summoned from St. George. St. George also has medical facilities.

Land status: Dixie National Forest; Bureau of Land Management, Dixie Resource Area.

Maps: USGS 7.5 minute quadrangles: Harrisburg Junction, Pintura, Signal Peak, and Washington, Utah; USGS 1:100,000 metric topographic series: St. George, Utah. (Bicycles Unlimited sells these and other maps detailing a number of cycling routes in and around St. George.)

Finding the trail: This route requires a vehicle shuttle, although experienced long-distance cyclists could make the ride a loop. Park at your discretion in St. George. Hop onto Interstate 15 at Exit 8 (St. George Boulevard) and drive 14 miles north to Exit 22/Leeds. Drive through town about a mile and turn left/north toward Silver Reef and Oak Creek Campground. Travel to the end of the pavement at the Dixie National Forest boundary. Park and embark.

Sources of additional information:

Dixie National Forest
Pine Valley Ranger District
196 East Tabernacle Street,
  Room 40
P.O. Box 2288
St. George, Utah 84770
(801) 673-3431

Bureau of Land Management
Cedar City District
Dixie Resource Area
225 North Bluff
St. George, Utah 84770
(801) 673-4654

Bicycles Unlimited, Inc.
90 South 100 East
St. George, Utah 84770
(801) 673-4492

The first bike shop in St. George 17 years ago, Mark McLaughlin's Bicycles Unlimited is one of southern Utah's finest. In an area where dirt roads outnumber paved 10 to 1, Bicycles Unlimited dedicates most of its interest and energy to mountain biking, catering to both the entire family and the most discerning cyclist. In addition to carrying the latest in mountain bike technology and top of the line components, Bicycles Unlimited boasts a professional staff in sales and service, and even a frame builder to modify a bike to your exacting specifications. The shop also sells popular area-USGS maps and displays a master map showing all the local favorite bike routes.

Notes on the trail: From the Forest boundary, pedal up the graded, gravel road past red cliffs and along rugged Leeds Creek. After 1.6 miles, turn west onto Forest Service Road 031 signed "Danish Ranch, St. George." Continue ascending through juniper and pinyon. Look back periodically to catch retreating views of the majestic towers of Zion National Park. A generous descent follows and dips into a rugged canyon drainage marking the head of Quail Creek. Pass by the apple orchard and pastures of Danish Ranch and then across another creek. A wooden Forest Service sign announces the Big Hollow trail. Just around the corner, a (usually) dry creekbed dives into a labyrinthine sandstone canyon. The canyon's walls are etched with swirling and checkerboard-style crossbeds. In the distant east are more views of Zion's Guardian Angels and Towers of the Virgin.

Thirteen miles into the ride, you will pass over a ridge marking the route's high point, followed by the Diamond Valley turnoff to the right. The route now bends south and begins an endless descent on FS 033 across the foothills above St. George. Pass the turkey farm on the left; then glide 6 more miles into town.

Time permitting, consider a side trip to the old Wells Fargo and Pony Express Station in Silver Reef. Silver Reef was a raucous mining town that produced millions of dollars of silver from the surrounding sandstone during the 1870s and 1880s. Once supporting a population of 1,500, the community of Silver Reef was a stark contrast to the sedate Mormon communities around it. The old mail transfer station is now home to Jerry Anderson's Art Gallery, where you can view paintings and sculptures based on southwestern themes.

RIDE 59 *WARNER VALLEY*

This easy ride is located just east of St. George. It is excellent for a family outing, since you make it as long as you want, depending on where you choose to park and embark.

The Warner Valley tour is loaded with history—human, prehistoric, and geologic. Before an era when great sand dunes blanketed southern Utah, some 200 million years ago, dinosaurs stomped through what was then a local flood plain. Evidence of these beasts is found at the route's end in a series of footprints stamped into a layer of Moenave siltstone. These three-toed impressions

RIDE 59 *WARNER VALLEY*

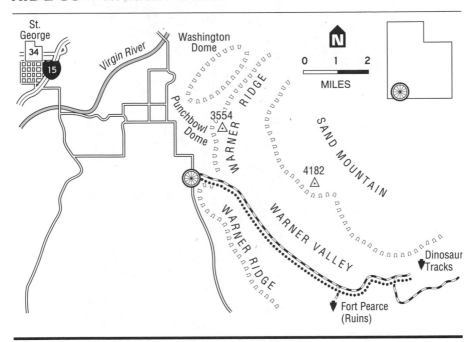

left by bipedal coelurasaurids and plateosaurids are considered some of the finest examples of footprints of their age in North America.

In more recent time, the Spanish Franciscan padres Dominguez and Escalante passed through here seeking a route between New Mexico and California missions in 1776. A century later, during the mid-1880s, Warner Valley was dubbed the Honeymoon Trail. Caravans of Mormon settlers (from towns as far away as Phoenix), including soon-to-be newlyweds, traveled to St. George, where the only Mormon temple in the territory existed at the time.

While Latter Day Saint immigrants colonized the region, they were persistently attacked by bands of marauding Indians. Such attacks increased during the Black Hawk Wars of 1865 to 1869. Consequently, pioneers constructed Fort Pearce as a defensive stronghold. You'll find the old stone fortress a short distance off the main bike route.

This 20-mile out-and-back tour follows maintained dirt and gravel roads. Technical difficulty is low and the entire route is well suited for novice/intermediate cyclists. Families with children may opt to drive out toward Fort Pearce to shorten the ride to the dinosaur tracks and back. Advanced bikers can head straight out from St. George on a 35-mile out-and-back tour.

Information on the Warner Valley tour was provided by Kent B. McDonald, St. George, Utah.

Three-toed dinosaur tracks (highlighted with water).

General location: Warner Valley is located 8 miles east of St. George.

Elevation change: The route begins at an elevation of 2,770′ and rises to 3,100′ twice: once just before the Fort Pearce turnoff and again at the foot trail for the dinosaur tracks. Except for one modest hill at the beginning of the Warner Valley dirt road, the majority of the route is quite level. Total elevation gain is about 450′.

Season: September through May is the best time of year to pedal through Warner Valley. The route is dusty and hot during the summer. Don't take this road if it's wet: its clay base can turn to viscous mud.

Services: There are no services along this route and all surface waters should be purified. St. George offers all visitor services, including bike shops.

Hazards: The route can be very warm, so always carry adequate water supplies. This route receives some vehicular traffic, so yield the right of way to motorists.

Rescue index: Emergency contacts will have to be made in St. George or from scattered residences along the route's access drive. St. George has medical facilities.

Land status: Bureau of Land Management, Dixie Resource Area.

Maps: USGS 7.5 minute quadrangles: St. George, The Divide, and Washington Dome, Utah. (The foot trail to the dinosaur tracks is not shown.)

Finding the trail: From St. George, drive east on 700 South and turn south onto River Road toward Bloomington Hills. Just past the Virgin River Bridge, turn left off River Road onto 1450 South heading east toward Washington Fields. After 2 miles, the road veers sharply right; immediately thereafter, you will fork left/east. Follow signs for Warner Valley and Fort Pearce. Five and one-half miles from turning off River Road, more signs direct you left onto a maintained dirt road that rises up a hill into Warner Valley. Park here at your discretion.

Sources of additional information:

Bureau of Land Management
Dixie Resource Area
225 North Bluff
St. George, Utah 84770
(801) 673-4654

Notes on the trail: From the parking area, where the Warner Valley Road turns to dirt and gravel, begin with a modest hill that rises up through a notch in Warner Ridge and into Warner Valley. Pedal southeast through this back valley beneath the looming red cliffs of Sand Mountain. About 5.2 miles from the beginning of the dirt road, turn right and pedal half a mile to historic Fort Pearce.

Upon returning from Fort Pearce, continue on the Warner Valley Road eastward for 2 miles, then fork left onto a dead-end road. A short 200-yard hike leads to the dinosaur tracks and a sign describing them. Return through Warner Valley in the opposite direction.

RIDE 60   *GUNLOCK RESERVOIR TO DAMMERON VALLEY*

The Gunlock Reservoir to Dammeron Valley ride passes through southwestern Utah's Dixie country, which is marked by volcanic terrain and high deserts. Despite the heat vapors you see rising off the parched land, this route passes three reservoirs. Upper and Lower Sand Cove Reservoirs are quite small but worthy of soaking your feet. Gunlock Reservoir (named after the famous Western marksman "Gunlock Bill" Hamblin) offers boating, fishing, picnicking, and swimming.

Mountains can be seen all around. The Pine Valley Mountains to the east host a Wilderness Area and are snowcapped during winter months. Small hills that surround the road are composed of contrasting yellow, orange, and red

RIDE 60 *GUNLOCK RESERVOIR / DAMMERON VALLEY*

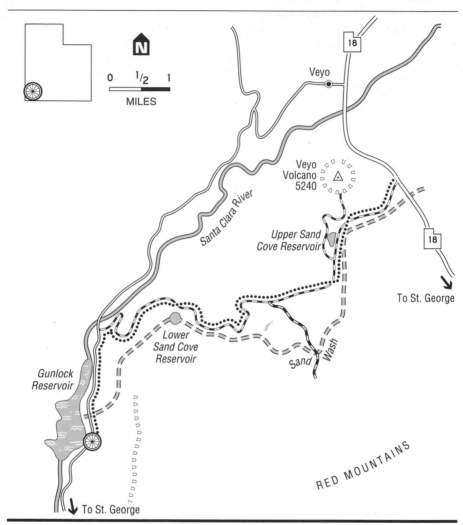

sandstones. Other areas are covered with a black crust of blocky lava, which flowed presumably from the nearby extinct Veyo Volcano.

This 22-mile out-and-back route begins with 2 miles of paved road followed by a hard-packed dirt and gravel road, which is suitable for passenger cars. You'll encounter two short climbs that are both of little consequence. The rest of the route is quite level and not technically difficult. This route is a good novice/intermediate-level ride.

Route information was provided by Mark McLaughlin, St. George, Utah.

Tricia explores a side route near Lower Sand Cove
Reservoir.

General location: This route connects Gunlock Reservoir, located 20 miles
northwest of St. George, with the Veyo Volcano, located 16 miles north of St.
George on UT 18.

Elevation change: Gunlock Reservoir resides at 3,585′. The route rises to
4,600′ at the turnaround point near the Veyo Volcano and UT 18.

Season: This route is rideable throughout the year, but spring, fall, and most of
winter are the best times. Summer temperatures commonly exceed 100 degrees,
so carry plenty of water.

Services: There are no services along this route. Water may be purified from
Upper and Lower Sand Cove Reservoirs or Gunlock Reservoir, or in an emergency obtained from residences in the town of Gunlock. Food is available at the
steakhouse in Dammeron Valley near the trailhead on UT 18. St. George offers
all visitor services, including bike shops. Developed USFS camping is available

at Pine Valley, located on the northwest side of the Pine Valley Mountains, or at Snow Canyon State Park, 10 miles north of St. George on UT 18.

Hazards: This route is very warm during midsummer, so carry plenty of water. Use plenty of sunscreen as well. Southwestern Utah is plagued with a pesky sticker weed called the goathead. This pea-sized burr can easily puncture mountain bike tires. Be sure to carry tire liners, tube sealants, spare tubes, and (at the very minimum) a fresh patch kit.

Avoid this route when it's wet; the fine sand and clay-base road turns to viscous mud, which can eat derailleurs and jam drive trains.

Rescue index: The route is not often traveled by motorists. Fishermen and boaters frequent Gunlock Reservoir. A telephone might be found at residences in the townsite of Gunlock or at the steakhouse on UT 18 near the route's midpoint.

Land status: Bureau of Land Management, Dixie Resource Area.

Maps: USGS 7.5 minute quadrangles: Gunlock and Veyo, Utah.

Finding the trail: From St. George, travel north on UT 18, then west on UT 91. Pass the turnoff for Ivins, then bear right at the Y intersection near the Shivwits Indian Reservation. Gunlock Reservoir is about 8 miles north. Parking is available near the boat launch.

Sources of additional information:

Bureau of Land Management
Cedar City District
Dixie Resource Area
225 North Bluff
St. George, Utah 84770
(801) 673-4654

Bicycles Unlimited, Inc.
90 South 100 East
St. George, Utah 84770
(801) 673-4492

Notes on the trail: You can start this out-and-back route from the east at UT 18, near the Veyo Volcano in Dammeron Valley, or from the west at Gunlock Reservoir. Gunlock Reservoir is an inviting starting point since it offers parking and aprés-ride swimming.

From the eastern shore of Gunlock (near the dam), pedal north 1.8 miles on the paved road. Immediately before the road crosses over the Santa Clara River, turn right onto a dirt and gravel road that rises steeply up through a dugway. After 2.5 miles, the road passes Lower Sand Cove Reservoir, a sizeable pond with a shade tree or two. Pass the power plant and up a second small dugway.

The road winds past Upper Sand Cove Reservoir and past the Veyo Volcano, an extinct cinder cone. Upon intersecting UT 18, turn around and enjoy coasting downhill back to Gunlock Reservoir.

RIDE 61 *BARLETT WASH*

There is a generally accepted but scientifically unproven theorem that states, "The more time spent mountain biking in Moab, the farther from town your explorations will lead." Ride the big name trails first, by all means, then pursue lesser known and infrequently visited areas to round out your Moab portfolio. Bartlett Wash supports a second corollary: "Not all slickrock is created equal." Bartlett's abbreviated but wavelike expanse of barren sandstone provides hours of mountain bike gymnastics.

Bartlett Wash lies on the northern fringe of Canyon Country, where colorful sandstones dissipate into bleak and hopelessly unproductive sagebrush plains and shallow, charcoal-colored washes. The slickrock along this route is a member (or subdivision) of the Entrada Sandstone, which forms the wonderful creations that give Arches National Park its name. Here, the grey-, tan-, and salmon-hued Entrada delights the eye with both soft color and smooth form. Compared to the Slickrock Bike Trail, which rolls over geologically older and stratigraphically lower Navajo Sandstone, Bartlett Wash might be likened to riding on fine rather than coarse sandpaper.

This out-and-back route is only four miles long, as the crow flies; but because of its free-flowing, create-a-route-as-you-go nature, fat-tire antics can last nearly all day. Its physical and technical difficulty is based on your desire to defy gravity and experiment with traction. Overall, Bartlett Wash is at least intermediate in difficulty.

General location: Bartlett Wash is located about 17 miles north of Moab and west of US 191.

Elevation change: The trail begins at 4,620′ and rises to 5,000′ at the turnaround point. Simple subtraction yields a total gain of 380′, but because of the route's freestyle nature, expect to gain several hundred feet of additional vertical.

Season: Spring (March through June) and fall (September through October) are the best times of the year to pedal in the greater Moab area. Midsummer can be uncomfortably warm and bugs may be annoying, especially near water sources. Certain times in winter can be enjoyable, but wet slickrock can be dangerous and can make accessing the trailhead difficult.

Services: There are no services along this route, and what little water can be found in Bartlett Wash should be purified. Moab, located 17 miles to the south, offers all visitor services and medical facilities. A gas station/small convenience store is located at Crescent Junction, 15 miles north of Bartlett Wash at the junction of US 191 and Interstate 70.

Hazards: Bartlett Wash's main attraction, slickrock, doubles as the route's greatest peril. The sandstone's smooth surface and swirling, platy crossbeds can provide excellent traction—or lack of traction—depending on how it's

RIDE 61 *BARTLETT WASH*

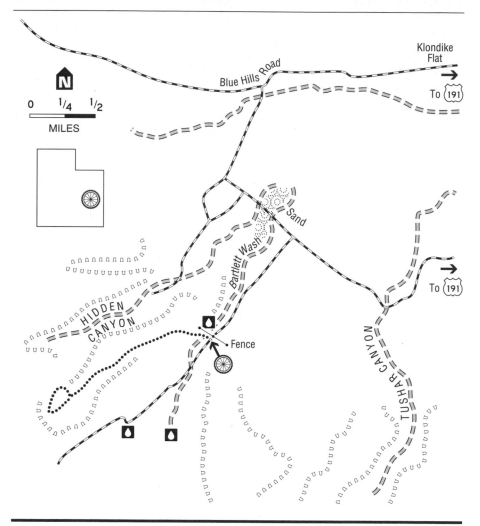

exposed. Be prudent when you are pursuing "Zen and the Art of Fat-Tire Friction."

Rescue index: Although located just a few miles from heavily traveled US 191, Bartlett Wash is not often visited and is considered remote. Solitude is common. A telephone can be found at Crescent Junction, located 15 miles north at the junction of US 191 and I-70. Moab has medical facilities.

Land status: Bureau of Land Management, Moab District.

Bob "gets a grip" on the Bartlett Wash slickrock.

Maps: USGS 7.5 minute quadrangle: Jug Rock, Utah. (The route is not mapped.)

Finding the trail: About 17 miles north of Moab, or 15 miles south of I-70, turn west off US 191 onto Blue Hills Road (near milepost 143). After 2.2 miles along this improved dirt and sand road, turn left/south. Less than a mile ahead there is a three-way junction; fork left again. Pass the spur branching right to Hidden Canyon, then cautiously approach a sandy wash bottom. If you're apprehensive about crossing this in your vehicle, simply park here; otherwise, continue up a small hill and take the right spur that drops into Bartlett Wash. Park at your discretion. The trail begins about 1 mile south at a fence line marked by a dead cottonwood and small grassy meadow. Look for a slickrock ramp to the right.

Sources of additional information:

> Bureau of Land Management
> Grand Resource Area
> 92 East Dogwood
> Suite G
> Moab, Utah 84532
> (801) 259-8193

Notes on the trail: At the fence line that crosses Bartlett Wash, turn right toward the old cottonwood and cross the small meadow. In the brush is a slickrock ramp that provides access to the sandstone playground. Within a half mile to the south, trudge through a long sandtrap and back onto the salmon-hued slickrock. Continue southwestward beneath the mesa overhead, which is capped with sandstone bonnets and lithified elephant toes.

You are on your own to construct a feasible route; there are no paint-on-rock dashes to provide direction. Improvisation is prerequisite to pursuing hours of bicycle frivolity. There are numerous arcuate bowls to surf in, solution pockets to dodge, and protracted slopes to test muscle against balance against the coefficient of friction.

About 1.5 miles from Bartlett Wash, the lens of slickrock wraps around the mesa's abutment. Hidden Canyon cuts in from the west. The route ends a half mile farther, where broken cliffs plunge down to the valley floor. Turn around and retrace your tracks or follow your bliss—diving, dodging, and generally feeling free on two wheels.

RIDE 62   *WILLOW SPRINGS*

The Willow Springs loop through Arches National Park harbors all the redrock wonderment captured in postcards, movies, and especially one popular Saturday morning cartoon. More than likely, you won't encounter frolicking roadrunners and devious coyotes, but it is easy to envision their comical antics on desert terrain that, in reality, is not overly exaggerated in the loony tune.

Initially, the route parallels massive cliffs flooded with shades of deep orange and red and streaked with black patina. There is a smattering of slickrock (rolling, lithified sand dunes) as the route makes its way around the heads of dead-end canyons. You'll even see an anvil-shaped rock perched precariously on a squashed pedestal. The route concludes on a winding paved road through one of the Southwest's most distinctive desert landscapes, Arches National Park. Views of Balanced Rock, North and South Windows, Double Arch, Three Gossips, Park Avenue, and the distant La Sal Mountains are certainly more impressive from the saddle of a bike than behind a bug-splattered windshield!

RIDE 62 *WILLOW SPRINGS*

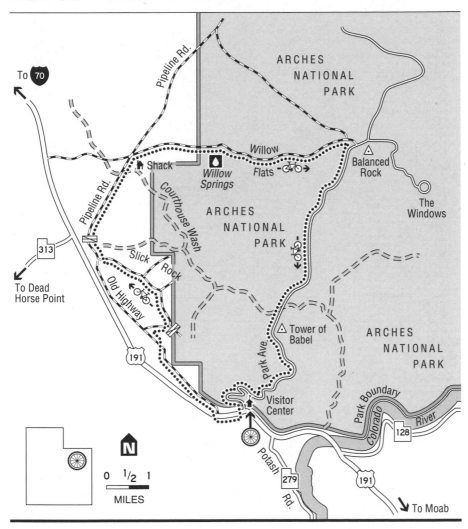

This 26-mile loop (clockwise) follows paved roads, an old highway that combines broken pavement and dirt, sandy double-track, and even a short segment of single-track. Most of the off-road pedaling is low in technical difficulty, except for intermittent pavement bedrock early in the route. The last 11 miles follows the paved Scenic Drive through Arches National Park. Early segments require good route-finding skills; the remainder is easy to follow.

As a loop, this route is intermediate to advanced level. An optional 5.5-mile out-and-back spur to the park's Windows Section is highly recommended, for

A side trip to the Windows Section in Arches National Park.

it is full of the park's namesake features. An alternate 19-mile point-to-point configuration might be suitable for strong novice riders.

General location: The Willow Springs/Arches National Park route begins 5 miles north of Moab.
Elevation change: The entrance to Arches National Park marks the route's lowest elevation at 4,100′. The route tops out at 5,040′ at Balanced Rock within the park. Total elevation gain is about 1,800′.
Season: March through mid-May and September through November are the most enjoyable times to bike around the Moab area. June through August can be uncomfortably warm and insects may be a nuisance. Carry plenty of water regardless of the season.
Services: Drinking water is available only at Arches National Park's Visitor Center (trailhead and end point). No other services are available, so carry an ample supply of water. Moab offers all visitor services.
Hazards: Always carry plenty of water, apply sunscreen liberally, and pack along a small container of insect repellent. The off-road section is generally low to moderate in technical difficulty. Use caution when pedaling the Scenic Drive through Arches National Park: stay to the far right, pedal in single file, and yield to motorists. The Scenic Drive's final descent to the Visitor Center is fast and rounds tight switchbacks; watch for oncoming traffic.
Rescue index: The first 9 miles of this loop are within a short distance of heavily-traveled US 191. The 6-mile-long Willow Springs road connects US 191

with the park's Scenic Drive. Motorists are common on the Scenic Drive and you can get emergency assistance from the park's Visitor Center. Park patrols are infrequent. Moab has medical facilities.

Land status: Arches National Park; Bureau of Land Management, Moab District.

Maps: USGS 7.5 minute quadrangles: Gold Bar Canyon, Merrimac Butte, Moab, and The Windows Section, Utah. (Initial portions of the route are not mapped.)

Finding the trail: Travel 5 miles north of Moab on US 191 to the entrance of Arches National Park. Park at the Visitor Center (a fee is required) or continue up US 191 half a mile to a pulloff on the right. This is the old highway and beginning of the route's off-road segment.

Sources of additional information:

Superintendent
Arches National Park
P.O. Box 907
Moab, Utah 84532
(801) 259-8161

Bureau of Land Management
Grand Resource Area
92 East Dogwood
Suite G
Moab, Utah 84532
(801) 259-8193

Notes on the trail: Entrance fees are required for traveling through Arches National Park: vehicles $4, bicycles $2. Carry your receipt or a few dollars with you; a park ranger may ask for one or the other. Within Arches National Park, mountain bikes are restricted to roads designated for vehicular traffic. Bikes are not allowed on foot trails.

From the Visitor Center, pedal north on US 191 not more than a half mile. Peel off to the right at a large pulloff and begin up the old highway's gentle to moderate grade. Broken pavement mixed with sand and gravel is the fare. Three miles up, there is a junction. The old highway, which is one option you can take, continues straight/north. But for the more adventurous, more scenic, and by far more challenging-to-navigate route, turn right/east, and plug in your homing device.

Double-tracks branch in all directions, but in half a mile the main road splits. Stay left, then shortly ahead bend northward. You should now be traveling northward on a double-track whose distinguishing features are low, sage- and grass-covered red knolls to the immediate left/west and barren slickrock to the immediate right/east. Make a mental image of this roadside dichotomy, for it is key to pursuing the next few miles. (Note: if you encounter a park fence line you have ventured too far southeast.)

Over the next 2 miles, don't be tempted by the two roads that fork right/east twice across slickrock. Remember, the route heads northward along the sage-and-soil/slickrock interface. Pass a (rather) obvious, anvil-shaped rock on the left. Beyond, the route will soon peter out across intermittent slickrock. Again stay near the soil/slickrock interface. Be sure to ride cleanly by keeping tires solely on rock and not on microbiotic soils. *Leave no trace.*

The route narrows to single-track as it rounds the head of dead-end Sevenmile Canyon. Cross a wire fence line and continue on the double-track (pipeline corridor) that gradually angles northeast away from nearby US 191. In half a mile you'll want to stay straight/northeast at a junction of double-tracks. Plunge over ledgy cliffs and into the wide, sandy bottom of upper Courthouse Wash. Just beyond the opposing embankment, fork right/east on the sandy Willow Springs road (The junction here is marked by a corrugated shack on the right).

Pedal 6 miles east on the Willow Springs road to the paved Scenic Drive at Balanced Rock. Turn right/south to return to the Visitor Center 11 miles away. But first give strong consideration to the 5.5-mile out-and-back spur from Balanced Rock to the Windows Section (left); the scenery is unparalleled.

Final note: To bypass the initial exasperating reconnoiter from the old highway to the Willow Springs road, car-top 8.5 miles north on US 191 from the Visitor Center. The resulting route is a 19-mile point-to-point tour via the Willow Springs road and Scenic Drive. (The Willow Springs road stems *unobtrusively* from UT 191 between mileposts 138 and 139 and is marked by a vertical orange pipe and a tubular steel/wire gate. When you reach the pipeline junction, which is marked by a corrugated shack, stay straight/east to venture into the park.)

RIDE 63 *GEMINI BRIDGES*

The Gemini Bridges (two large parallel arches) are the main attraction on this ride, but the scenery and geologic wonders are outstanding along the entire length of the trail. There are views of Monitor and Merrimac Buttes and Klondike Bluffs to the north, Gold Bar Rim and Arches National Park to the east, and the La Sal Mountains, Amasa Back, and Behind the Rocks area to the southeast. You can look down into beautiful Bull Canyon from Gemini Bridges (or, as an option, ride into Bull Canyon and look up at Gemini Bridges). The route traverses equally beautiful Little Canyon and passes innumerable interesting rock formations including other small arches and "the Gooney Bird" in Little Canyon.

This 13.7-mile, novice- to intermediate-level route travels on mostly good four-wheel-drive roads. Since this is generally configured as a point-to-point ride, a vehicle shuttle or similar arrangements are necessary. There are some sandy spots near Gemini Bridges and in Little Canyon. Ledgy bedrock outcrops in the road near the Bridges produce moderately technical conditions. Navigation is often the biggest challenge for the first-time rider.

RIDE 63 *GEMINI BRIDGES*

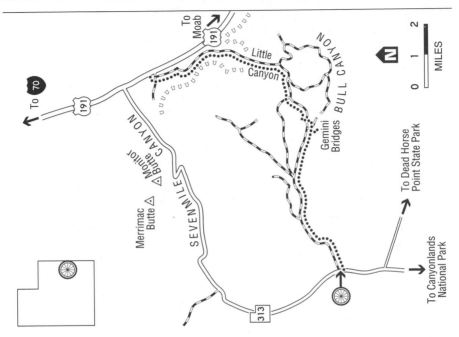

Information for this chapter was provided by John Groo,[*] Moab, Utah.

General location: Gemini Bridges is located in the northern end of the Island in the Sky area, northwest of Moab.

Elevation change: The trail's beginning at UT 313 is at 5,940′. The trail drops

---

[*]For no apparent reason, John Groo migrated to Salt Lake City from New England in 1973, then moved to Moab in 1977. Like many people, John had put away his Schwinn Varsity forever on the day long ago when he got his driver's license. But he rediscovered the bicycle in his late thirties as both an efficient and pleasant means of transportation, and as a tool for exploring the spectacular backcountry around his home. Working out his excess energies in USCF and NORBA racing, his real love remains anchored in traveling the backcountry roads and trails of southern Utah by mountain bike.

In 1986, John started Rim Tours, a company that offers a variety of supported mountain bike tours in southeastern Utah's Canyon Country and the mountains of Colorado. Although he has since sold his share to his partners, he continues to do some work for them. John now spends a large amount of time on his business, The Synergy Company, on local environmental affairs and politics, as Mayor of Castle Valley, and on the Board of Directors of the Grand County Water Conservancy District. What little time he has left over he spends working on his homestead in Castle Valley.

A lone rider approaches the "Gooney Bird."

to 4,500′ at UT 191 for an elevation loss of 1,400′. The climb out of Little Canyon is the only hill of any consequence.

Season: March through early June and September through early December are the best times to ride Gemini Bridges. There are often days during the winter when it is possible (and quite enjoyable) to ride this trail. Summer is usually too hot for an enjoyable or safe ride. Be aware of current weather patterns, take extra clothing if needed, and always take plenty of water.

Services: There are no services or water along this route. Moab offers all visitor services.

Hazards: There is no reliable water source along the route, and the generally dry climate dehydrates active bodies quickly. Always take plenty of water. It is relatively easy to get lost in this area, so obtain accurate maps and instructions before you head out.

Rescue index: Rescue depends on your timing. On a nice spring or fall weekend, there are almost always others in the area. During off seasons, weekdays,

John Groo. What, no helmet?! *Photo: Dennis Coello.*

or periods of marginal weather, there might not be another person in the area for days. Moab has medical facilities.

Land status: Bureau of Land Management, Moab District.

Maps: USGS 7.5 minute quadrangles: Gold Bar Canyon and The Knoll, Utah; There are other good maps available at the Moab Visitor Center.

Finding the trail: Travel 8.5 miles north of Moab on US 191. The end of the signed trail where you leave your vehicle is located on the left/west side of the highway adjacent to the railroad tracks. In your shuttle vehicle, drive about 1 mile farther north and turn left/west on UT 313 signed "Dead Horse Point," then 12.5 miles to the trailhead (located about 1.5 miles before UT 313 intersects with the Island in the Sky road).

Sources of additional information:

> Bureau of Land Management
> Grand Resource Area
> 92 East Dogwood
> Suite G
> Moab, Utah 84532
> (801) 259-8193

> Rim Cyclery
> 94 West 1st North
> Moab, Utah 84532
> (801) 259-5333
> Rim Cyclery, a company that offers a variety of supported mountain bike
> tours in southeastern Utah's Canyon Country and the mountains of
> Colorado, is well known as the outdoor center for southeastern Utah.
> This bustling establishment serves cyclists, climbers, hikers, and river run-
> ners with the best equipment and considerable personality.

Above and Beyond Slickrock, by Todd Campbell (Wasatch Publishing,
Salt Lake City, Utah)

RIDE 64 *POISON SPIDER MESA*

Few Moab-area rides are as mentally and physically rewarding as Poison Spider
Mesa. The route affords astonishing vistas of Behind the Rocks, where an
entourage of sandstone fins and ribs march in echelon toward the idyllically
emplaced La Sal Mountains. From rim-side vantage points, the Moab Valley
sprawls out below, sliced by the Colorado River, which slips between confining
cliffs of the Portal. In the distance, Arches National Park displays a wonderment of Nature's architectural talent. Poison Spider is a navigational challenge
that calls for collective route-finding techniques. Even a short lapse of attentiveness may prompt an anxious voyage across a nondescript land bound by
unscalable cliffs. You'll gain physical gratification that rivals that of the
Slickrock Trail; there are conditions here that demand unfaltering skills.
Conversely, superlative slickrock exposures provide endless freeform antics
and bicycle gymnastics.

Highlighting the loop is the infamous Portal Trail single-track—an exhilarating descent for the intrepid and adept biker, and an unforgiving one for the
timid and tentative. This precarious path boasts of severe exposures coupled
with a barrage of highly technical maneuvers. In many respects, the Portal Trail
transcends the staple guidebook adjective "challenging." If you take a look at

RIDE 64 *POISON SPIDER MESA*

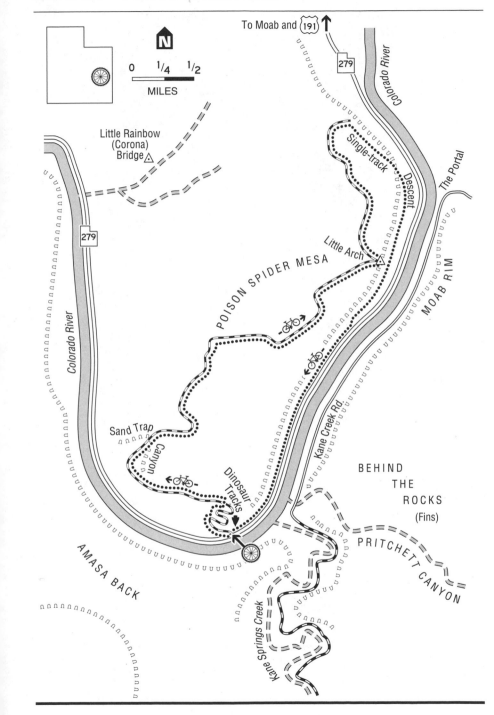

To Moab and 191

279

Colorado River

Little Rainbow
(Corona)
Bridge △

N

0   1/4   1/2
MILES

279

Colorado River

Single-track

Descent

The Portal

Little Arch

POISON SPIDER MESA

MOAB RIM

Sand Trap

Canyon

Kane Creek Rd.

Dinosaur
Tracks

BEHIND
THE
ROCKS
(Fins)

AMASA BACK

PRITCHETT CANYON

Kane Springs Creek

Finding a route across Poison Spider Mesa.

the definition of *wicked* in the dictionary, you will be convinced that whoever defined the word had this ride in mind:

> wick-ed (wik´-id) adj. 1. exceeding the limits of what is normal or tolerable. 2. giving trouble or anxiety. 3. marked by a high level of ability or skill. 4. involving the possibility of injury, pain, or loss. 5. having, showing, or indicative of intense, often vicious, ill will, *a wicked descent*.

The 13.5-mile Poison Spider Mesa loop (clockwise) is moderately to highly technical in nature, consisting of double-track punctuated with deep sand traps, bedrock ledges and stairsteps, plus open slickrock. Descending the Portal Trail is reserved for advanced cyclists and should not be taken lightly. (It has already claimed the life of one mountain biker.) Intermediate bikers can, however, revel in a 12-mile out-and-back route with Little Arch as the targeted turnaround.

General location: Poison Spider Mesa is located 4 miles southwest of Moab, as the crow flies, or 10 miles by over-ground transport.

Elevation change: The trailhead/parking area is at the route's lowest elevation at 3,960′. The route rises to 5,000′ at the Portal's rim, which overlooks the Colorado River. Estimated total elevation gain exceeds the net gain of 1,040′.

Season: March through May and September through October are the most enjoyable times to mountain bike in and around Moab. Midsummer tends to be oppressively warm and insects are annoying. Winter can be enjoyable when the route is dry and weather cooperates. (Note: Due to the Portal Trail's protected exposure, snow and wet conditions may last on it longer than on the part of the route that approaches it.) Always carry plenty of water regardless of the season, and use a liberal amount of sunscreen.

Services: There are no services or reliable water sources along this route. Carry plenty of water supplies with you. Moab offers all visitor services.

Hazards: Poison Spider is technically challenging, so be especially attentive when you approach more difficult sections. The Portal Trail descent varies from moderately to extremely technical. Portions are narrow, clogged with boulders and steplike drops, and exposed to precipices. Dismounting and walking the more difficult sections are *strongly* advised. Use good judgment.

Use caution when pedaling the 2 miles of highway from the Portal Trail back to the parking area; the Potash Road has a narrow shoulder and gets quite a bit of traffic, including trucks.

Rescue index: This route is quite popular, especially on weekends and holidays. The Potash Road is regularly traveled and visited by campers, rock climbers, and sightseers. Moab has medical facilities.

Land status: Bureau of Land Management, Moab District.

Maps: USGS 7.5 minute quadrangles: Gold Bar Canyon and Moab, Utah. (Only part of the route is mapped. The Portal Trail is not shown.)

Finding the trail: From Moab, travel north on US 191. Cross over the Colorado River and turn left after 1.5 miles onto UT 279 for Potash. The trailhead and roadside parking area are located 6 miles down the road near the "Dinosaur Tracks." The route begins up a double-track next to a wire fence. A trail register box, where you can write your name, destination, and comments, is provided.

Sources of additional information:

Bureau of Land Management
Grand Resource Area
92 East Dogwood
Suite G
Moab, Utah 84532
(801) 259-8193

Notes on the trail: From the roadside parking area at the "Dinosaur Tracks," the route begins on the sandy and rock-studded double-track behind the wire fence. Your initial views of Behind the Rocks are photoworthy, but save the film for later.

Not more than a mile along, an ugly, gravel- and cobble-strewn pitch precedes a narrow slot of ledgy bedrock that requires both finesse and brute strength. This is the fare for the day. Farther ahead, the double-track enters into a constricted canyon flooded with sand. Although it might be rideable when it's dry, it saps tremendous energy reserves. Beyond is a stairstep stunt that warrants a replay if you fail on your first try. Immediately thereafter, turn right to follow directional carsonite posts. You'll be doing creative ledgework maneuvers until the route levels on the mesa.

Cross directly over these shallow slickrock humps that resemble sandstone whales breaching the ocean's surface for a quick breath. A carsonite post points you in the correct direction, but keep an eye out for stenciled jeep icons painted on the bedrock; these are the "official" trail markers henceforth. Burn some film here, for the parade of fins, ribs, slots, and darkened creases—with the La Sal Mountains towering behind—is prizeworthy. The curious scattering of rounded chert and volcanic pebbles evidence an ancient erosional era when water blanketed the mesa.

Speed across the alluvial bench blanketed with sage, desert grass, and a peppering of juniper. After a descent, the trail splits at a pair of carsonite posts; stay straight. You'll have to "sniff out" the trail beyond this point. Watch for jeep icons painted on the slickrock and previously-laid bicycle tire tracks. In *most* cases, the greater the concentration of bike tracks going in a particular direction, the better off you are to follow. You will want to angle toward a prominent asymmetrical sandstone dome almost due east. (Head to its more blunt north slope.) Following painted jeep icons and occasional rock cairns will get you in the vicinity, but keep an eye out for two black arrows that signify the trail's split. Keep to the right.

Little Arch is a small eye in the Navajo Sandstone that keeps watch over the Colorado River. The slickrock that encloses the arch is steep, so a cautious approach is a prudent approach. Hike up the arch's northern abutment for a vertigo-inducing view of the Portal Trail angling down beneath the cliffs, the life-giving and canyon-crafting Colorado River, and cliff-bound Portal through which the Colorado leaves Moab Valley.

To continue the loop, return to the slickrock play area before Little Arch and continue north by northwest. Watch for telltale signs of the trail, including rock cairns, painted jeep icons, and a concentration of bike tracks. Just less than 2 miles from Little Arch, you will encounter a wire fence line on your right and a "multi-use" carsonite trailmarker; bikers turn right/northeast. Confronting you is a one last grunt-of-a-climb on a double-track littered with loose cobbles. After a half mile, you will reach Gold Bar Rim, which affords God-sent views of the Moab Valley, the Portal (Moab Rim), and Behind the Rocks—all framed by the La Sal Mountains. A left/north turn leads you out along Gold Bar Rim, an abusive endeavor; don't go that way. Instead, turn to the right/southeast to begin the Portal Trail's infamous descent.

One thousand feet of vertical emptiness stand between you and the Colorado River. Take in all your sightseeing now because once you begin your descent, both eyes should be glued to the trail. But do stop periodically to marvel at the precariousness of this route. After a mile, a ledge overlook is marked by an ironic BLM sign reading "Portal Overlook, end of maintained trail." One more mile of gnashing rocks and jackhammer stunts dump you out onto the Potash Road and a trail register box, where you can enter your name, home town, and comments. One rider wrote "I don't think we are in Kansas anymore Toto"; a second wrote "A 9 on the sphincter scale." What do you think?

Two miles of road and riverside pedaling lead back to the trailhead.

RIDE 65 *AMASA BACK*

Amasa Back is a relatively short and direct ride offering visual perspectives of Utah's desert sanctuary that transcend those offered by many other area rides. Poison Spider Mesa, the Portal, Moab Rim, Behind the Rocks, Kane Springs Canyon, Jackson Hole, Shafer Basin, Island in the Sky District, plus the ever-present La Sal Mountains collectively compete for your attention while you pedal. There are opportunities to dangle your feet over 1,000′ cliffs, become mesmerized by a company of marching sandstone fins, and spy on other cyclists creeping up distant trails.

The "Back" is a thumb-shaped mesa bound on three sides by a gooseneck-bend in the Colorado River. Over millions of years, the Colorado River shaped this land-locked peninsula. Within a short span of geologic time (long after our species succumbs to extinction) the river will undoubtedly bisect Amasa Back's narrow neck as it seeks the shortest route of flow. Amasa will then exist as a "rincon" encircled by a silted-in moat of the Colorado's abandoned meander, much like Jackson Hole (that is, Jackson Hole west of and below Amasa Back, not Wyoming.)

This out-and-back route is 13 miles long (round-trip). (Tack on about 2 miles for 2 must-do spurs, plus 9.5 out-and-back miles if you begin in Moab.) The route begins on an improved sand, gravel, and washboarded road, then jumps onto the old prospector's jeep road leading up to and out along Amasa Back. Packed and loose sand coupled with ledgy sandstone outcrops are the norm. The trail's terminus is largely broken slickrock marked intermittently with cairns. Route-finding (and route-creating) skills are necessary if you pursue the Back's northernmost reach. To clean the entire ascent requires adept skills, but most obstacles simply offer you a chance to unclip and stretch the legs a bit.

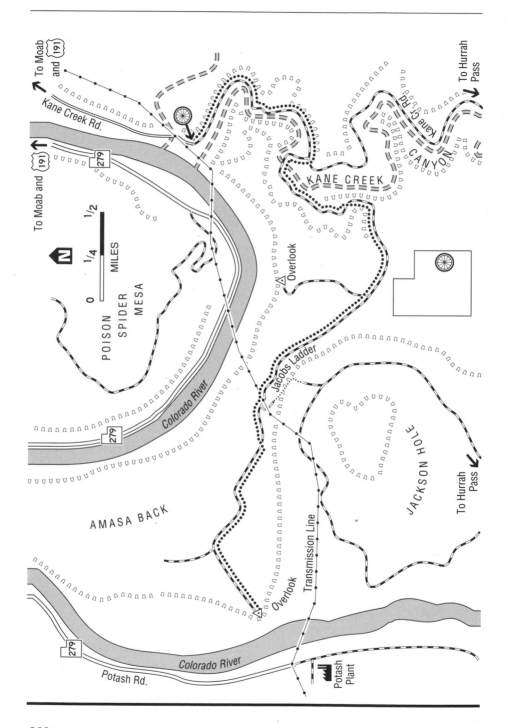

To Moab and 191

Kane Creek Rd.

To Moab and 191

279

POISON SPIDER MESA

N

1/4 1/2

0

MILES

Colorado River

279

AMASA BACK

279

Potash Rd.

Colorado River

Potash Plant

Transmission Line

Overlook

Jacobs Ladder

Overlook

KANE CREEK

Kane Cr. Rd.

CANYON

To Hurrah Pass

JACKSON HOLE

To Hurrah Pass

Riding the rim above Jackson Hole.

Intermediate-level riders will enjoy this route.

General location: Amasa Back is located 6 miles southwest of Moab off the Kane Creek Road.

Elevation change: The parking area resides at 4,000'. The Amasa Back trail leaves Kane Creek Road at an elevation of 4,160'. The highest elevation of Amasa Back you'll be able to reach reasonably is 5,050'. Total elevation gain is about 1,100'.

Season: Spring (March through June) and fall (September through October) are the best times of the year to pedal in the greater Moab area. Midsummer can be uncomfortably warm and bugs may become annoying, especially near water. Always carry plenty of water regardless of the season. Winter can be enjoyable when the route is dry.

Services: There are no services along this route and all surface waters should be purified. Moab (where many prefer to begin this ride) offers all visitor services, including top-flight bike shops and medical facilities, in addition to the usual amenities.

Hazards: Be especially attentive on the ascent to (and descent from) Amasa Back, which is moderately to highly technical. You'll have several outstanding views from the rims of numerous cliffs. Be aware of loose rocks and overhanging ledges. Use caution when pedaling Kane Creek Road (the paved portion from town especially), stay in single file, and yield the right of way to motorists.

Rescue index: Amasa Back is remote and difficult to reach. You won't see many motorists along the dirt section of the Kane Creek Road but you will along the paved section leading to town. Moab has medical facilities.

Land status: Bureau of Land Management, Moab District.

Maps: USGS 7.5 minute quadrangles: Gold Bar Canyon and Moab, Utah. (The route is not shown on these maps.)

Finding the trail: From the center of Moab, travel west on 1st North to 100 West (at Rim Cyclery). Turn south and immediately west on Williams Way. At the T intersection turn left/south on 500 West. Turn right on Kane Creek Road and enter into the Portal of the Colorado River. Pavement turns to dirt almost 5 miles from town. There is a parking area (with an information board) shortly ahead where the road turns into Kane Springs Canyon.

Sources of additional information:

> Bureau of Land Management
> Grand Resource Area
> 92 East Dogwood
> Suite G
> Moab, Utah 84532
> (801) 259-8193

Notes on the trail: From the parking area on Kane Creek Road (shortly after pavement turns to dirt), pedal out the dirt road. The (unsigned) Amasa Back Trail is about 1.2 miles ahead. It dives off the Kane Creek Road about halfway up the gentle hill. The old prospector's road begins with a short descent over ledgy bedrock to Kane Springs Creek. Stay left and next to the creek a short distance; cross the creek, then begin the ascent that rises quickly above the canyon. Rock cairns mark the way when the route periodically crosses barren slickrock.

Two miles from Kane Creek Road, the route reaches a summit and crosses over to Amasa Back's western side. Immediately ahead is a Y junction: the road forking left is the main route; the double-track spurring right crests a small hill, then descends half a mile to a compelling viewpoint. Here the hummocks of Navajo sandstone comprising Poison Spider Mesa are a backdrop for the Colorado River corridor. Eastward, a parade of fins and sandstone ribs march in echelon toward the La Sal Mountains. Despite some sand traps along the way, this is a must-do spur.

When you return to the main route, continue out Amasa Back along the edge of 1,000´-deep Jackson Hole. Hop over the gas pipeline, then pass under power lines, both of which descend into Jackson Hole and to the Potash Plant. The double-track spurring left/west leads to the top of infamous Jacobs Ladder—an improbable bike-on-shoulder portage out of Jackson Hole. (This "route" makes a loop ride out of the Hurrah Pass trail; see Ride 66.)

Beyond the spur to Jacobs Ladder there is about 2 miles of pursuable trail; however, the road dissipates into broken slickrock, marked periodically with cairns. How far you go out on the Amasa peninsula depends largely on your own route-finding, and route-making, creativity. A western rim, which affords overwhelming vistas of Jackson Hole, Colorado River, Island in the Sky District, Behind the Rocks and the La Sal Mountains, is worth striving for.

RIDE 66 *HURRAH PASS*

All this talk about Slickrock: precision gruntwork, interval straining; friction, stiction, and traction; cant and ratchet; inside pedal up, butt off the back, nose to the bars; pitch and twitch, potato chip, crotch split; rock rash; prodigious, profound, and improbable maneuvers; protracted acclivities, free-falling declivities; sandstone surfing.

If you long for a straightforward, scenically captivating ride, head out to Hurrah Pass. Here you'll have opportunities for viewing petroglyph panels, hiking to a secluded arch, quenching your thirst at a fern-encrusted spring, plus a whole lot of canyon country viewing.

This 20-mile out-and-back ride is a local favorite for strong novice and intermediate cyclists. The route follows improved dirt and gravel roads, with about two miles of intermittent pavement bedrock near Hurrah Pass. Technical difficulty is generally low, which means you can spend more time sightseeing than worrying about whether you might "stuff" your front wheel.

General location: The Hurrah Pass trail begins 5 miles southwest of Moab on the Kane Creek Road.
Elevation change: The route's parking area is at 4,000′. Hurrah Pass rises to 4,800′. A midroute descent and consequent rise increase the total elevation gain to about 1,300′.
Season: Spring (March through May) and fall (September through October) are the most enjoyable seasons to mountain bike in the Moab area. Midsummer tends to be oppressively warm and insects are bothersome. Winter can be enjoyable when the route is dry and weather cooperates. Always carry plenty of water regardless of the season and apply sunscreen liberally.
Services: There are no services along this route and all surface waters should be purified. There is a spring 2.2 miles into the ride that provides potable water and a good soaking upon your return. Moab offers all visitor services.
Hazards: Overall, the route is quite low in technical difficulty. The final approach to Hurrah Pass crosses intermittent pavement sandstone that is not too technical but requires attentiveness just the same. Vehicular traffic is light near the trailhead and less so farther out. Always carry plenty of water, use a liberal amount of sunscreen, and pack along insect repellent. Biting flies tend to hover near the creek.

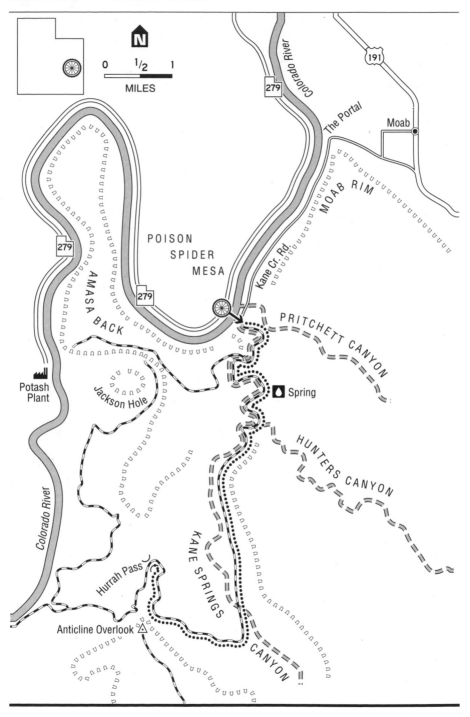

N

0 ½ 1
MILES

Colorado River

279

The Portal

191

Moab

POISON
SPIDER
MESA

MOAB RIM

Kane Cr. Rd.

AMASA BACK

279

279

PRITCHETT CANYON

Potash
Plant

Jackson Hole

Spring

HUNTERS CANYON

Colorado River

KANE SPRINGS

Hurrah Pass

Anticline Overlook

CANYON

Rescue index: This route is popular, so you are likely to encounter other bikers. Vehicular traffic is light from the trailhead to the Kane Springs Creek crossing 7 miles out. Thereafter, you won't see many motorists. Moab has medical facilities.

Land status: Bureau of Land Management, Moab District.

Maps: USGS 7.5 minute quadrangles: Moab, Shafer Basin, and Through Springs Canyon, Utah.

Finding the trail: From the center of Moab, travel west on 1st North to 100 West (at Rim Cyclery). Turn south, then immediately west on Williams Way. At the T intersection, turn left/south on 500 West. Turn right on Kane Creek Road and enter into the Portal, where the Colorado River leaves the Moab valley and penetrates sandstone palisades. Pavement turns to dirt almost 5 miles from the center of town. There is a parking area (with an information board) shortly ahead where the road bends away from the Colorado River and enters into Kane Springs Canyon.

Sources of additional information:

Bureau of Land Management
Grand Resource Area
92 East Dogwood
Suite G
Moab, Utah 84532
(801) 259-8193

Notes on the trail: From the parking area at the mouth of Kane Springs Canyon, follow the dirt and gravel road into a corridor of vertical sandstone glowing warmly in the midday sun. Kane Springs Creek nourishes shade-giving cottonwoods that interrupt pervasive desert hues with mellow emerald tones. The spur to Amasa Back branches right after 1.2 miles, about midway up a gentle rise. Drop through a pair of switchbacks and past a quenching spring.

For another mile, the road follows deep within the erosional architecture of Kane Springs Creek, then the canyon widens to a rim-bound valley. A gentle but noticeable incline is capped by roadside Turk Rock. Gather prudent speed to carry you through the Kane Springs Creek crossing up ahead. Once you've crossed, you'll notice a double-track that spurs left and up the remaining length of Kane Springs Canyon; don't take that spur. Instead, bear right/west to begin ascending the canyon's western slope to Hurrah Pass. As you approach Hurrah Pass, the route affords compelling views of the canyon through which you have just traveled.

You'll have incredible views of the Colorado River corridor once you reach Hurrah Pass. Westward, the river flows past Pyramid Butte and trapezoid-shaped, aquamarine settling ponds of the Potash plant. Southward, the river meanders through the Island in the Sky's layer-cake strata toward a passionate mating with the Green River. The Canyonlands' Anticline is clearly visible and the Overlook pavilion can be spotted high above on a southern point.

RIDE 67 *JUGHANDLE LOOP*

The Jughandle Loop is a continuous scenic highlight; it follows the Colorado River corridor downstream, traveling along spectacular benchlands above the river. Overhead, the jutting cliffs of the Island in the Sky reveal eons of geologic history lithified in the terraced rock strata. The trail passes Pyramid Butte and veers close (within a few feet) to the edge of the river canyon where the Colorado meanders through a gigantic "gooseneck." Above is the Dead Horse Point overlook; to the south is Canyonlands' Needles District.

The effort of climbing the Shafer Trail is rewarded by an incredible view to the east, matched perhaps only by the view from the top of upcoming Long Canyon. The last four miles of the ride is the descent of Long Canyon (through "Pucker Pass"), one of the best anywhere.

This 38-mile loop (clockwise) requires low technical skills with some intermediate-level ones mixed in; but it also offers one quite formidable climb marked by the 1,200´ ascent of the infamous Shafer Trail switchbacks. The route combines 9 miles of paved roads with 29 miles of dirt roads, most of which are in good condition. In Shafer Canyon, just outside Canyonlands National Park and in Pucker Pass, expect rough and eroded conditions, particularly after heavy rainstorms. You'll also be traveling a somewhat uncomfortable 1.5-mile stretch of packed river gravel just after you leave the pavement at the beginning of the route at the Moab Salt Plant.

This chapter on the Jughandle Loop was provided by John Groo, Moab, Utah.

General location: This route travels through the Colorado River Canyon, its benchlands, and the Island in the Sky area, all located about 15 miles southwest of Moab.

Elevation change: The start/finish point (Jughandle Arch) is at 3,960´. The high point of the ride (at UT 313/Island in the Sky) is at 6,190´. Much of the gain is made in the ascent of the Shafer Trail (including more than 1,000´ up the final set of switchbacks), and much of the loss is in the descent of Long Canyon. There are also several small hills and rolling terrain throughout the ride.

Season: Spring (March to early June) and Fall (September to early December) are the best times to ride. Winter riding is possible, and quite enjoyable, when weather permits. Summer is usually too hot for an enjoyable or safe ride, unless you start very early. Be aware of current weather patterns and bring extra clothes as needed. Always carry plenty of water.

Services: There are no services along the route, but the Park Service contact station for the Island in the Sky district is half a mile off the route at the top of the Shafer Trail. Their water is trucked in, so don't go looking for any unless it is an emergency. Moab has all visitor services, including bike shops.

RIDE 67 *JUGHANDLE LOOP*

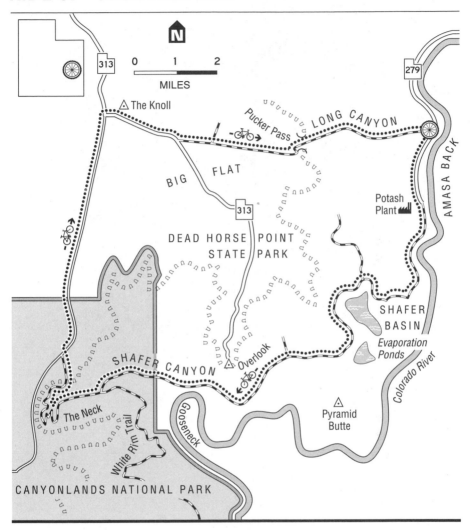

Hazards: There are no reliable water sources along this route, and the hot, dry climate dehydrates active bodies very quickly. Always take *plenty* of water—at least two large bottles.

Keep in mind that this is a long ride. Take food for sustained energy and allow yourself at least five hours to complete the loop.

Rescue index: Emergency assistance on this ride depends on your timing and where you are when you need help. The section of the route that lies outside the park is not frequently traveled; but on a nice spring or fall day there are almost always some other people in the area. During off-season, weekdays, or periods

A rider drops through Pucker Pass.

of marginal weather, there might not by another person in the area for days. There are no regular patrols.

Inside the park and on all sections of paved road, traffic (of one sort or another) is regular during all but the most disagreeable weather periods. (What would you be doing there then?) The park is patrolled, particularly along the Shafer Trail. Patrols are more sporadic from the Park entrance/boundary on the Potash Trail to the foot of the Shafer Trail.

Land status: Bureau of Land Management, Moab District; Canyonlands National Park. Keep in mind that you should ride only on the main, designated route. You are subject to fines if you take your bicycle off the main route in the park.

Maps: USGS 7.5 minute quadrangles: Gold Bar Canyon, Musselman Arch, Shafer Basin, and The Knoll, Utah; USGS 1:100,000 metric topographic series: La Sal and Moab, Utah. Good trail maps and guidebooks are available at the Moab Visitor Center, bike shops, public land agencies, bookstores, and other retail outlets in Moab.

Finding the trail: This ride begins and ends at Jughandle Arch, located at milepost 2 along UT 279 (the Potash Road), 13.5 miles from its intersection with US 191 north of Moab.

Sources of additional information:

Bureau of Land Management
Grand Resource Area
92 East Dogwood
Suite G
Moab, Utah 84532
(801) 259-8193

Above and Beyond Slickrock, by Todd Campbell (Wasatch Publishing, Salt Lake City, Utah)

Notes on the trail: Beginning at Jughandle Arch, follow the paved road south past the Moab Salt Plant and continue on a stretch of packed river gravel that the locals call "The Moab Roubaix." Thereafter, the dirt road turns west away from the Colorado River. Continue straight at the intersection with the brackish ponds and "Welcome to Potash Plant" sign, then up an eroded stretch of road. The main road levels and passes by Pyramid Butte to the south. The road swings close to cliffs overlooking the Colorado River. About 13 miles into the ride, take a short spur left for overlooks of the Colorado River Gooseneck. A mile beyond the Canyonlands National Park boundary is the junction with the White Rim Trail. A 1,200′ climb up the Shafer Trail switchbacks brings you to pavement.

Pedal north on the Island in the Sky road, then turn right on UT 313 towards Dead Horse Point. After about 2 miles, just before the paved road bends right/south, fork left onto a dirt road. The dirt road descends gradually but consistently eastward, then drops quickly through Pucker Pass and down the length of Long Canyon, your just reward.

RIDE 68 *SLICKROCK BIKE TRAIL*

For most people, the Slickrock Bike Trail (synonymous with Moab) needs no introduction. The trail lies atop a stairstep mesa, two sides of which are defined by the Moab Valley and the Colorado River. Besides having a constant reference to the 12,700′-plus La Sal Mountains, you can dangle your feet from an 800-foot overhanging cliff above the Colorado River. (Some Darwinist with a crude sense of humor dubbed this "Natural Selection Viewpoint.") Several giant arches are visible in the National Park of the same name across the river. The view made most famous by magazine articles is that showing bikers in front of the backdrop where the Colorado meanders through a portal defined by two

RIDE 68   *SLICKROCK BIKE TRAIL*

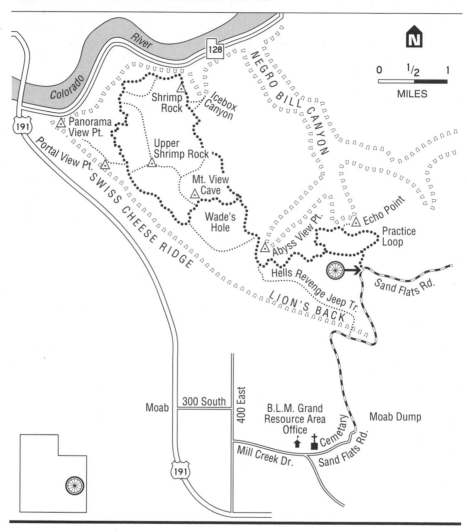

looming cliffs, as it flows on toward the classic western skyline of Canyonlands National Park.

The remarkable scenery of the Slickrock Trail is often over-shadowed by the opportunity of finding "impossible" paths or cleaning audacious two-wheeled moves. The fact that mountain bike manufacturers test their bikes on the Slickrock Bike Trail's steep, frictional surfaces is a tribute to its legendary difficulty. But don't be daunted; virtually any mountain biker can ride the majority of the trail. The first-time rider especially will have to walk some of the techni-

Returning from the Colorado River Overlook.

cally and physically demanding sections. Bike handling skills can make up for lack of brute strength, and vice versa.

The main trail is 12.3 miles long—a 5-mile out-and-back segment with a 7.3-mile loop at its far reaches. The practice loop is 3.1 miles. But, putting an exact mileage on Slickrock is presumptuous, for the clearly marked paint-on-rock aspect of the trail allows free-form exploring adjacent to it. The trail is almost entirely on barren sandstone, or slickrock (which is not slick, but smooth), punctuated occasionally by sandy depressions, known locally as "runaway bike ramps."

This chapter on the Slickrock Bike Trail was provided by the illustrious Todd Campbell,* Moab, Utah.

General location: The Slickrock Bike Trail is located about 4 miles east of downtown Moab.

---

*Like many canyon folk, Todd Campbell kept visiting the Moab area until he finally just stayed (actually his car broke down). The profound simplicity of form, color, and contrast in the redrock keeps him spellbound, "sandstoned," if you will. To Todd, the mountain bike is the preeminent tool for exploring the intricacies of Utah's Canyon Country, although his favorite places are still only accessible on foot, or "by crawling, on bloodied knee, if necessary," as Edward Abbey said.

As the author of the "guidebook to God," *Above and Beyond Slickrock,* Todd is particularly sensitive to the charges of environmental degradation caused by mountain

The author spends a "day at the office."

Elevation changes: Although no point on the trail is more than 150′ higher than the trailhead (4,650′), the undulating nature of the trail produces some 2,000′ of climbing. These climbs are usually short bursts that will convince you that you are in interval "straining" (as opposed to interval training).

Season: Early spring and fall are the best times to ride the Slickrock Trail. Recent rains can pack the sand deposits and clean loose matter off the rock's surface. Early winter is good, too, unless the trail becomes icy. Freezing and thawing in late winter can leave lots of loose sand on and at the base of sand-

---

(continued from page 293)
bikes. His quest is to share the desert he loves, not facilitate its trashing. "Life is fragile in this harsh environment; its beauty is realized by reverence."

Besides his work as a backcountry bike tour guide, Todd is a seasoned photographer and operates Moab Outabouts, a company specializing in backcountry photography tours throughout remote southeastern Utah.

stone slopes, thus reducing the tires' critical traction. Because of the heat and threat of sudden, intense electrical storms, a summer's ride should probably end by 9 A.M. or begin after 7 P.M.

Services: Although BLM (Bureau of Land Management) lands have historically had a camp-where-you-please policy, the impact of camping near the trailhead has forced a change to designated campsites. Campers should be mindful of the fragile desert environment and refrain from forging new roads, collecting wood, building new fire rings, etc. All visitor services are available in Moab.

Hazards: The biggest hazard on Slickrock is lack of preparedness. You will find no water on the trail or at the trailhead, and little shade anywhere during the ride. Carry at least 2 quarts of water, and be prepared to turn back when you start to run low. Always wear a helmet! The rock is as hard as cement, and falls can be deadly! The most challenging sections are marked with cautionary "fried eggs"—yellow dots within the white dashes. And remember, use reasonable judgement when you're choosing the parts of Slickrock you want to attempt; in many places a single lapse of concentration or mechanical foul-up can be costly.

Make sure your bike, especially your brakes, are well tuned. In addition to the standard tools you normally pack, carry extra cables and brake pad mounting nuts and screws. When you abandon a steep climb, jump over the side of the bike so you don't get caught rolling backward while still straddling the top tube. First-time Slickrock Trail riders, and especially those bikers relatively new to ATBs, should *not* ride alone.

Rescue index: There are bikers on the trail at almost all times. You may see an occasional jeeper and motorcyclist. The town of Moab lies 4 miles from the trailhead. Half-mile increments painted on the main trail aid search-and-rescue teams, and allow riders to gauge their progress.

Land status: Bureau of Land Management, Moab District.

Maps: USGS 7.5 minute quadrangle: Moab, Utah. (The Slickrock Trail is not shown on this map.) The local BLM office and several bike shops in Moab have Slickrock maps.

Finding the trail: From any of the stoplights in Moab, go east to 400 East. Turn right (south), then left on Mill Creek Drive. Bear left onto Sand Flats Road when Mill Creek Drive jogs right, and follow a sign for Slickrock. At the trailhead parking lot various interpretive signs describing the desert environment in which you're riding are worth reading.

Sources of additional information:

Bureau of Land Management
Grand Resource Area
92 East Dogwood
Suite G
Moab, Utah 84532
(801) 259-8193

Moab Outabouts
P.O. Box 314
Moab, Utah 84532
Moab Outabouts specializes in backcountry tours throughout remote southeastern Utah. Services range from trip photography for commercial outfitters to interpretive services of canyon country's natural and historical setting.

Above and Beyond Slickrock, by Todd Campbell (Wasatch Publishing, Salt Lake City, Utah)

Notes on the trail: Novice riders usually improve tenfold over the course of their first ride as they realize how the superb traction on the undulating Navajo Sandstone allows bikes their fullest expression. Observant cyclists will find "cheater" (and sometimes wiser) routes around many of the most difficult moves. Fatigued (but still functioning) riders can simply turn around at any point along the trail, and follow the painted dots and/or dashes back to the trailhead.

Interrupting the trail's pervasive sandstone pavement are exquisite pocket gardens of twisted juniper, squawbush, and cactus enveloped in a carpet of fragile, black microbiotic soil underneath. Microbiotic soils are the building blocks of desert soils; they help prevent erosion and fix critical nutrients that help establish larger plants. Avoid riding or stepping on the soil, for long-term actual damage (and even longer visual damage) will occur.

There are a few cottonwood trees on the trail that turn a radiant golden color in the fall. The salmon-hued rock will surprise you with its color variation of cream, gold, and lavender.

Note: During the spring of 1989, 4 miles of connectors and spurs were added to the route to enable more cross-country exploring. The new segments are marked with white dots; the original trail is still marked with white dashes.

RIDE 69 *PORCUPINE RIM*

This route takes you into relatively high country and offers scenic views in all directions. But, the real highlights are unusual rock formations and terrain, including stunning and surprising views of local geological phenomena from improbable vantage points. At one point, the trail swings down a small hill and contacts the rim of Castle Valley. Quite without warning you will find yourself on the edge of this beautiful valley looking down into and across it to the Priest and Nuns, Adobe Mesa, and monolithic Castle Rock. Similarly startling is the airy perspective from where the single-track crosses a terrace several hundred feet above the Colorado River. Add fine close-ups of upper Negro Bill Canyon

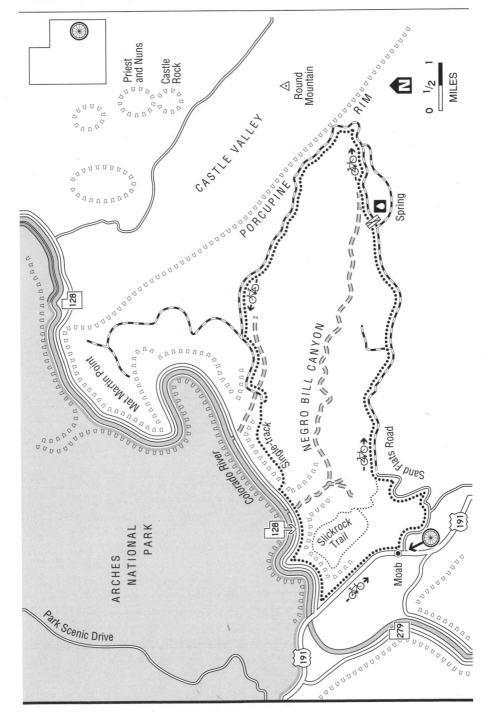

Priest
and Nuns

Castle
Rock

CASTLE VALLEY

Round
Mountain

PORCUPINE   RIM

Spring

128

Mat Martin Point

NEGRO BILL CANYON

Single-track

Colorado River

128

Sand Flats Road

191

Slickrock
Trail

Moab

ARCHES

NATIONAL

PARK

Park Scenic Drive

191

279

MILES

0   1/2   1

N

Descending single-track high above the Colorado River.

and Jackass Canyon, the La Sal Mountains, and Arches National Park, and you have a worldclass ride packed with dramatic highlights.

This 34-mile loop (counterclockwise) is a demanding ride, recommended for riders with more developed technical skills and good physical conditioning. It incorporates 9 miles of paved road and 25 miles of dirt, including a long climb on paved and then maintained but washboarded dirt and sand roads, followed by technical climbing and swooping descents on broken slickrock and packed-dirt double-track, and several miles of challenging single-track. Navigation can be tricky and you can be easily confused by the other inconsequential trail segments along Porcupine Rim.

This description of the Porcupine Rim Trail was provided by John Groo, Moab, Utah.

General location: Porcupine Rim is located in the highlands 10 miles east of Moab, along the rims of Castle Valley and the Colorado River canyon.

Elevation change: The route begins at 4,000′ in Moab and climbs to 6,800′ on Porcupine Rim above Castle Valley. Virtually all of the elevation gain is accomplished in the early part of the ride—on the 9-mile climb up the Sand Flats Road and the first 3 miles of the Porcupine Rim Trail itself. From there it is almost all downhill to the trail's end at the Colorado River/UT 128 with some level sections and short, abrupt hills (known locally as "bumps"). The ride back to Moab on pavement is flat.

Season: Spring (April to early June) and fall (September through November) are the best seasons. Because of elevation and exposure, this route is less enjoyable to ride than most until later in the spring. Summer is generally too hot for an enjoyable or safe ride. Be aware of current weather patterns, take extra clothing as needed, and always take plenty of water.

Services: Outside of Moab, which offers all visitor services, no services are available along this route. Water usually drips into the cattle tanks on Sand Flats Road at the beginning of the Porcupine Rim Trail. Matrimony Spring, located near the junction of UT 128 and US 191, is always cool and refreshing.

Hazards: The single-track section above Jackass Canyon is technical and challenging. Navigation can be tricky and you can be easily confused by a number of other inconsequential trail segments along Porcupine Rim. Inquire locally for specific information and/or detailed maps. Keep in mind that this is a long ride. Take some food for sustained energy, and allow yourself at least 5 hours to complete the ride.

Rescue index: The Sand Flats Road from Moab to its intersection with the Porcupine Rim Trail is fairly well traveled, and the paved road from the trail's end to town is quite busy (by local standards). Aid or rescue along these parts should pose no problem; however, the Porcupine Rim Trail itself is remote, seldom traveled, and hard to reach. Always leave word of your intended travels.

Land status: Bureau of Land Management, Moab District.

Maps: USGS 7.5 minute quadrangles: Big Bend, Moab, and Rill Creek, Utah; USGS 1:100,000 metric topographic series: Moab, Utah. Good trail maps are available locally at the Moab Visitor Center, bike shops, public land agencies, bookstores, and other retail outlets in Moab.

Finding the trail: The ride begins in Moab. The actual starting point for the Porcupine Rim Trail is at the watering tanks on Sand Flats Road, 9 miles from Moab. If you use a car shuttle, you can avoid the long ride up Sand Flats Road.

Sources of additional information:

Bureau of Land Management
Grand Resource Area
92 East Dogwood
Suite G
Moab, Utah 84532
(801) 259-8193

Above and Beyond Slickrock, by Todd Campbell (Wasatch Publishing, Salt Lake City, Utah)

Notes on the trail: From the intersection of Main and Center Streets in Moab, pedal east on Center. Turn right on 400 East and follow signs for Slickrock Bike Trail. Turn left on Mill Creek Drive, then left again on Sand Flats Road. You'll get a good warm-up climb past what's known as "America's Most Scenic Dump" to the trailhead for Slickrock. Continue on Sand Flats Road, which turns from paved to dirt/sand and is typically laden with sand traps, loaded with washboard, and littered with imbedded stones. Two and one-half miles past Slickrock, Sand Flats Road wedges between two sandstone fins and may be very rough for passenger cars.

Nine miles from town, look for water tanks, a wire fence line, and an old four-wheel-drive road forking left from the Sand Flats Road. This is the actual (unposted) trailhead for Porcupine Rim. After 3 miles of technical climbing over loose sand and broken bedrock, you'll reach Porcupine Rim. A grand view like this should not be hurried.

Double-track parallels the Rim for 2 miles, then veers toward Coffee Pot Rock. (The route is marked with a carsonite post reading "Porcupine Bike Trail and Jeep Road.") Shortly ahead, fork right following another carsonite post. (The left spur here leads toward Coffee Pot Rock.)

Head across "super polygrip ridge," where incessant broken outcrop sets your teeth to chattering. Swing through a pair of notably sharp turns, then welcome a reprieve of smooth, packed sand that affords large chainring cruising. Follow rock cairns across an evident patch of slickrock next to a prominent sandstone ridge, then stay left and slightly uphill. Up ahead, pass a carsonite post for the Wilderness Study Area. After it travels over a second slickrock exposure, the trail drops into a sandy gully followed by a quick uphill burst. Look for carsonite posts and/or rock cairns directing you right and onto the single-track section that hovers above the head of Jackass Canyon.

This unforgiving single-track requires good handling skills, attentiveness, and unclouded judgement, especially while you're trying to simultaneously absorb the spectacular composition of cliffs, river, and slickrock. When you reach paved UT 128, pedal riverside 3.4 miles to the junction at US 191 and then back to town.

RIDE 70 *WHITE RIM ROAD*

The White Rim Road is unequivocally the grandaddy of Utah mountain bike rides and the cadillac of multi-day fat-tire tours; in few other places is the sense of open space and clear light as overwhelming.

RIDE 70 *WHITE RIM ROAD*

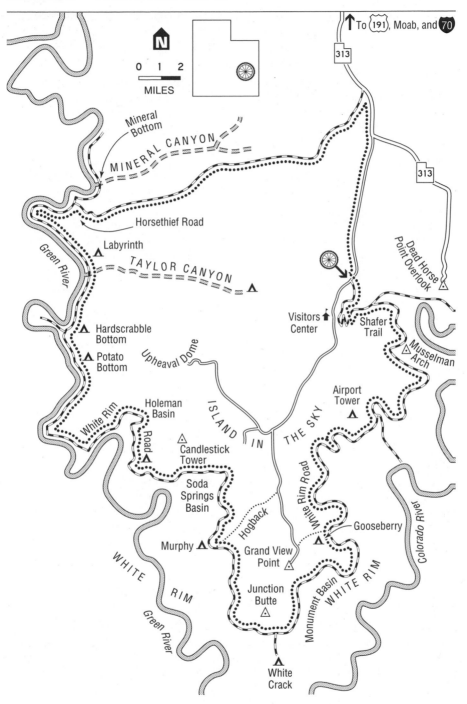

N

0 1 2
MILES

To (191), Moab, and (70)

313

313

Mineral Bottom

MINERAL CANYON

Horsethief Road

Green River

Labyrinth

TAYLOR CANYON

Dead Horse Point Overlook

Visitors Center

Shafer Trail

Musselman Arch

Hardscrabble Bottom

Potato Bottom

Upheaval Dome

Airport Tower

Holeman Basin

White Rim Road

ISLAND IN THE SKY

Candlestick Tower

Soda Springs Basin

Hogback

Murphy

Grand View Point

White Rim Road

Gooseberry

Monument Basin

WHITE RIM

Colorado River

WHITE

RIM

Green River

Junction Butte

White Crack

Scenic beauty is everywhere along the White Rim Road. You'll be awed by an ensemble of classic canyonlands-style rock formations ranging in color from orange and yellow to chocolate brown and fire red, to gold, purple, and green-blue. The allure of the White Rim is that you'll be exposed to several distinct geologic rock layers, each a chapter in the multi-million-year evolution of southern Utah's Canyon Country. You'll also have views of both the Green and Colorado Rivers as they flow to their confluence far from the trail. The "V" where the two rivers become one has created a three-tier slice of geologic "wedding cake"; the road travels along the middle layer.

The White Rim Sandstone, the trail's namesake, rests on top of a softer, brick-red member of the Cutler Formation. Being more resistant to the erosive effects of water than the underlying formation, the White Rim has created a landscape of sheer and overhanging white-capped cliffs, that appear to have been stamped by a cookie cutter. Numerous islands of White Rim Sandstone have withstood erosion such that they top 800′ freestanding monuments and spectacular buttes.

In addition to the panoramic captivity of the main route, some spur roads lead to memorable scenic overlooks, notably Musselman Arch, Colorado Overlook, and White Crack. Desert bighorn sheep are plentiful and reward the patient eye.

The White Rim Road is a 110-mile loop ride. Degree of difficulty depends on how fast or slow you plan to ride it and whether a support vehicle will be used; i.e., a four-day vehicle-supported trip is moderately difficult; whereas, a two-day unsupported trip is very difficult. (Some cyclists have completed the entire loop in a single day—an incomprehensible feat for the average biker.)

The White Rim Road, proper, is fairly level though it has several tedious hills; Murphy Hogback and Hardscrabble are the longest. Even mountain bikers unburdened by camping gear will probably have to walk these. Keep in mind that the White Rim Road is accessible only by 1,400′ switchbacks, one at either end (Shafer and Horsethief Trails), with 12 miles of dirt and 8 miles of paved road connecting them. The trail follows jeep roads throughout, and is punctuated occasionally with sandy stretches, loose rock, and minor bedrock exposures. For the most part, you can travel at a fast pace on these surfaces. All support vehicles should be high clearance and equipped with four-wheel-drive.

This description of the White Rim Road was provided by Todd Campbell, Moab, Utah.

General location: The White Rim Road is located in the Island in the Sky District of Canyonlands National Park, about 34 miles west of Moab.

Elevation change: The route's highest elevation (6,000′) is along the Island in the Sky road atop the Shafer Trail switchbacks. The trail dips to 3,900′ as it parallels the Green River. Over the course of the trip, expect to lose and regain approximately 3,000′, although about half of this occurs in one of two switchbacking climbs (on Shafer Trail Road or Horsethief Road) depending on direction of travel.

Season: Like all canyon country rides, spring and fall offer the most moderate temperatures. The White Rim, residing at over 5,000´, can be snowy in the winter and uncomfortably hot during midsummer. The gnats become a nuisance in mid- to late May, and can make an otherwise enjoyable trip miserable.

Services: There are no services along this route. Pack any necessities in your support vehicle or on your bike. Camping is restricted to designated, but primitive, sites. You must obtain an overnight permit for the White Rim Road. Call well in advance of your trip to ensure a campsite reservation. (Since mountain bikers are considered "vehicle users" it is illegal to camp backcountry at other than designated sites.) All visitor services and provisions are found in Moab.

Hazards: The lack of water is the single greatest limitation on the White Rim. The Park Service does not make water available for bike tour groups at the Visitor Center, so pack along all you will need in the support vehicle. In warm weather, plan on drinking a gallon and a half per person per day. Do not rely on sandstone potholes as a water source after rainstorms. Since there is very little relief from the beating sun, carry adequate sun protection.

During wet conditions portions of the route may become quite muddy, especially on the Green River bottomlands. All support vehicles should be high clearance and equipped with four-wheel-drive.

Rescue index: In recent years, overnight mountain bike travel has skyrocketed. Most bike groups have support vehicles, so help is usually not far away. Park rangers patrol the White Rim, but not on a regular basis. Numerous hiking trails, which are accessible by paved roads, connect the White Rim with the high rim overlooks above. Two key foot routes are Gooseberry Trail (on the east side of the ride) and Murphy Trail (on the west side of the ride). The park can arrange for helicopter rescue in the event of serious injury. Report all injuries to the Island in the Sky Visitor Center.

Land status: Canyonlands National Park; Bureau of Land Management, Moab District.

Maps: USGS 1:62,500 scale topographic map: Canyonlands National Park; USGS 1:100,000 metric topographic series: Hanksville, La Sal, Moab, and San Rafael Desert, Utah.

Finding the trail: From Moab, follow US 191 about 9 miles north to UT 313. Look for a sign for Canyonlands National Park and Dead Horse Point State Park. Travel west and south 25 miles to the parking area near the Island Visitor Center above the Shafer Trail Road switchbacks.

Sources of additional information:

Bureau of Land Management
Grand Resource Area
92 East Dogwood
Suite G
Moab, Utah 84532
(801) 259-8193

Canyonlands National Park
2282 S. West Resource Boulevard
Moab, Utah 84532
(801) 259-7164

Above and Beyond Slickrock, by Todd Campbell (Wasatch Publishing, Salt Lake City, Utah)

Notes on the trail: Backcountry permits issued by Canyonlands National Park are required for *all* overnight excursions. Call well in advance with a carefully planned itinerary, plus alternative dates, for a White Rim trip. By the first of the year, most of the prime dates and campsites will have been reserved for the coming spring and fall season.

Policies regarding White Rim excursions were changed, effective January 1995. Contact Canyonlands National Park for current policies and restrictions.

This loop can be ridden in either direction. When vehicle-supported, most bikers prefer to ride east to west—down the Shafer Trail Road first and up Horsethief Canyon last. If you tackle the route self-supported, you may prefer to travel west to east. In this direction, the 8 miles of pavement and an easy, but otherwise mundane, 15-mile stretch of dirt access road to the top of Horsethief Canyon are at the beginning of the ride. Then you can save the mind-boggling canyon displays for the heart of the trip. Also, you can stock up on water early in the trip along the Green River.

When planning your trip, make sure you know the distances between established campsites. Allow yourself three to five days to complete the entire trip, which includes time to explore many of the hidden treasures adjacent to the trail.

Special regulations:

Backcountry camping permits are required for all overnight White Rim bike tours. Canyonlands National Park begins accepting campsite reservations (permits) in July for the *following* calendar year. Call the park headquarters for current reservation procedures. Have a carefully planned itinerary plus backup dates. A $25 non-refundable fee is required for a permit application. (A park entrance fee, per vehicle, is collected at the Island in the Sky Visitor Center.)

No more than 3 vehicles and 15 persons are allowed at each campsite along the White Rim Road. Larger parties must reserve more than one campsite. Pets are not allowed in the park's backcountry, so they may not accompany you on the White Rim. Wood fires are prohibited. Use a gas stove or charcoal with a fire pan. All ashes (and trash) *must* be packed out.

Bicycles must stay on the White Rim Road and on designated spur roads. Cross country travel is strictly prohibited. When hiking, stay to trails, slickrock, or sandy washes to avoid trampling microbiotic soils. And as always when riding and visiting canyon country, practice minimum impact techniques. (See "Preface, Special Issues.")

RIDE 71 *DEADMANS TRAIL / HORSESHOE CANYON*

With a name like Deadmans Trail, one might envision the terrain on this ride fraught with gloom and despair, a hopelessly forsaken land where not even a jackrabbit could make a living. You *will* pass through some of Utah's most remote and desolate backcountry on Deadmans Trail, but your destination, Horseshoe Canyon, is a special place full of intrigue.

At first glance, Horseshoe Canyon alone is indeed an impressive sight. You'll see that a spring-fed creek nourishes desert flowers, succulent grasses, and tenacious sage; magnificent cottonwoods shade the canyon floor; and sheer sandstone walls glow with brilliant radiance. But if you take a closer look, you'll discover that Horseshoe Canyon is much more than a precious sanctuary amidst an arid wilderness. It hosts what many consider the most significant, and certainly most spectacular, prehistoric Indian rock art in North America. There are several displays in Horseshoe Canyon but the Great Gallery panel is far and away the most bewildering. The pictographs on this panel include dozens of well-preserved, life-size figures. Armless, mummy-shaped humanoids with either blank faces or hollow, sunken eyes are the motif along with trapezoid-shaped antelope and indecipherable shapes. Many figures are adorned with intricate shields and breastplates. Are these mysterious paintings the exaltation of deities? Are they the souls of the dead floating up to the heavens, visitors

RIDE 71 *DEADMANS TRAIL / HORSESHOE CANYON*

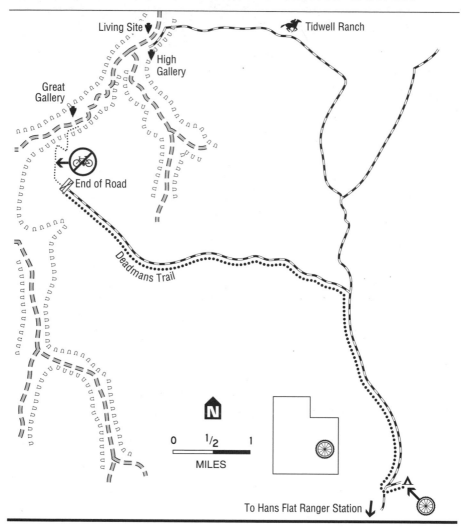

from another world, demons bearing omens, or simply artistic expressions? Whatever the answer, the images will leave you with a lasting impression.

This 14-mile out-and-back route follows sandy, four-wheel-drive roads across desert terrain. Technical difficulty is generally low, but isolated sections are rough and challenging. Sand traps are intermittent. Overall, it is a good intermediate-level ride.

From the turnaround point, a three-mile out-and-back foot trail leads into Horseshoe Canyon and to the Great Gallery. This primitive path crosses sloping desert and barren slickrock, then descends into the canyon via a bouldery

Part of the Great Gallery in Horseshoe Canyon.

path. Be sure to have shoes that are comfortable for biking *and* hiking. The hike is moderately strenuous; bring extra water and food.

General location: Horseshoe Canyon is a northern annex to the Maze District of Canyonlands National Park, south of Green River and northeast of Hanksville via 60 miles of dusty and lonely dirt roads.

Elevation change: The trailhead for Deadmans Trail is at 5,760′. The route's turnaround point drops to 5,360′. Adding in the road's undulations, total elevation gain is about 800′, the majority of which is on the way out. The hike into Horseshoe Canyon descends about 600′ over its 1.5-mile length.

Season: Spring (March through June) and fall (September through October) are the most pleasant times to visit Utah's Canyon Country. Midsummer temperatures can be oppressive (100s midday) and bugs annoying. Early and late winter can be enjoyable when the route is dry and weather is cooperative. Always carry plenty of water both on the bike and in the car, regardless of the season.

Services: Anything you may need along the trail will have to be stuffed into your vehicle. There are no services along the route and all surface waters should be purified. There is no water at Hans Flat Ranger Station. Camping is restricted to a handful of designated primitive sites within the National Park. Limited visitor services (inexpensive motels, food, and gasoline) are available at Hanksville, located 65 miles west and south of Hans Flat. Green River, nearly 100 miles away, has more extensive services. The closest bike shop is in Price.

Hazards: This is one of the most remote areas of Utah. Visitors are not common and access can be difficult. Thoughtful preparedness is mandatory. The maintained dirt road to Hans Flat Ranger Station is suitable for passenger cars when *dry*, but is impassable when wet. Heed this warning! The access road from Hans Flat to the Deadmans trailhead is restricted to high-clearance vehicles. If you plan to travel four-wheel-drive roads by vehicle to the far reaches of Maze country, stock a good spare tire, sturdy jack, extra gasoline, water, and food, plus a generous helping of common sense.

The bike route is low to moderate in technical difficulty. The hike down into Horseshoe Canyon crosses open slickrock. Be sure to wear shoes that are good for desert hiking *and* biking.

Rescue index: Visitors are not common in Horseshoe Canyon and less so along the Deadmans Trail since hikers usually get to the canyon via a western trailhead. Hans Flat Ranger Station, located 13 miles from the Deadmans trailhead, has radio communication. Green River has a medical clinic, but it is nearly 100 miles and several hours away by vehicle.

Land status: Canyonlands National Park.

Maps: USGS 7.5 minute quadrangles: Head Spur and Sugarloaf Butte, Utah.

Finding the trail: From Green River, travel 12 miles west on Interstate 70 and take Exit 147/UT 24, Hanksville, Capitol Reef. Travel 25 miles south on UT 24 to the turnoff for Rooster Flat, Flint Trail, the Maze, etc. (The turnoff is located between mileposts 137 and 136, half a mile south of the Goblin Valley/Temple Mountain junction, or about 20 miles north of Hanksville.) Drive southeast on the maintained dirt, sand, and washboarded road. After 25 miles, fork right at a sign for "Hans Flat Ranger Station 21" (right) and "Horseshoe Canyon foot trail 7" (left). Seven miles south, fork left at a junction signed "French Spring 15, Flint Trail 25, Maze 50" (all left); "Ekker Ranch 7" (right). Hans Flat Ranger Station is about 14 miles to the left.

From Hans Flat, travel north (past the outhouses) on a rough, sandy road signed "Horseshoe Canyon 22." A jeep road spurs left/west to Head Spur after 3.7 miles. In 10.5 miles near the top of a small rise, a designated but unsigned (and quite discreet) primitive campsite forks right/east. This is a good parking area; otherwise, Deadmans Trail (signed) is another 2.5 miles north on the "main" road.

Sources of additional information:

Canyonlands National Park
2282 S. West Resource Boulevard
Moab, Utah 84532
(801) 259-7164

Hans Flat Ranger Station
c/o Canyonlands National Park
2282 S. West Resource Boulevard
Moab, Utah 84532
(801) 259-7164

Notes on the trail: All regulations pertaining to Canyonlands National Park apply to the park's Horseshoe Canyon annex. For this information, contact the Canyonlands National Park. (See "Sources of additional information.")

Backcountry permits (free) are required for overnight camping or hiking within the park and are available at the Hans Flat Ranger Station.

From the primitive campsite/parking area, pedal northward on the access road 2.5 miles to the signed turnoff (left/west) for Deadmans Trail. This double-track undulates across a rolling high desert plateau. Knolls striped with tan, orange, and purple sediments enliven such desolation. Monumental buttes and canyons entombed by white sandstone spark curiosity and justify continued pursuit.

After 4.5 miles, the road ends at a small parking area signed "Deadmans Trail, Canyon Bottom 1.5, no vehicles or dogs allowed." (Locking up bikes is recommended; this area is seldom visited, but better safe than sorry. If you don't want to lock your bike, at least *carry* it cross country and stash it at a less-than-conspicuous location.) Take the primitive foot trail that heads northwestward toward a widening canyon. Posts and cairns periodically mark the way. You'll need to scramble over steep slopes of barren slickrock before you pass through a wire fence and drop down a bouldery path into the drainage bottom. Follow the braided path north/down canyon about half a mile to the Great Gallery (on the left.) Hike 2 miles north to additional rock art sites.

The panel here is flooded with sunlight during the morning hours but is draped in shadow by early afternoon. For photographs, you will probably need a polarizing lens when the panel is exposed to direct sunlight. Use a tripod when it's in shadow.

You can extend this route to a 34-mile, advanced-level out-and-back by starting at the Hans Flat Ranger Station. You will encounter easy cruising on the way out but gradual climbing on the return (1,000′ from Deadmans Trail to Hans Flat) and occasional deep sand. Budget all day and a gallon of water for the trip.

Final note: Since rock art is extremely fragile, avoid touching it; even the best intentioned visitors can cause permanent damage to these treasures. Please make an effort to preserve the site's scientific and aesthetic value for future generations. Defacing, collecting, or destroying Indian rock art, ruins, and artifacts is prohibited and punishable by law.

RIDE 72 *PANORAMA POINT*

From atop the 1,000′-tall Orange Cliffs, Panorama Point affords dizzying and confounding views of the tortuously incised Maze District of Canyonlands National Park. The Maze is replete with confusing and hostile terrain; its topography is an inverted and tangled wilderness of sandstone canyons that appears impossible to reconnoiter. Around every bend in its interwoven network of convolute canyons stands a wall. Every wall opens to more corri-

RIDE 72 *PANORAMA POINT*

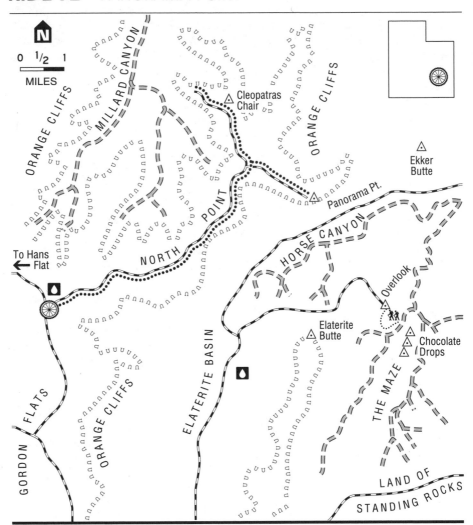

dors, some continuous, many boxed-in by sheer cliffs. Direct cross-country travel is impossible and becomes a matter of trial and error. Although Moab and the La Sal Mountains are less than 50 miles away by line of sight, Canyonlands' four districts (Island in the Sky, Needles, Rivers, and Maze) force the wayward traveler to circumnavigate by hundreds of miles.

Cliff-bound Panorama Point extends from the North Point mesa like the thumb extends from the hand and the hand extends from the arm. The North Point mesa, in turn, is connected to an expansive plateau, except the margins of this plateau are scarped with a series of coalescing recesses and rock-rimmed

Rimrocked at Panorama Point.

alcoves. Millions of years ago, the plateau once covered the entire region, including the Maze. Over time the Colorado and Green Rivers, their intermittent tributaries, plus rain, groundwater, and wind have caused the plateau's fringe to slowly recede. Elaterite, Bagpipe, and Ekker Buttes, along with other outlying spires and free-standing chimneys, are remnants of the plateau that have now distanced themselves into solitary isolation.

This 16-mile out-and-back route follows double-track composed primarily of hard-packed and soft sand. The route is generally low in technical difficulty, but it is interrupted periodically by broken pavement bedrock that forms patchy slickrock and ledges clogged with loose cobbles. Drift sand may force a dismount or two and some walking. Riding out to Panorama Point and back is intermediate level. If you tack on the optional spur to Cleopatras Chair, the difficulty rating approaches advanced level.

General location: Panorama Point is located in the Maze District of Canyonlands National Park, south of Green River and northeast of Hanksville via 48 miles of dusty and lonely dirt roads.

Elevation change: The trailhead/parking area is at 6,600'. The North Point Road descends gently to Panorama Point at 6,160'. Accounting for a few undulations, total elevation gain is about 800'. (Tack on about 300' of vertical if you plan to venture out-and-back to Cleopatras Chair.)

Season: Spring (March through June) and fall (September through October) are the most pleasant times to visit Utah's Canyon Country. Midsummer temperatures can be oppressive (100s midday) and bugs annoying. Early and late winter can be enjoyable when the route is dry and weather is cooperative. Always carry plenty of water both on the bike and in the car, regardless of the season.

Services: There are no services along this route nor any reliable sources of water other than French Spring, located half a mile before the trailhead. Visitor services are limited to what can be stuffed into your vehicle. There is no water at Hans Flat Ranger Station. Camping is restricted to a handful of designated primitive sites within the National Park. Limited visitor services (inexpensive motels, food, and gasoline) are available at Hanksville, located 60 miles west and south of Hans Flat. Green River, nearly 100 miles away, has more extensive services. There are no bike shops in the vicinity.

Hazards: This area is very remote. Visitors are not common and access can be difficult. Be prudent in your preparation. The maintained dirt road to Hans Flat Ranger Station is suitable for passenger cars when *dry,* but is impassable when wet. Heed this warning! The dirt and sand access road from Hans Flat to the North Point Road is suitable for passenger cars when they're driven with caution. The North Point Road is restricted to high-clearance vehicles, preferably equipped with four-wheel-drive. If you travel on four-wheel-drive roads by vehicle to the far reaches of Maze country, stock a good spare tire, sturdy jack, extra gasoline, water, and food, plus a generous helping of common sense.

The North Point Road is low to moderate in technical difficulty because it is mainly broken pavement outcrop and drift sand.

Rescue index: Panorama Point is seldom visited. Hans Flat Ranger Station, located 2.5 miles from the trailhead, has radio communication. Green River has a medical clinic, but it is nearly 100 miles and several hours away by vehicle.

Land status: Glen Canyon National Recreation Area.

Maps: USGS 7.5 minute quadrangles: Cleopatras Chair, Elaterite Butte, and Gordan Flats, Utah.

Finding the trail: From Green River, travel 12 miles west on Interstate 70 and take Exit 147/UT 24, Hanksville, Capitol Reef. Travel 25 miles south on UT 24 to the turnoff for Rooster Flat, Flint Trail, Maze, etc. (The turnoff is located between mileposts 137 and 136, half a mile south of the Goblin Valley/Temple Mountain junction or about 20 miles north of Hanksville.) Drive southeast on the maintained dirt, sand, and washboarded road. After 25 miles, fork right at a Y junction and a sign for Hans Flat Ranger Station 21 (right); Horseshoe Canyon foot trail 7 (left). Seven miles south, fork left at a junction signed "French Spring 15, Flint Trail 25, Maze 50" (all left); "Ekker Ranch 7" (right). Hans Flat Ranger Station is about 14 miles to the left.

From Hans Flat, travel southeast on the main access road signed "Flint Trail 14." After 2 miles, a turnoff to the left/east leads to French Cabin and French Spring, where water can be gathered as it flows out of a plastic pipe. Immediately past, is the signed junction for North Point Road, Panorama Point, and Cleopatras Chair. Limited parking is available.

Sources of additional information:

Glen Canyon National
  Recreation Area
P.O. Box 1507
Page, Arizona 86040
(602) 645-8200

Hite Ranger Station
c/o Glen Canyon National
  Recreation Area
P.O. Box 1507
Page, Arizona 86040
(801) 684-2457

Canyonlands National Park
2282 S. West Resource Boulevard
Moab, Utah 84532
(801) 259-7164

Hans Flat Ranger Station
c/o Canyonlands National Park
2282 S. West Resource Boulevard
Moab, Utah 84532
(801) 259-7164

Notes on the trail: All regulations pertaining to Canyonlands National Park apply to Glen Canyon National Recreation Area, through which this route travels. For this information, contact Canyonlands National Park. (See "Sources of additional information.") Backcountry permits (free) are required for overnight camping or hiking and are available at the Hans Flat Ranger Station.

From the parking area, pedal northward on the North Point Road across this high desert peninsula speckled with sage, juniper, and pinyon. Through the scattered foliage are distant views of the Orange Cliffs (Wingate Sandstone), which form the prominent vertical escarpments in this area.

In 6.5 miles from the parking area, the road forks. Turn right at the sign for Panorama Point. You'll reach the Point after about 1.5 miles of near-level pedaling. When you feel visually satiated return to the previous junction. To extend the ride by 6.5 miles, turn right and follow the double-track out-and-back to Cleopatras Chair. The route's surface is packed and loose sand, punctuated with moderately technical sections and periodic pavement bedrock. The road wraps around the butte's (Cleopatras Chair's) south side, then continues about a mile before dissipating on a mesa arm overlooking Millard Canyon. Turn around and go back to the Panorama Point junction, then do 6.5 miles of gradual but tedious climbing back to the parking area.

RIDE 73 *THE MAZE OVERLOOK*

The Maze District, located just west of the Colorado River, is Canyonlands National Park at its wildest. Its name conjures up striking images of convolute topography: dead-end canyons and twisted corridors and contorted terrain etched deeply into a sandstone floor. The Maze is Nature's jigsaw puzzle cut into stone.

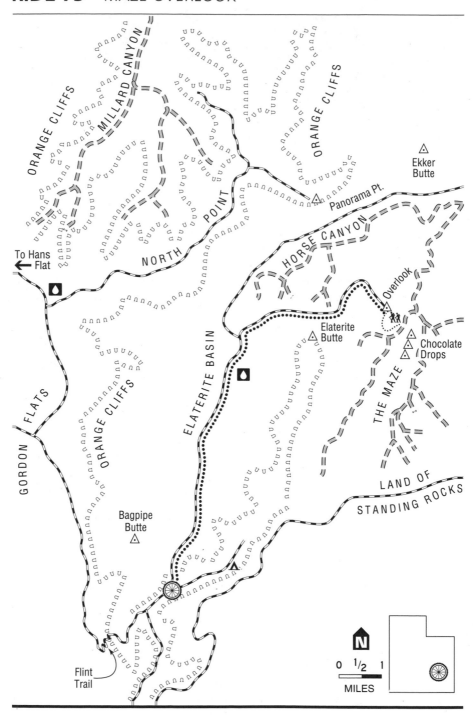

ORANGE CLIFFS

MILLARD CANYON

ORANGE CLIFFS

Ekker
Butte

Panorama Pt.

To Hans
← Flat

NORTH POINT

HORSE CANYON

Overlook

ELATERITE BASIN

Elaterite
Butte

Chocolate
Drops

THE MAZE

GORDON FLATS

ORANGE CLIFFS

LAND OF
STANDING ROCKS

Bagpipe
Butte

Flint
Trail

N

0 1/2 1
MILES

Tortuous canyons of the Maze District.

Few regions in Utah, if not the nation, are as remote and inaccessible. To some, the Maze is a stark and inhospitable land; to others, this hostile terrain sparks intrigue and offers many earthly pleasures—solitude, silence, and challenges of self-reliance—not found within the confines of civilization.

Today recreationists visit the Maze to seek temporary liberation from urban lifestyles, but this area has a history of inhabitation by outlaws, ranchers, and miners. And long before modern cultures attempted a living or sought refuge in the Maze, ancient Native Americans prospered in the canyon bottoms. Ruins, artifacts, and rock art panels dispersed throughout the region are irreplaceable vestiges of these archaic peoples.

This 24-mile out-and-back route follows sandy double-track. Although the initial descent off the mesa into Elaterite Basin is steep and technical, the remainder of the route is generally low in technical difficulty. A few dry wash crossings can be arduous. This is a down-and-back-up route where nearly all the elevation gain is attained on the ride out. From the turnaround point, an optional two-mile out-and-back footpath leads down into this redrock intaglio. The hike is an adventure across barren sandstone, through cracks and over ledges, and down tiny footholds chiseled into the sloping sandstone. The sandy conditions of the trail and the optional hike make this an advanced-level ride.

General location: The route to the Maze Overlook is located in the Maze District of Canyonlands National Park, south of Green River and northeast of Hanksville via 60 miles of maintained dirt and four-wheel-drive roads.

Elevation change: This route's trailhead is also at its highest elevation at 6,040´. The trail drops to 5,000´ at the north end of Elaterite Basin prior to the Maze Overlook. Total elevation gain is about 1,300´, almost all of which you'll have to tackle on your return from the overlook.

Season: Spring (March through May) and fall (September through October) are the most pleasant times to visit Utah's Canyon Country. Midsummer temperatures can be oppressive (100s midday) and bugs annoying. Early and late winter can be enjoyable when the route is dry and weather is cooperative. Always carry plenty of water both on the bike and in the car, regardless of the season.

Services: There are no services along this route nor any reliable sources of water. There is a spring midway along the route. In early spring, small pools of water may collect in the Maze's canyon bottoms, but they tend to dry up as summer approaches. Carry *lots* of water, even if you plan a short hike through the Maze.

Carry whatever supplies you may need in your vehicle. There is no water at Hans Flat Ranger Station. Camping is restricted to a handful of designated primitive sites within the National Park. Limited visitor services (inexpensive motels, food, and gasoline) are available at Hanksville, located 60 miles west and south of Hans Flat. Green River, nearly 100 miles away, has more extensive services. There are no bike shops in the region.

Hazards: Do not underestimate your body's need for water. You'll need *at least* two large water bottles to last the entire bike route. If you plan on extending the day by hiking into the Maze, budget another quart to half gallon, *per person,* especially during warm weather.

To get to the trailhead you have to negotiate the Flint Trail, a series of steeply descending switchbacks dropping 800´ over the edge of the Orange Cliffs. Four-wheel-drive and a stalwart driver are strongly recommended. The Flint Trail can be impassable when wet and is subject to washout during spring thaw and after severe storms. Contact the Hans Flat Ranger Station *before* venturing onto the Flint Trail.

The bike route is low to moderate in technical difficulty, except for the initial steep, ledgy descent off the mesa platform.

Hiking the Maze Overlook Trail into the canyons below involves crossing slickrock, wedging through narrow slots and cracks, and climbing precariously placed "Moki" steps (small footholds chipped into the barren sandstone).

Rescue index: The Maze Overlook is a base camp and jump-off point for hikers venturing out into the Maze, but visitors are rare. Self-sufficiency is vital. Hans Flat Ranger Station, located 18 miles from the trailhead, has radio communication, but the notorious Flint Trail lies in between. Green River has a medical clinic, but it is nearly 100 miles and one-half day away by vehicle.

Land status: Canyonlands National Park; Glen Canyon National Recreation Area.

Maps: USGS 7.5 minute quadrangles: Clearwater Canyon, Elaterite Butte,

Spanish Bottom, and Teapot Rock, Utah.

Finding the trail: From Green River, travel 12 miles west on Interstate 70 and take Exit 147/UT 24, Hanksville, Capitol Reef. Travel 25 miles south on UT 24 to the turnoff for Rooster Flat, Flint Trail, Maze, etc. (The turnoff is located between mileposts 137 and 136, half a mile south of the Goblin Valley/Temple Mountain junction or about 20 miles north of Hanksville.) Drive southeast on the maintained dirt, sand, and washboarded road. After 25 miles, fork right at a Y junction, where Hans Flat Ranger Station 21 is to the right and the Horseshoe Canyon foot trail 7 is to the left. Seven miles south, fork left at a junction signed "French Spring 15, Flint Trail 25, Maze 50" (all left); "Ekker Ranch 7" (right). Hans Flat Ranger Station is about 14 miles to the left.

From Hans Flat, travel southeast on the main access road signed "Flint Trail 14." There is a pullout/parking area atop the Flint Trail. Lock in your four-wheel-drive hubs. (This point is generally accessible to passenger cars; points beyond require four-wheel-drive.) It is 1.7 miles to the bottom of the Flint Trail. One mile farther, turn left at a junction signed "Golden Stairs 2, Maze Overlook 12" (left); "Highway 95 33 mi., Standing Rocks, Doll House" (right). The road to the Golden Stairs splits after 1 more mile; the left (unsigned) fork is the trailhead to the Maze Overlook.

Note: There are 2 roads out of the Maze: the Flint Trail/Hans Flat Road to the west or the Hite Road to the south. Be forewarned. Although the Hite Road is only 33 miles long from this route's trailhead, it takes a good 3 hours to travel. High clearance, preferably four-wheel-drive, is required, and the double-track is painstakingly slow. Rarely will you shift out of second gear! Sure the switchbacks of the Flint Trail can be daunting, but once you surmount them, cross-country travel is relatively swift when the Flint Trail becomes Hans Flat.

Sources of additional information:

Superintendent
Canyonlands National Park
2282 S. West Resource Boulevard
Moab, Utah 84532
(801) 259-6111

Hans Flat Ranger Station
c/o Canyonlands National Park
2282 S. West Resource Boulevard
Moab, Utah 84532
(801) 259-2652

Glen Canyon National
  Recreation Area
P.O. Box 1507
Page, Arizona 86040
(602) 645-8200

Hite Ranger Station
c/o Glen Canyon National
  Recreation Area
P.O. Box 1507
Page, Arizona 86040
(801) 684-2457

Notes on the trail: All regulations pertaining to Canyonlands National Park and Glen Canyon National Recreation Area apply to this route. For this information, contact the Canyonlands National Park or the Glen Canyon National Recreation Area. (See "Sources of additional information.") Backcountry permits (free) are required for overnight camping or hiking and are available at the Hans Flat Ranger Station.

From the parking area, pedal north. Immediately, the road dives off the terraced mesa along a steep, highly technical descent. When you reach the desert plain of Elaterite Basin, the route is a fast double-track descending gently. After about 5.5 miles, stay left; the road to the right dead-ends at a backcountry campsite and spring. Drop into a wash bottom a mile ahead, staying right for the Maze Overlook. (Anderson Bottom is to the left.) Pass through the Canyonlands National Park boundary and wrap around the head of slickrock-bound Horse Canyon. Three miles ahead, around the northern point of Elaterite Butte, is the Maze Overlook (and the route's turnaround point).

To hike into the Maze, start at the trailhead to the north of Maze Overlook. (If stashing bikes out of sight, be inconspicuous by *carrying* bikes while stepping only on rock. There is no point in leaving evidence of your bike's whereabouts.) The 2-mile out-and-back foot trail descends into the canyon bottom. But en route, you will have to cross open slickrock, wedge through tight creases, and scramble down a set of "Moki" steps. Explore the canyon bottom, then return to your bikes and pedal back through this romantically wild country of desert growth, redrock fortresses, and blue sky.

RIDE 74 *CONFLUENCE OVERLOOK*

Canyonlands National Park is located near the heart of the Colorado Plateau, which encompasses the greater Four Corners region. The confluence of the Colorado and Green Rivers divide Canyonlands into three districts: to the north, Island in the Sky; to the west, the Maze; and to the southeast, the Needles. This route leads to a rim-side view of the districts' intersection.

The Needles District is a jumble of colorful rock formations eroded into a startling and diverse landscape of spires, arches, canyons, and valleys. Stirring the imagination are features named Angel Arch, Elephant Hill, Paul Bunyan's Potty, and Devil's Kitchen. The route to the Confluence Overlook penetrates a region of vertical walls topped with peculiar knobs and needles, separated by grass-laden desert valleys. This route, like many of the hiking trails that lead to more remote reaches, rewards the adventurist with geologic wonderments that border surrealism.

An added bonus is nearby Newspaper Rock Historical Monument, located midway along the Needles' access road. An alcove is covered with both ancient and modern Indian petroglyphs (etchings on rock) ranging from hunting scenes to footprints and handprints, concentric circles, and numerous anthropomorphs (trapezoid-shaped humanoids) to coils, swirls, and indecipherable shapes. Newspaper Rock has perhaps the greatest concentration of Indian rock

RIDE 74 CONFLUENCE OVERLOOK

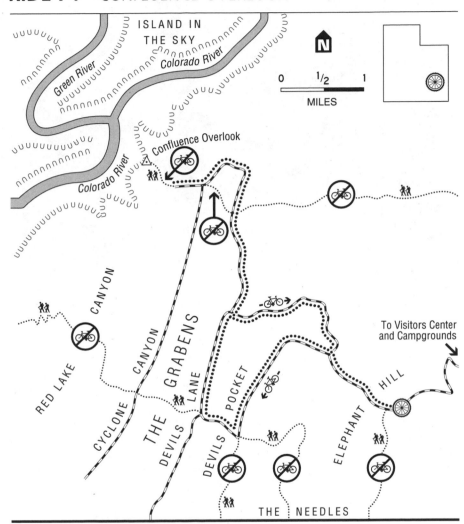

art at a single location on the Colorado Plateau; the Navajo call it Tse Hani (or "rock that tells a story").

This 15-mile combination out-and-back/loop follows double-track throughout. Based solely on its preponderance of sand, the route is rated as moderately difficult. Factoring in numerous moderately to highly technical sections of ledgy bedrock, plus the general nastiness of Elephant Hill, the difficulty level rises to advanced.

The needles enclose Devils Lane.

General location: The route to the Confluence Overlook is located 80 miles south and west of Moab in the Needles District of Canyonlands National Park.
Elevation change: The trailhead/parking area is at an elevation of 5,200´. The route's lowest elevation is 4,800´ at the Confluence Overlook. There are numerous climbs and descents along the way that yield a total elevation gain of about 800´.
Season: Spring (March through May) and fall (September through October) are the most enjoyable seasons to visit Canyonlands. Midsummer tends to be oppressively warm and insects may become a problem. Winter can be enjoyable when the route is dry and weather cooperates. Always carry plenty of water regardless of the season and use a liberal amount of sunscreen. Because of the excessive amount of sand comprising the route, the best time to pedal the ride is a day or so after rain (but not when the route is saturated).
Services: There are no services along this route nor reliable water sources. The parking area/trailhead has a pit toilet. Developed Park Service campgrounds are available 3 miles before the trailhead. Water is available at the Visitor Center and at campgrounds. Limited (and pricey) camping supplies, groceries, gasoline, and showers can be found at the Needles Outpost, located a mile before the Visitor Center. Monticello is the closest full-service town, located 55 miles (and nearly 2 hours by vehicle) from the trailhead.
Hazards: Carry ample water supplies (2 oversized bottles minimum), high-energy food, appropriate tools, and clothing; this is remote desert bicycling. Use a liberal amount of sunscreen. Sections of the route, especially Elephant Hill,

Newspaper Rock—a sandstone tabloid.

are highly technical because of ledgy and stairstep bedrock exposures; other sections are pocketed with drift sand. Cliff areas at the Confluence Overlook can be dangerous.

Rescue index: This area is not regularly patrolled by park personnel. Others may be found at the trailhead and perhaps along the route. The route does not receive much motorized traffic (four-wheel-drive). Rescue will be difficult and costly due to extremely rough conditions, even for four-wheel-drive vehicles. Emergency contacts can be made at the park's Visitor Center, located about 6 miles from the trailhead. Monticello and Moab have medical facilities.

Land status: Canyonlands National Park.

Maps: USGS 7.5 minute quadrangles: Druid Arch, Spanish Bottom, and The Loop, Utah. (Non-topographic trail maps are available at the Visitor Center.)

Finding the trail: From Moab, travel 40 miles south on US 191. Turn right/west on UT 211 signed "Canyonlands National Park, Newspaper Rock." Newspaper Rock is 13 miles in and the Needles Visitor Center is 35 miles in. After paying the park fee at the Visitor Center, continue west 3.5 miles, following signs for Elephant Hill. Before you enter into campground B, turn right onto a maintained but washboarded dirt road that leads 2.7 miles to the Elephant Hill trailhead/parking area. (If you're camping in the park, this makes for a good warm-up ride.)

Sources of additional information:

Manti–La Sal National Forest
Moab Ranger District
2290 S. West Resource Boulevard
Moab, Utah 84532
(801) 259-7155

Notes on the trail: A park entrance fee must be paid at the Visitor Center. Within the park, mountain bikes are restricted to roads designated for vehicular traffic. Bikes are prohibited from hiking or foot trails.

From the trailhead/parking area, the route begins immediately and without opportunity for warm-up with a merciless, technical climb over Elephant Hill. Attack with vigor. The descent off the sandstone fin is more confounding. (If you were to negotiate this "route" in a jeep you would need an intrepid driver adept at such white-knuckle endeavors.) Remember, Elephant Hill must be tackled again at the route's end.

At the junction for the one-way loop, stay left/west. The return route enters from the right/north. Slide unrestricted through a sandstone corridor. Judging from tire marks at the base of opposing walls and scratchings on bedrock from undercarriages, vehicles cannot do the same. At the Devils Kitchen junction, turn right/west for Devils Lane and descend gradually.

Devils Lane is indicated by a T junction signed "Chesler Park 5" (left/south), "Confluence Overlook 4" (right). An option arises; you can either go left or right. Turn left/south to pursue a 2-mile out-and-back spur laden with thick sand that leads to the Cave of 100 Hands. Positive images of brick-red handprints (plus many reserve-image outlines) dot the inside of a small cave.

Devils Lane is one of many parallel valleys pinned between opposing ridges known collectively as the Grabens ("graves" in German). This geologic structure is the product of parallel faulting and slumping of alternating crustal blocks. The underlying Paradox Formation (300-million-year-old evaporites) accentuated this process when the weight of overlying sediments, coupled with the uplift and tilt of the Colorado Plateau, caused this lens of subterranean salt to flow like toothpaste. This action fractured the overlying rocks and some sections sank. Further erosion by water, wind, and alternating freezing and thawing carved up a vicissitude of spires, towers, fins, furrows, and long valleys. The fanciful and intricately ornamented Needles District is an expression of the Cutler and Cedar Mesa Formations, an interfingering of red land-derived sediment and white beach deposits, respectively.

To continue to the Confluence Overlook, pedal north along Devils Lane to a junction signed "Confluence Overlook 3" (straight/north), "Elephant Hill 3" (right/east). The route makes a large, box-shaped U-turn to the head of Cyclone Canyon, another graben. Turn right and pedal half a mile to the Confluence trailhead, marked by a sole picnic table sheltered beneath a lowly pinyon. A short half-mile hike (marked with cairns) leads to the 800′-high viewpoint where the Green River joins the Colorado. The Maze resides downstream and across the Colorado; the Needles is to the southeast; Island in the Sky is north.

Return to the Elephant Hill junction at the north end of Devils Lane, then turn left/east. Two miles ahead is the junction for the one-way loop; turn left again to finish the route with the cursed assault on Elephant Hill.

RIDE 75 *KOKOPELLI'S TRAIL*

Imagine mountain biking 130 miles across the remote desert backcountry, over sun-drenched redrock, through deep river canyons, and past forested mountain slopes. Dream of a premier mountain biking trail that connects two states but recognizes no border between them. Picture volunteers and private businesses banning together—without a budget, without bylaws, and without bickering. Think of federal land agencies lending feverish support, cutting through often beleaguering red tape to approve the construction of hand-built single-track. And, envision the Hopi Indians performing a sacred dance to bless the route.

In as little as six months all of these "would-be" dreams came true for a dedicated group of bicycling enthusiasts under the guidance of the Colorado Plateau Mountain Bike Trail Association (COPMOBA). With the assistance of the Bureau of Land Management, U.S. Forest Service, private businesses, and dozens of volunteers, Kokopelli's Trail—a visionary trail linking Grand Junction, Colorado, with Moab, Utah—was created and built. Fueled by undying motivation and ceaseless determination, COPMOBA has created a trail system that will become an inspirational model to future trail builders.

"Mountain biking is a vehicle to promote low impact outdoor recreation, natural history education, bike safety, and land use ethics on the Colorado Plateau. We believe mountain biking is not a fad, it is the future because it combines fun, fitness, and fantastic scenery—always with an eye on protecting the land we love," asserts COPMOBA.

Kokopelli's Trail, like the mystical hunchbacked flute player of Hopi legend, wanders across the Colorado Plateau, crossing deserts, canyons, and mountainsides along the way. The trail is 130 miles of canyon country travel at its best. The route combines all aspects of mountain bike travel from improved dirt roads to rugged four-wheel-drive roads to exacting single-track. Kokopelli's Trail caters to a wide variety of ability levels: expert cyclists can tackle the entire route self-supported, midroute access points provide access for vehicle-supported tours, and a number of segments can be pursued as individual day trips.

Information on Kokopelli's Trail was provided by Pat Weiler, Salt Lake City, Utah.

RIDE 75 *KOKOPELLI'S TRAIL*

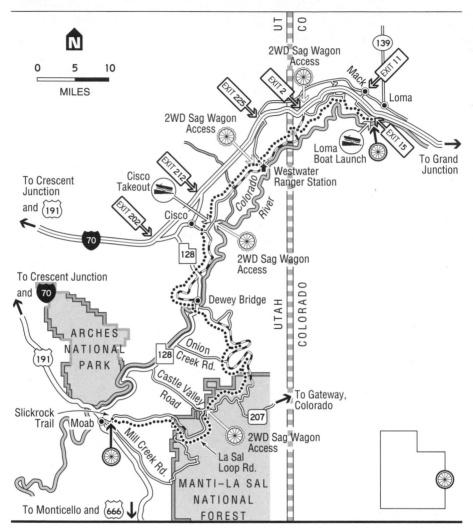

General location: Kokopelli's Trail begins at Loma, Colorado (15 miles west of Grand Junction), and ends in Moab, Utah (or vice versa, since it can be ridden in either direction).

Elevation change: The elevation of the Loma trailhead is 4,460´; the elevation of the Slickrock trailhead in Moab is 4,600´. You'll reach the highest elevation of 8,400´ between Beaver and Fisher Mesas. Total elevation gain greatly exceeds net elevation by thousands of feet, for the route crosses canyons, tops mesas, climbs the flanks of the La Sal Mountains, and drops back to the desert over its lengthy course.

Miles from nowhere on Kokopelli's Trail. *Photo: Pat Weiler.*

Season: Early spring (March through mid-May) and fall (September through October) are the best times of the year to plan a Kokopelli's trip. Midsummer brings very warm desert temperatures (100s) along with pesky insects. Snow may close high elevation segments during early spring and, likewise, cause high runoff during spring thaw. Contact the BLM for current trail conditions.

Services: Grand Junction (located 15 miles from the Loma trailhead) and Moab (located downhill from the Slickrock trailhead) offer all visitor services, including bike shops. Both cities have medical facilities. Along the route, services are essentially nonexistent. Although Kokopelli's Trail passes near Cisco, this rail-side townsite does not offer any services. So, pack all necessities in with you (and pack all leftovers *out* with you).

Hazards: Lack of preparedness and lack of water are two of the greatest hazards faced on Kokopelli's Trail. Riders should be well equipped, both on bike and in support vehicles, for all emergencies. Do not skimp on water consumption. The combination of strenuous activity, dry climate, and warm temperatures can cause dehydration and heat exhaustion. Carry sufficient water supplies on the bike and in the vehicle (if supported), and be aware of water sources along the route. Conversely, high elevations and cool tempera-tures can cause hypothermia. Pack along clothes that provide good thermal insulation and dry fast. Rainstorms may occur, especially at higher elevations, so carry rain gear.

Portions of the route are rough and technical. Honestly assess both your physical fitness and skill level before you embark on this ride.

Pat Weiler of Recreational Equipment, Inc. (REI).

Rescue index: Much of Kokopelli's allure lies in its remoteness, which means emergency contacts and assistance are few and far between. A telephone *might* be found at the Westwater Ranger Station (seasonal) or at a residence in Cisco. The trail crosses several roadways, but motorists are not common. Remember, self-sufficiency is the key. Medical facilities are located in Moab and Grand Junction.

Land status: Bureau of Land Management, Grand Junction and Moab districts.

Maps: USGS 7.5 minute quadrangles (east to west): Mack and Ruby Canyon, Colorado; Bitter Creek Well and Westwater, Utah/Colorado; Agate, Big Triangle, Cisco, Dewey, Blue Chief Mesa, Fisher Valley, Mount Waas, Warner Lake, Rill Creek, and Moab, Utah; USGS 1:100,000 scale topographic series: Grand Junction, Colorado; Westwater and Moab, Utah.

Finding the trail: To the eastern trailhead (Loma): Loma is located 15 miles west of Grand Junction, Colorado, along Interstate 70. Take Exit 15/Loma, cross over I-70 to the south, and turn east away from the Port of Entry. The Loma Boat Launch (parking area) is a short distance down the gravel road.

To the western trailhead (Slickrock Bike Trail, Moab): From the center of Moab, travel east on 100 North, turn right/south on 400 East, turn left/east on Mill Creek Road, then fork left onto Sand Flats Road. Slickrock Bike Trail is a few miles up the hill.

For midroute access points, consult the sources listed below.

Sources of additional information:

Bureau of Land Management
Grand Junction Resource Area
2815 H Road
Grand Junction, Colorado 81506
(303) 244-3050

Bureau of Land Management
Grand Resource Area
92 East Dogwood
Suite G
Moab, Utah 84532
(801) 259-8193

Colorado Plateau Mountain Bike Trail Association (COPMOBA)
P.O. Box 4602
Grand Junction, Colorado 81502
(303) 241-9561

The Utah-Colorado Mountain Bike Trail System, Route 1, Moab to Loma—Kokopelli's Trail, by Peggy Utesch (Canyon Country Publications, Moab, Utah)

Notes on the trail: Providing a turn-by-turn description of Kokopelli's Trail would be exasperating, so the following are some of the highlights. Remember to contact the BLM and COPMOBA for route information, obtain the appropriate maps, and consult the trail's guidebook (see "Sources") when planning your Kokopelli's trip.

Heading out from the Loma Boat Launch, the route cuts through grey and purple shales of the dinosaur-graveyard Morrison Formation as it roughly parallels I-70. The route alternates between easy four-wheel-drive roads and difficult single-track, which both afford spectacular views of Horsethief Canyon, where the Colorado River flows several hundred feet below. Rim-riding and a short section of slickrock precede the difficult descent to Salt Creek. (In years past, Salt Creek challenged riders with a thigh-deep ford, but during November 1993 a foot bridge spanning the creek was erected.) The foot bridge is located about 1 mile from the previous water crossing via new single-track trail along the creek.

Beyond Salt Creek, the trail bushwhacks through willow-infested sand and up what is perhaps the steepest climb along the route—a 2-mile, 20 percent grade. Its summit affords you splendid views of the austere Book Cliffs towering to the north while the Colorado River slips through Westwater Canyon to the southwest.

As you continue south toward the river, grayish-green shale gives way to pink sandstone formations, and Rabbit Valley opens up to rolling grasslands. The route travels through the Bittercreek drainage, climbs across the rim of a mesa, then follows the access road to the Westwater Ranger Station and parallels the railroad tracks. From a high point, an incredible view of the Priest and Nuns formation in distant Castle Valley is beautifully framed by the La Sal Mountains. Rolling hills punctuate the route as it passes near the 1950s railroad boomtown of Cisco, now reduced to a few shacks in the desert. Single-track heads east to McGraw Bottom where Kokopelli's meets UT 128.

The main route leaves the highway and heads up Yellow Jacket Canyon. Gorgeous Entrada Sandstone bluffs tower above sculpted slickrock at the top of the canyon. To get there you must endure a steep, sandy, 10-mile slog through cow country. The alternative is to stay on UT 128 for a leisurely 10-mile stroll to the historic Dewey Suspension Bridge. (From 1916 to the mid-1980s, this span of white washed boards and steel cables provided the only crossing of the Colorado River between Grand Junction and Moab.) Presently, the historic bridge is open to foot and bike traffic; vehicles are directed to a modern bridge nearby. You are now halfway into the trail (or halfway out of, depending on your perspective).

From the Dewey Bridge, the route climbs Entrada bluffs up Sevenmile and Blue Chief Mesas. There is a fine slickrock playground off to the side that adds some excitement to an otherwise long climb. A scenic detour from the main road leads into deeply-notched Upper and Lower Cottonwood Canyons. Although the descent is loose and the opposing stair-step ascent is taxing, the scenery and the chance you'll spy wildlife are worth the effort. Atop Sevenmile Mesa, you can practically retrace with your eyes the entire length of Kokopelli's back toward Grand Junction.

The next section you'll travel is perhaps the route's most remote, surrounded by scenic canyons and sage-covered valleys at the base of the La Sals. Traverse Sevenmile Mesa and pursue the steep, rocky descent along the edge of a second Cottonwood canyon, which is deeper and narrower than the first. Use caution here! A fall could be disastrous. Overviews of Fisher Valley are gained as the route climbs out of the depression and intersects with Onion Creek Road (which bails out to UT 128). Cacti and sage give way to ponderosa and aspen as the route rounds Cowhead Hill and scales the flank of the La Sals. White sandstone escarpments announce Polar Mesa; beyond is North Beaver Mesa. You are nearly 100 miles into the journey.

As you round the head of Fisher Valley, you'll enjoy a great view of the redrock monuments of Fisher and Castle Rock towers interrupting the valley below and the La Sal's mighty peaks piercing the sky overhead. Congratulations, this is the route's highest point. A screaming descent leads down the Castleton-Gateway Road to the junction of the La Sal Mountain Loop Road. It is a dirty trick, but one more obnoxiously steep climb (to Mason Draw) is between you and Moab. Fortunately, it is on pavement. The remainder of the route is generally downhill on dirt roads but hardly anticlimactic, for views into Castle Valley from the trail, or from Porcupine Rim, are decidedly Kokopelli highlights. And if your legs have not been ground to hamburger after 130 miles, take a lap around the Slickrock Bike Trail (Ride 68).

RIDE 76   *THREE LAKES*

The Three Lakes loop explores the La Sal Mountains' Geyser Pass region, which is the topographic break separating the central and northern group of peaks. Although there is a section of dirt road thrown in, most of this route follows single-track, and at times, *rather elusive* single-track. Be forewarned, these trails are not the buffed-out tracks of the Wasatch Range or even spirited paths of Brian Head; these are exacting trails that test mind-set against muscle against metal against mountain. But those who are ambitious and patient enough to pursue these La Sal offerings will be rewarded with immediate gratification.

The trip passes three small lakes: Oowah, Clark's, and Warner. Each is nestled in a distinctively pristine alpine setting. Between the lakes, much of the ride threads through forests of aspen and fir that engulf a patchwork of meadows sprinkled with flowers. You'll be impressed as well by desert views that extend 100 miles or more from the mountainside across Canyonlands to distant plateaus; and mountain views of treeless peaks that sputter throughout the forest canopy, reflect off motionless lakes, or reign above breezy fields.

This 14-mile, figure eight-shaped loop is a good initiation to La Sal single-tracks. The route is advanced level based on a few steep climbs, technical trail conditions, and need for some route finding. You may have to dismount occasionally and shoulder your bike in some places. Nearly every type of single-track challenge can be expected; these trails exist in a semi-primitive condition and do not receive regular maintenance. The Geyser Pass Road is marked by gravel, washboarded sections, and hard-packed dirt.

General location: The Three Lakes loop begins at Oowah Lake in the La Sal Mountains, located about 30 miles east of Moab.

Elevation change: Oowah Lake sits at 8,800′. The figure eight's first loop rises up to Geyser Pass (elevation 10,600′), then drops back to Oowah Lake. Elevation gain is about 2,400′. The figure eight's second loop begins at Oowah Lake and rises to Warner Lake (elevation 9,360′), then descends to 8,080′ on the Oowah Lake Road. Elevation gain for the second loop is 1,280′. Total gain for the day is 3,680′.

Season: This route is rideable from June through October, depending on seasonal snowmelt and snowfall. Midsummer is quite pleasant because of high elevations, but nights may be cool if not utterly freezing. Both early summer and fall afford spectacular colors. Portions of the trail (especially Geyser Pass to Oowah Lake) can be quite damp during early season.

Services: Oowah Lake has a USFS non-fee campground with 6 sites and an outhouse, but no water taps. Warner Lake is a USFS fee-area campground with 20 sites and water taps. No other services are available along the route and all

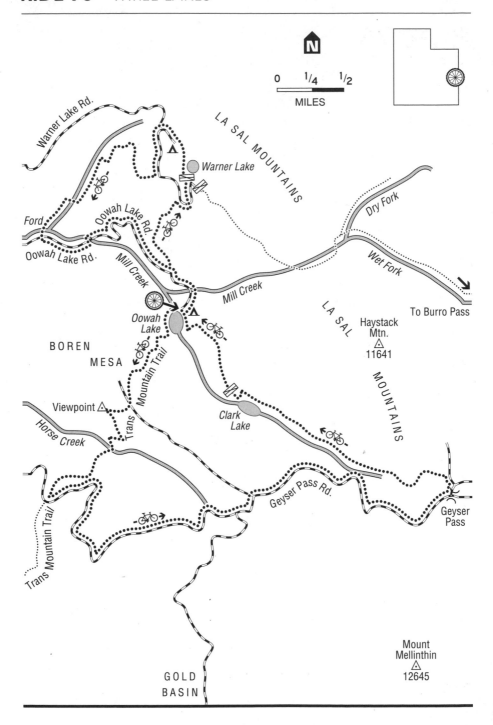

N

0   1/4   1/2
MILES

Warner Lake Rd.

LA SAL MOUNTAINS

Warner Lake

Dry Fork

Ford

Oowah Lake Rd.

Oowah Lake Rd.

Mill Creek

Mill Creek

Wet Fork

To Burro Pass

Oowah Lake

LA SAL

Haystack Mtn.
11641

BOREN

MESA

Trans Mountain Trail

MOUNTAINS

Viewpoint

Clark Lake

Horse Creek

Trans Mountain Trail

Geyser Pass Rd.

Geyser Pass

Trans Mountain Trail

Mount Mellinthin
12645

GOLD
BASIN

Spindly aspens form an eerie tunnel.

surface waters should be purified. Moab offers all visitor services, including bike shops and medical facilities.

Hazards: Single-track on this route is in a semi-primitive condition and does not receive maintenance on a regular basis. Expect to encounter multiple obstacles, including loose and imbedded rocks, root networks, water bars, deadfall, narrow tread, off-camber trail, steep slopes, sharp switchbacks, and bedrock stairsteps, to name a few. Portions may require dismounting, walking, and/or shouldering your bike.

Near the route's end, the Shafer Creek Trail crosses Mill Creek just before it joins the Oowah Lake Road. This is a wet crossing that requires portaging through calf-deep waters. During spring runoff, the creek may flow swiftly, be icy cold, and thigh deep. Carry a pair of "wading" shoes or be willing to sacrifice your pricey bike shoes.

Rescue index: Recreationists frequent Oowah and Warner Lakes, especially on weekends and holidays. A Forest Service ranger is stationed at Warner Lake, but his whereabouts (and mood for the day) are noted by a sign on the guard station: "In residence, a soft knock will suffice . . . hiking a trail, be back in a few hours . . . grouchy, does not wish to speak to you." Geyser Pass is much more remote.

Land status: Manti–La Sal National Forest.

Maps: USGS 7.5 minute quadrangles: Mount Peale, Mount Tukuhnikivatz, and Warner Lake, Utah. (Some portions of the route are not shown.)

Finding the trail: From the center of Moab, travel 8 miles south on US 191. Turn left/east at milepost 118 onto County Road 126 at a sign for La Sal Mountain Road, Oowah Lake, etc. Immediately ahead at the T junction, turn right/south for La Sal Mountain Loop and pass by the Red Rock Speedway. Stay left at the Pack Creek junction and begin ascending out of Spanish Valley up a sandstone hogback. (Treat yourself to the fascinating view of mountains, stream-fed valleys, and redrock palisades from the Spanish Valley Overlook.) About 1.5 miles past the turnoff for Geyser Pass, turn right/east onto Forest Service Road 076 and travel 3 miles to Oowah Lake.

Sources of additional information:

Manti–La Sal National Forest
Moab Ranger District
125 West 200 South
Moab, Utah 85532
(801) 259-7155

Notes on the trail: From Oowah Lake, cross over the dam and start up the protracted Trans Mountain Trail. After 1 mile, the rutted trail reaches the open tabletop of Boren Mesa and crosses a double-track. Head *due west* on the less-than-obvious single-track toward a carsonite post marked "trail." At the fourth marker, the trail turns left/south for a highly technical descent. But first, take a long quaff of Canyonlands' visually intoxicating brew. The Moab Rim, denoted by rusty palisades topped with sandstone dollops, bounds Spanish Valley. Into the Moab Portal slips the Colorado River. The terraced land of plateaus topped with mesas, which the Colorado River carved up millions of years ago, fades into the western haze. Over 100 miles away, the horizon is shaped by lofty highlands of the Aquarius, Fish Lake, and Wasatch plateaus, and the Henry Mountains.

The single-track descends to a signed T junction. Turn right, drop through a dogleg left and down to Horse Creek. Follow "trail" markers to the Geyser Pass Road. It is 5 miles of sustained climbing on gravel, washboarded sections, and hard-packed dirt to Geyser Pass. At the pass, turn left/north toward "Forest Boundary" on a double-track marked with a bike emblem. Within 200 yards, turn left/north again onto a second double-track. One hundred feet ahead (at the interface between aspen and open slope), fork left onto a primitive single-track/game trail. (Do *not* climb the steep hill northward).

Pass through a haunting corridor of twisted sapling aspen and across more meadows. Drop into a marshy clearing marked by a cattle salt lick, which is actually half of a 55-gallon drum. Turn right/west (90 degrees) and head toward a young pine that has a split trunk about 3 feet from its base. Avoid the temptation to cross a stream .6 miles ahead; instead, follow the stream down through the woods and across more meadows.

Carefully descend (or preferably walk) the switchbacks *down* to Clark Lake, then head westward on more single-track. After passing another cattle salt lick, the trail drops to a creek crossing filled with willows and shrubs (the crossing is actually 50′ back uphill), then heads north into the forest once more. Your ride culminates in advanced-level, fat-tire antics down to Oowah Lake.

If you still feel fresh, continue on to the Warner Lake loop. Coast down the Oowah Lake road .4 miles. Dump your chain into a granny gear and fork right/uphill onto a steep, single-track ramp signed "Warner Lake Guard Station 1.5." At first, the trail is rideable but then turns into a bike-on-shoulders portage for a few hundred yards as it becomes clogged with outcropping bedrock and huge boulders. Cross a double-track and continue the uphill battle to a trail registration box and carsonite post. Upon intersecting a good four-wheel-drive road (should be posted "Oowah Lake"), turn right. Shortly ahead is a junction marked with an orange gate signed "Burro Pass, Beaver Basin" (right). Follow the narrow path northward alongside a wooden fence to Warner Lake.

Pedal to the campground's entrance and turn left on a double-track signed "Dead End." When you break out of the aspens, there are good views of La Sals' high peaks. Here a sign tacked to an aspen (on your left) announces "Shafer Creek Trail, Mill Creek 2." Turn right/west onto the faint single-track marked with wooden directional arrows. (If you continue straight on the double-track, you will loop back to the orange gate and then to Warner Lake.)

The single-track weaves northward through aspens and descends into Schuman Gulch. (Hmmm, so shouldn't this be called the Schuman Gulch Trail instead of the Shafer Creek Trail?) The seldom-used path is loaded with advanced-level maneuvers plus lots of fresh "guacamole." (Cattle travel this route more than recreationists.) Parallel Schuman Creek a bit, then come to its confluence with Mill Creek. Shoulder your bike and trudge straight across an irrigation ditch and into the swamped-out riparian jungle draping Mill Creek. Oowah Lake road is atop the creek's embankment (marked with another sign for Shafer Creek Trail). Finish the adventure with 2 miles of moderate climbing to Oowah Lake.

And now for the geology lesson for the day: The La Sal Mountains, like the Abajo and Henry Mountains, were formed when chambers of magma sought the Earth's surface millions of years ago. Stymied by the excessive weight and continuity of the overlying sedimentary crustal rocks, the molten mass could do no better than bow the cap rocks and spread laterally between their layers. Geologists call this laccolithic intrusion. To the layman the La Sals are simply volcano wannabes. Erosion, primarily by streams and glaciers, has hence exposed the massif's crystallized core and carved the range into a trio of sovereign crowns. The central cluster hosts the La Sal's monarch, Mt. Peale, which rises to 12,721′.

RIDE 77 *BURRO PASS*

To most fat-tire zealots who seek divinity on Moab's lithified dune field, the La Sal Mountains are little more than an idyllic backdrop to countless Slickrock photographs. During spring and fall when Canyon Country is blessed with comfortable climes, and when most of us embark on our semi-annual pilgrimages to Utah's mountain bike mecca, the La Sals are largely unapproachable. Triumphant 12,000′-plus peaks harbor snow well into late spring, and by autumn are dusted by pre-winter flurries. A midriff of verdant forests overlain by snowy caps separate the ultramarine sky from a sun-baked mélange of sandstone fins and towers, mesas and plateaus, canyons and valleys. This is how the mountainous island is portrayed time and time again in postcards of and photo essays on Canyonlands. And this is how most bikers recall the La Sals when they are reminiscing about their Moab excursions from distant abodes.

Return to the Rock during midsummer and your brain will sizzle like a fried egg in an anti-drug commercial. By now snow in the La Sals has receded to the protected confines of high-elevation cirques, and the mountains entice the bedraggled desert biker with promises of crisp alpine breezes wafting through dense timber; of peaks, ridgelines, and glacially-molded tarns; of uninterrupted solitude, other than the dewy-eyed gaze of deer; and of pursuable mountain bike terrain replete with profound vistas. Along the Burro Pass loop, you will experience the allure of the La Sal Mountains.

This 12-mile loop (counterclockwise) combines highly technical single-track with good double-track and segments of hard-packed dirt roads. Single-tracks are generally semi-primitive and maintained on an irregular basis. You'll need sharply honed bike handling skills coupled with acute judgement, plus rudimentary route-finding skills. The demanding ascent to, and sketchy descent off, Burro Pass may require periodic dismounting. The final part of the loop, Warner Lake Trail, is notorious for bedrock stairsteps that can buck even the most gifted (or most resolute) mountain biker. Burro Pass is categorically advanced level and exemplifies fat-tire adventures that penetrate the La Sal Mountains' backcountry.

General location: The Burro Pass loop begins at Oowah Lake in the La Sal Mountains, located about 30 miles east of Moab.
Elevation change: The elevation of Oowah Lake is 8,800′. Geyser Pass rises to 10,600′ followed by the struggle to Burro Pass at 11,180′. Thereafter, it is

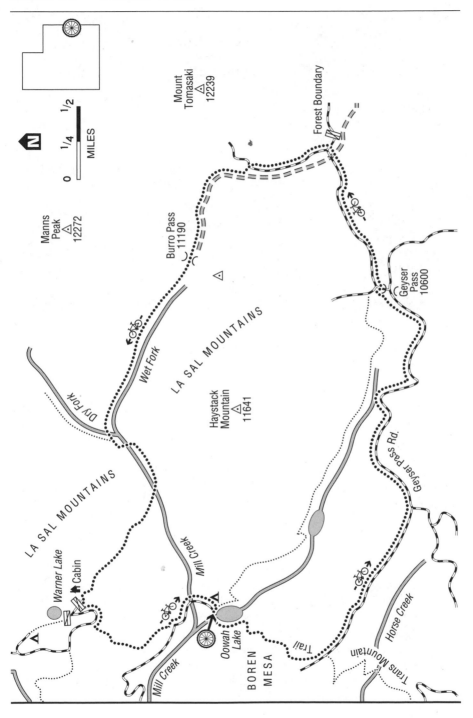

Mount
Tomasaki
△
12239

Forest Boundary

Manns
Peak
△
12272

Burro Pass
11190

Geyser
Pass
10600

LA SAL MOUNTAINS

Wet Fork

Dry Fork

Haystack
Mountain
△
11641

LA SAL MOUNTAINS

Geyser Pass Rd.

Warner Lake

Cabin

Mill Creek

Oowah
Lake

BOREN
MESA

Trail

Trans Mountain

Horse Creek

Mill Creek

N

1/2

1/4

0

MILES

Mount Tomasaki.

generally downhill to Warner Lake and finally Oowah Lake. Total elevation gain is 3,600′.

Season: This route is rideable from late June/early July through September, depending on seasonal snowmelt and snowfall. Midsummer is quite pleasant because of high elevations, but nights will be very cool. Both early summer and fall are exceedingly colorful. Portions of the trail (especially the descent from Burro Pass) can be quite wet during the early season. Midsummer may bring chilling afternoon rainstorms, often accompanied by lightning.

Services: There is a developed USFS campground at Warner Lake (with water taps) and a semi-developed USFS campground at Oowah Lake (no water taps). There are no other services along this route and all surface waters should be purified. Moab offers all visitor services, including bike shops and medical facilities.

Hazards: Single-track sections can be highly technical and require both advanced handling skills and good judgement. Portions may require dismounting and pushing your bike up steep slopes. You may need to walk (or shoulder) your bike down steep grades and over bedrock stairsteps. Deadfall and lingering snowdrifts may block the trail, especially near avalanche-prone Burro Pass.

Rescue index: A Forest Service ranger is stationed at Warner Lake, but his whereabouts (and mood for the day) vary. One of the following notes he marks with a colored pin on his door will give you a clue: "In residence, a soft knock will suffice," or "hiking a trail, be back in a few hours," or "grouchy, does not wish to speak to you." Warner and Oowah Lakes are popular with campers and fishermen, especially on weekends and holidays. Burro Pass is remote and doesn't get many visitors. Moab has medical facilities.

Land status: Manti–La Sal National Forest.

Maps: USGS 7.5 minute quadrangles: Mount Peale, Mount Tukuhnikivatz, Mount Waas, and Warner Lake, Utah.

Finding the trail: From the center of Moab, travel 8 miles south on US 191. Turn left/east at milepost 118 onto County Road 126 at a sign for La Sal Mountain Road, Oowah Lake, etc. Immediately ahead at the T junction, turn right/south for La Sal Mountain Loop and pass by the Red Rock Speedway. Stay left at the Pack Creek junction and begin ascending out of Spanish Valley up a sandstone hogback. (Treat yourself to the fascinating view of mountains, stream-fed valleys, and redrock palisades from the Spanish Valley Overlook.) About 1.5 miles past the turnoff for Geyser Pass, turn right/east onto Forest Service Road 076 and travel 3 miles to Oowah Lake.

Sources of additional information:

Manti–La Sal National Forest
Moab Ranger District
2290 S. West Resource Boulevard
Moab, Utah 84532
(801) 259-7155

Notes on the trail: From Oowah Lake, cross over the dam and begin with an arduous ascent up the Trans Mountain Trail. After 1 mile, the rutted path reaches the treeless tabletop of Boren Mesa and intersects a double-track. (The Trans Mountain Trail heads due west, a viable but extremely technical route to Geyser Pass Road.) Turn left/southeast and follow the double-track along the interface between aspens and meadows, then pedal through dispersed forests 1 mile to Geyser Pass Road. Forested Geyser Pass is 2 miles ahead (to the left).

At Geyser Pass, fork left/north onto a rock-studded four-wheel-drive road toward "Forest Boundary" (note the carsonite post with a bike decal), then stay right when a second double-track peels off to the left. (This second left is the trailhead for the Clarks Lake/Oowah Lake single-track; see Ride 76.) Descend quickly eastward through vast meadows for just over a mile. The route becomes engulfed by La Sal peaks. Haystack Mountain and Mount Tomasaki embrace the topographic void of Burro Pass to the north, and the sky above Burro is blocked by the bouldery crown of Manns Peak. Southward across Geyser Pass, Mount Mellenthin commands the scene with Mounts Tukunikivatz and Peale peering over its shoulders.

Immediately before you reach the Forest Boundary, turn left/north up FS 240. At the fence line where a sign reads "Burro Pass Trail, Warner Lake CG," the route can be confusing. Pass through the gate, then parallel the fence to the left/west a few feet. Just before you drop into the shallow gully, look carefully for the faint trail that scales Burro Pass. At the pass a sign welcomes you. The short but vertical scramble toward Manns Peak offers rewarding perspectives of a blazing desert and fading mesas resting more than a vertical mile below these timbered slopes.

The single-track descent off Burro Pass is "upbeat," to say the least, and periodically red-lines the crash-and-burn meter. Use good judgement not only to ensure your own safety but to limit unnecessary trail erosion. During midsummer, a profusion of wildflowers drape the trail, concealing obstacles that await your front tire.

Upon joining Dry Fork (a misnomer, for is flows with confidence), continue downstream. Shortly past the wire fence line and gate, a pile of strategically placed rocks indicates that the trail crosses Mill Creek. Cross the creek and, within a half mile, cross back over Mill Creek and then the Wilson Ditch (an earthen canal). Follow the double-track up through aspens and past a trail register box. Cut across a small clearing, marked by a cabin on the right, to an orange steel gate and a trail sign reading "Burro Pass, Beaver Basin; Oowah Lake."

Before you complete the loop, take the very short spur paralleling the log fence to Warner Lake. Generously named, Warner Lake is a small aquatic mirror framed by tall, luxuriant grasses. Groves of spindly aspen, steel-gray talus enshrouding Manns Peak, and a deep blue sky overhead reflect off its glassy surface. Fishermen line its bank, rhythmically casting flies to unsuspecting trout.

Return to the orange gate and turn downhill on double-track toward Oowah Lake. Within 200 yards, look for a post on the left (where a sign for Oowah Lake should be) that marks the Warner Lake Trail down to Oowah Lake road. A little common sense goes a long way; the trail's midsection is choked with rude exposures of bedrock stairsteps that require dismounting and shouldering the bike a short distance. The trail goes left onto Oowah Lake road abruptly, so use caution here. Oowah Lake is half a mile left and uphill.

RIDE 78 *HOVENWEEP NATIONAL MONUMENT*

Hovenweep National Monument is ideal for the solitude-seeking mountain biker. But, just because it isn't as popular as, say, Mesa Verde National Park, where wondrous Anasazi cliff dwellings are the finest examples of ancient Native American adobe architecture, doesn't mean it doesn't have anything to offer; in fact, the series of dirt roads you'll be riding lead to satellite ruins of early Pueblo-style, coarse-stone masonry that stand in haunting silence.

Hovenweep, a Ute (pronounced "yōōt") word meaning "deserted valley," offers ruins that feature square, oval, circular, and D-shaped towers. Many are perched on cliff rims or balanced delicately on massive boulders. Some multi-

RIDE 78 *HOVENWEEP NATIONAL MONUMENT*

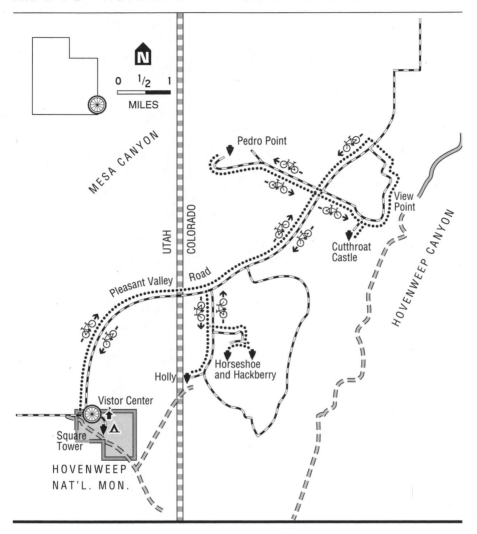

room structures were apparent living quarters or possibly used for sacred ceremonies. Curious-looking towers, which have no windows or doorways, had a
use for which you'll have to use your imagination. This population farmed,
collected wild plants, and hunted animals. there also were expert craftsmen and
artists among them. Hardships, whether brought on by drought or warfare,
forced them to abandon their homes almost 700 years ago.

This 31-mile tour is a combination of 2 spurs and 1 loop branching from the
main Pleasant View road and caters to intermediate cyclists. You can shorten
the route by visiting selected sights instead of all three. The maintained dirt and

Boulder House *(foreground)* and Great House *(background)*—Holly Ruins.

sand Pleasant View road is low in technical difficulty. Side roads, which are restricted to high-clearance vehicles, can be mixed with moderately technical sections.

General location: Hovenweep National Monument is located in the Four Corners region on the Utah/Colorado border (about 45 miles east of Blanding and Bluff, Utah, or about 40 miles west of Cortez, Colorado).

Elevation Change: The Visitor Center is at an elevation of 5,240′. The Pleasant View road rises imperceptibly to 6,040′ over 10 miles. A few hills are encountered on side routes leading to ruin sites; most are inconsequential. Total elevation gain out-and-back on the main road plus side trips is about 1,600′.

Season: Resting on a broad plateau in the high desert, Hovenweep National Monument is accessible year round. Spring (March through June) and fall (September through October) are the best times of year. Midsummer can be very warm. A winter visit is possible, but expect cool temperatures during the day and below freezing temperatures at night. Snowfall is intermittent and usually does not linger.

Services: There are no services or water along this route, although the Visitor Center offers a soda vending machine. The monument has a small but developed campground with outhouses and water taps. The last outposts for supplies and overnight accommodations are in Blanding and Bluff, Utah, and Cortez, Colorado, each more than an hour away by vehicle. Limited supplies and gasoline *may* be found at Hatch and Ismay Trading Posts.

Hazards: Although the majority of the route is low in technical difficulty, isolated sections of four-wheel-drive roads that lead to Cutthroat Castle and Pedro Point are rough. Do not climb on any ruins; the ancient masonry is fragile and may crumble. Use caution exploring along and under cliffs and ledges. Be aware of falling rock when others are on the cliffs above or below you. Late spring and summer bring insects. Rattlesnakes may be in cliff recesses and under rocks.

Dirt roads that take you to the area may become impassable when wet. Call for current weather conditions and forecasts. Vehicular traffic on the Pleasant View road is common.

Rescue index: Because of their remoteness and sometimes rough access roads, outlying ruin sites are seldom visited by tourists and park rangers alike. Emergency contacts can be made at the Visitor Center, but medical attention must be sought in Cortez, Colorado.

Land status: National Park Service, Hovenweep National Monument; Bureau of Land Management, San Juan Resource Area.

Maps: USGS 7.5 minute quadrangles: Ruin Point, Utah/Colorado, and Negro Canyon, Colorado.

Finding the trail: From US 191 (which connects Blanding with Bluff), follow UT 262 east for Hovenweep National Monument and Four Corners. After about 9 miles, a series of secondary paved and maintained dirt roads pass through the Navajo Indian Reservation. Signs for Hovenweep dot the 32-mile approach route.

From Cortez, Colorado, the most direct route (on relatively high-quality roads) is south a few miles on US 160/666, west for 30 miles on McElmo Road, then 12 miles on secondary paved and maintained dirt roads to Hovenweep.

A third access route originates from Pleasant View, Colorado, located 19 miles north of Cortez on US 666. Travel west on County Road BB signed "Hovenweep National Monument." After 6 miles turn left (at a sign for Hovenweep) and follow the maintained dirt Pleasant View road 20 miles to the Visitor Center.

Sources of additional information:

Hovenweep National Monument
McElmo Route
Cortez, Colorado 8132
(303) 562-4248

Mesa Verde Country Tourism
 and Convention Bureau
928 East Main1
Cortez, Colorado 81421
(303) 565-3414 (in Colorado)
(800) 346-6528 (outside Colorado)

Hovenweep National Monument has a small bicycling guide of its outlying ruin sites and surrounding area.

Notes on the trail: Before embarking on this bike tour, spend plenty of time at the Monument's main attraction, Square Tower Ruin, to learn about the masonry and living conditions of this ancient Indian culture.

From the Visitor Center, pedal north on the Pleasant View road. After 3.5 miles, a cattle guard marks the Utah/Colorado border. One-half mile beyond is a spur signed "Hovenweep," which leads to the Horseshoe/Hackberry group and Holly ruins. (This out-and-back spur is about 5.2 miles.)

The Horseshoe ruins consist of a half-circle-shaped structure composed of a large central room adjoined by 3 smaller rooms; none are connected by windows or doors. A short trail leads past a retaining dam, handprints on a wall, and a small kiva. Holly ruins feature Tilted Tower and Boulder House, two stone structures built atop huge boulders. The main attraction is Holly Great House, a large structure where archaeologists have unearthed a plastered floor with a fire pit, grinding stones, and ceramic vessels.

Return to the Pleasant View road and turn right to continue the tour. Pedal 3.2 miles to a junction (crossing 2 more cattle guards along the way). Immediately beyond the second cattle guard the obscure road to Cutthroat Castle branches right, next to a "Carbon Dioxide Pipeline" sign. Portions of the road can be rough. (This side loop is 5.5 miles long.)

Cutthroat Castle is a large kiva situated directly on the edge of an overhanging cliff. It is surrounded on one side by a wall forming an attached room. (Kivas are used in modern Pueblo villages for ceremonies, to store dance costumes, accessories, and sacred objects, and as social centers.) From Cutthroat Castle, pedal right/south for a half mile. The road then turns north and rises up a small hill. Atop this hill, look for a short spur to the right that leads to a cliff-edge viewpoint of upper Hovenweep Canyon and the La Plata Mountains. If you have a sharp eye, you will spot Painted Hand Ruin tucked just below the overhanging cliff. From the viewpoint, return to the Cutthroat Castle Road and pedal north to its junction with the Pleasant View road. Turn left on the Pleasant View road and pedal back to the original turnoff for Cutthroat Castle. Time and endurance permitting, pedal out-and-back to Pedro Point (6 miles round-trip). The spur branches westward from the Cutthroat Castle turnoff near the carbon dioxide pipeline sign. About 2.3 miles out along the Pedro Point road, fork left. This double-track will soon turn northward, hugging the rim of Cross Canyon, and lead to a small group of ruins. Thereafter, return to the Visitor Center to reminisce the day's explorations under the setting sun.

Remember, under the 1906 Federal Antiquities Act, it is unlawful to appropriate, excavate, injure, or destroy "any historic or prehistoric ruin or monument, or any object of antiquity" on federal lands. Violators are punishable by fines and/or imprisonment.

RIDE 79 *VALLEY OF THE GODS*

Valley of the Gods is a prelude to Monument Valley and the Four Corners Area, where space is open and endless, and where the air is filled with a lucid sense of remoteness. Dispersed throughout these perpetually hapless desert plains are sporadic features of positive relief: a monolithic tower or a castle cameo, what look like troops of soldiers displaced from their platoon, rock formations that evoke imaginary animals, and statues of exalted gods. Bounding a small wedge of this circumferential view is a line of lobate cliffs and deep alcoves forming the burnt amber ramparts of Cedar Mesa. As erosion slowly but continually attacks the abrupt escarpment of Cedar Mesa, the fanciful features of Valley of the Gods are gradually liberated.

Stemming from the loop is a side trip to the Goosenecks of the San Juan overlook. Geologists consider this one of the finest examples of "entrenched meanders" in the world. The San Juan River's looping pattern originated several million years ago when it flowed sluggishly over a relatively flat plain, much like the Mississippi River. When the Colorado Plateau was slowly uplifted, the San Juan followed its initial course, cutting downward 1,000´.

This 27-mile loop (counterclockwise) is a good intermediate-level outing. The improved dirt road is low in technical difficulty with localized drift sand and washboard. Paved highways roll gently. (A vehicle shuttle can eliminate riding on the highway and make the route a 16.5-mile point-to-point trip.) Tack on an additional 7 miles total (out-and-back) if you decide to pedal to the Goosenecks overlook, which follows a paved roadway.

General location: Valley of the Gods is located in the far southeastern corner of Utah (18 miles west of Bluff, 28 miles south of Natural Bridges National Monument, or 30 miles north of the Utah Arizona border near Monument Valley).

Elevation change: The Valley of the Gods' eastern trailhead off US 163 is at an elevation of 4,440´. The dirt road rises to 5,130´ at Castle Butte, drops to an intermediate low of 4,660´, then rises back up to 5,300´ at its western trailhead.

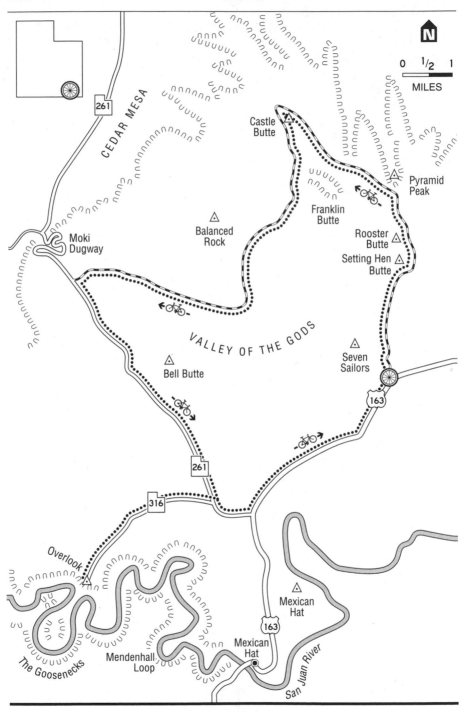

The Goosenecks of the San Juan River.

The paved highway then drops gradually downhill (with a few gentle uphill pulses) back around to the eastern trailhead. Total elevation gain for the loop is about 1,600′. Add on an extra 700′ of vertical for the spur to the Goosenecks.

Season: Spring (March through mid-June) and fall (September through November) are the best times of the year to visit the Four Corners area. Expect warm days and pleasant nights. Use lots of sunscreen. Midsummer is very hot and bugs can be a nuisance, especially near water sources. Depending on snowfall and subsequent drying, winter months might be enjoyable.

Services: There are no services along this route, nor any reliable water sources. Water should be purified out of Lime Creek at the route's eastern trailhead; that is, if there is any water to be purified. Carry ample water supplies on your bike and in your car. You'll find limited visitor services in Bluff, located 18 miles east on US 163, or in Mexican Hat, located 10 miles south on US 163. Neither has a bike shop. Backcountry camping is allowed along the Valley of the Gods road or at the Goosenecks overlook, but no water is available. A primitive BLM campground is located at Sand Island just south of Bluff.

Hazards: Running out of water will be your greatest concern. Carry plenty of water supplies both on your bike and in your car. (Stock up on ice, too.) The Valley of the Gods road is low in technical difficulty. Use caution when pedaling paved highways, for there is frequent high-speed RV traffic and shoulders are narrow to nonexistent.

Rescue index: Recreationists and motorists are few and far between along the Valley of the Gods road. There is frequent vehicular traffic along paved highways. A phone *may* be found at the Valley of the Gods bed-and-breakfast (Lee's Ranch on topographical maps), but *do not* seek water or refreshments there. Both food and water are trucked in and valued highly by the owners and their guests.

A medical clinic is located at Goulding (22 miles south of Mexican Hat, then a few miles west of Monument Valley).

Land status: Bureau of Land Management, San Juan Resource Area. All land south of the San Juan River lies within the Navajo Indian Reservation. Camping and off-road travel is not recommended without prior and explicit permission from the Navajo Nation!

Maps: USGS 7.5 minute quadrangles: Cedar Mesa-South, Cigarette Spring Cave, Mexican Hat, and The Goosenecks, Utah; USGS 1:100,000 metric topographic series: Bluff, Utah.

Finding the trail: The Valley of the Gods' eastern trailhead is located 18 miles west of Bluff along US 163 (milepost 29). Its western trailhead is 28 miles south of Natural Bridges National Monument along UT 261 (1 mile below the steep switchbacks of Moki Dugway). Both ends of Valley of the Gods road are signed. Park at your discretion.

From the south (Arizona approach), head north on US 163 past Monument Valley to Mexican Hat. Continue north on US 163 3.5 miles to its junction with UT 261. The Valley of the Gods' eastern trailhead is 4 miles farther on US 163, and its western trailhead is about 6.5 miles along UT 261. Park at your discretion.

Sources of additional information:

Bureau of Land Management
San Juan Resource Area
435 North Main
Monticello, Utah 84535
(801) 587-2141

Notes on the trail: You can ride this loop clockwise or counterclockwise. The direction you decide to take depends largely on whether you want to pedal on dirt or pavement first and whether you prefer gentle climbing or descending on pavement. The counterclockwise version of the loop is descibed here. You'll start at the eastern trailhead off US 163 on dirt road; you'll finish with a mostly gentle descent on pavement.

From US 163, pedal generally northward 7 miles toward looming orange-brown cliffs lining Cedar Mesa. It is slightly uphill and easy pedaling to where the road bends southward at Castle Butte. About 5 miles of upbeat descending are followed by a 4-mile, shallow rise to UT 261. Turn left/south and catch a tail wind (hopefully) down the paved highway. Take the turn for the Goosenecks after 5.5 miles. An additional 7 miles total (out-and-back) lead to the overlook.

Continue southward on UT 261 about a mile to its junction with US 163. Your vehicle is 4 miles to the north along the rolling highway.

RIDE 80 *MONUMENT VALLEY NAVAJO TRIBAL PARK*

Monument Valley is a sublime landscape, one full of astonishing vastness and intangible beauty. In this denuded valley stand rock monuments, buttes, and mesas of majestic form and rich color, 400′ to 1,000′ in height. When you pedal past Mitten Buttes, Three Sisters, and Totem Pole, round Rain God Mesa, or stop to appreciate the utter silence and ethereal tableau from Artist's Point or North Window, you'll truly be awed. You will, at the very least, contemplate the possibility that divine intervention by some Great Architect had something to do with their creation. It is of little wonder that the Navajo Indian Nation (who call themselves "the Dinah," or "the people") look upon Monument Valley with sacred reverence.

Both amateur and professional photographers find that Monument Valley seduces the camera's lens. Not only has the valley's splendor been the subject of countless postcards, calendars, and commercials, it has been the backdrop in a number of movies, including the 1936 John Ford classic "Stagecoach" (featuring John Wayne), "How the West was Won," and "Back to the Future III."

This 12-mile loop follows maintained dirt and sand roads that are generally suitable for passenger cars. You may encounter sand traps that can force even strong riders to dismount and walk a bit. The first mile or so descends steeply and is an arduous climb when you exit the loop. The rest of the loop is essentially flat. Overall, the loop makes for a good intermediate-level ride.

General location: Monument Valley Navajo Tribal Park is located in the Four Corners area on the Utah/Arizona border.
Elevation change: The elevation of the Visitor Center (parking area/trailhead) is 5,600′. The scenic drive drops to 5,200′, then loops through the park with little elevation change. Total elevation gain is 800′. Half of that gain comes during the 2.5-mile climb from the loop road back to the Visitor Center.
Season: Spring (March through mid-June) and fall (September through November) are the best times of year to visit the Four Corners area. Expect warm days and pleasant nights. Use lots of sunscreen. Midsummer is very hot and bugs can be annoying. Depending on snowfall and subsequent drying, winter months can be enjoyable. Early morning and late afternoon/early evening are spectacular times to pedal through Monument Valley; the sun's low angle rays intensify the glowing warmth of the valley's features. Visitor Center hours in Summer are (April through October) 7 A.M. to 7 P.M.; in Winter (November through March), 8 A.M. to 5 P.M.
Services: A small convenience store is located in the Visitor Center. Developed camping is available at the park's entrance. There is no water along Monument Valley's scenic road. Several miles west of the park's entrance is Goulding's

RIDE 80 *MONUMENT VALLEY NAVAJO TRIBAL PARK*

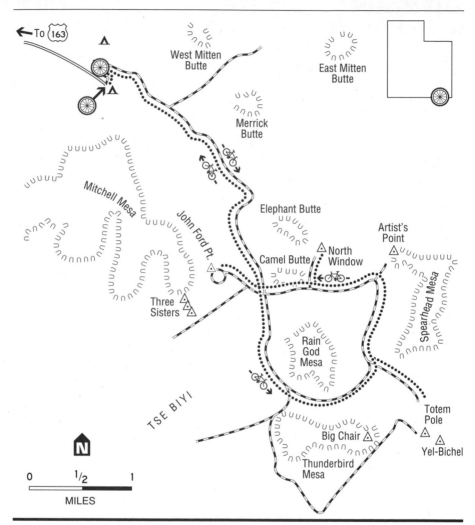

Trading Post, which offers lodging, dining, private campgrounds, showers, and limited supplies.

Hazards: The maintained dirt scenic road is low in technical difficulty and generally suitable for passenger cars. With that in mind, be aware of motorists and tour operators. The route may be very warm, so carry plenty of water. Also, use lots of sunscreen.

Rescue index: Emergency assistance can be summoned from the Visitor Center. Motorists frequent the scenic drive. You might hitch a lift with a tour

Mitten Buttes.

operator, but expect to pay a hefty fee for his or her services. Goulding's Trading Post has medical facilities.

Land status: Navajo Indian Nation.

Maps: USGS 7.5 minute quadrangle: Mitten Buttes, Arizona/Utah.

Finding the trail: The turnoff for Monument Valley is located about 22 miles south of Mexican Hat along US 163, or about half a mile north of the Utah/Arizona border. The park entrance is 3 miles to the east. Parking is available at the Visitor Center.

Sources of additional information:

> Monument Valley Navajo Tribal Park
> P.O. Box 360289
> Monument Valley, Utah 84536
> (801) 727-3287/3353

Notes on the trail: From the Visitor Center, pedal past the steel gate and begin the quick descent into the park. After about 3.5 miles is the turnoff for John Ford Point and the beginning of the loop road. Ride the loop in a counterclockwise direction with the flow of traffic. Wrap around Rain God Mesa and go past the spur for the Totem Pole and Sand Springs. Continue around the loop while taking must-do spurs to Artist's Point and North Window. Both offer distinct perspectives of this wonderfully vacant land. Merrick and Mitten Buttes guide you back to the Visitor Center.

Vehicular and bicycle travel is restricted to the main loop road, unless you are accompanied by a tour operator. Abide by all signs restricting travel. Photography for personal use is allowed; however, permission is required to photograph the Navajo residents and their property, and a gratuity is expected.

Author Gregg Bromka.

A native of upstate New York, Gregg Bromka ventured west to pursue graduate studies in geology at the University of Utah in Salt Lake City.

Although initially hesitant about mountain biking, in the mid-1980s Gregg was reluctantly persuaded to venture on his first off-road ride, fittingly on Moab's famous Slickrock Bike Trail. By day's end, a grin on his face and eyebrows raised, Gregg knew he was hooked. The thrill and exhilaration of fat-tire cycling led to the immediate purchase of his own ATB, scotching any thoughts of moving back East.

What had begun merely as a hobby, searching out new and enticing mountain bike terrain throughout Utah and the Intermountain West, mushroomed into a free-spirited career resulting in several publications, including *Mountain Biking Utah's Wasatch and Uinta Mountains, Mountain Biking Utah's Canyon and Plateau Country,* and *The Mountain Biker's Guide to Colorado* (co-authorship with Linda Gong). Rarely will Gregg be found out on the trail without a note pad and camera in his pack.

For information on these publications and related photographs, contact Off-Road Publications, 1590 South 1400 East, Salt Lake City, Utah 84105.

Appendix I

MOUNTAIN BIKE FESTIVALS

Canyonlands Fat Tire Festival (late October)
Canyon Country Cyclists
c/o Rim Cyclery
94 West 1st North
Moab, Utah 84532
(801) 259-5333

Thin Air Fat Tire Festival, Torrey (early June),
Brian Head Bash (July 24th), and
Fish Lake in the Fall Mountain Bike Rally (early September)
c/o ClearKreek Cycle and Tours
36 North Main
Richfield, Utah 84701
(801) 896-9300

San Rafael Swell Festival (late April)
Carbon County Recreation
625 East 100 North
P.O. Box 793
Price, Utah 84501
(801) 637-5092

Utah Fat Tire Festivals
2448 East Campus Drive
Salt Lake City, Utah 84121
(801) 582-4425

MOUNTAIN BIKE ORGANIZATIONS

International Mountain Bike Association (IMBA)
P.O. Box 421043
Los Angeles, California 90041
(818) 792-8830

National Off-Road Bicycle Association (NORBA)
One Olympic Plaza
Colorado Springs, Colorado 80909
(719) 578-4717

Utah Mountain Bike Association (UMBA)
476 East South Temple, Suite 246
Salt Lake City, Utah 84111
(801) 531-7703

Wild Bunch Bike Club
384 North 700 East
Price, Utah 84501

Appendix II

RECOMMENDED READING

Travel, description, and history:

Abbey, Edward. *Desert Solitaire*. New York: Ballantine Books, 1968.

————.*Slickrock*. New York: Sierra Club/Charles Scribner's Sons, 1971.

Aitchison, Stewart. *Utah Wildlands*. Salt Lake City, Utah: Utah Geographical Series, Inc., 1987.

Bruhn, Arthur F. *Southern Utah's Land of Color*. Bryce Canyon, Utah; Bryce Canyon Natural History Association, 1962.

Carr, Stephen L. *The Historical Guide to Utah Ghost Towns*. Salt Lake City, Utah: Western Epics, 1972.

Crampton, C. Gregory. *Standing Up Country: The Canyon Lands of Utah and Arizona*. New York: Alfred A. Knopf, 1964.

Hayward, C. Lynn. *The High Uintas: Utah's Land of Lakes and Forest*. Provo, Utah: Monte L. Bean Life Science Museum, 1983.

Hinchman, Fred. *Bryce Canyon National Park*. Bryce Canyon, Utah: Bryce Canyon Natural History Association.

McClenahan, Owen. *Utah's Scenic San Rafael Swell*. N.p.: n.p., 1986.

Porter, Eliot. *The Place No One Knew: Glen Canyon on the Colorado*. Salt Lake City, Utah: Peregrine Smith Books, 1988.

Reynolds, Katherine. *Park City. A 100 Year History: Silver Mining to Skiing*. Park City, Utah: The Weller Institute for the Cure of Design, Inc., 1984.

Smart, William B. *Old Utah Trails*. Salt Lake City, Utah: Utah Geographical Series, Inc., 1988.

Stegner, Wallace. *Beyond the Hundredth Meridian: John Wesley Powell and the Second Opening of the West*. Lincoln, Nebraska: University of Nebraska Press, 1954.

Telford, John, and Terry Tempest Williams. *Coyote's Canyon*. Salt Lake City, Utah: Gibbs Smith, Publisher, 1989.

Van Cott, John W. *Utah Place Names*. Salt Lake City, Utah: The University of Utah Press, 1990.

Weir, Bill. *Utah Handbook*. Chico, California: Moon Publications, 1988.

Wharton, Tom and Gayen. *Utah*. Oakland, California: Compass American Guides, Inc., 1991.

Wilson, Ted. *Utah's Wasatch Front*. Salt Lake City, Utah: Utah Geographical Series, Inc., 1987.

Archaeological and geological references:

Barnes, F. A. *Canyon Country Geology for the Layman and Rockhound*. Salt Lake City, Utah: Wasatch Publishers, 1978.

———.*Canyon Country Prehistoric Rock Art*. Salt Lake City, Utah: Wasatch Publishers, 1982.

Barnes, F. A., and Michaelene Pendleton. *Canyon Country Prehistoric Indians: Their Culture, Ruins, Artifacts, and Rock Art*. Salt Lake City, Utah: Wasatch Publishers, 1979.

Bloom, Arthur L. *Geomorphology: A Systematic Analysis of Late Cenozoic Landforms*. Englewood, New Jersey: Prentice Hall, 1978.

Castleton, Kenneth B. *Petroglyphs and Pictographs of Utah*. Vol. 1. Salt Lake City, Utah: Utah Museum of Natural History, 1978.

Chronic, Halka. *Roadside Geology of Utah*. Missoula, Montana: Mountain Press Publishing, 1990.

Dutton, Clarence. E. *Tertiary History of the Grand Cañon District*. Washington, D. C.: United States Geological Survey, 1882. Reprinted by Peregrine Smith, Inc., Santa Barbara and Salt Lake City, 1977.

———.*Report on the Geology of the High Plateaus of Utah*. Washington, D. C.: U. S. Geographical and Geological Survey of the Rocky Mountain Region, 1880.

Foster, Robert J. *General Geology*. Columbus, Ohio: Charles E. Merrill Publishing Company, 1978.

Hintze, Lehi F. *Geologic History of Utah*. Provo, Utah: Brigham Young University, Department of Geology.

Schaafsma, Polly. *Indian Rock Art of the Southwest*. Santa Fe, New Mexico: School of American Research, 1982.

Stokes, William Lee. *Geology of Utah*. Salt Lake City, Utah: Utah Museum of Natural History, Occasional Paper no. 6, 1986.

Mountain biking, hiking, and recreational:

Barnes, F. A., and Tom Kuhne. *Canyon Country Mountain Biking*. Moab, Utah: Canyon Country Publications, 1988.

Bickers, Jack. *Off-Road Vehicle Trails: Maze Area*. Moab, Utah: Canyon Country Publications, 1988.

Bromka, Gregg. *Mountain Biking the Wasatch and Uintas*. Salt Lake City, Utah: Off-Road Publications, 1989.

———.*Mountain Biking Utah's Canyon and Plateau Country*. Salt Lake City, Utah: Off-Road Publications, 1992.

Campbell, Todd. *Above and Beyond Slickrock*. Moab, Utah: Moab Outabouts, 1991.

Coello, Dennis. *Mountain Bike Rides of the West*. Flagstaff, Arizona: Northland Publishing, 1989.

Hinchman, Sandra. *Hiking the Southwest's Canyon Country*. Seattle, Washington: The Mountaineers, 1990.

Kelsey, Michael R. *Hiking Utah's San Rafael Swell*. Provo, Utah: Kelsey Publishing, 1986.

Kelly, Charles, and Nick Crane. *Richard's Mountain Bike Book*. New York: Ballantine Books, 1988.

Lambrechtse, Rudy. *Hiking the Escalante*. Salt Lake City, Utah: Wasatch Publishers, Inc., 1985.

McCoy, Michael. *Mountain Bike Adventures in the Four Corners Region*. Seattle, Washington: The Mountaineers, 1990.

Ringholz, Raye Carleson. *Park City Trails*. Salt Lake City, Utah: Wasatch Publishers, Inc., 1984.

Utesch, Peggy. *The Utah-Colorado Mountain Bike Trail System: Route 1, Moab to Loma—Kokopelli's Trail*. Moab, Utah: Canyon Country Publications, 1990.

Glossary

This short list of terms does not contain all the words used by mountain bike enthusiasts when discussing their sport. But it should serve as an introduction to the lingo you'll hear on the trails.

ATB
all-terrain bike; this, like "fat-tire bike," is another name for a mountain bike

ATV
all-terrain vehicle; this usually refers to the loud, fume-spewing three- or four-wheeled motorized vehicles you will not enjoy meeting on the trail—except, of course, if you crash and have to hitch a ride out on one

bladed
refers to a dirt road which has been smoothed out by the use of a wide blade on earth-moving equipment; "blading" gets rid of the teeth-chattering, much-cursed washboards found on so many dirt roads after heavy vehicle use

blaze
a mark on a tree made by chipping away a piece of the bark, usually done to designate a trail; such trails are sometimes described as "blazed"

blind corner
a curve in a road or trail that conceals bikers, hikers, equestrians, and other traffic

BLM
Bureau of Land Management, an agency of the federal government

buffed
used to describe a very smooth trail

catching air
taking a jump in such a way that both wheels of the bike are off the ground at the same time

clean
while this may describe what you and your bike *won't* be after following many trials, the term is most often used as a verb to denote the action of pedaling a tough section of trail successfully

combination
This type of route may combine two or more configurations. For example, a point-to-point route may integrate a scenic loop or out-and-back spur midway through the ride. Likewise, an out-and-back may have a

loop at its farthest point. (This configuration looks like a cherry with stem attached; the stem is the out-and-back, the fruit is the terminus loop.) Or a loop route may have multiple out-and-back spurs and/or loops to the side. Mileage for a combination route is for the total distance to complete the ride

dab touching the ground with a foot or hand

deadfall a tangled mass of fallen trees or branches

diversion ditch a usually narrow, shallow ditch dug across or around a trail; funneling the water in this manner keeps it from destroying the trail

double-track the dual tracks made by a jeep or other vehicle, with grass or weeds or rocks between; mountain bikers can ride in either of the tracks, but you will of course find that whichever one you choose, and no matter how many times you change back and forth, the other track will appear to offer smoother travel

dugway a steep, unpaved, switchbacked descent

endo flipping end over end

feathering using a light touch on the brake lever, hitting it lightly many times rather than very hard or locking the brake

four-wheel-drive this refers to any vehicle with drive-wheel capability on all four wheels (a jeep, for instance, has four-wheel drive as compared with a two-wheel-drive passenger car), or to a rough road or trail that requires four-wheel-drive capability (or a *one*-wheel-drive mountain bike!) to negotiate it

game trail the usually narrow trail made by deer, elk, or other game

gated everyone knows what a gate is, and how many variations exist upon this theme; well, if a trail is described as "gated" it simply has a gate across it; don't forget that the rule is if you find a gate closed, close it behind you; if you find one open, leave it that way

Giardia shorthand for *Giardia lamblia*, and known as the "back packer's bane" until we mountain bikers expropriated it; this is a waterborne parasite that begins its life cycle when swallowed, and one to four weeks later has its host (you) bloated, vomiting, shivering with chills, and living in the bathroom; the disease can be avoided by "treating" (purifying) the water you acquire along the trail (see "Hitting the Trail" in the Introduction)

gnarly a term thankfully used less and less these days, it refers to tough trails

hammer to ride very hard

hardpack a trail in which the dirt surface is packed down hard; such trails make for good and fast riding, and very painful landings; bikers most often use "hard-pack" as both noun and adjective, and "hard-packed" as an adjective only (the grammar lesson will help you when diagramming sentences in camp)

hike-a-bike what you do when the road or trail becomes too steep or rough to remain in the saddle

jeep road, jeep trail a rough road or trail passable only with four-wheel-drive capability (or a horse or mountain bike)

kamikaze while this once referred primarily to those Japanese fliers who quaffed a glass of saké, then flew off as human bombs in suicide missions against U.S. naval vessels, it has more recently been applied to the idiot mountain bikers who, far less honorably, scream down hiking trails, endangering the physical and mental safety of the walking, biking, and equestrian traffic they meet; deck guns were necessary to stop the Japanese kamikaze pilots, but a bike pump or walking staff in the spokes is sufficient for the current-day kamikazes who threaten to get us all kicked off the trails

loop This route configuration is characterized by riding from the designated trailhead to a distant point, then returning to the trailhead via a different route (or simply continuing on the same in a circle route) without doubling back. You always move forward across new terrain, but return to the starting point when finished. Mileage is for the entire loop from the trailhead back to trailhead

multi-purpose   a BLM designation of land which is open to many uses; mountain biking is allowed

ORV   a motorized off-road vehicle

out-and-back   a ride where you will return on the same trail you pedaled out; while this might sound far more boring than a loop route, many trails look very different when pedaled in the opposite direction

pack stock   horses, mules, llamas, et cetera, carrying provisions along the trails . . . and unfortunately leaving a trail of their own behind

point-to-point   A vehicle shuttle (or similar assistance) is required for this type of route, which is ridden from the designated trailhead to a distant location, or end point, where the route ends. Total mileage is for the one-way trip from trailhead to end point

portage   to carry your bike on your person

pummy   volcanic activity in the Pacific Northwest and elsewhere produces soil with a high content of pumice; trails through such soil often become thick with dust, but this is light in consistency and can usually be pedaled; remember, however, to pedal carefully, for this dust obscures whatever might lurk below

quads   bikers use this term to refer both to the extensor muscle in the front of the thigh (which is separated into four parts) and to USGS maps; the expression "Nice quads!" refers always to the former, however, except in those instances when the speaker is an engineer

runoff   rainwater or snowmelt

scree   an accumulation of loose stones or rocky debris lying on a slope or at the base of a hill or cliff

signed   a "signed" trail has signs in place of blazes

single-track   a single, narrow path through grass or brush or over rocky terrain, often created by deer, elk, or backpackers; single-track riding is some of the best fun around

slickrock   the rock-hard, compacted sandstone that is *great* to ride and even prettier to look at; you'll appreciate it even more if you think of it as a petrified sand dune or seabed, and if the rider before you hasn't left tire marks (from unneces-

	sary skidding) or granola bar wrappers behind
snowmelt	runoff produced by the melting of snow
snowpack	unmelted snow accumulated over weeks or months of winter—or over years in high-mountain terrain
spur	a road or trail that intersects the main trail you're following
squid	one who skids
switchback	a zigzagging road or trail designed to assist in traversing steep terrain; mountain bikers should *not* skid through switchbacks
talus	the rocky debris at the base of a cliff, or a slope formed by an accumulation of this rocky debris
technical	terrain that is difficult to ride due not to its grade (steepness) but to its obstacles—rocks, logs, ledges, loose soil . . .
topo	short for topographical map, the kind that shows both linear distance *and* elevation gain and loss; "topo" is pronounced with both vowels long
trashed	a trail that has been destroyed (same term used no matter what has destroyed it . . . cattle, horses, or even mountain bikers riding when the ground was too wet)
two-wheel-drive	this refers to any vehicle with drive-wheel capability on only two wheels (a passenger car, for instance, has two-wheel-drive); a two-wheel-drive road is a road or trail easily traveled by an ordinary car
washboarded	a road that is surfaced with many ridges spaced closely together, like the ripples on a washboard; these make for very rough riding, and even worse driving in a car or jeep
water bar	an earth, rock, or wooden structure that funnels water off trails to reduce erosion
whoop-de-doo	closely spaced dips or undulations in a trail; these are often encountered in areas traveled heavily by ORVs
wilderness area	land that is officially set aside by the federal government to remain *natural*—pure, pristine, and untrammeled by any vehicle, including mountain bikes; though mountain bikes had not been born in 1964 (when the United States Congress passed the Wilderness Act, establishing the

National Wilderness Preservation system), they are considered a "form of mechanical transport" and are thereby excluded; in short, stay out

wind chill a reference to the wind's cooling effect upon exposed flesh; for example, if the temperature is 10 degrees Fahrenheit and the wind is blowing at 20 miles per hour, the wind-chill (that is, the actual temperature to which your skin reacts) is *minus* 32 degrees; if you are riding in wet conditions things are even worse, for the wind-chill would then be *minus 74 degrees!*

windfall anything (trees, limbs, brush, or fellow bikers) blown down by the wind

DENNIS COELLO'S AMERICA BY MOUNTAIN BIKE SERIES

Happy Trails

Hop on your mountain bike and let our guidebooks take you on America's classic trails and rides. These "where-to" books are published jointly by Falcon Press and Menasha Ridge Press and written by local biking experts. Twenty regional books will blanket the country when the series is complete.

Choose from an assortment of rides—easy rambles to all-day treks. Guides contain helpful trail and route descriptions, mountain bike shop listings; and interesting facts on area history. Each trail is described in terms of difficulty, scenery, condition, length, and elevation change. The guides also explain trail hazards, nearby services and ranger stations, how much water to bring, and what kind of gear to pack.

So before you hit the trail, grab one of our guidebooks to help make your outdoor adventures safe and memorable.

Call or write
Falcon Press or Menasha Ridge Press
Falcon Press
P.O. Box 1718, Helena, MT 59624
1-800-582-2665
Menasha Ridge Press
3169 Cahaba Heights Road, Birmingham, AL 35243
1-800-247-9437

FALCON™

Menasha **Ridge Press**